The Book and the Text

18.95

D0813935

The Book and the Text

The Bible and Literary Theory

Edited by
Regina M. Schwartz

Basil Blackwell

Copyright © 'Sodom as Nexus', Robert Alter 1986; copyright © 'On Prophetic Stammering', Yale University Press 1987; copyright © 'Joseph's Bones and the Resurrection of the Text', PMCA 1988; copyright © 'The Song of Songs: Lock or Key?', Daniel Boyarin 1990; copyright © 'Time and Space in Biblical (Hi)story Telling', Meir Sternberg 1990; copyright © 'The Gospel in Greco-Roman Culture', Mary Ann Tolbert 1990.
All other material: copyright © Basil Blackwell 1990.
First published 1990
Basil Blackwell, Inc.
3 Cambridge Center
Cambridge, Massachusetts 02142, USA
Basil Blackwell Ltd
108 Cowley Road, Oxford, OX4 1JF, UK

All rights reserved. Except for the quotation of short passages for the purpose of criticism and review, no part of this publication may be reproduced, stored in a retrieval system, or transmitted, in any form or by any means, electronic, mechanical, photocopying, recording or otherwise, without the prior permission of the publisher.

Except in the United States of America, this book is sold subject to the condition that it shall not, by way of trade or otherwise, be lent, re-sold, hired out, or otherwise circulated without the publisher's prior consent in any form of binding or cover other than that in which it is published and without a similar condition including this condition being imposed on the subsequent purchaser.
Library of Congress Cataloging in Publication Data
The Book and the text: the Bible and literary theory/edited by Regina M. Schwartz.
p. cm.
ISBN 0–631–16861–3 ISBN 0–631–16862–1 (pbk.):
1. Bible as literature. 2. Bible-Criticism, interpretation, etc.
3 Criticism. I. Schwartz, Regina M.
BS535.B66 1990
220. 6'6–dc20

British Library Cataloguing in Publication Data
A CIP catalogue record for this book is available from the British Library.

Typeset in 10½ Sabon
by Hope Services (Abingdon) Ltd.
Printed in Great Britain by
T. J. Press Ltd., Padstow

Contents

List of Figures   vii

List of Contributors   viii

Acknowledgments   xi

Introduction: On Biblical Criticism
Regina M. Schwartz   1

1 Dealing/With/Women: Daughters in the Book of Judges
Mieke Bal   16

✓ 2 Joseph's Bones and the Resurrection of the Text:
Remembering in the Bible
Regina M. Schwartz   40

3 On Prophetic Stammering
Herbert Marks   60

4 Time and Space in Biblical (Hi)story Telling:
The Grand Chronology
Meir Sternberg   81

5 Sodom as Nexus: The Web of Design in Biblical Narrative
Robert Alter   146

✓ 6 The Keeping of Nahor: The Etiology of Biblical Election
James C. Nohrnberg   161

7 The Hermeneutics of Midrash
Gerald L. Bruns   189

8 The Song of Songs: Lock or Key?
Intertextuality, Allegory and Midrash
Daniel Boyarin   214

9 J. L. Austin and the Book of Jonah
   Terry Eagleton   231

10 Interpretative Narrative
   Paul Ricoeur   237

11 The Gospel in Greco-Roman Culture
   Mary Ann Tolbert   258

12 'Buried with Christ': The Politics of Identity and the
   Poverty of Interpretation
   Sheila Briggs   276

Index   305

List of Figures

1.1 Egyptian relief, found on Semitic territory. From P. Derchain, 'Les plus anciens témoignages de sacrifices d'enfants chez les Semites occidentaux.' Reproduced by permission from *Vetus Testamentum* 20 (no. 3): 351–55. 1977 by E.J. Brill.

6.1 'These are the generations of . . .'

6.2 The major patrilineal descent in Genesis, and their ethnographic tripartition at the locus of epochal displacement and reorigination.

List of Contributors

Robert Alter is Class of 1939 Professor of Comparative Literature at the University of California at Berkeley. He has written on a variety of aspects of the novel, from Fielding to Stendhal to Nabokov. His books include *The Art of Biblical Narrative* and *The Art of Biblical Poetry*, and he is the co-editor, with Frank Kermode, of *The Literary Guide to the Bible*.

Mieke Bal is Professor of Comparative Literature and Susan B. Anthony Professor of Women's Studies at the University of Rochester. She has published on narrative theory, on feminist criticism, and her books on the Hebrew Bible include *Lethal Love: Literary Feminist Interpretations of Biblical Love Stories*, *Murder and Difference: Gender, Genre and Scholarship on Sisera's Death*, and *Death and Dissymmetry: The Politics of Coherence in the Book of Judges*. She is presently completing a study of word and image relations, entitled *Reading 'Rembrandt'*.

Daniel Boyarin teaches Talmud and midrash at Bar-Ilan University. He has published articles on midrash and literary theory in the *Buchnell Review*, *Poetics Today* and *Representations*. His book, *Intertextuality and the Reading of Midrash*, of which the present paper forms a chapter, will be published in the spring of 1990. He is presently working on a book on Eros and religion in Talmudic Judaism.

Sheila Briggs teaches courses on gender and theology in the School of Religion at the University of Southern California. She has contributed to *Analyzing Gender* and *Immaculate and Powerful: The Female in*

Sacred Image and Social Reality. She is currently working on a book entitled *God, History and Emancipation.*

Gerald Bruns is Professor of Literature at Notre Dame. He has written on hermeneutics and literary theory, classical rhetoric, Victorian literature and modern poetry. His works include *Inventions: Writing, Textuality, and Understanding in Literary History* and *Heidegger's Estrangements: Language, Truth, and Poetry in the Later Writings.*

Terry Eagleton is Fellow of Linacre College, Oxford, and University Lecturer in Critical Theory. He is the author of *The Function of Criticism, Literary Theory: An Introduction, William Shakespeare, Against the Grain, Marxism and Literary Criticism,* and *The Ideology of the Aesthetic* will be published this year. He is also author of a novel, *Saints and Scholars,* and a play, *The Fall of Oscar Wilde,* produced in Ireland and London in 1989.

Herbert Marks is Associate Professor of Comparative Literature, English, and Near Eastern Languages, and director of the Institute for Biblical and Literary Studies at Indiana University. He is working on a book on poetic etymology.

James Nohrnberg is Professor of English at the University of Virginia, where he teaches both Bible and Renaissance literature. He has written on Homer, the Bible, Dante, Milton and Pynchon, given the Gauss Lectures at Princeton on the Bible, and he is the author of *The Analogy of The Faerie Queene.*

Paul Ricoeur is Professor of Philosophy and Theology at the University of Chicago. Among his publications on hermeneutics are *The Symbolism of Evil, Freud and Philosophy, Freedom and Nature: The Voluntary and the Involuntary, Essays on Biblical Interpretation, The Conflict of Interpretations* and, most recently, the three volumes of *Time and Narrative.*

Regina Schwartz is Associate Professor of English at Duke University, where she teaches the Bible, Renaissance literature, and literary theory. She has published on Milton, the Bible and theory in *Milton*
contd

Studies, *PMLA* and *ELH*, and is the author of *Remembering and Repeating: Biblical Creation in Paradise Lost*. She is currently working on a book on the Bible entitled *Can These Bones Live?*

Meir Sternberg is Professor of Comparative Literature and Poetics at the University of Tel Aviv. He is the author of *Expositional Modes and Temporal Ordering in Fiction*, and other studies in narrative. He has written on the Bible for *Hasifrut* and is the author of *The Poetics of Biblical Narrative*.

Mary Ann Tolbert is Associate Professor of New Testament and Early Christianity at the Vanderbilt University Divinity School. She holds graduate degrees in English and biblical studies. Her publications include *Perspectives on the Parables*, *Semeia 28: The Bible and Feminist Hermeneutics* (ed.), and *Sowing the Gospel: Mark's World in Literary-Historical Perspective*.

Acknowledgments

This volume began with the Conference on the Bible and Literary Theory which I directed at the University of Colorado in Boulder in 1986. I would like to thank the University of Colorado for its generous funding of that event: the President's Fund for the Humanities, the Offices of the Chancellor and Vice-Chancellor, the College of Arts and Sciences, the Graduate School, the Center for Theory, and the departments of English, Religion, and Comparative Literature all contributed. I also want to thank Buck McMullen for his invaluable help, the conference speakers for their energizing presentations, and the audience for their enthusiastic participation.

With the advice of readers from the publisher, I have added more essays, ones that approach the Bible in ways that were not represented at the conference, and I am grateful to those contributors for joining the project. Thanks to Patrick Melson for his meticulous work with the preparation of the manuscript, to Kim Didonato and Jan Chamier for helping with many details, and to Naomi Wood and Karla Shargent for their assistance in the final stages. The following essays have been reprinted with permission from their presses: Herbert Marks, 'On Prophetic Stammering', first published in *The Yale Journal of Criticism*, vol. 1, no. I; Robert Alter, 'Sodom as Nexus', in *Tikkun* vol. 1, no. 1; Regina Schwartz, 'Joseph's Bones and the Resurrection of the Text', *PMLA*, March 1988. Finally, I would like to thank the inspiration behind it all, James S. Ackerman, Professor of Hebrew Bible at Indiana University, whose teaching during my graduate Bible studies and whose summer institutes on the Bible as/and Literature at Indiana University in the seventies provoked this activity, and who led our discussion on the book of Numbers (his essay was published in *The Literary Guide to the Bible*) at the Colorado Conference.

Introduction: On Biblical Criticism

Regina M. Schwartz

The essays assembled in *The Book and the Text* are not intended to offer a 'literary reading' of the Bible. Such studies, both the efforts by individual interpreters and collections by various hands, already exist: *The Literary Guide to the Bible*, edited by Alter and Kermode, is one of the more recent guides, and it is designed to take the reader by the hand through the Bible, book by book. The editors of that collection have carefully delimited their project, and what they have chosen to exclude offers an indication of what this volume on the Bible and theory includes. They explain that

> critical approaches mainly interested in the origins of a text in ideology or social structure are not represented here; nor is Marxist criticism . . . or psychoanalytic criticism. . . . we have not included critics who use the text as a springboard for cultural or metaphysical ruminations, nor those like the Deconstructionists and some feminist critics. . . . The general validity of such approaches is not at issue here, only their inapplicability to our project as we have defined it.[1]

Amid the growing focus on the Bible in literary studies, this book offers the complementary strain, for its essays are deliberately engaged in a dialogue between currents in contemporary theory – structuralism, deconstruction, semiotics, hermeneutics, feminism, psychoanalytic interpretation and political thought – and the Bible. In practice, what that means is that the contributors do not subscribe to a self-evident notion of what a 'literary approach' to the Bible might mean. There are only approach*es*, and even these are questions they engage rather than a collection of settled concerns.

When the Bible first made its way into English departments, there seemed to be some common understanding about what a course title like 'The Bible as Literature' might mean: there would be attention to figurative language, to characterization, to plot. In 1975, when

Robert Alter began to call the attention of literary scholars to the
Bible in what was, at the time, a ground-breaking essay, he began
with the observation that 'It is a little astonishing that at this late date
there exists virtually no serious literary analysis of the Hebrew Bible.'
Then he proceeded to describe what 'serious literary analysis' would
constitute:

> By serious analysis I mean the manifold varieties of minutely discriminating
> attention to the artful use of language, to the shifting play of ideas,
> conventions, tone, sound, imagery, narrative viewpoint, compositional units,
> and much else; the kind of disciplined attention, in other words, which
> through a whole spectrum of critical approaches has illuminated, for
> example, the poetry of Dante, the plays of Shakespeare, the novels of
> Tolstoy.[2]

In the current theoretical climate 'literary analysis' no longer evokes
such stable formulations; we speak more often of discourse, of
textuality, and we derive the vocabulary of that discourse from
decidedly extra-literary sources: from developments in continental
philosophy, linguistics, anthropology, psychoanalysis and political
theory. But if it is timely for the Bible to be brought into an encounter
with literary theory, that does not mean that in the following essays
theory will be 'applied' to the text. On the one hand, only the
reduction of theories to 'techniques' could allow imagining such
applications – we cannot *apply* gender studies, Marxism or
hermeneutics any more than we can *apply* ideology – and on the
other hand, most theoretical perspectives would concede that
whatever the Bible is, it is not stable enough to receive any such
application. Instead, theoretical problems are reconceived in their
dialogue with the Bible, even as such reflection reshapes what 'the
Bible' might be. In the essays that follow, the book and text are
engaged in an encounter.

Furthermore, while the contributors were selected with the
principle of theoretical eclecticism in mind, most would be leery of
accepting any strict label. In some, the emphasis is on theory, with the
Bible offering examples; in others, closer scrutiny is paid to the
narrative workings of the text, and theory is left more implicit. As a
key figure of the Tel Aviv school of poetics, Sternberg's debt to
Russian formalism is clear, but his approach to the problem of how
biblical narrative approaches chronology is his own.[3] Then, too,
when we read Bal's work as feminist criticism, we still have not begun
to categorize it: she has taken pains to distinguish herself from some
obvious comparisons with biblical critical-historical feminist scholars;[4]
besides, there are many feminisms. Here she explores how marriage

economies in biblical patriarchy result in the victimization of women and the silencing of the female subject in narrative. Bruns and Ricoeur share an interest in hermeneutics, in the interpretive function of narrative, but Bruns focuses on midrashic hermeneutics, arguing that it is a historical process, not a method, a 'social practice', not a logical exercise, while Ricoeur finds an 'indissociable union of kerygmatic and narrative aspects' in the passion account. If, from our historical position, placing midrash and the New Testament side by side in a common hermeneutics may appear like a quiet gesture, it is not.[5] Boyarin contrasts the activity of midrashic interpretation with the more familiar allegorical one of the Song of Songs. In their Marxist approaches, Eagleton and Briggs further the exploration of the relation between social practice and interpretation: in her discussion of the value of hermeneutics for praxis, Briggs focuses on the ways that Paul negotiates the conflict between baptismal identities and existing social identities in the early Church. Eagleton sees in Jonah the dilemma of how to constitute the subject as one who can act meaningfully. Nohrnberg is preoccupied with kinship structures in his essay but structural anthropology would not adequately describe his argument in which identity is constituted, and genealogy is drawn, by blood or by adoption. In his more structural approach, Alter speaks of the 'pointed activation of one [biblical] text by another', of intratextual allusion that forms a narrative design. Tolbert's focus is more historicist, setting the Gospel of Mark in the context of ancient popular culture to show how the gospel plays on expectations of ancient romance novels. If Marks's and my own piece are postmodern, Marks turns to sublimity – prophetic stammering concentrates attention on the status of the utterance, the hearer and speaker. My own interest is in postmodern process: the activity of forgetting and remembering allies my thinking with psychoanalytic dynamics of repression at the same time that it characterizes the biblical vision of history. But if these essays resist the categories imposed by the academy for the ready consumption of critical theory, that need not be frustrating; instead, their range may be the best testimony to their value.

Added to the difficulty of situating these essays in the contemporary critical climate is another problem: that context – complicated as it is – is not the only one where we should locate *The Book and the Text*. There is another dimension: not contemporary, but historical. If less well known to literary scholars, the history of biblical interpretation is no less central; for when we understand interpreting the Bible as an act of reappropriating, reconceiving and rewriting, we have attached ourselves to a long and illustrious lineage of biblical interpreters. The vocabulary of medieval and reformation biblical exegesis may not be borrowed from continental philosophy or linguistics, but the issues are strikingly familiar: the authority for our interpretations; the relation of the text to the reader; the relation of the text to history; the political force of our interpretations; the question of the boundaries of the text and canon formation.

This story of biblical interpretation begins in the Bible, where the prophets rework the exodus narratives, the New Testament interprets the 'Old' (the construction of those categories was itself a major interpretive event), and Paul offers allusive remarks about the letter and the spirit that are to influence subsequent patristic principles of exegesis. Paul's 'The letter kills but the spirit maketh life' (II Cor. 3:6) leads to formulations and reformulations of what the 'letter' and the 'spirit' might be; if the letter refers to literal meaning and the spirit to figural meaning, what, then, do figural and literal mean? Even as the school of Antioch attacked the Alexandrians for their allegorizing of scripture, the two schools understood the provinces of allegory and literalism differently. The Alexandrians understood 'literal' to mean essentially concrete: the 'arm of God' meant that God has an arm, and at least one of the impulses informing their allegorizing was to combat such anthropomorphism. In Antioch, on the other hand, the literal meaning could include metaphor and with that broader spectrum of sense, such 'literal meanings' were less troubling to uphold. Nonetheless, Chrysostom, a key figure in that school of Antioch where literalism was advanced, writes that 'we must not examine the words as bare words else many absurdities will follow, but we must mark the mind of the writer'. Needless to say, this medieval version of intentionalism is fraught with the same problems its more modern versions confront: how do we gain access to the mind of the writer? In short, while the fourfold medieval method seems to have systematized interpretation formally, the bounds of allegorical, literal, tropological and anagogical exegesis were at least as blurred as our contemporary theoretical categories.

Furthermore, the disjunctions between medieval *theory* of exegesis and *praxis* show how troubling the 'application' of even medieval principles was. In the fifth century, Vincent of Lerins offered one of the most influential theories of exegesis. He asserted that 'the rule of interpretation be laid down in accordance with the norm of ecclesiastical and Catholic understanding' (*Commonitorium*, II, 3) and that this understanding is what has been held 'everywhere, always, and by everyone'. 'Everywhere, always, and everyone' meant tradition (with a capital T): the doctrines espoused by the Fathers, sanctioned by the medieval Church, hence, believed to be everywhere, always, and by everyone. But even this effort to elevate the ideal of universal consensus to an exegetical principle did little to quell the factionalized debates over the meaning of the text. If the tropological meaning is the moral implication, what and who adjudicates it – in the absence of a consensus everywhere, always, and by everyone? Allegory was invoked to neutralize morally troubling passages: Bernard of Clairvaux explained the passage, 'the virgins love thee' from the Song of Songs, by elaborating why God is loved by angels, archangels, virtues, powers, principalities, dominions, cherubim and seraphim. But the functions of allegory were not always so quaint: on other occasions, allegorical interpretation was asked to serve, if not confer, political power. Bernard interpreted the two swords of Luke 22:38 as the 'spiritual' and 'material' weapons to be wielded respectively at the bidding of the clergy and the command of the emperor, and that interpretation was used as authoritative justification for the powers of pope and emperor.

In rabbinic exegesis the impulse was less to delimit meanings than to justify their proliferation. 'The exegesis of verses of Scripture defined a convention in Israelite life even before books of holy writings attained the status of scripture.'[6] Polysemy prevailed, both in the expositions of rabbinic law, *halakhah*, and in the more homiletic or narrative midrashim, *aggadah*. Nonetheless, all proceeds, for the Rabbis, from the 'oral Torah', that revelation at Sinai that accompanied the written one and is passed from generation to generation. According to the sages, this revelation included every interpretation of the Bible, even contradictory ones. 'Verses receive not just one but many interpretations, which indicates not the rejection of previous explanation but the simultaneous legitimacy of a number of meanings', says Judah Goldin.[7] That simultaneity of conflicting interpretations is evident in the famous portrayal of the fierce debates between the exegetical schools of Hillel and Shammai. Unable to agree for years about their interpretation of the law, the dispute was 'settled' by a heavenly oracle that decreed, 'The words of both Houses are the word of the living God, and the law is like the House of Hillel.' When the Rabbis asked why, if the words of both houses are the words of the living God, the law is decided by the House of Hillel, they answered, 'Because they were peaceful and humble men, and they taught the teachings of the House of Shammai as well as their own, and even more than that, they taught the teachings of the House of Shammai before they taught their own.'[8] Another frequently cited expression, 'Turn it and turn it, for all is in it', describes not only the sense of ceaseless activity on the book but also the comprehensiveness of the book. In halakhic commentary, where legal concerns and prescribed courses of action were foremost, there was ostensibly close attention to what the sages called *peshat*, 'literal meaning'; philology and Hebrew grammar entered discussions; rules of interpretation were followed – of course, different rules for different schools.

Aggadah, the freer, more narrative mode of exegesis, had conventions of its own, stemming largely from its sermonic setting. The *petihta*, or proem, usually ends with the first verse of the weekly reading and begins with a verse from a very different context. The interpreter's virtuosity lay in connecting, in whatever roundabout way possible, the two verses. Scripture, then, was not only interpreted by recourse to tradition; whether halakhic or aggadic, scripture was interpreted by scripture. Rhetorical devices were common: punning, homophones, acronyms and methods borrowed from ancient dream interpretation. While these procedures may sound atemporal, political and polemical impulses informed Judaic scriptural exegesis no less than Christian. Judaism was being defined through these very acts of interpretation, defined and defended against such ideological cross-currents as the Christians, who claimed that they were the authentic inheritors of the biblical tradition, the Karaites, who rejected the authority of the oral Torah in favor of the written scripture alone, Greek pragmatism, and Alexandrian culture. Meanwhile, authorizing the tradition of interpretation – the oral Torah – shed new light on the canon. What constitutes the authoritative text is redefined when its interpretations are also authorized. That problem did not only belong to the Rabbis.

Biblical authority, the issue implicit throughout medieval debates over allegorical and literal interpretation, became explicit – and explosive – during the Reformation. Upon what authority does any interpretive activity rest? Luther denounced the view that interpretation belongs to the church alone, that the scripture must be mediated by the clergy. 'The Church', wrote Luther, 'is daughter born of the Word, not the mother of the Word.'[9] A doctrine of 'sola scriptura' could not solve differences in interpretation, and neither could professing the perspicuity of scripture. Given its supreme authority, the Bible may be more urgent to interpret, but no easier. At the Diet of Worms when Luther was asked to recant, he invoked the 'testimony of scripture' to distinguish his guiding authority from the church, but he also spoke allusively of the guidance of his reason and conscience:

Unless I am convicted of error by the testimony of Scripture or (since I put no trust in the unsupported authority of Pope or of councils, since it is plain that they have often erred and often contradicted themselves) by manifest reasoning I stand convicted by the Scriptures to which I have appealed, and my conscience is taken captive by God's word, I cannot and will not recant anything, for to act against our conscience is neither safe for us, nor open to us.[10]

Later he would distrust reason, only to invoke the Spirit to help interpret the Bible. 'Scripture alone' may have meant without tradition, but it did not mean without bringing another principle to the text. Calvin laid even greater emphasis on the illumination of the Spirit. But even with the guidance of the Spirit, the Bible seemed to mean different things to different Reformers – a diversity of interpretations that only induced ever more acute awareness of ideological differences among them. Generally speaking, doctrine did not follow exegesis; doctrine came first, determining what the Bible ostensibly said. True enough, Luther spoke with conviction about the importance of the literal meaning (he called it the grammatical sense), with impatience about the allegorical excesses of Origen, but he would not hesitate to indulge in allegory himself when it suited his purpose. The Bible taught the doctrine of faith in Christ, and he found that doctrine not just in the New Testament but in Genesis and in the Psalms.

There was another consequence of this investment in the authority of scripture: it inevitably induced a new crisis over the text itself. When Calvin claimed that the Spirit was expressed in the Word, the transmission and corruptibility of the Word were at issue. He notes that Paul misquotes Psalm 68:18 in Ephesians 4:8, but, Calvin explains, that is because he is not interested in the words of the psalm, but in its sense. 'We see with what freedom the apostles permitted themselves to quote scripture passages. The apostles were not so scrupulous [in quotation] as to decline to accommodate their language to the uninformed.'[11] Throughout their proofs and counterproofs of biblical inerrancy, and in their elevation of the 'grammatical sense' of scripture, the Reformers turned to the study of the original biblical languages. Renaissance humanism left the Reformers its legacy, with its painstaking Greek and Hebrew studies. These biblical exegetes were grammarians first; their interpretations required ancient language competence. Soon, biblical interpretation would be chiefly that, an exercise in language competence, and theology would begin to go underground in biblical studies. Even Calvin had formally separated his biblical commentary from his theology, the *Institutes*, thereby helping to usher in the distinction between philology and theology that would come to dominate interpretation throughout the eighteenth, nineteenth and into the twentieth centuries.

The distinction between scientific approaches to the Bible and theological ones deepened in the eighteenth century, a period that made an unprecedented investment in the 'factuality' of the Bible. The focus turned to the apparent inconsistencies in Scripture, to say nothing of the difficulty of reconciling the new science with the old word. This was the era when the movement that came to be called historical criticism first emerged. Bacon and Descartes had already insisted on the supremacy of reason; Spinoza had maintained that the Bible must be treated like any other book. Nonetheless, it is important to recall that initially, rationalism was not a movement outside the church, at war with religion. Reason was not used to unseat the Bible; rather, reason was called upon to reconcile revelation to the dictates of logic. Locke's title *The Reasonableness of Christianity* is indicative. When dispute arose, it was over the question of whether there was a supernatural revelation of truth beyond 'natural religion'. The Deists asserted that human reason was adequate for discovering religious truth; hence, John Toland's *Christianity Not Mysterious: or, A treatise shewing that there is nothing in the gospel contrary to reason, nor above it: and that no Christian doctrine can be properly call'd a mystery*, and Matthew Tindal's *Christianity as Old as the Creation, or, The Gospel, a Republication of the Religion of Nature*. Their influence was felt in France and Germany where efforts to reconcile natural reason to revelation became less accommodating in the second half of the century. Some (like Reimarus) found them completely incompatible: a specific revelation could not address a universal religion, and miracles, in particular, were an affront to reason.

But it was a complex period, and biblical studies mirrored the prevailing cross-currents of philosophy. If dogma was beseiged by rationalism on one front, it was attacked by pietism on the other. The notion of a 'heartfelt' or subjective experience of religion (founded, of course, on intimate Bible study) spread throughout Germany, into England where it contributed to the founding of Methodism, and into the New World. Then, too, the end of the century witnessed the flowering of Romanticism; the Romantics attacked orthodox dogma on one side and rationalism on the other. So, Herder's oft-quoted injunction to empathize rather than analyze when approaching the Old Testament:

Become with shepherds a shepherd, with a people of the sod a man of the land, with the ancients of the Orient an Easterner, if you wish to relish these writings in the atmosphere of their origin; and be on guard especially against abstractions of dull, new academic prisons, and even more against all so-called artistry which our social circles force and press on those sacred archetypes of the most ancient days.[12]

Nevertheless, it was the 'science' of biblical exegesis that would prevail, the demand to investigate each biblical narrative in its historical context. One of the pioneers of the historical inquiry into the Bible, J. S. Semler (1725–91), illustrates the paradox engendered by historicizing doctrines that had been regarded as timeless: 'for him the Bible as a book is *no longer inspired* and can therefore be viewed impartially with the eyes of the historical investigator, without endangering *the Word of God*, which he wishes at all costs to guard' (my emphases).[13] That safeguarding of 'the Word of God' became increasingly difficult as biblical criticism did its work. Philology, textual criticism, grammatical analysis and historical criticism made it apparent that many ideas had been attributed to biblical writers for dogmatic and theological reasons, without historical grounding. J. P. Gabler's approach to the dilemma was to distinguish true (*wahre*) theology – a historicized Bible, contingent upon time and place – from pure (*reine*) theology – God's eternal truths, the timeless biblical ideas. To derail eternal truth from the historicized Bible was to take a key step toward a growing sense that biblical scholarship need not be concerned about eternal truth at all. There were other truths: the truths of history.

The so-called higher criticism of the Bible (as distinguished from lower, textual study) came of age in the context of nineteenth-century German historiography, sharing its assumptions, its methods, its goals. In 'On the Task of the Historian' (1822) Wilhelm von Humboldt summarized many of the positions that would become characteristic: 'every human epoch bears its own, uniquely individual character' and the historian's task is to chart the spiritual progress of this national individuality. Empiricism is not enough; the historian must work 'as a poet' to capture the unique character of an epoch. Following suit, Leopold von Ranke wrote that the historian's task is 'to portray what actually happened', but such empiricism is meant to uncover the transcendent design, 'the hand of God' in history. Throughout, these histories presuppose a story of development. While Johann Gustav Droysen denies that he is Hegelian, in his *Principles of History* (1868) he speaks of the 'supra-empirical level of spirit' and of the necessary logic of a progressive moral development. When it is not spiritual, the development is moral. In other words, the story of nineteenth-century historiography is largely the story of an uneasy alliance between efforts toward a historical 'science' and commitment to an idealistic historical philosophy.[14] We can see these forces in one of the most prominent biblical scholars of the late nineteenth century, Julius Wellhausen, when he writes in the introduction to his *Prolegomena to the History of Ancient Israel*, 'It is necessary to trace the succession of the three elements [the Jehovist, the Deuteronomic, and the Priestly] in detail, and at once to test and to fix each by reference to an independent standard, namely, the inner development of the history of Israel.' That inner development suggested something like 'the moral development'.

Wellhausen's *Prolegomena* is most openly indebted to those biblical scholars who began the work of fixing the sources of the Bible. Critical-historical scholarship – devoted to determining the extent and character of the various documents composing the text, their date, and authorship – is often traced to the physician to Louis XV, Jean Astruc, who noted two separate uses of appellations for God in Genesis, Yahweh and Elohim, positing that two different documents had been joined, but it was the work of systematic scholars like Eichhorn, De Wette, Reuss, Vatke and Graf that created a methodology. De Wette asserted that the proper study of the Bible is the study of the history of the text. A wealth of data poured forth to argue the dating of various sources; the prophets were dated before the law, the Pentateuch separated into separate strands, and other units of material in the Hebrew Bible were fixed chronologically, only to be re-fixed. In New Testament studies, Schleiermacher was largely responsible for initiating 'the quest for the historical Jesus'. For him, the Bible's authority was superseded by that which 'flows immediately from the person of Jesus Christ'. Uninterested in arguing for the historical accuracy of the gospel stories, David Strauss advocated that they be read as legendary narratives, and Ferdinand Christian Bauer asked that the ideology of the writer be examined instead of the historicity of his story; both incited further research on the origins of New Testament literature.

The advantages of the critical-historical approach were evident: history need not be waived in this age of historicism, but neither did the Bible have to be indicted as historically untrue. Instead of asking if the gospels or exodus narratives were historically correct, scholars now asked what was the correct history of those narratives. During the Reformation, the Bible reader might encounter difficulties in the text, obscurities in Paul or in Isaiah, but he believed that the deficiency was his, attributable to his lack of spiritual understanding. The Bible was perspicuous to believers, illuminated to those who possessed the light. With the advent of historical criticism, when the common reader found difficulties, he could only assume that he lacked the special expertise that would offer him historical explanations.

Procedures that were essentially excavative – including archae-ology – were honed in the criticism of the late nineteenth and early twentieth centuries. The cultural contexts of ancient Israel and the early church began to be fleshed in as archaeological discoveries of ancient Mesopotamian and Egyptian documents were uncovered.

These documents, in turn, enabled research in comparative philology and in textual criticism, with its efforts to restore the primitive text of the Bible. In source criticism, scholars continued to search out the documentary sources of the Bible; redaction criticism focused on biblical editorial hypotheses; form criticism turned to biblical genres and the 'life situations' in which they were generated (the *Sitz im Leben* of Gunkel). When form criticism was applied to the gospel traditions, it linked various genres to the homiletical and political needs of the early communities. If the Bible could still be regarded as allegorical in all this research, it would only be loosely; for the tropological and anagogical categories of the medieval exegetes have given way to a historical world the Bible ostensibly encodes. While the Bible did not survive the age of science as a historically valid record, nonetheless, historical validity – both the history of the production of the text and the culture that produced it – have become paramount. The major work of the influential form-critic Sigmund Mowinckel, *The Psalms in Israel's Worship*, was devoted to ascertaining the cultic setting for each of the psalms, and its title is symptomatic of how little interest there was in interpreting the poetry of the psalms in any other light: its original Norwegian title was *Offersang og Sangoffer*, 'Song of sacrifice and Sacrifice of song'.

In *The Eclipse of Biblical Narrative*, Hans Frei has offered a compelling scheme for this long history of biblical interpretation. For the early exegetes, the Bible was the arbiter of all meaning, an inclusive world to which 'extra-biblical' history – including their own – had to be accommodated. 'Biblical interpretation became an imperative need, but its direction was that of incorporating extra-biblical thought, experience, and reality into the one real world detailed and made accessible by the biblical story – not the reverse.'[15] Figurative interpretation had to be infinitely inventive to allow the Bible to embrace any and all historical experience. According to Frei, with the 'higher criticism' (so-called to distinguish its scientific pursuits from mere theological interpretation) the frame of reference moved from the world inside the Bible to a world outside, and the project became one of fitting the Bible to those external data.

Our current understanding of textuality has broken down the distinction between these worlds. That does not mean that the Bible is privileged, that it can subsume a non-biblical world: we do not try to cram the world into the pages of the Bible. Nor does it mean that some historical realm is privileged: we do not use the Bible to footnote the text of history. Rather, the pages of both are contiguous, and the categories themselves – biblical and non-biblical – have become obsolete. Ideological (or theological) concerns are not separable from historical ones, and excavations of the past do not replace interpretation for they are understood to be an interpretive procedure. If theology went underground in the age of excavative biblical research, it is returning in the guise of theory. Along with this renewed interest in ideology and interpretation are theoretical controversies about the ground of meaning that sound remarkably familiar – from early theological debates.

That brings me to the third story that should be understood as another context for this volume: the story of institutions. Much of the history of biblical interpretation is part of the history of the Church and the history of Judaism, at once propelling major changes in those institutions and being propelled by those changes. But it may be less obvious – because it is too close to home – that just as the Reformers' displacement of medieval exegesis tells a story about shifting power, so the movement of biblical interpretation from religious institutions to the academy is both driven by our theoretical concerns and shapes those concerns. That academic setting requires further refinement: scriptural interpretation is pursued in departments of divinity, departments of religion, Near Eastern studies, and departments of English and literary criticism. It seems to me that the Bible's travels from one setting to another within the academy recapitulates the above narrative: a theological/ideological frame is explicit in departments of divinity, engaged as they are in vocational training of the clergy. In contrast, departments of religion have largely clung to those excavative-historical procedures ushered in by the age of enlightenment. Bible students in religion departments learn of the Hyksos period, the Amarna Age, the discoveries of Mari and Nuzi, and here, embarrassment over theology led to a recent contribution, *The Bible Without Theology*,[16] which makes an explicit virtue of that rejection. And what are the constraints bearing upon the study of the Bible in the institutional setting of English departments? Like the prophet Amos, who denounces the enemies of Israel as if he were going to contrast their faults to Israel's virtues, only to turn his strongest critique against Israel herself, I cannot report that the study of the Bible in departments of English has fulfilled the promises held out in the 1970s. 'The Bible as Literature' is a course title fraught with dangers: it suggests that we know what literature is, what the Bible is, and with all these confident formulations behind us, we can now make them analogous, or even equate them, as the case may be. To construct a poetics of the Bible, as we would for Shakespeare, Dante or Tolstoy, is valuable; but there can be no poetics that does not have ideological implications. The project of biblical poetics, as Bal has shown, can be historical in the deepest sense, obstructing universalism, or it can be narrowly formal and disappointingly unreflective about its own assumptions.[17] A decade after Robert Alter noticed the almost complete lack of interest in biblical narrative in the academy, Adele Berlin described a very different scene:

We are now in the aesthetic, or literary age. The most avant-garde books on the Bible are studies of narrative or poetry, or applications of literary theory to the biblical text. Even in more staid areas of research – commentaries, textual criticism – account is now taken of literary issues such as the poetic needs and impact of a work, and the literary (not only historical) logic behind its formation.[18]

If, as Berlin says, we are still 'applying' theory and comfortably distinguishing literary from historical concerns, then the project still has a long way to go. Meanwhile, this volume should attest that an infusion of literary theory in biblical studies is changing its shape. We only hope that in this latest encounter between the book and the text, the song need not be sacrificed.

In one sense, all this volume demonstrates is that the Bible is now being subjected to the same theoretical questions we ask of other texts. But in another sense, doing just that signals a radical departure from business-as-usual in biblical studies, another genuine rupture in the history of interpreting the text. It has happened before. In the eighteenth and nineteenth centuries, the importation of 'foreign methods' meant that the Bible was asked to answer, for the first time, to the historical-critical examination that any other text from antiquity would. 'All that happened', in other words, is that the unchallenged authority of the Bible was challenged – powerfully and systematically. My own sense is that in the course of the critical-historical Bible scholarship that ensued, that authority was reinscribed, albeit in a disguised fashion. Whether the approach was historical or philological, the Bible was the focus of sustained, loving attention. Efforts to determine the cultic setting of psalms, to date the book of Daniel, to attribute various verses to various hands and to correlate those hypothetical authors with events in ancient history, did not so much pose a challenge to the Bible's authority as they presupposed that authority, for only a commitment to the centrality of the Bible could authorize that exhaustive activity. Nonetheless, that authorizing motive was closeted, all the more so because scientific inquiry into the Bible became a discipline set apart – apart from questions of faith, of theology, of biblical authority, and in this way the historical approaches were unable to touch – or injure – them. That separation was even institutionalized: departments of religion asked historical and philological questions, leaving theology to schools of divinity.

Hence, this most devastating challenge to biblical authority, this threat posed by the rise of historicism, was resisted on both fronts: on the one hand, faith in the Bible was deflected into scientific commitment to it, and on the other, the Bible's truths were preserved from the encroachments of scientific scepticism.

It is early to predict the effects of bringing literary theoretical discourse to bear upon the Bible. However, certain tendencies are betrayed by even this growing interest. Recent concerns are not borrowed from science; no 'hard facts' of philology or archaeology in literary theoretical approaches, will pose a challenge to the Bible's authority. But the growing appearance of Barthes, Derrida, Lacan, Foucault, feminist, and Marxist criticism on the shelves of biblical scholars indicates that questions of interpretation are foregrounded. And these questions – about the design of the narratives, about gender construction, about repression in the Bible, about prophetic sublimity, about multiplicity of interpretations, about the politics of interpreting, about decentered subjects, about the Bible in ancient popular culture, and about biblical understanding of space and time – these questions are difficult to cordon off from the preserve of biblical theology and hermeneutics, even when they are broached from a secular perspective. Even biblical history will not be left untouched by this new theoretical discourse; now the question will be how to theorize history. Biblical authority is not safe from all of these questions – in part because theological questions are more difficult to separate from literary theory than they were from the discoveries of archaeologists and philologists; in part because questions of faith are matters of theory. Before we know it other hard questions will be asked that have their immediate source in literary theory: why has this text been authorized at all? What institutional purposes were served by that authorization, what power is garnered by authorizing any text, this text, by whom and how, and harder still, why does the Bible still persist to hold that stature in our culture, even residually, among unbelievers?

NOTES

1 Robert Alter and Frank Kermode (eds), *The Literary Guide to the Bible* (Harvard University Press, Cambridge, Mass., 1987), p. 4.
2 Robert Alter, 'A Literary Approach to the Bible', *Commentary*, December 1975, pp. 70–1.
3 See Meir Sternberg, *The Poetics of Biblical Narrative* (Indiana University Press, Bloomington, 1986).

4 Mieke Bal, 'The Bible as Literature: A Critical Escape', *Diacritics*, 16(4), pp. 71–9.

5 See Geoffrey Hartman and Sanford Budick (eds), *Midrash and Literature* (Yale University Press, New Haven, 1986).

6 Jacob Neusner, *Judaism in the Matrix of Christianity* (Fortress Press, Philadelphia, 1986), p. 89. My brief remarks necessarily obsure the diversity and evolution in rabbinic thought.

7 Judah Goldin, 'Midrash and Aggadah', *Encyclopedia of Religion*, ed. Mircea Eliade (Macmillan, New York, 1987), pp. 509–15.

8 The Babylonian Talmud, quoted among other places in David Stern, 'Midrash and Indeterminacy', *Critical Inquiry*, 15 (Autumn 1988), pp. 132–60, esp. p. 140. The relation of rabbinic exegesis to contemporary literary theory has been pursued more fully recently than the relation of the Bible to literary theory. See the helpful collection of essays in Hartman and Budick (eds), *Midrash and Literature*, and Susan Handleman, *The Slayers of Moses: The Emergence of Rabbinic Interpretation in Modern Literary Theory* (State University of New York Press, Albany, 1982).

9 Martin Luther, *Lectures on Genesis*, 7:16–24 Werke, Weimar Edition, vol. 42, p. 324.

10 In Henry Bettenson, *Documents of the Christian Church* (Oxford University Press, London and New York, 1943), p. 201.

11 John Calvin, *Opera, Corpus Reformatorum* (C. A. Schwitsche, Brunsvig, 1863).

12 Johann Gottfried von Herder, *Briefe, das Studium der Theologie betreffend*, pt I, in *Sammtlichte Werke*, ed. Bernhard Supan (Weidmann, Berlin, 1877–1913), vol. 10, p. 14, cited in Hans Frei, *The Eclipse of Biblical Narrative* (Yale University Press, New Haven, 1964), p. 185.

13 Werner Georg Kummel, *The New Testament: The History of the Investigation of Its Problems*, tr. S. McLean Gilmour and Howard Kee (Abingdon Press, Nashville, 1972), p. 68.

14 See the discussion by Robert Oden, *The Bible without Theology* (Harper & Row, New York, 1987), p. 14.

15 Frei, *The Eclipse of Biblical Narrative*, p. 3.

16 Oden, *The Bible without Theology*.

17 Mieke Bal, 'The Bible as Literature: A Critical Escape.'

18 Adele Berlin, 'Narrative Poetics in the Bible', *Prooftexts*, 6 (1986), pp. 273–84, esp. p. 273.

1

Dealing/With/Women: Daughters in the Book of Judges

Mieke Bal

The role of critical theory

The question of the relations between the Bible and critical theory is not one of application. Critical theory can be no more or no less meaningfully 'applied' to the Bible than to any other ancient body of texts. But since theories are bodies of language of the same order as the text, I do not think there can be a question of application. At the most, theories can be brought into a dialogue with texts. In this sense, I would like to take the conjunction 'and' in the theme of this volume on the Bible and critical theory, as I like to take the Hebrew conjunction '*waw*': at face value. I do not want to take it as a false coordination that conceals some other, 'logical' relation, some subordination, on either side.

'And' stands for dialogue, for two equals speaking to each other, listening to each other, in an attempt to learn something from the encounter: to change. The success of the dialogue will be measured in this chapter in terms of relevance and of limits – and of the relevance of limits. The theory I will use, which is my own version of narratology,[1] will be brought to the text as a subtext, one that speaks with, or through, the biblical text, one that opens the text up, asks it questions. I will assess the relevance of this encounter against the theory's capacity to raise problems rather than solve them, to make it more interesting, make it speak more excitingly, than it used to do without the theory. It is to be challenged on its own terms. But the text, in response to that challenge, will challenge the theory, point out its limits, and force it to go beyond itself. As a result, the very dialogue between narrative theory and a body of biblical texts leads to a transgression of disciplinary boundaries. A fruitful encounter between critical theory and the Bible will end, I will argue, in an interdisciplinary venture. The only *critical* literary theory, then, criticizes itself, too. It must be an open, dialogic theory.

Killers and victims

When I first read the Book of Judges as a whole, I was surprised to see that the famous wicked woman, Delilah, had two colleagues in evil. Two other women tricked a male hero into a trap and killed him. In spite of her participation in the 'right' cause, Yael, the murderess of Sisera, is generally criticized by commentators. She is blamed for breaking the sacred laws of hospitality and for the cruelty of her method of killing.[2] In fact, we need only to reverse the perspective and take the side of the Philistines to become aware of the close resemblance between the two murder stories. A third murderess is not so much blamed for her deed by commentaries, but fits the schema pretty well: the woman-with-the-millstone who, in 9:53, kills Abimelech. Although her deed is liberating, the victim himself thematizes the gender issue that underlies the event, and that is also elaborated in the prose version of Yael's act in chapter 4. It is shameful to be killed by a woman.

I had a hard time, as a feminist, defending these killers against attacks, and I agree that the impression of excessive violence in relation to gender is undeniably evoked by the book. I worked for quite some time on these female killers in the hope to understand better what issues underlie these stories.[3] It was only after concentrating on female violence that I became aware of another structure of violence in the same book. The impression of violence as a gender issue is at least as much caused by two other cases of violence: the sacrifice of Jephthah's daughter, and the rape, torture and murder of an innocent 'concubine' in Judges 19. At first sight, again, there is a contrast: the daughter of Jephthah, although killed, is a 'pure' victim of a sacred murder. She is sacrificed to Yhwh. The 'concubine' is, in the common view, a woman of lowly status, a status defined by her sexuality. Certainly not a virgin, she is killed in a way that repeats her degradation. Instead of being purified by fire and being devoted to the deity, she is debased, by men, raped to death. The horror of the two stories, the murder of two innocent women, match pretty well.

It was only after my attention – and my strong emotional response – had been drawn by these two stories, that I discovered a third case of a female victim. Just as the woman-with-the-millstone could only be inserted in the series of female killers after the establishment of the series – in other words, after we saw the similarities between the first two – similarly, this third victim almost escaped attention, and came to the fore once the similarities between the fate of the two other victims had been enhanced. Our third victim is Samson's bride, who was killed for the sake of male violence, too. Both third cases, almost hidden, will turn out to be in some sense the crucial ones, the ones that summarize the two others of the series. The narrative proximity between this victim and Delilah struck me as significant. Married, but not really, a virgin but not really, killed not by but with her father, she precedes the murderess who is not really the actual murderess of her victim, and who is, of the three killers, also the most clearly a lover of her victim – just as the bride is a lover of her indirect killer.

Three female killers, three female victims: a structure seems to emerge,[4] a structure that accounts for the excessively violent impression the book makes, a structure which I will replace for the coherence of history and theology that is usually the guideline for readings of the book as a whole. Indeed, although the difficulty of establishing a chronology of the book is acknowledged,[5] attempts continue to be made. The best analysis of the book that I know of, that of Gooding,[6] starts with a convincing refutation of the assumption that a dumb editor rather than a clever one composed the book; his own interpretation is as yet based on the assumption of the domination of the isotopies of war and theology. It will be my contention in this essay that in spite of the historical, political and theological mainline of the book as a composition, there is an underlying interest that may have had at least some influence on the selection of the available material. I read the book for the counter-coherence of violence and gender. Given the restrictions of time and the work previously done, I will focus here on the victims, and try to return to the killers briefly at the end.[7]

Narrative theory will help raise the questions, enhance the problems. I enter the analysis with the key question of narrative theory: the question of the subject. The subject is involved in narrative at three levels: the subject of speech, the subject of vision, the subject of action. In other words, who speaks? who sees (I call it, technically, who focalizes)? who acts? I use these questions to overcome a naïvely realistic reading, in their capacity to account for narrative form. I also use them to overcome a fallaciously repetitive reading that would remain within the ideology of the text rather than criticize it. In other words, I will use them to try to overcome the paralyzing opposition, so common in biblical scholarship, between historical and literary approaches. The questions help to account not only for what happens in the stories but also for the responsibility for both events and their narrative rendering.

The figuration of the subject

The first surprise that the question of the subject has for us is the problem of anonymity. The three victims, as if by coincidence, have no names. No names; no narrative power. They are subjected to the power of, mostly named, men. The first act that awaits us, then, is to provide the victims with a name. A name that makes them into subjects, that makes them speakable. Naming the victims is an act of insubordination to the text. Is it a distortion? In fact, the problem of naming is a useful way to become aware of the need of readerly activity. But my goal is not to embellish the text; only to account for its effect. Therefore the names to be given have to be acceptable within the text, while also emancipating the reader – and the characters – from it. Jephthah's daughter is defined by her daughter-hood. Her fate is a metonymic extension of her father. She will be given the name of *Bath*, which means 'daughter' (*bat*). The 'concubine' of chapter 19 is, as we shall see shortly, not a concubine in the now common sense. In order to grasp her status, we have to realize how her fate is connected to the house. Coming from Beth-lehem, the house of bread, she is moved from house to house, thrown out of the house, and signified, in her utter victimhood, when she drags herself to the threshold of the very house she was kicked out of. What else can her name be but *Beth*, which alludes to 'house' (*bayit*)? For Samson's bride, a character we will only meet briefly, the obvious name is *Kallah*. The word means 'bride', but I wish it to be a pun on *kalah*, which means 'consumption', 'complete destruction'. And indeed, the destruction of her is complete, both physical and symbolical. She is consumed by fire, and her remembrance is overshadowed by that of Delilah. The one who destroyed Samson's heroic strength is remembered, not the one who is its victim. Naming these women, then, is a first gesture to counter their oblivion. It is a first stage of their reinstatement into the history of gender relations as we try to reconstruct them. To rewrite these victims back into history is a way to correct the excessive and exclusive place the murderesses have been assigned in it.

It will not be possible to analyze the stories comprehensively. I will focus on an appropriate phenomenon which I call 'narrative condensation', a term I will explain below. I will try to convince the reader of the following points. First, Bath and Beth are not only victims. They are also subjects, more fully than one would suspect, although within the limits of the patriarchal power that kills them. Second, their reputation is false and in itself evidence of a modern patriarchal ideology that repeats the repression the text stimulates. Third, the issues at stake in the stories concern primarily the power of the father. This has been repressed by the enhancement of the themes of obedience (Bath) and hospitality (Beth). These interpretations are quite common, and are both evidence of the 'repetition-compulsion' that is in my view the basic strategy of ideological readings that my analysis argues against. These three points will be argued through the tiny textual details that exemplify the figure of condensation that is so appropriately iconic where the condensation, the being-one, of father and daughter is at stake.

Condensation is a figure of style and of thought that expresses two or more completely different ideas in a single expression. It is, of course, in the first place a figure in Freudian rhetoric. Freud claimed that condensation is used as a form of censorship. Those ideas that the subject cannot afford to acknowledge, are repressed from consciousness and return in a defigured form. Condensation is one such form, displacement is another. *Narrative* condensation is the same figure, two or more ideas expressed in one expression, but then, narratively: in one narrative act. *The* narrative condensation is the one that conflates two different, often incompatible subject-positions. The following will illustrate this, thus demonstrating the critical power of narratology.[8]

Bath, Beth and virginity

How are Bath and Beth introduced? Bath is first represented, not only without a name, but conditionally, unknown, characterized only by the *firstness* that is so crucial to our idea of virginity: the first one to meet the hero after victory. She is the object of a vow. As a speech-act, the vow is a combination of trade and promise.[9] The promise concerns the future, the trade concerns a deal. The deal, here, exchanges Bath's life against a military victory which Jephthah feels unable to accomplish himself. He needs support from Yhwh. Yhwh, then, is the real victor. According to the tradition that we see at work, for example in Judges 1, the victor is entitled to the chief's daughter as a bride. Just as Othniel, there, deserves Achsah, chief Caleb's daughter, Yhwh deserves Bath. The wording of the vow is quite similar in both cases and so is the situation: a difficult military situation that calls for the testing of the hero, the *gibbor*. Robert Alter would call it a type-scene.[10] The vow ends with a difference: Bath will not be given as a bride but as a burnt offering, not to a husband but to another, higher father (11:30–31).

Similarly, Beth is given away conditionally. The reversal of the situation only stresses the resemblance. The hero is in danger, but no military victory, only escape from danger is at stake. The same insecurity, however, highlights the same structure, shows the scene as a variant, by antithesis, of the type-scene whose structure is set in Judges 1. This woman is not given as a bride either, but as an object of sexual abuse. She is not given to the real victor, but to the strongest party. Strangely, the 'concubine' is offered as a gift *together* with a virgin: 'behold, my daughter, a virgin, and his concubine'. Again, a woman is given away to insure safety, this time not of the army but of an individual man. And again, the status of that woman (virgin? concubine?) seems to be important. They are given *as* women, and for their specific womanhood.

What is virginity? In a well known, but not yet enough criticized essay, Freud in 1918 tried to explain the taboo of virginity. Why is it that 'primitive people' shun defloration, while 'civilized men' cherish it? In spite of Freud's attempt to establish a difference between the 'savage' and his own kind, a difference that will then allow the similarity not to hurt too much, in both cases, and that is the important point, virginity, or rather, defloration, is an issue. Why, and how? Let us first turn to the status of these women, a 'virgin' and a 'concubine'. The word usually translated as 'virgin' (*betulah*) is used by Bath herself, not by Jephthah or by the narrator. The question 'who speaks?' can be rephrased as 'who speaks virginity?' and may be a crucial question. The narrator ends his presentation of the story with the words, 'and she had known no man'. Bath says something else. Her sentence is usually translated as 'let me bewail my virginity' and is then interpreted as 'bewail my childlessness, my futility'. I am not so sure that this is the issue for Bath; this sounds like a male concern. In order to focus this problem clearly, we have to make a brief excursion into language problems. This is, then, the first limit narratology forces us to transgress.

In the land of wandering rocks

The verb translated as 'to bewail' has not, in Hebrew, a direct object. Hence we may as well give it an absolute meaning: to lament. The noun *betulah* is preceded by the same preposition as 'mountains' in the same sentence: '*al*. The two segments '*al* the mountains, '*al* my *betulah*, although separated, may be considered as a broken parallelism.[11] This preposition is among the most variable in Hebrew. In one dictionary, one which is sometimes looked down upon but for which I shall argue later, it has at least twenty-eight meanings, one of which is to be a synonym of *'el*, for which the dictionary gives twelve meanings. It is clearly one of those words that shift with their context. With a spatial referent, it can mean upon, unto. The combination with the verb 'let me go down upon' is odd. It seems quite plausible, given this uncertainty, and in accordance with one of its frequent uses to give it a meaning of confrontation and directionality: 'towards' 'in order to be confronted with'. Towards the mountains, away from the father. If we extend that feature of directionality to the other noun, as the Septuagint suggests we may,[12] interpreting it as temporal, it could mean, there, 'towards my *betulah*', 'until I will be confronted with it'.

The noun *betulah* itself is subject to scrutiny for four reasons. It is often accompanied by the phrase: 'she/who had not known man'. In the episode of the bride-capture, at the end of the book, the description is even more explicit: 'four hundred young girls, *betulah*, who had not known man by lying with him' (21:12). This is usually translated as 'young virgins': the two nouns, *na'arah* (young, unmarried girls) and *betulah* are then considered synonyms. If that were the case, the description would be four times repetitive; which seems excessive, even for the Hebrew Bible. The juxtaposition of these expressions makes me suspect they each add a feature to the described brides. A second reason to sense a different meaning in *betulah* is the quoted verse 'my daughter, *betulah*, and his "concubine"'. If being a virgin is a recommendation, then being a concubine is not; both women are, however, offered on an equal footing, as a gift valuable enough to compensate for the man. The third reason is that the narrator uses the description while Bath herself uses the noun. The fourth reason is now sufficiently strengthened: the absence of the accusative form and the use of the preposition-shifter, that takes the ideas of confrontation and directionality from its previous use.

These arguments all point at the same idea: that *betulah* refers, for Bath, to a state, a life-phase, that does not end, but towards which one goes, which one confronts. This points to a view, a vision, different from the one expressed by the narrator. If conceived this way, Bath's *direction* is what she is concerned with. 'Leave me alone': she turns away from the father, and goes, in the direction of the mountains, the wilderness, and *betulah*, a phase. Her expression, then, is more independent from the narrator's than we are accustomed to assume possible, used as we are to a realistic, psychological narrative discourse. I contend that the biblical discourse, with its heterogeneous background and composition, could very well accommodate what I like to call *wandering rocks*. Expressions, words, fragments of discourse that circulated within the culture even if they were, perhaps, no longer understood, resemble those glacial tilts that travelled with the ice and landed in an alien place where they were put to a use foreign to their origin. Yet, they remained undestructible. Just so, Bath's discourse, expressing a female conception of *betulah*, of the life-phase of ripeness, so thoroughly recuperated by the trade between men, yet still there, as a wandering rock, indestructible but used in an alien way.

It is well-known practice among many people, and our culture is no exception, to mark the transitions in the life of the individual by a ritual, a rite of passage.[13] Rites of coming-of-age, *bar-mitzvah*, first communion, are replaced, in secular culture, by graduation ceremonies. Among mothers and daughters, the first menstruation is often secretly celebrated. In many societies the rites of passage are very elaborate, and, as Victor Turner has pointed out in his structuralist interpretation of the rites,[14] the transition, a temporal moment, is often symbolized in a spatial form, by the wilderness where the initiate is kept in separation from the world of childhood, often for several months. In Bath's request, the latter aspect is present, as is the former.

Seen in the light of rites of passage, Bath's request receives an altogether different meaning. Coming out of the house of her father to celebrate the victor, her situation is similar to Achsah's. She can be expected to be given in marriage to the victor. This is how she obstinately, and justly, interprets her fate – as a wandering rock, out of place. She knows, then, that she has reached the age of transition. Taking leave from the father, she prepares for the next phase of her life, the *nubile* state, by organizing the rite of passage that belongs to it. The problem of her 'not having known man', of her being due to the victor but whose identity is unclear, since the father failed as a *gibbor* and invoked divine rather than human help, is not her concern. The same event, then, receives a completely different, alien if not opposed meaning, according to the subject whose view is expressed. This is a first case of narrative condensation. The wandering rock of Bath's language, her almost formulaic speech, is not acknowledged as different any more, and readers take only the male view of virginity into account.

The concept of *betulah* comes to stand in a series of which *na'arah* is the preceding and *'almah* the following term: unmarried, marriageable, recently married. It will be shown to be a dangerous series: it indicates the phases in life wherein the ripeness of women becomes the bone of contention between men who struggle for her possession. I will turn to the concept of 'concubine' shortly, but already we know that the 'concubine' of chapter 19, Beth, is a recently married woman.

The gift offered by the host in that story consists, then, of two women, both young, but of age: *sexually usable.*

Now we can see what comprises the narrative condensation. Bath speaks one language, the narrator another. Bath's is the language of the female subject who prepares for the future, for the next phase of her life. The narrator is concerned with virginity in the now common sense, which is not oriented towards the future but to the past, not a beginning but an end, not positive but negative. What can the importance be of this negative, male view of the woman in transition?

The logic of possession

In the already mentioned essay on the taboo of virginity, Freud, who is not only the justly praised discoverer of the importance of unconscious motivations in cultural behavior, but also the spokesman of contemporary male ideology, expresses the long-held view of virginity in the following words: 'The demand that a girl shall not bring to her marriage with a particular man any memory of sexual relations with another is, indeed, nothing other than the logical continuation of the right to exclusive possession of a woman, which forms the essence of monogamy, the extension of this monopoly over the past'.[15] The 'logic' Freud expresses here, in the relation he establishes between sex and memory, is quite revealing. It is also, 'logically' problematic, and in that sense it comes close to a Freudian slip. The Hebrew language expresses the same idea in what we have always considered to be a euphemism: 'to have known no man'. I do not think it is a euphemism, an expression that softens the crudeness of its content. I think, to the contrary, that it is a specification that sharpens the content. What the expression conveys is, in the light of Freud's 'logic', that from sexuality conceived as 'sexual possession' there is no escape. The motivation for the concern with virginity is not so much, in Freud's view, the often-held idea that sexuality is defiling, hence that sex makes the woman less valuable because it pollutes her.

In a short paper, G. J. Wenham[16] argues that Mary Douglas's interpretation of defilement[17] is too narrowly symbolic. The loss of semen is a loss of life-liquid, and therefore takes a (less serious) place in the series of other losses of life-liquid, like blood in childbirth and menstruation. In this conception the defiling effect of sex pollutes the man in the first place. The woman, then, is defiled by contagion, I would say, metonymically. What makes the experience of sex devalue the woman is, rather than the bodily change, literally memory, that is knowledge, but knowledge of the past. This knowledge turns the woman into an *other*, an autonomous subject. It is that subjectivity that comes with sexual experience that apparently threatens the exclusivity of the possession. What matters *is* knowledge, what threatens purity is the contamination of the mind, what the male view of virginity is concerned with is basically the past, not the future. This is expressed in Hebrew in other words than the description of virginity. The Hebrew word for male is, significantly, *zakar*. Whether or not this is a homonym of different origin, the word does mean 'to remember', and given the Hebrew use of the singular masculine as the root, 'he will remember'. To remember is a male prerogative, denied the women.

The male role in procreation is, indeed, something that has to be remembered, as opposed to the female role that is visible. Remembering is an urgent business, since paternity is never certain, while maternity is always sure. Expressions for sexuality and for maleness both enhance the importance of paternity. But, and this is the interesting detail that disturbs, this is a shift, a shift from husband to father. As Freud points out, the purpose of virginity is to make a new start, to bring no memory of any other man, including, we might now suggest, the father. This becomes particularly pointed since the recent discovery of widespread father–daughter rape as a modern patriarchal practice. It also helps us understand the reluctance of fathers to let their daughters go to another man – to give her away, as the jargon of marriage ceremonies has it. There is a condensation here; not a narrative one, although with narrative consequences, but a linguistic one, a condensation that conflates the position of father and husband, of possession in the present and possession in the past or, in yet another tune, of temporary possession and possession forever. Bath's sacrifice is a solution, be it a fatal one, to this dilemma: the father gives her away, but to a higher father, not to a man. And if Bath has been remembered as the virgin-daughter, it is because her view of what she is, her subjectivity, has been repressed in the subsequent readings of her story. Of the double view of *betulah*, the female view of her own life-phase has been repressed and only the negative concern with her possession has been preserved.

Beth's marriage

The state of Beth is equally interesting. It is visible, even to an outsider, that her presentation is massively misunderstood. The sentence that introduces her is usually translated as, 'a Levite from

Ephraim took to him a concubine from Beth-lehem'. Literally, however, it says, 'he took to him a woman, a 'concubine' from Beth-lehem'. As many scholars have pointed out, the order of the words 'woman' and 'concubine' seems odd. More 'logical' would be, 'he took to him a concubine, a woman from Beth-lehem', but we have learned to suspect logic. Another solution would be, 'he took as his wife a concubine from Beth-lehem', but there is no indication that this is meant. In my view, these problems are caused by the anachronistic assumption that 'concubine' means concubine. Again, it is the word that expresses the woman's status that is the trouble-maker. Note that two local indications, judged irrelevant by some scholars, are the figuration of an opposition that is also at play in the previous and the following chapters. The opposition can be interpreted right now through the meaning of the names: *Ephraim* is derived from a word meaning 'pasture land' (Aramaic: *'aphra*) while *Beth-lehem* means 'house-of-bread'. I will come back to those meanings that will provide the background for the problematic statement about the woman.

The word translated as 'concubine' is the central problem in this presentation of the woman. The 'logic' of translation that chooses, first, the latinate word 'concubine' and gives it the meaning that it literally has in Latin, bedmate, is anachronistic. It becomes circularly so when it is, next, assumed to refer to a lowly status. There is very little evidence for this connection. Phyllis Trible is among those who uncritically accept this meaning.[18] She makes great case of the lowly status of the woman on the basis of extremely thin evidence. This is an example of the way scholars sometimes tend to repeat each other, and of the dangerous consequences of this uncritical attitude. Trible, who works for a feminist hermeneutics, does the feminist cause a small favor by this acceptance.

Let us try to approach the word from the point of view of narratology, and keep in mind that this woman is the subject of an action described in verse 2. The opposition between the husband's pasture land and the house-of-bread of the father is the setting of the first part of the story. If we are faithful to the order of the words, and keep this opposition in mind, we must assume that the first description of Beth means something like, 'he took to himself a wife, a (specification) from Beth-lehem'. The specification can then be assumed to specify *what sort of wife* he took, and Beth-lehem apparently is relevant information there. In other words, he took a wife according to the tradition that was usual in Beth-lehem.

The dictionary gives several meanings of this non-semitic noun, and suggests a connection with the Arabic word for 'queen'. Koehler and Baumgartner mention as a first, ancient meaning, 'wife who, after marriage, remains with her father'.[19] This form of marriage is known from nomadic societies. The husband, who had no stable place to live, wandered around with his flocks, and visited his wife at irregular intervals. As early as 1921 and 1931, Morgenstern examined quite a few cases of the type of marriage he calls *beena* marriage. Although the noun *pilegesh* seems to refer to a secondary wife (Gen. 22:24; 25:6), most of the occurrences make much more sense as cases of this type of marriage. I will contend in this article that the competition between this and the more usual type of marriage is the major anthropological issue in the book of Judges. This brings us, from narratology via philology, to anthropology as a discipline useful and necessary to understand these disturbing stories.

The term used by Morgenstern, *beena* marriage or *matriarchat*, suggests that the background of *pilegesh* is a matriarchal society. This is an interesting case of repression in anthropological discourse. Indeed, in many anthropological studies on kinship structure, matrilocal marriage is opposed to virilocal marriage, and matrilocal is easily confused with matriarchy. This is a false conflation. In other studies the marriage form at stake is called duo-local. In both cases, however, the husband is, again, conflated with the father. The woman is attributed much more power than she probably had, and many features of the stories remain unexplained. Morgenstern does not deal with Judges 19, which I consider the founding story for the transition that is at issue. In order for some clarity to emerge, we can call this marriage form *patrilocal* marriage, and oppose it, not to matrilocal but to virilocal marriage.

If we take it that *pilegesh*, in this probably very ancient story, refers to this type of wife, many elements found problematic by scholars suddenly fall into place. First, the introduction of Beth in verse 1: he took to him a wife, a patrilocal wife from Beth-lehem. The specification becomes meaningful: as a man from a pasture land, without stable dwelling, he took a wife firmly established in the house of her father. The rest of the story becomes, not only coherent, but extremely meaningful as an account of institutional transition.

The translation of verse 2 is even more problematic. Two translations compete: 'she played the harlot against him'[20] and 'she became angry with him'. The first translation is derived from Hebrew texts, the second from the Greek translation. The difference involves Beth's position as either culprit or offended party, hence, her subject-position on the level of action. Instead of being alarmed by this disagreement that entails ideological conclusions, Trible never questions the tendency of both translations. In the light of the crucial importance of the meaning of the verb for the interpretation of the story, I find it an almost comical problem. The same preposition whose flexibility was so helpful in Bath's story is the troublemaker here. It never occurs elsewhere with this verb, *zanah*. Its spatial meaning was, in chapter 11, directional: toward. We get, then: she . . . toward him, with a nuance of confrontation. Now the verb has to illuminate the problem. It is generally assumed to mean 'to be unfaithful'. Although it is often used in relation to sexual unfaithfulness, this is not always so. And although it usually refers to women, it also refers to men (e.g. Num. 25:1). Koehler and Baumgartner, referring to Winckler's *Geschichte Israels*, cite, as a first possible meaning, 'means originally, that the husband does not live in his wife's tribe'. I confess I was flabbergasted by the coincidence; if there is an evolution, from the context of patrilocal marriage to regular prostitution, we glimpse an ideological evolution that affects the semantics of the word. The meaning 'to become angry' is given, in my dictionary, as derived from Akkadian while the many other cases derive their meaning from the Aramaic. For the Akkadian, Judges 19 is the only case, and I feel justified to doubt this uniqueness. Comparative philology is not meant to solve problems prematurely, nor should it be used to cover up interesting possibilities.

Let us assume, for our story, the meaning 'to be unfaithful', and given the coincidence between *pilegesh* and the ancient meaning of *zanah*, this unfaithfulness may have to do with the transition from patrilocal to virilocal marriage. Narratology draws our attention to Beth's status as the subject of the action of the verb. She is, then, unfaithful, not *against* her husband, but *toward* him, in the directional, confrontational and spatial sense. She is unfaithful because she *goes to* her husband. This makes sense, too, in connection with the next statement, that has it that she leaves him, but after this 'unfaithfulness'. To whom is she unfaithful, then? To her father, who had the 'right of exclusive possession'? This woman acted as a relatively autonomous subject. She went to visit her husband – whether or not on his instigation, that we cannot know. After the visit, she went back to the father where she belonged, according to the institution of marriage that binds her. The uncertainties in the translation and interpretation reflect the problematic, uncertain situation Beth entered. As we will see, she will be crushed between the men who compete for her exclusive possession. This is the narrative condensation *par excellence*, the one that conflates father and husband.

Beth's father

This possibility explains an otherwise odd detail, frequently noticed but never satisfactorily dealt with. The most thorough analysis I know of is by Niditch, but she does not manage to explain the story as a whole either, and especially not the details that concern me here.[21] When, later, the husband comes to the house of the father, the latter is very happy to see his son-in-law and insists that the couple remain in the house of bread. The reception he gives the husband does not seem plausible for the case of the lowly woman, similar to a slave, bought from poor families, that the *Interpreter's Dictionary of the Bible* presents as 'concubine'.[22] Why, many have asked, is he so happy to see the husband of the either shamefully repudiated or infuriated daughter? And if so, why his insistence, why does he harass him to stay against his wish? My answer is simple: he is happy, because now, the husband is behaving according to the rules, because the threatened institution which guarantees his exclusive possession of the daughter, is back in order. Second, the reason that he insists is because he does not want the transgression to happen again. The rich reception in the house-of-bread displays his power, and indeed, the husband in turn, trying to compete with this powerful father, displays his own possessions. A third detail has a sad explanation as well. From the moment that the two men are together, Beth disappears from the story, only to reappear as the victim of the climax of violence of the book. The phrase 'he went after her to her father's house to speak to her heart' is often mistakenly translated or interpreted as a sign of the husband's kindness. The heart, however, is the site of reason rather than of feelings, and the goal of the visit must be interpreted as persuasion, not conciliation. This is not a modern psychological novel.

Beth's marriage reflects the competition between patrilocal and virilocal marriage. This competition is more often at stake in the Hebrew Bible than is generally assumed. The wooing of Rebekah has virilocality as its condition, and Jacob had to integrate himself in a patrilocal environment for a long time, before he managed to emancipate himself from Laban. Father and husband, in these cases, compete over the 'memory' of the daughter. Within the preoccupation of biblical ideology, that competition concerns the question: whose memory will she perpetuate, whose will her children be, which name will she serve? Not her own, in any case; of that, the writers who deprived Bath and Beth of a name, have taken care. But they overlooked what female subjectivity can accomplish, even within the limits of the struggle between two forms of patriarchy.

It is time to introduce briefly a character who plays a role in Bath's story, and who is strikingly absent in Beth's, although not in its aftermath: Yhwh, the true hero, the 'fiancé' of the chief's daughter. As the addressee of Jephthah's vow and the beneficiary of her sacrifice, he does not speak. Attempts to argue that his silence is evidence for his condemnation of the sacrifice do not seem convincing. If he does not speak for it, he does not speak against it either. In his alleged omniscience, he could have foreseen the outcome of the vow. If Jephthah accomplished the victory, it was, in the eyes of the *gibbor*, thanks to Yhwh's help. And, finally, while Yhwh knew how to prevent Isaac's sacrifice, he refrains from preventing Bath's. Yhwh is undeniably a father figure. Jephthah, we might conjecture, prefers to give up his daughter altogether rather than to give her to a man of the next generation. Giving her to the superfather, he keeps her at least at the 'proper' side: the side of the fathers. The side of absolute property, of property with a *past*. The image of the deity that emerges from this story is that of a father figure who complies with the structure of power that trades daughters for military victory, who does nothing against this priority of business over life.

Now that we have become aware of this anthropological structure that figures these stories, it is easy to insert our third victim in this series. In fact, Kallah the bride exemplifies the issue. Her father almost gave her away to a husband, but he took her back, in order to give her to someone who would at least accept the rules of patrilocal marriage. This explains the strange fact that when Samson comes to visit her, she does live with her father but her father claims to have given her away already.[23]

Between men

In Beth's case, the husband seems to end up winning: he manages to take Beth out of the house-of-bread, to the pasture land. But social changes produce dangerous situations, and the dangers in this case are very tough. In fact, the husband shows that he is not up to his newly acquired status. He is not able to see the daughter safely home. Hosted by another father, in other words, returning, out of weakness, to the father's house – again a house full of bread – he gives up his position. Beth is taken over by the father when the latter offers her, as well as his own nubile daughter, for sexual abuse. The gift has to be this double gift, not only in order to play the story off against Genesis

19 (Niditch calls it, ironically I would hope, more successful than the Lot story[24]), but mainly, in order to signify the gift as a fatherly act; the father gives daughters, his own and somebody else's alike. The inhabitants of the city are not satisfied with the women. They want the man. It is the man who has to be punished for subverting the institution. They want to teach him a lesson – about sex, knowledge and possession; about sex as knowledge and possession.

This explains another strange detail. The men refuse to accept the two women from the hand of the father. When the husband throws his wife out, they do accept that gift. Why would they refuse two women, and accept one? Because they are concerned with a symbolic victory. The subversive husband has to be punished, either by being raped himself or by giving up his bone of contention. Taking the women from the father would obscure the issue. And if punishment is at stake, why does it have to take the form of rape? First, it seems naïve to suppose that the entire male population of both Sodom and Gibeah is homosexual. As Niditch point out, in this culture homosexual rape is seen as a form of extreme humiliation: it is, in these stories, the destruction of the subject that the men want to perform, and is there a worse destruction possible than to treat a male as a female? But there is another, deeper motivation thinkable. In the eyes of the patrilocal ideology, the bond between father and daughter is the only 'natural', acceptable one: possession with a past. To go away from the father, to be 'unfaithful towards a man', is to go with any man; it is arbitrariness as opposed to naturalness. And from 'any man' to 'every man' is but one step, a step that even today is often made. A woman who divorces, or takes a lover, is often assumed to be public property, since, in the eyes of those who follow this 'logic', she has shown herself by her act of autonomy to be 'available'. The punishment against this particular transgression, then, can be of only two kinds: either confinement, return to exclusive possession and the impossibility ever to enter the compromise situation of marriage (Bath); or gang-rape, public, mass abuse (Beth). Both punishments lead to the death of the female subject.

One question has to be answered still. Why does the father figure protect the husband? Why, in other words, this excessive hospitality? The father may compete with the husband; the very competition is a business between men. When it comes to a confrontation, the father will take the side of the other man, who may be of a different generation, but who still is of the same sex: the one that has interest in memory. Offering to give the daughters, Bath the Second and Beth, the father wins on both fronts: he protects the man, but he strips him of his otherness. Taking the patrilocal wife away from him, he turns him into a 'normal' young man: he has submitted to the power of the father, yet he is a man, who may raise up seed for the father, a man with a future father-position.

The husband, in his turn, displays the cowardice that we know. His distorted report, later, shows that he is well aware of what he is doing. He has lost the struggle with the father, he must give up the woman, but at least he can confirm, in the very gesture of giving her up, his power over her. Power over the weaker compensates for the loss of power, for the humiliation that goes with submission. This we know to happen in other circumstances all the time. It explains why oppressed men oppress their women rather than fighting, with her, against the oppressing power. The gesture of throwing Beth out is thus a narrative condensation on the level of action: the act of submission and the act of exercising absolute power are conflated in one act. The gesture is of the same order as the one it inverts. Beth had been 'unfaithful' against the father/towards him; he throws her back, towards the father's side, away from himself, submitting to the father, but, within the extreme violence that goes with revolutionary chaos, *over her dead body*.

The daughters' sacrifice

Three young, nubile women are sacrificed. Sacrificed: given up, in a symbolic gesture, to a higher power. Green defines sacrifice as 'the voluntary or involuntary termination of human life in a ritualistic manner or for ritualistic purposes.[25] Turner stresses the symbolic aspect of sacrifice;[26] Girard its violence,[27] and Jay calls it 'a remedy for having been born of woman'.[28] All these theories of sacrifice fit our three women extremely well; none mentions them. That the 'remedy' necessarily involves the 'founding violence', hence, that Jay's and Girard's theory need each other, clarifies our three victims. Bath is burned to death, rather than given in marriage. Beth is momentarily taken away from the father, but given up, back, later. Kallah is burned to death *with* her father. The executioner of Bath is her father himself. Kallah is executed by a collective that represents the tribe of the father and the age-group, the generation of the husband. Beth is killed by . . . that is unclear.[29] She is offered by the father, actually given up by the husband, raped and tortured by the collective that punishes the intruder in the name of the father. But who kills her?

The initiative that Beth took to go and visit her husband in the beginning of the story, is mirrored by her second 'visit' at the end. She has been eliminated as a narrative subject, only to act again as what she then is: bereaved of all her 'property', she can only fall down, but she does it at the threshold of the house, the house that is neither her father's nor her husband's, but that is owned by the father and inhabited by the husband. Is she dead, when she does not answer her husband's display of power when, refreshed by a good night's sleep, he *orders* her to stand up and come *home*? We do not know, and we are not supposed to know. Because this time, the executioner has to remain ambiguous. The husband does act as the sacrifical agent. Repeating his first gesture of violence, he now cuts her to pieces. This sacrificial gesture is equivalent in violence to the story as a whole. The gesture is symbolic. It turns Beth into a symbol. To speak with Shoshana Felman: Beth is *the scandal of the speaking body*. The gesture is also ambiguous. If Beth is still alive, the husband is her actual murderer. That cannot be, since the next chapter presents the war against the Benjaminites as a justified revenge on this intrusion upon the Benjaminites themselves,[30] a war that starts with an unacceptable sacrifice, that is led by Yhwh and whose final scenes of the purity laws. There is no way to redeem this man. But then, there is no way to redeem the following episode, the civil war, that ends in the enforcement of the new, virilocal marriage institution, upon the Benjaminites themselves.[30] A war that starts with an unacceptable sacrifice, that is led by Yahweh and whose final scenes of bride-capture are often seen as a 'merry end' of the book, in spite of the violence against women it entails. The three sacrifices, considered in this respect, are all three 'improper'. Bath is killed by someone who is not a priest. Samson transgressed the purity laws in his eating of the honey from a dead lion. Beth, the founding victim who undergoes all violence thinkable, is slaughtered by the hand of a priest who does wrong either way.

Counter-rituals

If, in these stories, the men accomplish the ritual sacrifice of the women for whom there is no proper place in their competitive encounters, Beth and Bath, both within the limits of the subject-positions assigned to them, ritually counter the oblivion they are condemned to. Beth's gesture, her hand on the threshold, points in accusation to her murderer. She also claims entrance into the house. Whether or not she is already dead at the moment she is found there does not really matter. Her last act, as an already destroyed subject, is to claim her place in the house, to accuse the inhabitants of the house of their repudiation of her. What she points at is, ultimately, the house as the site of power and of male competition. The house is, to use a Freudian key term, *unheimlich*: a spooky place because it is familiar yet alien, dangerous in its very promise of safety.

Bath, who, condemned to death, has some more power to act out her subjectivity, initiates another ritual. Taking her companions with her to the initiation rite, towards the mountains, towards nubility, she becomes the occasion of a ritual of remembrance. It is, ironically, her, not her father that Israel, through the doing of her daughters, must remember. It seems typical, to me, that this apparently innocent passage is generally distorted and explained away as an etiological tale with no real ritual.[31] It is not a custom, as many translations have it, but a task, not to lament, but to sing or recount Bath–Jephthah.

And what about Kallah, the third nameless victim? At the time of her wedding, she was already crushed between the different male parties, her groom and her brothers. Rembrandt, who may very well be considered Holland's most interesting biblical scholar, painted the wedding scene on the model of Da Vinci's *Last Supper*. Isolated from the men around her, who are involved in their own deals, the woman sits in the middle, with a crowned head, in the position of Christ. This is not an ordinary typological interpretation. It is not Kallah who prefigures Christ, it is Christ who reminds us of Kallah, of her sacrifice, the desacralizing sacrifice of pure revenge. At the moment of her execution we see her neither act nor speak. How will *she* be revenged?

This leads us back to the question of the beginning. The triangular situations in which the daughter is crushed to death between the men who strive for her possession display a spectacular absence. Where is Clytemnestra, as Marianne Hirsch in her paper on maternal anger rightly asked?[32] Where is Jephthah's daughter's mother? Where are the mothers who might have protected, or if they could not, have avenged their daughters' sacrifice? Absence can only signify negatively, thus promoting fantasy to take the place of the repressed. Reading a short article on child sacrifice I stumbled across a drawing which set my fantasy in motion (see fig. 1.1).

This is a sketch of an Egyptian relief, found, like many similar ones, on semitic territory.[33] What do we see? A tower, closely threatened by the enemy who is already busy climbing it. The situation is described in Judges 9:52. What does one do when the enemy is so close to the tower of defense? On the relief, the men stop fighting. They sacrifice to the god. They sacrifice, to be precise, children. Daughters. Between the men on the upper level, we see the women. They sit, and occupy an inferior position. According to Derchain, women, mothers, were not supposed to lament the sacrifice of their

Figure 1.1 Egyptian relief, found on Semitic territory. From P. Derchain, 'Les plus anciens témoignages de sacrifices d'enfants chez les Semites occidentaux.' Reproduced by permission from *Vetus Testamentum* 20 (no. 3): 351–55. 1977 by E. J. Brill.

children.[34] Mothers, then, are utterly powerless, unable to protect their own flesh. Now, let this image trigger a story.

Try to imagine that at some point one of the mothers stands up. She pushes the men aside, with contempt for their inefficient strategy that kills their own memory rather than the enemy. Instead of looking up away from the battle, she looks down and faces it. At the moment that Abimelech approaches her tower too closely, she throws not a child but a millstone.[35] This, then, is the answer of the mother to the male way of dealing with daughters, wives and warfare. The woman-with-the-millstone thus exemplifies the avenging mother that the Greek tradition stages in Clytemnestra. Her mighty body that is stronger than the *gibbor* who claims kinghood through his father, is represented in the tower that is its metaphor.

The figure of the avenging mother is, maybe, not absent from the book of Judges, but displaced. Displacement, the accompanying term for condensation, is the translation of the German *Entstellung*.[36] The word means both distortion and dislocation. The local dimension of the stories has already become obvious. The house as the site of the competition between men is the space where Bath meets her death sentence, Kallah her death, and Beth her expulsion, her death and her dismemberment. The mother, who 'normally' lives inside that house, is pushed out of it, repressed. There is no place for her in the competition over the daughter. But the repressed returns, distorted, in the guise of the enemy Delilah, or the heroine Yael. Both women have maternal features and their actions in the encounter with the men are colored by nursing and mothering.[37] Dislocated, the mother returns, on the top of the tower of safety from which she had been expelled.

If we view the murderesses in the book as avenging mothers, the excess of violence attached to them becomes understandable. Since they avenge the excessive violence done to the daughters, their role has to be, in turn, displaced. But where repression covers oppression, violence cannot but increase.

Conclusion

I have tried to convince the reader of the interest of a narratological reading of the book of Judges, a reading that starts from the premise that the *subject* of narrative is a relevant category in that it responds to socially available subject-positions. In the course of the analysis, we have met with problems of language and philology. In their turn, those problems pointed at underlying, ancient struggles that disappear in translations that hastily try to solve problems instead of enhancing them and using them as heuristic tools. What we encountered was a social change of anthropological interest. The relation between social reality and narrative structure, then, turns out to be more complex than a naïvely realistic assumption would suggest.

If the book of Judges is historiographic, it is not only, not even predominantly, because it recounts wars and conquests. It is deeply historical in that it stages a social change of profound historical consequences. The change from one form of patriarchy to the next is the pre-text that needs to be remembered. It is in danger of oblivion when feminists and others tend to cover up historical change under the one term of patriarchy, and make it seem eternal, hence, unchangeable. It is only when the disciplines that study ancient texts are open to interdisciplinary collaboration – and biblical scholarship with its rich tradition could and should play a leading role in that endeavour – that the social function of narrative and the narrative function of social changes, the ideological function of ritual and ritual function of ideology, can be properly analyzed and understood. It is only on this condition that we can hope to undermine the language of power, and restore to the anonymous women the power over language.

NOTES

This article is a condensed section of my book *Death and Dissymmetry: The Politics of Coherence in the Book of Judges* (University of Chicago Press, Chicago, 1988).

1 Mieke Bal, *Narratology: Introduction to the Theory of Narrative* (University of Toronto Press, Toronto, 1985).
2 See Alberto J. Soggin, *Judges: A Commentary* (SMC Press, London, 1981), and Robert Boling, *Judges: A New Translation with Introduction and Commentary* (Doubleday, Anchor Bible, Garden City, NY, 1975).
3 See Mieke Bal, *Murder and Difference: Gender, Genre and Scholarship on Sisera's Death* (Indiana University Press, Bloomington, 1988).
4 See Bal, *Death and Dissymmetry* for a full-length study of this structure.
5 See, for example, Boling, *Judges*.
6 D. W. Gooding, 'The Composition of the Book of Judges', *Eretz-Israel*, 16 (1982), pp. 70–9.
7 Again, for a more detailed analysis, see Bal, *Death and Dissymmetry*.
8 For more about Freud's concept of condensation, see Sigmund Freud, *The Interpretation of Dreams* (first published in 1900), in *The Standard Edition of the Complete Psychological Works of Sigmund Freud* (24 vols), ed. James Strachey (Hogarth, London, 1953), vol. 5, and Samuel Weber, *The Legend of Freud* (University of Minnesota Press, Minneapolis, 1982).
9 Austin's view of performativity is defended by Shoshana Felman, *Le Scandale du corps parlant. Don Juan avec Austin ou la séduction en deux langues* (Edition de Seuil, Paris, 1980). I use their concept rather than that redefined by others.
10 Robert Alter, *The Art of Biblical Narrative* (Basic Books, New York, 1981).

11 See James Kugel, *The Idea of Biblical Poetry* (Yale University Press, New Haven and London, 1981); Adele Berlin, *The Dynamics of Biblical Parallelism* (Indiana University Press, Bloomington, 1985); and Robert Alter, *The Art of Biblical Poetry* (Basic Books, New York, 1985).

12 K. H. Keukens, 'Richter 11.37f: Rite de Passage und Übersetzungs-probleme', *Biblische Notizen*, 19 (1982), pp. 41–3.

13 Arnold van Gennep, *The Rites of Passage* (University of Chicago Press, Chicago, 1960).

14 Victor Turner, *The Forest of Symbols: Aspects of Ndembu Ritual* (Cornell University Press, Ithaca, 1967) and *The Ritual Process: Structure and Anti-structure* (Cornell University Press, Ithaca, 1968).

15 Freud, 'The Taboo of Virginity', p. 193.

16 G. J. Wenham, 'Why Does Sexual Intercourse Defile?', *Zeitschrift für die Alttestamentliche Wissenschaft*, 95 (1983), pp. 432–4.

17 Mary Douglas, *Purity and Danger* (Praeger, New York and Washington, 1966).

18 Phyllis Trible, *Texts of Terror: Literary-Feminist Reading of Biblical Narratives* (Fortress Press, Philadelphia, 1984).

19 L. Koehler and Walter Baumgartner, *Lexicon in Veteris Testamenti Libros* (Brill, Leiden, 1958).

20 A. Slotki, Commentary on Judges, in *Joshua and Judges: Hebrew Text and English Translation with Introduction and Commentary*, ed. A. Cohen (The Soncino Press, London, Jerusalem and New York, 1980), p. 279.

21 Susan Niditch, 'The "Sodomite" Theme in Judges 19–20: Family, Community and Social Disintegration', *Catholic Biblical Quarterly*, 1982, pp. 365–78.

22 O. J. Baab, 'Concubine', *The Interpreter's Dictionary of the Bible* (Abingdon Press, Nashville, 1962), p. 666.

23 Julian Morgenstern, 'Additional Notes on "*Beena* Marriage (Matriarchat) in Ancient Israel"', *Zeitschrift für Alttestamentliche Wissenschaft*, 49 (1931), pp. 46–58.

24 Niditch, 'The "Sodomite" Theme', p. 376.

25 Alberto Ravinell Whitney Green, *The Role of Human Sacrifice in the Ancient Near East* (Scholars Press, Missoula, Montana, 1975), p. 17.

26 Victor Turner, 'Sacrifice as Quintessential Process: Prophylaxis or Abandonment?' *History of Religions*, 16 (1977), pp. 189–215.

27 René Girard, *La Violence et le sacré* (Grasset, Paris, 1972).

28 Nancy Jay, 'Sacrifice as a Remedy for Having Been Born a Woman', in *Immaculate and Powerful: The Female in Sacred Image and Social Reality*, ed. Clarissa Atkinson, Constance H. Buchanan and Margaret R. Miles (Beacon Press, Boston, 1985), pp. 283–309.

29 Robert Polzin, *Moses and the Deuteronomist* (Seabury Press, New York, 1980), pp. 200–2.

30 The relation between the story of Beth and the bride-captures, as the reversal and revenge of the imposition of one institution over the other,

was established by Teresa Cooley, student in my seminar on Ideo-stories at the Harvard Divinity School.

31 See Slotki, in Cohen (ed.), *Joshua and Judges*.

32 Marianne Hirsch, 'Clytemnestra's Children', lecture, Dartmouth College, Hanover, New Hampshire.

33 Ph. Derchain, 'Les plus ancien témoignages de sacrifice d'enfants chez les sémites occidentaux', *Vetus Testamentum*, 20 (1970), pp. 351–5.

34 Ibid., and see Derchain's bibliography.

35 Mieke Bal, *Lethal Love: Reading Biblical Love-Stories, Differently* (Indiana University Press, Bloomington, 1987).

36 Weber, *The Legend of Freud*.

37 Bal, *Murder and Difference*.

2

Joseph's Bones and the Resurrection of the Text: Remembering in the Bible

Regina M. Schwartz

Bertha could not imagine what Jews believed now; and had a dim idea that they rejected the Old Testament since it proved the New.

Daniel Deronda

The rabbis taught: Come and see how dear were the good deeds of Moses. While all Israel plundered Egypt, Moses devoted himself to the search for Joseph's bones. He went to Serah the daughter of Asher the only survivor of that generation and he said to her 'Do you know where Joseph is buried?' She said to him: 'The Egyptians made him a metal coffin and sank it into the Nile so that its waters become blessed.' Moses went and stood on the bank of the Nile. He said to him: 'Joseph, Joseph, the time has arrived of which the Holy One, blessed be He, swore that "I shall redeem you!" And the oath has come which you made Israel swear [to carry his bones back to Israel]. If you show yourself, good and well; if not, behold, we are freed of your oath.' Instantly, the coffin of Joseph swam up . . . Moses took it and carried it with him, and all those years that Israel wandered in the desert, these two boxes, one of the dead Joseph and the other of the Ark of the Covenant went side by side. And they asked, is it just that the bones of the dead should travel with the living ark? And they answered, the contents of this box fulfilled what is written in this one.

Babylonian Talmud

I

Interpretation is life-giving in the Joseph story. Joseph's ability to interpret dreams allows him, first, to be released from prison; next, to develop an agrarian policy that saves all of Egypt from famine and eventually enables him to dispense food throughout the world; and finally – and even more important for the biblical writer – to feed his family who will bear the promised nation. His interpretations lay claim to authority: 'Do not interpretations come from the Lord?' (Gen. 40:8) he explains, as he proceeds to interpret. While later interpreters of Joseph's interpretations make no such claim, they often locate the Joseph story within a schematic design that confers another kind of authority: typology. In typological readings, distinctions between provisional and 'fulfilled' meanings, between shadows and truth, are construed. The Joseph story assigns no such distinctions. Interpretation does not proceed from partial to definitive meaning and then come to rest; instead, interpretation is depicted as an ongoing process. In the Joseph story, and by extension, in the Hebrew Bible, interpreting is depicted as an activity of repressing and reconstructing, of forgetting and remembering, and that activity, by its very nature, resists completion.[1] It is no accident that Joseph's interpretations are life-giving, for what is at stake in his narrative is not truth – veiled only to be revealed – but survival: the continued life of Joseph, of his people, and of the ancient text that tells their story. I will contrast a typological reading of the Bible with an understanding of repetition that is at once more contemporary and more ancient, for the roots of our recent understanding of textuality can be discerned in the Bible itself.

In typology, meaning is conferred retrospectively; those early instances have a provisional status until, at last, a last one confers their ultimate meaning. The emphasis on 'fulfillment' in patristic typology is frequent and explicit.

The Jews wandering in the wilderness did not know that manna prefigured the Eucharist, nor did Joshua know that in leading his people into the Promised Land he was a type of Jesus leading His people into Heaven. Hence, the meaning of a type cannot be known until it has been fulfilled in its antitype.[2]

Irenaeus isolated what he called the 'consummative' nature of typological thinking, its drive to formalize and complete: 'The Son of God became the son of David and the son of Abraham, perfecting and summing up this in himself, that he might enable us to possess life'.[3] God's plan for the Hebrew nation is consummated, that is, it is perfected and concluded, by Christ. And he could turn to a text like Matthew 5:17 for corroboration: 'Do not imagine that I have come to abolish the Law or the Prophets. I have come not to abolish but to complete them.'[4] Acts 8 depicts just such a scene of interpretation: an Ethiopian eunuch sits on his chariot reading the prophet Isaiah as he returns from Jerusalem. Philip runs up and, meeting the chariot, asks, 'Do you understand what you are reading?' The eunuch admits that he cannot interpret without a guide, and so Philip explicates the text from Isaiah 53 by explaining the 'Good News of Jesus' to him. Thus guided, the eunuch finally understands.

The same drive to conclude gives rise to a corollary feature of such thinking: provisional meanings. Definitive meaning and provisional meaning – notions usually attached to contradicting visions – are interdependent in typological readings, for the very notion of fulfillment suggests that things must *be* fulfilled, and are not yet. Whether 'fulfillment' suggests primarily the unveiling of hidden meanings (as for the Alexandrian Fathers) or temporal completion (the Antiochine Fathers) or combinations of the two, Paul's language of provisionality is pervasive.[5] In Corinthians he refers to the Hebrews in the desert as *typoi hemon* or 'figures of ourselves', and to early biblical events as *skia* or 'shadows' of the coming of Christ (I Cor. 10:6; 11); in Romans, Adam is the *typos* or 'figure' of Christ (5:14); and the classic image for partial understanding, for a glimpse of meaning, is that of a veil: Corinthians refers to the *kalymnos* or the veil that covers scripture when the Jews read it (II Cor. 3:14).[6] In turn, the suggestion that such scripture can be unveiled, can, that is, be made apparent, is linked to finality: *apocalypse* means 'to uncover'. On another level, the work of typologists is necessarily incomplete for the definitive event has not yet arrived. The interpretive activity itself mocks the very totality it presupposes, adding shadows to shadows, veils to veils.

In practice, the drive for fulfillment and definitive meaning in typological readings does not foreclose the opportunity for invention; on the contrary, the cast of characters who make up types is ever-changing, for the system is large enough, incorporative enough, to accommodate.[7] In order to see Miriam as a type of Mary, Gregory of Nyssa saw her timbrel as a sign of her virginity.[8] When Sandys rehearsed types of Christ in his Christmas sermon, he left virtually no one out:

This is that seed of the woman which breaketh the serpent's head, that meek Abel murdered by his brother for our sin, that true Isaac whom his father hath offered up to be sacrifice of pacification and atonement between him and us. This is that Melchisedech, both a King and a Priest that liveth forever, without father or mother, beginning or ending. This is that Joseph that was sold for thirty pieces of silver. This is that Samson full of strength and courage, who to save his people and destroy his enemies hath brought death upon his own head . . . . This is that Bridegroom in the canticle . . . . This is that Lamb of God, pointed at by John . . . . This is the child that is born for us.[9]

Governed by the logic of similitude, but with no laws to legislate what constitutes 'the similar', typological thinking can, with enough

ingenuity, make anything fit anything else. What is fulfilled need not be precisely what was promised, for the promise itself can be reconfigured retrospectively to make it prefigurative.

Discussions of typology take up the center of Northrop Frye's book on the Bible, *The Great Code*, where he fashions himself the most recent apostle of patristic typology.[10] The history of typological exegesis is complex and varied,[11] and Frye's debt is often remote, but there are at least three basic points of continuity. Like his forebears, Frye reads the Christian Bible, a work in which the Hebrew Bible has become an 'Old' Testament to be read through the lenses of the New; he reads it analogically; and the terms in his analogy do not have equal status – type and antitype are respectively provisional and definitive. Frye's system – and his drive to systematize may exceed even that of his Fathers – describes a U-shaped structure of ascent and descent: Israel descends into apostasy and bondage, proceeds to repent, and then begins its ascent to deliverance and the promised land. Frye tells us that this structure encompasses the Bible as a whole, a 'divine comedy' characterized by a final restoration after an initial loss. The garden in Eden is denied us, to be replaced by a 'paradise happier far' – if not 'within', then above. Exodus is the type of this deliverance – as Frye so wonderfully puts it, 'Mythically, the Exodus is the only thing that really happens in the Old Testament'.[12] The descent into Egypt, subsequent repentence and finally the deliverance at the Red Sea complete the structure. The narrative of Christ's life fits the same pattern, with its descent of the incarnation and ascent of the resurrection. In this sense, the resurrection is the only thing that really happens in the New Testament. The 'double mirroring' of the testaments creates a lucid structure for Frye: the entirety of the Bible boils down to the resurrection as the antitype of the exodus.

But Frye's drive to create pattern glosses over a stubborn difference, glosses over all difference, for his analytical model is not tuned to the music of distinctions. When the Israelites emerge from the wilderness, it is not to attain anything like the final triumph of a resurrection. He does acknowledge, in an aside, that at what he deems the sixth stage in this story, deliverance, the Hebraic and Christian patterns diverge. However muted, that aside draws an enormous distinction:

For Christianity, Jesus achieved a definitive deliverance for all mankind with his revelation that the ideal kingdom of Israel was a spiritual kingdom; for Judaism, the expulsion from their homeland by the edict of Hadrian in 135 AD began a renewed exile which in many respects still endures.[13]

In order to conclude, the New Testament must launch its structure beyond history into a new and separate plane, an ideal realm, a heaven. Vertical metaphors are often invoked to describe this move: M. H. Abrams speaks of the 'right angle' of biblical history in order to separate the horizontal, historical domain of the Hebrew Bible from the cataclysmic turn vertically at the incarnation and resurrection.[14] Auerbach and Frye follow suit: a typological approach 'points to future events that are often thought of as transcending time, so that they contain a vertical lift as well as a horizontal move forward.'[15] But recently, the historian Michael Walzer has argued just the opposite, that the idea of the exodus stands as an alternative to such verticality. In his reading of the book of Exodus, the promised land is a nation with a political configuration, not an Eden in the heavens; the deliverance it depicts is from human oppressors, not from the bondage of the flesh. And that deliverance is far from final. 'Exodus thinking' implies future revolutions and future redemptions: 'The Exodus did not happen once and for all . . . in fact, the return to Egypt is part of the story, though it exists in the text only as a possibility: that's why the story can be retold so often'.[16] It would seem that we must choose a captain back to Egypt.[17] There is no definitive conclusion in the pattern he would draw for the Hebrew Bible; the drama of exile and exodus persists.

Walzer is reading the exodus in the Hebrew Bible instead of in the Old Testament of a Christian Bible, and the difference between his iterative understanding of the exodus and Frye's sense that it is a type of conclusive deliverance raises another question. If we do not invoke typology, how are we to read those repetitions in the Hebrew Bible that have proved such a rich resource for typological readers of the Old Testament? Joseph's story is an especially apt example because, on the one hand, it has invited readings in which Joseph is a type to be fulfilled, and, on the other, it is given to interpretations that would avoid the language of 'fulfillment' altogether, to opt for a sense of textuality more compatible with rabbinic, psychoanalytic and post-modern thinking.

For Frye – and I offer what follows as a hypothetical reading – the Joseph story would constitute a biblical romance, fitting the descent–ascent structure aptly. Joseph is thrown down into a pit; from there he is sold into bondage, into Egypt, a deeper pit yet, and through the false witness of a woman, he lands in the pit of a prison (he makes the comparison between that first pit and his imprisonment explicit to his brothers). Then, Joseph rises from his first pit to become the aide of the Egyptian Potiphar, rises from his pit-prison to become first the adviser to Pharaoh and then overseer of the land, and ultimately rises to save Egypt and his family from a world famine. Not only does *Joseph* endure a series of descents and ascents, he also makes his *brothers* repeat them: they come down to Egypt, and before he allows them to go up to Israel, he recreates the experience of his own captivity in the person of his younger brother, Benjamin. The Joseph narrative is punctuated by dreams, oaths, testimonies, tokens of recognition (all hallmarks of Frye's 'secular scripture', romance); the famous coat used as false witness of Joseph's death reappears as an 'outer garment' used to indict him for a staged seduction of Potiphar's wife, and yet he is awarded, and awards his brothers, festal garments in the end. In other words, the coat itself follows the pattern of descent and ascent: torn and bloodied, it will be made whole. To read Joseph's descent into the pit as a descent into the underworld is not at all strained. When his father, Jacob, grieves over Joseph, he speaks of going down to Sheol, where he will mourn his son. The Hebrew word used for descent throughout the narrative, *yrd*, is also the psalter's term of choice for a descent into the underworld. And so the temptation to see Joseph as prefiguring or shadowing other descents, culminating in the final one of the incarnation, was not to be resisted, – not by the New Testament, not by the Fathers, and not by Frye.[18]

But let us note some differences. While Joseph may parallel Jesus in his descent, he does not rise in the same way. No tomb is left empty. There is no resurrection. Instead, Joseph's dying words – and a last testament has special power in the Bible – stipulate a provision about his bones. 'I am about to die,' he says. 'God will surely remember you and take you up from this land to the land that he promised on oath to Abraham, Isaac, and Jacob' (Gen. 50:24). Paul asks, who will deliver me from this body of death? Joseph asks that his body *be delivered*, not that he be delivered from it: 'then Joseph put the sons of Israel under oath saying, "When God remembers you, be sure to take up my bones from here"' (50:25). And then Joseph is embalmed and laid in his coffin. Joseph is buried in the ground, bound to that horizontal plane; and while he will be carried to the promised land, he will be trans*planted* there and not translated. The detail is not dismissed readily: we learn that at the exodus, Moses takes with him the bones of Joseph, and the book of Joshua ends with the burial of those bones in the promised land. This emphasis on burial is reinforced in the account of Jacob's extensive funeral. Militating against any hint of an ascension, the narrator offers rich detail concerning his place of burial. 'Thus Jacob's sons did for him as he had instructed them. His sons bore him to the land of Canaan and buried him in the cave of the field of Machpelah, facing on Mamre, the field that Abraham had bought from Ephron the Hittite for a burial site' (50:12,13). The burial plot of Jacob is, significantly, the only piece of land that Abraham – the first to be blessed with the promise of land – inherited in his lifetime; and the cave of Machpelah is full, not empty.

II

We can describe patterns in the Joseph narrative, but instead of ascents and descents, partial and conclusive meanings, dim apprehension and definitive understanding, they could be approached with the more Hebraic terminology of forgetting and remembering.[19] A dialectic of forgetting and remembering, loss and recovery, is so frequently depicted in the text and enacted by the text that it informs each of the 'scenes of writing' the Bible offers. Deuteronomy tells the story of the exodus, with a second Moses repeatedly enjoining his hearers to remember and retell the story themselves.[20] But the injunctions of Deuteronomy are forgotten. The text is lost. Even the reminder to remember is forgotten. During a religious reform that included the restoration of the Temple, the lost book is found amid debris, according to the account in II Kings, and with the recovery of the book, the contents – to remember and what to remember – are remembered.[21] This lost-and-found phenomenon recurs for another text: the scroll of Jeremiah. After reading the first twenty-five chapters of Jeremiah, we are told how they came to be, and not to be, and to be again. As each page is read to the king, it is torn off and burned in the fire in his winter apartments. Despite this destruction, Jeremiah and his scribe begin all over again. The text persists. Another book suffers the same fate: the Torah. When Moses receives the tablets of the law, before he even begins to promulgate it, he dashes the tablets to pieces. The Torah is rewritten; thus, all we have from the beginning is a copy, one that proliferates further copies. Silencing the narrative, forgetting the past, obliterating any account of it: memory is the Hebrew Bible's way of coping with this ever-pressing crisis of discontinuity. The Book itself is imperiled, lost over and over. And so it must be remembered, recovered, rewritten, and rediscovered over and over, in a perpetual activity that defies the grand designs of fulfillment constructed by typology.

All of the varieties of repression that these texts suffer – destroying, forgetting, and losing – have roles in Joseph's story. His father assumes that Joseph has been destroyed, torn to pieces by a wild animal; and his brothers forget him. 'Our brother is no more,' they tell the unrecognized harsh-speaking stranger before them – not knowing that they speak to this one who 'is no more' (Gen. 42:13). Losing an object is not so very different from forgetting it, from forgetting where we have put it; and destroying, while characterized by an act of aggression that may not attend misplacing or forgetting, issues in the same result: the object is gone. Part of the thrust of the Joseph story is to equate, or at the very least to relate, these kinds of losses: to forget Joseph is to lose him, to destroy him: 'Our brother is no more.' To find him is to remember him, that he might live; and to be remembered by him is to survive, for Joseph literally rewards his brothers' memory with sustenance.

Throughout all the forgettings and rememberings, losses and recoveries, Joseph interprets. He interprets the dreams of his fellow prisoners and of Pharaoh, he interprets his brothers' selling him into slavery, and he interprets his brothers' responses to his plot when they appear in Egypt. These threads do not merely coexist; rather, the process of losing and finding, of forgetting and remembering, describes the process of interpretation. The resistance and repression described *in* the text – the losing and finding of Joseph and his brothers – are paradigmatic of the fate *of* the text. Our modern dream interpreter, Freud, wrote that, descriptively speaking, interpretation fills in gaps in memory; dynamically speaking, interpretation overcomes resistances due to repression.[22] And he was to further refine the relation between interpretation and repression: one does not simply overcome the other, for the two are subtly and thoroughly interdependent. I invoke Freud, and will often, because he opens his great project of dream interpretation, *Die Traumdeutung*, by invoking Joseph, calling up the ancient authority of dream interpreting to clear the ground: Joseph was wrong to interpret thus, Freud will interpret so.[23] But we would be as naïve to take this rejection of Joseph at face value as we would to accept Freud's denial of his debt to Nietzsche. Freud claims to have deliberately shunned Nietzsche because the proximity of the philosopher's insights might have threatened Freud's 'independence of mind.'[24] But he himself taught us to read such denials as affirmations, as a debt admitted only to be denied only to be admitted. Perhaps his relation to Joseph the dream interpreter is similarly complex. There may be a deeper affinity in their technique than Freud wanted to be fully aware of: Joseph may not only simplistically substitute one code, a predictive one, for another, the dream (as Freud would have it). Perhaps *Joseph* also demonstrates that interpretation is bound to repression.[25]

To understand the future as dependent on our recovery of a repressed past may create more problems than it solves. Freud reminisces about the early days of analysis when the 'old technique' of hypnosis prevailed: 'In these hypnotic treatments the process of remembering took a very simple form. The patient put himself back into an earlier situation, which he seemed never to confuse with the present one, and gave an account of the mental processes belonging to it'.[26] No such simplicity is possible now. On the one hand, we know that what is found is never the same as what is lost. Neither time nor language will indulge such identity. On the other, we cannot speak of an 'accurate' memory, as though memory could recover the contents of the past. We cannot re-cover any more than we can – to return to the image of a veil that conceals a definitive truth – uncover. That effort is born of nostalgia, for the object we long to recover is forever receding behind us, just as it forever recedes before us in desire. In this sense, nostalgia is a kind of temporally inverted desire, and in both cases, the object forever recedes because it was never there. All we have, all we *can* have, are reconstructions, re-, and we must include that hyphen, -memberings. Again, like desire, nostalgia holds forth not just frustration but an eternal invitation: the invitation to interpret. 'The dream as nocturnal spectacle is unknown to us,' says Ricoeur; 'it is accessible only through the account of the waking hours. The analyst interprets this account, substituting for it another text which is, in his eye, the thought-content of desire.' He concludes, not surprisingly, that 'it must be assumed . . . that dreams in themselves border on language, since they can be told, analyzed, interpreted'.[27] The inaccessible dream gives rise to elaborations, to 'accounts' and accounts of accounts, that is, to interpretation, to writing. Repression not only invites interpretation, it enables it, and the accounts of accounts become re-creations rather than a quest for a definitive truth. 'When Freud made the unconscious the key to our psychic life, he made the repressed material – or, the very act of repression however voluntary or involuntary – a key to interpretation.[28] In Derridian parlance, 'writing is unthinkable without repression'.[29]

This contemporary sense of the role of repression in all its various forms – forgetting, censoring, losing and misreading, voluntarily or involuntarily – can help us decipher the biblical phenomenon. Instead of seeing the forgetting of texts, their loss or destruction, only as failures, we could also see them as occasions for remembering, for interpreting, that is, for re-creation.[30] In Freud's early work *The Psychopathology of Everyday Life*, he wrote that his ruminations on the forgetting of names led him not only to 'forgetfulness, but also to false recollection; he who strives for the escaped name brings to consciousness others – substitutive names – which although immediately recognized as false, nevertheless obtrude themselves with great tenacity'.[31] His judgments here are ringing: substitutive names are false, they obtrude, they are incorrect. But of course later he will come to understand such displacements as the ground of his entire project. Forgetting will constitute remembering just as the life and death drives constitute one another.[32] Similarly, while the Bible seems to depict its moments of loss as failures, it also seems to insist on them as necessary, as 'structural and founding'. Joseph does: 'And now, do not be distressed and do not be angry with yourselves for selling me here, because it was to save lives that God sent me ahead of you' (45:5). He might well have added, 'What is success when the possibility of failure continues to constitute its structure?'[33]

III

I return to the story of Joseph with this inquiry into the role of repression in mind. First, his disappearance. What happened to him? Can we discern what happened? The scene of abandonment (Gen. 37) is a complicated business, marked by deflections and displacements. The brothers plot to kill Joseph, but one, Reuben, intervenes to save him: 'Let us have no bloodshed. . . . Throw him into this pit in the wilderness, but do him no bodily harm.' They agree, but then a few verses later another brother, Judah, speaks up with no indication that he has heard another defender: 'What shall we gain by killing our brother and concealing his death? Why not sell him to the Ishmaelites?' The sale is similarly confusing. After Judah's suggestion that the brothers sell him to the Ishmaelites, it is the Midianites – not the brothers or the Ishmaelites – who come along and draw Joseph from the pit and sell him to the Ishmaelites for twenty pieces of silver, and it is the Ishmaelites, not the Midianites, who take him to Egypt. But then we learn that the *Midianites* sell him, not to the Ishmaelites but to the Egyptian Potiphar. Even a summary is confusing. Critical-historical scholars found a ready solution to the contradiction in the documentary hypothesis: Speiser tells us that 'all of this narrative confusion is dissipated automatically once the narrative is broken up into two originally independent versions'.[34] In one (E), Joseph's defender is Reuben and the traders are the Midianites; in the other (J), Joseph's defender is Judah and the traders are the Ishmaelites. Nonetheless, Speiser cannot explain why the redactor let these explicit contradictions stand. The result is that there is no accurate, privileged, original account of what happened to Joseph. Even the first account is marked by fluctuating casts of characters and roles, by substitutions and condensation. This apparent lapse on the part of the otherwise painstaking editor/writer may be instead an invitation – to read the event as a memory. However much we try to reconstruct a coherent account from memory, details elude us, some are lost altogether, others displaced. We do not reconstruct, we construct.

In contrast, Joseph's response to the event is not at all confusing: he makes a deliberate, willful effort to forget it. Joseph the dreamer and interpreter of dreams will repress this waking nightmare. Now, with his fortunes reversed, prospering in Egypt, he names his firstborn Manassah, saying, 'It is because God has caused me to forget all my trouble and all my father's household' (Gen. 41:51). But only seven verses later, the narrative begins to describe the return of that household and the instigators of his trouble: one senses that the brothers will not let Joseph forget. When they stand before him seeking grain – his identity concealed – they provoke a fascinating response. 'When Joseph saw his brothers he recognized them, but he made himself a stranger to them. . . . Although Joseph recognized his brothers, they did not recognize him' (42:7, 8). Their forgetfulness is emphasized with a pun on 'recognize' – *nkr* is also the root of 'stranger' – to forget Joseph's identity is to make him a stranger. But Joseph also *wills* that error in his ensuing plot, a plot designed to inspire more forgetfulness, this time of Benjamin, by the brothers: 'Then he remembered his dreams about them and said to them, "You are spies! You have come to see the nakedness of the land"' (42:9). Why should dreams of sheaves bowing down to a sheaf and of the sun, moon, and eleven stars bowing down to Joseph prompt this accusation? If Joseph wants to accuse his brothers, why, of being spies? This term for the 'nakedness' they would spy on refers not to nudity but to the sight of something that should remain hidden, something that is illicit to see.[35] Only Joseph's recent effort to repress his past can make sense of this response, for the very presence of the brothers violates what Joseph is trying to hide from himself: his memory of their abuse.[36]

Nonetheless, according to the narrator, the appearance of his brothers instantly reminds Joseph, not of their cruelty, but of his own dreams: 'then he remembered his dreams about them' (42:9). Joseph is not only forgotten and remembered, Joseph himself forgets and remembers – his dreams – and in the process he too demonstrates that remembering is reconstructing; as both analyst and analysand he confers a new interpretation on his own dreams. The images of sheaves and stars bowing down before him can no longer be construed as an arrogant youthful sign of hegemony over his brothers; now, with his brothers trembling, bowing, before him, the dream comes to signal his responsibility to save them.[37] Any hint of vindictiveness soon gives way to forgiveness and to far more: Joseph's complex plot to save his brothers from their worst instincts to prey on one another. Joseph will re-educate his brothers, encouraging them to revisit and reinterpret their past in order to ensure their future. Only when they achieve the awareness that they must be their brothers' keepers – the insight Cain so dramatically denied – are they qualified for divine enfranchisement. Cain is condemned to exile, but Joseph teaches his brothers to become the Sons of Israel.

But first, he must remember the dreams and remember the scene of abandonment they provoked. Instead of having a grand reunion, Joseph finds his brothers and is found by them in stages, each marked by losses – if only temporary – and each provoking interpretation. In what follows, Joseph acts out fragments from his repressed past with substitutes, and that acting out serves double-duty – as compulsive repetition and as education. He imprisons his brothers as he was imprisoned; he separates one, Simeon, from the others; he insists on parting another, Benjamin, from his father as he was parted. The powerful Egyptian governor selling grain during a world famine makes the condition of his sale to these supplicants that they bring their youngest brother, Benjamin, to Egypt (thereby demanding that they sell another brother into Egypt). This scheme induces his father to remember his mourning: 'You are robbing me of my children; Joseph is no more; Simeon is no more; and now you want to take Benjamin. . . . My son is not going down with you, for now his brother is dead he is the only one left [that is, the only other child born of Rachel] (42:36–37). The prospect of that loss also provokes his brothers' memory of another: 'They said to one another, "Surely we are being punished because of our brother. We saw how distressed he was when he pleaded with us for his life, but we would not listen; that's why this distress has come upon us"' (42:21). Joseph overhears (there was an interpreter between them). The interpreter who ostensibly promotes understanding is believed to inhibit it; and because that interpreter is a signal to the brothers that Joseph cannot understand, Joseph is allowed to understand. The presence of the interpreter enables their private admission to become a public confession, fulfilling the interpretive function after all.

Joseph's complex response casts him as both victim and victimizer: he weeps, for he is forced to remember pain he had repressed, and he picks out Simeon and has him bound before his brothers' eyes (42:24). Hearing his own story rehearsed by his brothers provokes Joseph to dramatize his imprisonment with Simeon. But because the brothers refuse to abandon Simeon – as they had Joseph – they agree to his captor's terms: they agree, that is, to bring Benjamin to Egypt. Joseph has instigated, not just one repetition, but a chain of substitutive hostages. And for all of his efforts to stand outside of his own painful story, as Egyptian vizier, as beneficent educator, it continually erupts in his reenactments of his injury. The narrative does not just depict a sovereign and self-sovereign Joseph manipulating his brothers in order to teach them lessons; it also shows him learning from them. When he should be in full control of his plot to make his brothers morally accountable, at the very moment when the brothers present Benjamin and the climax is at hand, Joseph collapses under the weight of his own history. He asks the wrong questions for a powerful vizier to ask, and he has no business blessing Benjamin, but he cannot help himself. Relational epithets abound as Joseph recovers his family identity.

[Joseph] greeted them [his brothers] kindly, asking, 'Is your father well, the old man you told me of? Is he still alive?' 'Your servant our father is well,' they replied 'he is still alive,' and they bowed low in homage. Looking up he saw his brother Benjamin, his mother's son. 'Is this your youngest brother,' he asked 'of whom you told me?' Then he said to him, 'God be good to you, my son.' Joseph hurried out, for his heart was moved at the sight of his brother and he was near to weeping. He went into his room and there he wept. After bathing his face he returned and, controlling himself, gave the order: 'Serve the meal.' (43:27–32)

Maintaining his Egyptian identity, Joseph is served separately, 'for Egyptians cannot take food with Hebrews, they have a horror of it' (44:32); but beginning to reclaim his Hebraic identity, he eats the same food, feeding his brothers from his own plate as he will feed them during the famine. And the narrator adds that they all drank together. Soon it becomes clear that separations are the means for reunions and reunions the condition for survival.

Joseph plots the final test, setting up Benjamin as a thief who must be enslaved for a crime he did not commit, as Joseph was. It is only when the brothers are threatened with losing Benjamin that Judah steps forward to attest to their mutual devotion. Separations prompt reconciliations that are moral as well as physical.

If I go to your servant my father now, and we have not the boy with us, he will die as soon as he sees that the boy is not with us, for his heart is bound up with him. . . . Now your servant went surety to my father for the boy. I said: If I do not bring him back to you, let me bear the blame before my father all my life. Let your servant stay, then, as my lord's servant in place of the boy, I implore you, and let the boy go back to his brothers. How indeed could I go back to my father and not have the boy with me? I could not bear to see the misery that would overwhelm my father. (44:30–34)

In turn, Judah's expression of mutual responsibility prompts a further reunion: now Joseph reveals his identity. The simple fact he offers to his dazed audience sounds like an impossible oxymoron in this new moral climate: 'I am your brother Joseph who you sold into Egypt.' And now Joseph's own separation from his brothers and his reunion to them enable the survival of Israel: 'Do not be distressed and do not be angry with yourselves for selling me here, because it was to save lives that God sent me ahead of you' (45:5). His repression of his past has enabled survival in another sense, becoming the ground of that fertile interpretation.

Another episode of losing and finding is embedded in the midst of the Joseph narrative, the story of Tamar and Judah (Gen. 38), and it demonstrates the same pattern: repression is the ground of interpretation that is in turn the ground of survival. Judah loses his seal, cord, and staff – hallmarks of his identity – to a prostitute he hires at the crossroad. He subsequently loses the prostitute: his messenger cannot find her to make the promised payment and retrieve his pledges. Judah may also lose his widowed and pregnant daughter-in-law, for he threatens to have her executed, convinced that she must have 'played the harlot and is with child from her harlotry.' When he recovers the lost seal, cord, and staff – when, that is, Tamar returns them – he also finds that the prostitute and his daughter-in-law are one. Only then does Judah understand Tamar's drastic effort in the face of his own negligence; Tamar had repressed her identity to ensure the survival of the family. 'She is more right than I' – that startling judgment from a patriarch saves Tamar and her progeny.

Remembering is persistently linked to survival. The future Walter Benjamin depicts must be nourished by the image of enslaved ancestors rather than that of liberated grandchildren.[38] Joseph asks a fellow prisoner to remember him in prison once the prisoner has been released; the implication is clear that to be so remembered is to be freed. The prisoner forgets Joseph, only to remember later. Joseph's brothers slowly recall their brother. The next installment in the Bible after the Joseph narrative, Exodus, begins with a pharaoh who 'knew nothing' of Joseph, and his poor memory issues in an extermination policy for the descendants of the forgotten one. But when we say that remembering is the condition of survival in the Bible, we cannot mean it in any naïve sense. With no such thing as accurate memory possible, dependence on such memory would enable no future at all. Rather, it is interpretation that becomes the ground of continuity, enabling a future, interpretation that is, in turn, enabled by repression. It is with such an elevated sense of interpreting, not as mere substitute for truth, that Edward Said wrote, 'only because man has lost does he write about it, must he write about it, can he only write about it.'[39]

If this is a deliverance, it is not the glorious and final deliverance that resurrection holds. Joseph instigates something far more modest: 'It was not you who sold me into Egypt,' explains Joseph; 'God sent me before you to ensure for you a remnant on earth, and to save your lives.' Survivors of a famine, a remnant, like Noah from the flood, Lot from the destruction of Sodom, the generation who survive the wilderness, the 'tottering hut' of the house of David that survives the exile, like Deuteronomy, the scroll of Jeremiah, and the Torah itself, surviving destruction. Memory, like typology, reconfigures events from the past, but its motive is more humble. It is not a drive to interpret authoritatively; the motive of memory is simply to preserve, and preservation, by its very nature, does not end. Once a type is fulfilled there is no need to remember; once we incorporate the body of Christ there is no need to recall the text.

Many interpretations of the Joseph narrative have relied on fundamental oppositions,[40] famine and fruitfulness, preservation and destruction, dreams of conservation (the imprisoned butler dreams that he squeezes his grapes into a cup) and dreams of waste (the baker dreams that birds eat his bread crumbs from his basket), fat cows and lean cows, full grain and thin grain – all pointing to the more fundamental distinction between life and death. Joseph's brothers who once plotted his death are saved by him. But the very notion of opposition has been subject to question. Nietzsche writes:

The fundamental belief of metaphysicians is the belief in the opposition of values. It may be questioned whether there are indeed any oppositions at all . . . rather than simply foreground estimations, preliminary perspectives. . . . Indeed, it might even be possible that what comprises the value of those good and respected things is precisely that they are insidiously related, tied to, interlaced with those wicked, seemingly opposed things, and perhaps even of the same essence.[41]

He goes on: 'Perhaps! But who is willing to worry about such dangerous perhapses. For that, we will have to wait for the arrival of a new kind of philosopher'.[42] Not so very new. Milton wrote long ago, 'It was from out the rinde of one apple tasted, that the knowledge of good and evil, as two twins cleaving together, leapt forth into the World'.[43] And perhaps forgetfulness and fruitfulness are also twin-born, like Manassah and Ephraim. If Joseph names his firstborn Manassah, saying, 'it is because God has made me forget all my trouble and all my father's household,' he names his second Ephraim, saying, 'It is because God has made me fruitful in the land of my suffering' (41:52).

Modern psychoanalytic theory teaches us that fictions of closure are linked to the death drive; that, as the end of desire, fulfillment is tantamount to death. Desire itself, however, perpetual desire, ensures textuality – in our parlance, script-uality. The Bible complicates this picture, for it gives us at once desire (the promised land is, after all, promised) and nostalgia. As to re-member presupposes that something has been dismembered, or lost, or forgotten, so, too, to repeat suggests that what is repeated is somehow discrete, and hence repeatable, instead of a mere continuation. One of the ironies that inhere in the notion of repetition is that only those things that are in some sense finished can be repeated. Biblical repetition, then, suggests at once discontinuity and continuity: discontinuity, because there must be a break to enable something to be repeated, just as something must be lost to be recovered, forgotten to be remembered; and continuity, because the fact of repetition, recovery, memory, ensures a living-on. In this sense, the idea of death and resurrection is not so much alien to the Hebrew Bible as it is terribly familiar. There are many dyings and risings rather than a single resurrection.

Thus there are more bones. In Ezekiel, the bones of the army of Israel come to life. Jacob's bones are buried at Machpelah, Joseph's lie in Canaan, but no one knows where the bones of Moses lie. For a typologist, those missing bones suggest the possibility of ascension; the absent grave is powerful testimony that Moses is the type of a resurrected Christ. To someone who subscribes to a less completing hermeneutics, the missing bones of Moses point to infinite Moseses and suggest that we, like Moses, will never reach the promised land of a definitive truth. With Milton, we can only hope to re-member her torn body.[44]

NOTES

This essay was written under the auspices of the University of Colorado's Center for Theory. It was delivered at the Colorado Conference on the Bible and Literary Theory in May, 1986 and at UCLA in the same year. I thank the audiences for their help. Published in *PMLA* in March, 1988, it is reprinted here with their permission. The work is part of a book-in-progress on the Bible entitled, *Can These Bones Live? Remembering the Bible*.

1 Rabbinic exegesis offers, naturally enough, a greater kinship to the textuality of the Hebrew Bible: activity is suggested by the term 'midrash' itself, taken from the root 'd-r-sh', 'to study, to seek'. The activity in question, interpretation, is endless and endlessly conflicting. According to one rabbinic saying, 'Solomon had three thousand parables to illustrate each and every verse: and a thousand and five interpretations for each and every parable' (*Pesikta Rabbati: Discourses for Feast, Fasts, and Special Sabbaths*, tr. William Braude, 2 vols, Yale University Press, New

Haven, 1968, Piska 14.9). The Talmudic excerpt at the beginning of this chapter offers an example of continuity: a fabulous tale of the recovery of Joseph's bones is spun out as a commentary on his story. The relation of rabbinic commentary to contemporary critical thinking has received much attention. See Gerald Bruns, 'The Hermeneutics of Midrash', in this volume; Geoffrey H. Hartman and Sanford Budick (eds.), *Midrash and Literature* (Yale University Press, New Haven, 1986); Susan Handleman, *The Slayers of Moses* (State University of New York Press, Albany, 1982).

2 William C. Madsen, *From Shadowy Types to Truth: Studies in Milton's Symbolism* (Yale University Press, New Haven, 1968), p. 5.

3 Ibid., p. 103.

4 All references to the Bible are to the Jerusalem Bible unless otherwise noted. My distinction is not between Jewish and Christian exegesis. While the New Testament could offer typologists support for their drive towards conclusive meaning, it also has a deep strain of the opposite logic. Deferral, rather than completion, is best exemplified by Hebrews 1:11, 'Now faith is the substance of things hoped for, the evidence of things not seen' (King James Version). Similarly, a typological drive is toward fulfillment is apparent in much interpretation in Judaism, notably the Qumran literature. My distinction is more specific, between patristic typology and interpretation in the Hebrew Bible, and even these large categories have exceptions. For a discussion of deferral in Protestant typology, see Schwartz, 'From Shadowy Types to Shadowy Types,' *Milton Studies*, 24, 1988, pp. 123–39.

5 Examples of such uses from Melito of Sardis, Origen, Chrysostom, and Cyril of Jerusalem abound in K. J. Woollcombe, 'The Biblical Origins and Patristic Development of Typology', in *Essays on Typology*, ed. G. W. H. Lampe and K. J. Woollcombe (SCM, London, 1957).

6 Erich Auerbach, 'Figura', *Scenes from the Drama of European Literature* (Meridian, New York 1959), pp. 11–76. Paul's exegesis of the Hebrew Bible was already turning it into an 'old' testament before the new one has even come into existence as such.

7 The creative and varied uses of typology during the Renaissance have been the subject of several studies. See Barbara Lewalski, *Protestant Poetics and the Seventeenth-Century Religious Lyric* (Princeton University Press, Princeton, 1979); Earl Miner (ed.), *The Literary Uses of Typology from the Late Middle Ages to the Present* (Princeton University Press, Princeton, 1977); Paul J. Korshin, *Typologies in England 1650–1820* (Princeton University Press, Princeton, 1982).

8 Gregory of Nyssa, *De Virginitate*, vol. 46 of *Patrologiae Graecae* (161 vols), ed. J.-P. Migne (Migne, Paris, 1863), 396B.

9 Edwin Sandys, *Sermons Made by the Most Reverend Father in God, Edwin, Archbishop of York, Primate of England and Metropolitan at London* (1585), ed. John Ayre (Cambridge University Press, Cambridge, 1841), pp. 7–8.

10 Northrop Frye, *The Great Code: The Bible and Literature* (Harcourt, New York, 1982), pp. 78–138.

11 The development of patristic typology is beyond the scope of this chapter, but such histories include those of A. C. Charity, *Events and Their Afterlife* (Cambridge University Press, Cambridge, 1966); J. S. Preus, *From Shadow to Promise: Old Testament Interpretation from Augustine to the Young Luther* (Harvard University Press, Cambridge, Mass., 1969).

12 Frye, *The Great Code*, p. 171.

13 Ibid.

14 M. H. Abrams, *Natural Supernaturalism* (Norton, New York, 1971), p. 36.

15 Frye, *The Great Code*, p. 82.

16 Michael Walzer, *Exodus and Revolution* (Basic Books, New York, 1984), p. 5.

17 John Milton, 'The Ready and Easy Way to Establish a Free Commonwealth', in *Complete Poems and Major Prose*, ed. Merritt Hughes (Bobbs, Indianapolis, 1957), p. 899.

18 Frye does apply the descent structure to Joseph explicitly but briefly: 'The Incarnation was a voluntary descent into the lower world repeated in the creation of Adam, hence Paul characterizes Jesus as a second Adam (I Cor. 15:45). There is in Genesis a type of such a descent, not wholly voluntary, in the story of Joseph, whose 'coat of many colors' suggests fertility-god imagery, and who, like Burns' John Barleycorn, is thrown into a pit.' (*The Great Code*, p. 196). Frye's own associative methods are not that different from Tertullian's: 'Joseph likewise was a type of Christ, not indeed on this ground . . . that he suffered persecution for the cause of God from his brethren, as Christ did from His brethren after the flesh, the Jews; but when he is blessed by his father in these words: "His glory is that of a bullock; his horns are the horns of a unicorn; with them shall he push the nations to the very ends of the earth" (Deut. 33:17), he was not, of course, designated as a mere unicorn with its one horn, or a minotaur with two; but Christ was indicated in him – a bullock in respect of both His characteristics: to some as severe as a Judge, to others gentle as a Saviour, whose horns were the extremities of His cross. For the antenna, which is a part of a cross, the ends are called horns; while the midway stake of the whole frame is the unicorn' (p. 336). Clearly, typology does not foreclose invention. Even Joseph's seduction by Potiphar's wife has been seen typologically, for Joseph was Christlike 'because he flourished as the flower of chastity in a gross and carnal age' (Testaments of the Twelve Patriarchs', in *The Ante-Nicene Fathers*, ed. Alexander Roberts and James Donaldson, 10 vols, [Scribner's, New York, 1906], vol. 8, p. 4).

19 For further discussion of the relation of remembering and repeating to ritual in the Bible and in *Paradise Lost*, see Regina M. Schwartz, *Remembering and Repeating: Biblical Creation in Paradise Lost* (Cambridge University Press, Cambridge, 1988).

20 On the offices of Moses and the Deuteronomic Moses, see James Nohrnberg, 'Moses', in *Images of Man and God*, ed. Burke O. Long (Almond, Sheffield, 1980), pp. 35–57, and 'On Literature and the Bible', *Centrum*, 2 (1974), 2, pp. 5–43.

21 Bruns discusses this scene with reference to the problem of canonicity in 'Canon': Gerald Bruns, 'Canon and Power in the Hebrew Scriptures', *Critical Inquiry*, 10 (1984), pp. 462–80.

22 Sigmund Freud, *The Standard Edition of the Complete Psychological Works of Sigmund Freud*, ed. James Strachey, 24 vols (Hogarth, London, 1953), vol. 12, p. 148. See also Sternberg's discussion of gap-filling in the Bible: Meir Sternberg, *The Poetics of Biblical Narrative* (Indiana University Press, Bloomington, 1985), pp. 186–263.

23 Freud, *Standard Edition*, vol. 4, p. 97; see also p. 334.

24 I simplify a rich discussion greatly. See ibid., vol. 20, p. 59. See also Jacques Derrida, *La Carte postale* (Flammarion, Paris, 1980), pp. 280–1; Samuel Weber, 'The Debts of Deconstruction', in *Taking Chances: Derrida, Psychoanalysis and Literature*, ed. William Kerrigan and Joseph Smith (Johns Hopkins University Press, Baltimore, 1984), p. 36.

25 In his 'return to Freud', Lacan has elaborated the complexity of the role of repression. For Lacan, repression is a figure for the difference that makes signification and narration possible: 'repression is not a simple event [in which conscious material is relegated to a darkened unconscious realm] but an ongoing process of marking and suppressing differences' (Robert Con Davis, 'Lacan, Poe, and Narrative Repression', *Lacan and Narration*, ed. Con Davis, Johns Hopkins University Press, Baltimore, 1983, pp. 983–4).

26 Freud, *Standard Edition*, vol. 12, p. 148.

27 Paul Ricoeur, *Freud and Philosophy: An Essay on Interpretation*, tr. Denis Savage (Yale University Press, New Haven, 1970), p. 15.

28 Harold Bloom, *A Map of Misreading* (Oxford University Press, New York, 1975), pp. 83–105.

29 Derrida, 'Freud and the Scene of Writing', *Writing and Difference*, tr. Alan Bass (University of Chicago Press, Chicago, 1978), p. 226.

30 The structural affinity of Freud's thought to the Hebraic narrative of repression runs deep. Freud himself wrote of interpreting dreams as interpreting 'Holy Writ'. Handleman traces Freud's methodology to rabbinic hermeneutics, reading psychoanalysis as a 'secular vision of the Talmud' (*The Slayers of Moses*, p. xv, see esp. ch. 5).

31 Freud, *Standard Edition*, vol. 6, pp. 1–2.

32 Jean Laplanche, *Life and Death in Psychoanalysis*, tr. Jeffrey Mehlman (Johns Hopkins University Press, Baltimore, 1976).

33 Jacques Derrida, *Margins of Philosophy*, tr. Alan Bass (University of Chicago Press, Chicago, 1982), p. 324.

34 E. A. Speiser (ed.), *The Anchor Bible: Genesis* (Doubleday, Garden City, NY, 1964), p. 293.

35 Ibid., p. 321, n. 9: 'nakedness in the sense of something that is unseemly

(Deut. 23:15) and improper to look at or expose (Gen. 9:22f; Lev. 18:5ff).'

36 See Robert Alter, *The Art of Biblical Narrative* (Basic Books, New York, 1981), pp. 160–77, on the subtle depiction of knowledge in this episode.

37 See Sternberg, *Biblical Narrative*, pp. 285, 306.

38 Walter Benjamin, *Illuminations*, ed. Hannah Arendt, tr. Harry Zohn (Harcourt, New York, 1968), p. 262.

39 Edward Said, *Beginnings: Intention and Method* (Basic Books, New York, 1975), p. 280.

40 See James S. Ackerman, 'Joseph, Judah, and Jacob', in *Literary Interpretations of Biblical Narratives*, 2 vols, ed. James S. Ackerman and K. R. R. Gross Louis (Abingdon, Nashville, 1974), vol. 2, pp. 85–113; and Donald Seybold, 'Paradox and Symmetry in the Joseph Narrative', in Ackerman and Gross Louis (eds), *Literary Interpretations*, pp. 59–73.

41 Friedrich Wilhelm Nietzsche, *Beyond Good and Evil*, tr. W. Kaufman and R. J. Hollingdale (Random, New York, 1967), p. 110.

42 Ibid.

43 John Milton, 'Areopagitica', in *The Complete Prose Work of John Milton*, 8 vols, ed. Don Wolfe et al. (Yale University Press, New Haven, 1953–8), vol. 2, p. 514.

44 Ibid., p. 549.

3

On Prophetic Stammering

Herbert Marks

Biblical prophecy is hard to read, harder even than biblical narrative, and the ostensible reasons are fairly obvious. The prophets, in Luther's words, 'have a queer way of talking, like people who, instead of proceeding in an orderly manner, ramble off from one thing to the next, so that you cannot make head or tail of them or see what they are getting at.'[1] Though critical analysis has improved on this formlessness, providing various mappings of oral and redactional intention, the impression of sheer accumulation, of forbidding non-sequential abundance, manages to persist. One might even argue that it helps account for the prophets' capacity to move us so powerfully, an effect that differs, at least in degree, from the continuous modulations of skillful reading, being more sudden and intermittent.

Christopher Smart, who knew as much about Hebrew poetry as Bishop Lowth or his scholarly successors, offers a profound comment on the method of these and his own cumulative add-orations in the third fragment of his revisionary psalter, the *Jubilate Agno*:

> For innumerable ciphers will amount to something.
>
> .   .   .   .   .   .
>
> For the mind of man cannot bear a tedious accumulation of
>   nothings without effect (C35–36).

Like his poetics of atonement, Smart's hermeneutic invites us to presume, in desire or aspiration, on the power of composition and the synthetic unity of form. It stresses the prerogatives of language, but it also acknowledges the transcendental agency in every act of assimilation. This presumption, which grounds the rationalists' stand against skepticism – against the radical discontinuity of all perception and the suspicion that causal relations are at best hypothetical – is the same which, strenuously exercised, allows us to read the prophets. Even the most minimal act of interpretation, as Augustine insisted, requires that we transform, or atone, succession into union. In reading the Bible, as in reading Smart's poem, we are forced to forego the prop of authorial intention (adjacent verses in the Bible may well be the work of different authors; in the *Jubilate Agno*, where the episodic schizophrenia of the author is confirmable, of radically disjunctive states of mind). But Smart's lines also remind us how tenuous the prop of intentionality can be, and that our opportunity in forgoing it is to move the battle with skepticism indoors: behind the essentially erotic problem of intercommunication to the stark arena where the one and the many would defy one another.

Rephrased in the language of contemporary idealism, Smart's rule conforms almost precisely to a more influential eighteenth-century theory, Kant's analytic of the sublime, particularly that subdivision sometimes known as the sublime of magnitude or the 'mathematical sublime'. In his third *Critique* Kant describes the sublime object as one 'whose representation determines the mind to think the unattainability of nature as a presentation of [reason's] ideas'.[2] The relation by means of which 'unattainability' (*Unerreichbarkeit*) becomes a mode of 'presentation' (*Darstellung*) depends on the substitution of a cognitive for a perceptual failure, but the same structure may be applied to objects outside nature, in the first place to literature, but in the end perhaps even to memory traces or to affective impulses that display the compulsive structure of repetition. Accordingly, Thomas Weiskel, who has given us the most probing exposition of Kant's theory, argues for a broadening of the definition: 'We call an object sublime,' he writes, 'if the attempt to represent it determines the mind to regard its inability to grasp wholly the object as a symbol of the mind's relation to a transcendent order'.[3] 'We call' simply records a linguistic fact; for in Kant's theory sublimity is properly referred to the *subject* and to the extension of its power, the 'supersensible destiny', that follows upon its collapse before the innumerable ciphers, and not to the ciphers themselves. The indefinite plural or unassimilable excess that defeats the ordinary understanding becomes the occasion of a reactive identification which depends on the negative relation of unattainability. In Weiskel's semiological translation: 'The absence of a signified itself assumes the status of a signifier, disposing us to feel that behind this newly significant absence lurks a newly discovered presence'.[4] Daunted initially by a repetition that defies assimilation, the mind posits the same potential infinity within itself, thereby both capitulating to repetition and defending against its ostensive form.

One of the virtues of Kant's theory is the ease with which it allows itself to be translated into a hermeneutic, to yield a 'reader's sublime' as well as a 'mathematical sublime', and it thus seems to me a useful model for approaching my proper topic – prophetic calling. A second model, from poetic rhetoric, will figure later on, but I believe that even here our operative categories are abstractions from our own experience as readers. The grammatical ambiguity in the conjunction of prophet and call is already thematic. 'Is the prophet subject or object,' we ask. But the voice that cries calls only 'Cry!' The cry itself is a repetition, and our understanding of the identity, or as we shall see, the identifications, that conditioned it must proceed via the dynamics of transference if we are to escape from the empty labelling of traditional scholarship.

In limit cases, what the prophet himself transfers or conveys is finally nothing more than the fact of conveyance itself, a reflexive figure that culminates in the gospel of Mark, whose content is its own proclamation, and in John's treatment of the messiah as the Word. The Kantian sublime might be said to operate by two submodes – negation and tautology – and the self-referential oracle is perhaps the strongest example of the latter, whose paradigm is YHWH's self-originating and self-circumscribed gloss on his own name, *'ehyeh 'asher 'ehyeh*, 'I will be what I will be' (Ex. 3:14). One example is the isolated but climactic oracle immediately preceding the first of the three doxologies strategically placed by the editors of Amos to solemnize the divine judgments:

> Therefore, thus I will do to you, O Israel;
>   because I will do this to you,
>   prepare to meet your God, O Israel! (Amos 4:12).

Here, the logical order, accusation and then threat, elsewhere followed by Amos (3:11; 5:11; 5:16; 6:7; 7:17), has been reversed, a metalepsis emphasized by the unusual conjunction (*'eqeb ki*) with its intensive force, 'precisely because'. Concurrently, the two ostensives, 'thus' and 'this', have no referent other than each other. The result is another *idem per idem* formula in which temporality is collapsed in a promise (or threat) of manifestation. Teased out, the logic of the oracle is double: 'because of God's action, therefore manifestation of God's action', with the floating sense of futurity in the imperfect aspect left to hover ambiguously between the two clauses. One is reminded of the Deuteronomic superscription in which what Amos sees is the word of Amos: 'The words of Amos . . . which he saw concerning Israel.'

Another example is God's response to the renewed complaint of Habakkuk, whose satisfaction must derive not from the vision but from the annunciation of the vision:

> And the Lord answered me:
>   Write the vision;
>   make it plain upon tablets,
>   so that he may run who reads it.
> For still the vision awaits its time;
>   it hastens to the end – it will not lie.
> If it seem slow, wait for it;
>   it will surely come, it will not delay.
> Behold, he whose soul is not upright in him shall fail,
>   but the righteous shall live by his faith. (Hab. 2:2–4)

– or, following Gerald Janzen, 'by his confidence in it [the vision]' (*be'emunato*, objective pronoun). In its literary context this vision may be the theophany described in the closing hymn – YHWH the divine warrior riding forth from Mount Paran attended by pestilence and plague; but the power of the prophetic word is independent of the content of the vision which in chapter 2 is indefinitely deferred in favor of attentiveness to the announcement itself – a purely kerygmatic program. Here no less than in the negative sublime the 'absence of a signified itself assumes the status of a signifier.' The epistemological breakdown is resolved by substitution, and we ourselves experience the freedom or power that corresponds to the *active* apprehension of terms independent of causality. To recall Kant's phrase, 'unattainability' becomes a form of 'presentation'.

A similar dialectic explains the effectiveness of the more prevalent submode of negation, where the paradigmatic instance for interpreters since Hegel is from Psalm 104: 'who coverest thyself with light as with a garment: who stretchest out the heavens like a tent'; but the 'great veil', as Maimonides calls the juxtaposition of revelation and concealment,[5] figures in all of the prophets where it is incident to, or even definitive of, prophetic speech: 'obscuris vera involvens' – the difficult ornament universally associated with prophecy.

I use this Renaissance commonplace ironically, for I want to contest the notion that the rhetorical forms that prophecy takes are secondary embellishments, or even parabolic correlatives of their object, as if this could be independently known. Obscuration corresponds rather to the moment of blockage that marks the mind's defeat before the unattainability of the object. It symbolizes not the transcendent order but the prophet's relation to the transcendent order, a relation that includes his mute intuition of his own infinitude. The rhetoric of obscuration which follows upon the prophetic call demonstrates – like the rhetoric of threat – the prophet's identification with the blocking agent that *he himself* has constructed in a reaction against the indefinite magnitude (Smart's 'innumerable ciphers') which threatens to overwhelm him. In the Kantian model, this magnitude is external, a sum of natural percepts or, in our hermeneutic translation, of legible signs. From a Freudian perspective we might rather say that an external effect provokes the deferred mobilization of unbound 'energy' – a metapsychological notion homologous to Weiskel's 'excessive signifiers' – which assails the mind from within. Defenseless against such an assault, the ego calls upon repression to block the excess to which no phenomenal signified corresponds.

In the dramatizations of prophetic calling, this central moment of blockage before the reactive identification takes place is represented by the prophetic stammer – the 'slow tongue' of Moses and its variations, the 'unclean lips of Isaiah', the demur of Jeremiah, the mutism of Ezekiel. The topos has had a full career in secular literature, invariably marking the subject's resistance to an overwhelming influx. Thus Dante, when abandoned to himself by Virgil towards the end of the *Purgatorio*, will stand mute, his voice broken 'like an overstretched bow', following the unique invocation of his proper name by Beatrice (his version of the prophetic call); while Vico, followed by Joyce, will make stammering the original utterance, an imitation of – but also a reaction to – the senseless iteration of the thunder. The complex dynamics behind all these uses are captured most subtly in the stammering of the bride in the *Cantico espiritual* of St. John of the Cross:

> Y todos cuantos vagan
> de ti me van mil gracias refiriendo
> y todos más me llagan,
> y déjame muriendo
> un no sé qué que quedan balbuciendo.

[And all who pass tell me as they go of your thousand graces, and each wounds me more, and I am left dying by I don't know what that they keep stammering.]

The thousand rumored graces of vague provenance which wound the poet provoke, by their unassimilable magnitude, a sense of inundation. Meaningless iteration is then projected out onto the others, who are represented as stammering ('balbuciendo'). In between, however, the ego's own blockage is figured by a phonic and grammatical stammer in the verse itself ('un no sé qué que quedan').

The most extraordinary representation of the prophetic stammer in the Hebrew Bible is Ezekiel's prophecy to the mountains of Israel in chapter 36, which with its disordered plethora of commissions to the prophet, summonses to attention, causal conjunctions and introductory formulas resembles nothing so much as the *qua qua* of Lucky's speech in *Waiting for Godot*. The effect may well be the result of editorial overlaying, but even Walther Zimmerli, the most perspicacious of Ezekiel's modern critics, confesses himself thwarted by the dense tangle of inceptions, each turning on the last, which precede the climactic announcement of YHWH's turning towards Israel in verse 9:

And you, son of man, prophesy to the mountains of Israel, and say, O mountains of Israel, hear the word of the Lord. Thus says the Lord God: Because the enemy said of you, 'Aha!' and, 'The ancient heights have become our possession', therefore prophesy, and say, Thus says the Lord God: Because, yea, because they made you desolate . . .; therefore, O mountains of Israel, hear the word of the Lord God: Thus says the Lord God to the mountains and the hills, the ravines and the valleys, the desolate wastes and the deserted cities, which have become a prey and derision to the rest of the nations round about; therefore thus says the Lord God: I speak in my hot jealousy against the rest of the nations, and against all Edom, who gave my land to themselves as a possession . . . . Therefore prophesy concerning the land of Israel, and say to the mountains and hills, to the ravines and valleys, Thus says the Lord God: Behold, I speak in my jealous wrath, because you have *suffered* the reproach of the nations; therefore thus says the Lord God: I swear [literally, *lift* my hand] that the nations that are round about you shall themselves *suffer* reproach. But you, O mountains of Israel, shall shoot forth your branches, and *bear* your fruit to my people Israel; for they will soon come home (36:1–8, my emphasis).

Here the conjunctions 'because' and 'therefore' give a promise of discursive movement, but in fact the phrases are logically independent. If one tries to analyze the speech grammatically, one finds only abstract patterns: the triple recurrence of the command to 'prophesy', as of the pseudo-illative 'because', suggesting one purely formal model; while the sixfold repetition of the phrase 'Thus says the Lord God', which with the injunction to 'hear the word of the Lord God' makes seven occurrences of the divine name, recalls the numerological schemes encoded in the priestly account of creation. As if in comment upon this extended epanaphora or 'carrying back', the actual oracle, marked by the long-delayed eruption of the first person ('I speak'), turns about the recurrent stem *nasa'*, 'to carry' ('suffer', 'lift', 'bear'), whose nominal form, *massa'*, 'burden', is in fact the technical term for oracle.

Ezekiel himself, in contrast to Isaiah, Jeremiah and many of the Twelve, never uses the nominal form *massa'*, but the verb occurs throughout the book as a figure for prophetic calling: 'Then the Spirit *lifted* me up' (3:12, 14; 8:3; 11:1, 24; 43:5). The meaning of this avoidance may be covertly at issue in our passage, which seems to allude to the celebrated speech by Jeremiah expressly prohibiting the use of *massa'* in prophetic discourse:

When one of this people, or a prophet, or a priest asks you, 'What is the burden of the Lord?' you shall say to them, 'You are the burden, and I will cast you off, says the Lord.' And as for the prophet, priest, or one of the people who says, 'The burden of the Lord,' I will punish that man and his household. . . . Surely I will *lift* you up and cast you away. (Jer. 23:33–39)

(Similar puns appear in Numbers 11 – a text concerned with the office of the prophet – where Moses resents the weight of the public 'burden' that has been placed on him and compares himself to a nurse who has to '*carry* a sucking child', a figure enlarged by the analogy between the prophetic word and manna in the same chapter.)

Since Jeremiah's speech, at least in the canonical arrangement, follows directly on his imprecation against prophets 'who steal my words from one another' (23:30), Ezekiel's appropriation is particularly sly. Yet the allusive strategy is darkly apposite given his larger revisionary project. Where 'reproach' and 'disgrace' in Jeremiah are to be the portion of the Israelites, who flaunt the verbal forms of prophecy while ignoring its ethos, Ezekiel, writing a few years later in the wake of the Babylonian conquest, has YHWH promise to turn the same threat against the surrounding nations (Ez. 36:6, 7, 15; the words echo those of Jer. 23:40 and stand moreover with the verb *nasa'*). For both prophets, however, the double sense of *massa'* represents their own ambivalence towards the prophetic commission.

The ambivalence that binds the stammerer is finely diagnosed by Gertrude Stein, St. John's modern admirer, who transposes it, in Kantian fashion, into the realm of aesthetics ('Pidgeons on the grass, alas'). In Stein's critique, stammering is a response to the crisis of inception, best represented in her early poem 'Orange In' (read 'origin') from *Tender Buttons*, whose final paragraphs oppose a premolecular 'pain soup' to the obstructed wish for a creation *ex nihilo* ('only excreate, only excreate a no since'). The result is a second stalemate: a spontaneous generation of non-sense, which refuses to abandon causality, and hence to proceed:

A no, a no since, a no since when, a no since when since, a no since when since a no since when since, a no since, a no since when since, a no since, a no, a no since a no since, a no since, a no since.

For many poets, the impasse of origination (inseparable from originality in the modern sense) is manifest primarily in the insistence of semantic phantoms, which gather about every rhythmically or phonetically modulated text like dead souls about a sacrifice. But the crisis of inception has a deeper structure, suggested most clearly in the striking figure used by the Priestly writer to signify the barrier of resistance or verbal blockage in his version of the call of Moses (Ex. 6). In this revision of the burning bush story, Moses is sent directly to Pharaoh: 'But Moses said to the Lord, "Behold, the people of Israel have not listened to me; how then shall Pharaoh listen to me, who am a man of uncircumcised lips"' (6:12)? To be like Moses *'aral sephatayim*, 'of uncircumcised lips', is to be vulnerable to the threat of annihilation, represented – in the symbolic structure that Freud wanted to call a phylogenetic inheritance – by the anxiety of castration. Weiskel, in his treatment of the psychology of the sublime, traces the sequential movement in which this anxiety takes its place:

in a first moment, the excessive object [in the Sinai prototype figured both by the burning bush and by the repetition of Moses' name] excites a wish to be inundated, which yields an anxiety of incorporation [marked by the divine warning to approach no nearer]; [next] this anxiety is met by a reaction formation against the wish which precipitates a recapitulation of the oedipus complex [a double movement elided by the Exodus text, although the transformation of the rod of authority into a serpent and the leprous contamination of the hand thrust into the bosom both suggest the redirection of an aggressive aim]; [finally this recapitulation] in turn yields a feeling of guilt . . . and is resolved through identification.[6]

The failure of speech which marks the final crossing in the prophetic call would, according to this scheme, be induced by a turning back upon the self of a destructive drive, a drive that testifies to the crucial moment of revulsion in which the prophetic ego reasserts itself, at considerable cost, against the original incommensurability of signifier and signified, form and content, outside and inside.

In the main, it is the initial and final terms of this sequence that are most apparent. Let us begin with the former. The 'excessive object' (excessive with regard to its recuperable meaning or relation to the self) is especially manifest in the visions of Isaiah and Ezekiel. In the throne vision in Isaiah 6, the mind is thwarted immediately by the supernumerary wings of the seraphim and the repetitiveness of the hymn they sing to one another, a redundancy reinforced by the one echoing word *qadosh*, 'holy', even before the magnitude of the calling voice makes itself felt and 'the [mental] house fills with smoke'. In Ezekiel 1 the inundation is even more violent. The *merkabah* or divine chariot is a paradoxical icon of mobility, a literal and figurative vehicle whose only goal is to evade by constant transference all recuperative translation. The superabundance of its external forms defies assimilation: four cherubs with four faces and four imbricated wings, all shadows of a disembodied spirit, and thus figures not of totality but of infinity. The sound they make is indefinable: 'like the sound of many waters, like the thunder of the Almighty, a sound of tumult like the sound of a host'. Neither the singing nor the words that were still prominent in the story of Micaiah ben Imla (I Kings 22) and in the call of Isaiah – the two precursory texts – are audible any more. In the expansion that follows in the middle of the chapter, each creature is further provided with a 'wheel upon the earth', the immanent extension or complement of the transcendent vehicle, yet no more comprehensible, 'their construction being as it were a wheel within a wheel', and the rims that might have marked their integral boundary being inset with eyes. If one were to take the chariot as an object for contemplative exercise, a higher instrument of accommodation rather than a vehicle of war, these eyes might seem to carry the incarnational movement a step further, evoking the notion of mutuality. Such a figure would resemble the statues which Rilke exhorts us to regard with total intensity until each surface begins to return our gaze. As Ezekiel's prostration shows, however, the eyes of the wheels work more like the gaze of the Medusa, turning back the effort of vision and transfixing the beholder.

In Jeremiah 1 the initial excess is represented by a temporal metalepsis rather than a visual paradox. The prenatal commissioning – 'Before I formed you in the womb I knew you, and before you were born I consecrated you' – implies an infinite regress of call and response in which the prophet's attention can never bind or catch up with the original invocation. Despite the difference in form, its effect is thus similar to the unassimilable visions on the Isaianic model. At the same time, its function within the context of the Deuteronomic redaction is rather to identify Jeremiah as the 'prophet like Moses' announced in Deuteronomy 18:18, a verse deliberately echoed in the unusual expression *natati debaray bephikha*, 'I have put my words in your mouth', in verse 9 (where normal usage would have rather required the verb *sim*). That such overdeterminations pose no obstacle to the prophet is confirmed by the final pun on *shaqed*, which points to the duplicity of the prophetic word itself. The almond (*shaqed*), an untimely bloomer, represents the word as seen by Jeremiah, likewise called to flower before his time. But YHWH takes back even this prerogative, incorporating the word into his own *shoqed*, a providential 'watching', which again objectifies the prophet and makes him into the spectacle (1:11–12). Moreover, the association with Moses will play a part in the antithetical or reactive movement of the identification, to which we may now turn, only pausing to note that in the two prophetic calls in the narrative books – the call of

Moses in Exodus 3 and the call of Samuel – the sublime of magnitude is conveyed most simply and effectively by the bare repetition of the prophet's name: 'Moses, Moses'; 'Samuel, Samuel'.

The identification that frees the prophet to speak is apparent in the very form of the oracle, and in the phrase 'word of YHWH', which occurs some 240 times in the Hebrew Bible, of which over nine-tenths relate to prophetic oracles. However, the underlying mechanism, which involves a double movement of introjection and projection, absorbing the desired presence and spitting out the destructive threat, is figured most dramatically in the scenes of oral incorporation in which the prophet actually eats the word or the scroll. YHWH places his – or perhaps Moses's – words in Jeremiah's mouth at his commissioning (1:9), but the trope is developed more fully in the course of his 'second lament':

> Thy words were found, and I ate them,
>   and they became to me a joy
>   and the delight of my heart;
> for I am called by thy name,
>   O Lord, God of hosts. (Jer. 15:16)

The name itself, with its military epithet, suggests the prophet's commission 'to pluck up and break down, to destroy and overthrow' (1:10), upon which even the word of mercy must build. In Ezekiel, a 'writing prophet' in the full sense, the divine words become a written scroll, which the prophet eats following his prostrating vision, 'and it was in my mouth as honey for sweetness' (3:3). Again, the ingested words are sweet, but the prophetic speech which they unleash is bitter, a dynamic contrast made explicit by the author of Revelation where this text is revised: 'it was sweet as honey in my mouth, but when I had eaten it my stomach was made bitter' (10:10). The two effects are rather complementary than sequential, although formally one might say that the projection of punishment precedes the introjection of presence. This was the pattern of Ezekiel 36, reconfirmed at the redactional level – the promise to the mountains of Israel having been split off from its original counterpart, the oracle of judgment against the same mountains at the beginning of the collection (Ez. 6), and attached to the judgment against Edom at the end. The same pattern is reflected by the conventional tripartite arrangement of several of the minor prophets and of the Greek text of Jeremiah. The Book of Zephaniah is particularly revealing by virtue of its strategically placed tropes of incorporation. Thus, in chapter 1 the imminent 'day of the Lord' is conceived, following Amos, as a 'day of wrath' on which Judah will be judged and the whole earth 'devoured [*te'akhel*] by the fire of his jealousy' (Zeph. 1:18). At the end of the central section of oracles against the nations – culminating with Assyria and Nineveh 'the oppressing city' – the same phrase recurs: 'for all the earth shall be devoured with the fire of my jealousy' (3:8); but now the judgment has been displaced onto the foreign nations who were the object of the preceding oracles. The ensuing gospel of redemption then culminates with a literal image of internalization in which YHWH the 'devourer' assumes a place 'in the midst' of Israel:

> The Lord has taken away the judgments against you,
>   he has cast out your enemies.
> The King of Israel, the Lord, is in your midst;
>   you shall fear evil no more . . .
> The Lord, your God, is in your midst,
>   a warrior who gives victory;
> he will rejoice over you with gladness,
>   he will renew you in his love;
> he will exult over you with loud singing. (Zeph. 3:15, 17)

Referred to the individual prophet, such incorporation is the active counterpart of the original anxiety produced by the desire for inundation, and the bitterness of the law derives its flavor from the intensity of the prophet's own defence against the intrusion of the sublime.

In the one place where Freud discusses stammering directly (the case history of Frau Emmy von N.), he traces it to a moment of childhood panic during which his patient had fought back a strong urge to scream. The convulsive inhibition of speech had then become a mnemic symbol, involuntarily repeated years later whenever there was an analogous conflict between an intention and an antithetic idea or 'counter-will'.[7] The prophetic stammer might be thought to mark a similar conflict between the wish to cry out and the fear of crying, except that in prophecy, which represents the abrogation of temporality, the three phases of the Freudian model – trauma, repression, and return in the symptom – would have to be collapsed.

The attraction of the hysterical model within the context of the Kantian sublime is that it develops from an initial overwhelming of the ego. The stammer is a secondary transposition of the psychical conflict provoked by the original influx; in economic terms, the energy released by repression (by the dissociation of idea and affect) is converted into a somatic symptom. The primary symptom of the first stage of hysteria, which always presupposes a passive experience of unpleasure, is fear 'accompanied by a *gap* in the psyche'.[8] It is because of the gap that the source or object of the fear is never accessible, as it would be in the case of an external danger, against which the primitive defense would be flight. (It is because Jonah is a devout student of biblical tradition, and thus clear about the source of his call, that he commits the mistake of fleeing.)

If the stammer resembles a hysterical response to YHWH's 'call', the call itself might rather come within the defensive structure of paranoia, in which 'the repressed affect seems invariably to return in hallucinations of voices'.[9] Since hallucinations are themselves irrepressible, they provoke a secondary defense on the part of the ego, which instead of dismissing them as alien, adapts itself through an often elaborate system of intellectual formations, which Freud called 'assimilatory' or 'interpretive' delusions.[10] This whole process is subsequent to an original act of projection, understood, at least in the early writings, as a form of *méconnaissance*, in which one escapes from self-reproach by only recognizing one's own forbidden tendencies as they appear in others.

Where hysteria begins with the overwhelming of the ego, paranoia leads indirectly to the same effect. Perhaps then the prophetic texts should be considered 'interpretive delusions', which in turn employ the hysterical model as a representational strategy. This would suggest that the tropes and displacements of representation, its endless deferrals and extraneous versions, are precisely the inaccessible 'experience' one seeks in vain as the original cause of defense. Such circular reasoning would narrow the divide between prophets and redactors, both of whom are excluded from knowledge of the first cause. More specifically, it would confirm our intuition that if the oracles 'bear witness', it is only insofar as they themselves are inspired interpretations – attempts to understand what such a thing as prophecy could be. Similar intimations of our exclusion from knowledge eventually led Freud to formulate a more radical model of defense – a 'splitting of the ego', in which disavowal and acknowledgment 'persist side by side'.[11] In disavowal (*Verleugnung*) the gap within the psyche is replaced by a gap between the psyche and the world. Thus 'what was abolished internally returns from without'[12] – from the inaccessible dimension both Lacan and the prophets would label 'the real'. Disavowal and the consequent splitting of the ego are brought about by experiences of presence *and* absence, in which self-preservation demands that the absence be denied. This returns us to the prophetic trope of circumcision; for Freud's prototypical instance involves sexual difference, and what the subject denies or disavows is castration.

If, like Freud and the biblical authors, we are prepared to take the bedrock of sexual difference figuratively, we may draw a further lesson on the stammering of the prophet from the uncanny story of the bridegroom of blood, which follows the call of Moses in Exodus:

> At an encampment on the way, the Lord met him and sought to kill him. Then Zipporah took a flint and cut off the foreskin of her son and touched his feet with it and said, 'Surely you are a bridegroom of blood to me!' So he let him go. At that time she said 'bridegroom of blood' in reference to the circumcision. (Ex. 4:24–26)

The passage seems to allude to a more extensive tradition, long since lost, but in its present context it concerns Moses on his way to Egypt to execute the prophetic commission he has only just received. Since there is no antecedent for the 'him' whom YHWH meets, we cannot say who precisely is threatened (a calculated uncertainty, as in the similar story of Jacob and the angel). However, the fact that the son is specified in the following verse suggests that the attack was originally against Moses. If we assume further that Zipporah's words are addressed to her husband and that it is thus his genitals she touches with the son's foreskin ('feet' is a conventional euphemism), we may interpret the scene as extending a symbolic, or second circumcision to Moses himself. Pre-critical interpreters, beginning with the ancient versions, read the circumcision as a symbolic sacrifice, in which the blood of the son shed by Zipporah atones for the guilt of Moses – incurred, as the rabbis made explicit, by his failure to perform the rite himself. The final verse, which appears to be an editorial gloss, tends to support this reading, the repetition drawing attention away from the demon-god, to whom the title 'bridegroom of blood' would originally have belonged, and redirecting it to his would-be representative.

In the Priestly version of Moses's call in Exodus 6, however, the need for circumcision is transferred back onto the scene of commissioning, where, as already mentioned, it interprets the prophet's stammer: 'slow of speech and tongue' (Ex. 4:10) in the earlier account becoming 'of uncircumcised lips' (6:12). This conflation opens up the possibility of a less ritualistic reading of the bridegroom passage, in which Zipporah's act is not a sacrificial atonement but, on the contrary, a symbolic castration. From the moment he removes his sandals at the burning bush, Moses is only alive and potent by virtue of the potency of YHWH. On the road to Egypt he has to come to terms with the reality of his new office – to renounce his own prerogative in favor of an otherness he is still tempted to disavow. The acknowledgement of castration is the recognition of that otherness, or of the other's presence as absent other; hence the urgency of the circumcision, which can only be carried out by the wife –

the one marked by absence here acting as surrogate for the absent one. For the prophet to repudiate circumcision would be to disavow the absence that assails him, and so to remain captive to the demonic power of the real which only symbolization can undo. Stammering is the sign of this 'captation' by the real, resolved in the passage through oral circumcision – a passage to the symbolic dynamics of projection and identification.

In Exodus 4 the circumcision is performed on the son, that is on the sign of the prophet's past encounter with the uncanniness of the surrogate in coition. This substitution of son for father, enlarged by the oscillation of the pronouns, qualifies the status of Moses as first or archetypal prophet, replacing origin with originary repetition. The initiation at Sinai is shadowed by the attack on the road to Egypt; YHWH's relation to Moses is shadowed by Moses's relation to Aaron, and so on. Such repetitions cut both ways. On the one hand, they provide against cultic fixation, thereby freeing us from the immobility of worship; but they also weaken the linearity of history, which can no longer be felt as progressive. In the Priestly call narrative, the description of Moses as 'of uncircumcised lips' at 6:12 is recapitulated, with the syntax reversed, at 6:30. Between the two verses, we are given the genealogy of the Levites, in which Aaron and Moses both appear. Biblical history is here the blank space within the stammering of the text. In Kantian terms, it passes from the mode of permanence into the mode of succession in pursuit of the mode of simultaneity. We cannot hear the voice of Moses except in the voice of Aaron; we cannot touch the bridegroom of blood but only those marked by his absence.

The identification of the prophet with YHWH is thus dependent on a second identification with the son, which defends against the pressures of historical supersession. Ultimately, this Oedipal son is a figure for the people Israel. A similar doubling of prophet and people is evident in the accounts of prophetic calling, though it is often obscured by the more obvious signs of antagonism. The call of Jeremiah, for instance, ends with a figure of fortification which can be read from two sides:

And I, behold, I make you this day a fortified city, an iron pillar, and bronze walls, against the whole land, against the kings of Judah, its princes, its priests, and the people of the land. They will fight against you; but they shall not prevail against you, for I am with you, says the Lord, to deliver you. (Jer. 1:18–19)

The 'bronze wall', which seems at first to be an image of separation between YHWH – or Jeremiah – and the Israelites, is also in the context of the Babylonian seiges, an image of protection: YHWH will make Jeremiah himself the wall of protection which the city lacks. In part then, Jeremiah identifies himself with the people, that is with the externalized object of condemnation required by the logic of prophetic transference. Such an identification is clearly second order, but it is the crucial movement that distinguishes prophetic calling from other manifestations of the sublime, whether mystical or aesthetic. One sees it most clearly at the beginning of Deutero-Isaiah, where the portrayal of the heavenly council is resolved into a call scene with the conversion of the indeterminate voice that generates or controls the various rhetorical voices into the voice of the 'herald Zion' (Isa. 40:1–9). The corporate title picks up and effectively transfigures the initial response of the solitary 'I' unable to reconcile the call to prophesy with the dire knowledge of his own mortality or limitation: 'A voice says, "Cry!" And I said, "What shall I cry? All flesh is grass . . . ."' The repeated phrase 'the grass withers' dramatizes not the influx of sublimity but the fixation of the blocked prophet before an inaccessible word until, in a paronomastic inversion of 'the word made flesh', the flesh that is grass (*habbasar ḥaṣir*) becomes the herald Zion (*mebasseret ṣiyon*).

I want to return in concluding to the perspective of the reader; for the prophet's heteropathic or centripetal identification with the people of Israel is as it were a mirror of the reader's own. The absolute importance of this element is that it distinguishes prophecy as a literary genre from lyric, in which the reader identifies with the poetic 'I' – most intensely perhaps when the poem pretends to address him or her as 'you'. Lyric poetry, in Mill's famous phrase, is always 'overheard'; but the word is only prophetic if it is heard directly. This is not a distinction that corresponds to biblical/classical or sacred/ secular, but is independent of the institutionalization of historical traditions and generic forms.

In classical rhetoric, apostrophe, the figure of direct address, is commonly placed beside prosopopoeia, the trope which 'gives a face' to inanimate objects and nonperceptual categories such as time. According to Quintilian, prosopopoeia may serve equally 'to bring down the gods from heaven and to raise the dead'.[13] Raising the dead is elsewhere the specific function of 'eidolopoeia', which may also refer to the petrifying impact the trope can have on the audience. Thus Paul de Man only develops a rhetorical commonplace when he writes of 'the latent threat that inhabits prosopopoeia, namely that by making the dead speak, the symmetrical structure of the trope implies, by the same token, that the living are struck dumb, frozen in their own death'.[14]

The same effect applies to the experience of hearing a prophetic oracle, as the example of Dante at the end of the *Purgatorio* 'turned to stone in the mind and stonelike' illustrates. Beatrice's command to the poet paralyzed by the prophecy of the DXV is to 'carry' the obscure words away within him – 'if not written, at least depicted' (33:76) – a command that seems designed to allay the poet's (or perhaps the reader's) misgivings about the imminent transition from direct address to literary inscription. The meaning of this transition is the obsessive concern of Romantic poetry, most overt in Wordsworth, and we may turn to it briefly here as a way of testing the relation of prophet to poet, hitherto simply assumed. The classic prooftext is the 'Intimations Ode', which revises the peculiar paradigm of prophetic calling at the end of Virgil's fourth eclogue (source for the blessed babe passage in the *Prelude* as well). The final lines of Virgil's 'messianic' poem mark at once the actual inception of the new age, invoked with perlocutionary force, and, in their chiastic structure, the impossibility of ever finding a point of entry into its perfected economy:

> incipe, parve puer, risu cognoscere matrem:
> matri longa decem tulerunt fastidia menses.
> incipe, parve puer: cui non risere parentes,
> nec deus hunc mensa, dea nec dignata cubili est.

[Begin, baby boy, to know thy mother with a smile – to thy mother ten months have brought the weariness of travail. Begin, baby boy! Him on whom his parents have not smiled, no god honours with his table, no goddess with her bed.] (trans. Fairclough)

Like the mutual infusions of the blessed Babe passage, the circulation of interdependent smiles has no obvious point of origin, unless it is the poet's own timely utterance, the 'incipe, parve puer'. The important difference is that in Wordsworth's work utterance can only follow the *disruption* of this interdependence. (Parodying a recent adage, we might say that in Wordsworth the subject indeed thinks with [by means of, by virtue of] its object, but can only *speak* without it.) Thus the babe that 'leaps up on his mother's arm' at the end of the joyous awakening in stanza 4 of the Ode may incite the poet to realize his calling – to pass from 'I have heard the call' to 'I hear, I hear, with joy I hear!' – but the leap, like the oracle that evoked it, is premature. As a result, the vision collapses before the end of the stanza, and composition is temporarily suspended.

I am inclined to read this intermittence in the Ode as a more extended version of the prophetic stammer, analogous to the mutism of Ezekiel, only at a somewhat higher level of abstraction – since it is now the entire scene of election, with its self-reflexive calls and conversions, rather than the more daemonic eruption of a personified demand, that constitutes the intolerable burden. Yet there can be no doubt that the poet's intimations extend to the very pattern of intermittence itself, which seems to have been an essential part of the poem's initial agenda. One cannot ignore the almost programmatic shrillness of the opening allegro, or discount the echo of Spenser's poignant address to Colin Clout on Mount Acidale, about to be bereft of his vision ('Pype iolly shepheard, pype thou now apace') in the reflexive apostrope at the end of stanza 3:

> Thou Child of Joy
> Shout round me, let me hear thy shouts, thou happy Shepherd Boy!

Wordsworth's defaults, on closer reading, are often ironically self-conscious, which is another reason why critics can speak of his tone as anti-apocalyptic. In his work, the shadow of the object has become so long that its darkness acquires a generic outline of its own, recognizable in the elegiac frame that at once limits and composes every representation of the call.

When the Ode picks up again two years later it is with a mythical account of the theory of anamnesis. Now, however, Wordsworth has a subtler attitude towards the 'Mighty Prophet' who is the youthful subject of this myth. Not yet schooled in the 'fallings' and 'vanishings' which will free him to remember and recreate his own life, he remains a captive to presence:

> Thou, over whom thy Immortality
> Broods like the Day, a Master o'er a Slave,
> A Presence which is not to be put by (11. 117–19).

Why this brooding, and why these figures of bondage? The allusion through Milton to the mysterious wind of God 'brooding' (*meraḥephet*) over the primal waters is only background for the figure, although the ambiguous identity of a spirit that impregnates after, or even *by*, incubating is analogous in several respects to a breeze, at once correspondent and creative, that 'vexes its own creation', or to a voice, both concordant and transgressive, that through the hollow of woven fingers inaugurates by mimicking. For the Boy of Winander, too, the dawn of consciousness, equivalent to a commissioning, is attendant upon the intermittence of sound and the concurrent access of vision: it is the *shadow* of the object that falls upon the ego. The suspension of voice, which marked the translation of the natural self in the original (first-person) Winander fragment, is represented again in the muteness of the poet, whose half-hour vigil by the grave recalls the half-hour of silence that ushers in the synaesthetic vision of trumpets and incense at the opening of the seventh seal (Rev. 8:1). Until immortality gives way to loss, the poet remains overmastered and silent. With the sobering of the eye, however, the soul that 'gathers passion' becomes the soul that recollects or reads, transcending that primordial

> Eye among the blind,
> That, deaf and silent, read[s] the eternal deep.

What becomes clear in these texts is that Wordsworth abandons the direct simulation of the prophetic call (in its Virgilian as well as its Hebraic mode) and represents us instead in our reading of the call. But he does so from the conviction that these two postures are ultimately the same. The history of the prophetic movement with its ever-mounting burden of intertextuality illustrates in the end a similar intuition. Against the tumult of its echoes, the current debates between the proponents of logos and the proponents of graphe are scarcely audible. The distinctive feature of the prophetic oracle is not, as Harold Bloom has suggested, its relative freedom from influence anxieties,[15] but simply its greater compression – the directness with which it addresses its audience. In the oracle, as opposed to the Romantic lyric, the temporal, narrative and allegorical dimensions are all omitted (or better, to use the language of the epitaph poem itself, 'bypassed', transgressed – though they still continue to operate at the level of expectation), and the threat revolves less literalistically around the concept of 'sin', a more difficult figuration for death.

To hear a prophetic oracle is to be totally arrested in the state of sin, which, it must be emphasized, is not an effect of some previous act or mental attitude, *but of the fact of being addressed*. The sinner is the one who stands arrested under the prophetic address – outside the temporal or natural continuity. The only possible consequences within the frame of the address itself are fixation or what the prophets figure forth as turning, and its emotional correlative, repentance. One might say therefore that within the prophetic frame, trope or conversion is the sufficient *and only* condition of life. The dead that are made to speak in Romantic lyrics are generally inanimate objects or forms of nature: prosopopoeia is a rhetorical function of animism. But just as theism can be seen as animism of a more abstract order (without thereby implying any evolution or hierarchy between them), so the prophetic oracle or divine word is a hyperbolic prosopopoeia. Theology represents the impulse to apostrophe as the initiative of the other. It is thus the other that both arrests and restores us by two movements of transformation. The critical reader, pondering all this, is in something of the position of Leontes in *The Winter's Tale*: he only recognizes the reality of the first transformation by witnessing the second.

The other has several modes in which it addresses us, however: besides the modes of judgment and promise (arrestation or literalization, and animation or trope), there is the important mode of command. Interpretation of this final mode must eventually become objective, as in the Abraham stories, for example, where it inheres in blind acts of obedience. It seems to have been the peculiar trick of the prophets (at least up to Jeremiah) to have projected the petrifying element of condemnation onto the audience, while personally responding to an interpreted command. Thus, for Amos, the fear of one who hears the lion's roar (Amos 3:8) – of one arrested before the sudden manifestation in the 'real' of the rent in the ego's relation to the world – is superseded by a fiction of authority. Amos must prophesy; it is Israel who must fear. The prophet needs the audience so that he can project the sense of judgment or threat involved in the apperception of the other, while retaining a sense of inalienable mission. If the mode were narrative or allegorical, it might be possible for the one called to respond to the command (as Abraham does in Genesis 12 and 22) without implicating an audience. It could become a command to *go*. But oracle, more radically even than lyric, suspends succession or movement. Its anti-temporal conventions prohibit the prophet from realizing the command within a narrative frame or translating it into the first term of a sequence (thereby opening the moment up to supersession). He is unable to evade the guilt by repressing it as Abraham does – by transforming it into the shrouded, inaccessible occasion for the drives; all he can do is to project it onto the audience – Israel.

The crisis of Jeremiah is bound to his recognition that command and accusation cannot be so readily separated. In him, for the first time, the reflexive basis of the prophet's aggression becomes fully apparent. Whether this is the cause or the effect of the fact that he no longer has any audience is hard to say. The pronominal agitation characteristic of all apostrophic modes here becomes a subjective confusion, in which the stammering cry *me'ay, me'ay,* 'My bowels, my bowels!' (Jer. 4:19) is simultaneously a transmission of divine pathos and an expression of personal outrage. Like Freud's psychotic Dr. Schreber unmanned by the *Gottesstrahlen*, he feels he has been 'raped' (*patah*, Jer. 20:7–9), and he responds with the full set of negations from erotomania to jealous delusion. Ezekiel likewise suffers schizophrenic episodes and a period of muteness. In their wake, post-exilic prophecy can be said to give up the oracle of judgment, to revert, in the words of the late exilic watchman, to the 'burden of silence' (*massa' duma*):

> To me, calling from Seir:
> Watchman, what of the night?
> Watchman, what of the night?
> The watchman says:
> Morning comes, and also the night.
> If you will inquire, inquire;
> return, come. (Isa. 21:11–12)

The call that comes here to the waiting prophet imposes a question rather than a command. Indeterminately emanating from a site of origin that seems to have become a land of alienation or exile, it manifests itself only as anxiety – or rather, since its subjective status is in doubt (not *qol qore*, 'a voice calls', as in Isaiah 40, but only the prophet's *'elay qore*, 'to me calling . . .'), it is under this mode that it is apprehended. Reiteration is its sign as well as its burden: in a sense, its burden has become a refrain.

Is this refrain fixation or the tautology representative of one mode of the sublime? An answer would only be possible if we could separate the active personae of the scene. To schematize briefly, there are three possible 'voices' here: those of YHWH, his people and the prophet. The scene offers only two personae, however: the one (off-stage) who questions the watchman, and the watchman who answers. If the 'me' addressed by the questioner is the prophet, the transition to the third person which introduces his response may again suggest the self-alienation that allows the threatened subject to escape fixation. Alienation enables the culminating identification which marks the watchman's response. His words are now YHWH's command to Israel in exile – but also an expression, albeit a weary one, of the prophet's ambiguous triumph. Henceforth, the prophetic stammer will be refigured less violently as temporal syncope, the poetic gap between an experience of presence and its recollection. We in turn are left with the agrammaticality of reading – 'un balbutiement, que semble la phrase' – in which, as Mallarmé insisted, 'unfailingly the blank returns'.

NOTES

1 Martin Luther, *Kritische Gesamtausgabe der Werke* (Weimar, 1883–), vol. 19, p. 350.

2 Emmanuel Kant, *Critique of Judgment*, section 29, *Gesammelte Schriften* (Berlin, Preussische Akademie der Wissenschaften, 1900–42), vol. 5, p. 228.

3 Thomas Weiskel, *The Romantic Sublime: Studies in the Structure and Psychology of Transcendence* (Baltimore and London, The Johns Hopkins University Press, 1976), p. 23.

4 Ibid., p. 28.

5 Moses Maimonides, *The Guide of the Perplexed*, 3.9, trans. S. Pines (Chicago and London, University of Chicago Press, 1963).

6 Weiskel, *The Romantic Sublime*, p. 105.

7 Sigmund Freud, *The Standard Edition of the Complete Psychological Works*, ed. and trans. James Strachey (London, Hogarth Press and the Institute of Psychoanalysis, 1953–74), vol. 2, pp. 57–8, 91–2.

8 Ibid., vol. 1, p. 228.

9 Ibid., p. 227.

10 Ibid., vol. 1, p. 227; vol. 3, p. 185.

11 Ibid., vol. 23, p. 203.

12 Ibid., vol. 12, p. 71.

13 Quintilian, *Institutio oratia*, 9.2.31, ed. H. E. Butler, Loeb Classical Library (London, William Heinemann, 1920–22).

14 Paul de Man, *The Rhetoric of Romanticism* (New York, Columbia University Press, 1984), p. 79.

15 Harold Bloom, *A Map of Misreading* (Oxford, Oxford University Press, 1975), p. 50.

4

Time and Space in Biblical (Hi)story Telling: The Grand Chronology

Meir Sternberg

The rule of chronology: biblical poetics *vs.* narrative theory

Chronological ordering has long suffered from a bad name as an inferior method of arrangement, if artistic or viable at all. Backed by the prestigious practice of Homer and Greek tragedy, Aristotle's *Poetics* already ranks the 'simple' plot, plodding from beginning through middle to end, below the 'complex' plot with its unexpected reversals and discoveries. And if Aristotle does not explicitly condition artistic form and effect on temporal displacement, his successors have done so in no equivocal terms. Renaissance and Neoclassical criticism doctrinally opposes the 'natural' or 'historical' to the 'poetic' order, elevating the jump *in medias res* into a distinctive feature of epic and literary storytelling in general. So do the Russian Formalists, with their numerous progeny and kindred spirits to this day, by appeal to a more sophisticated distinction: the orderly *fabula* underlying the work must be disordered in the finished *sujet* for the sake of aesthetic 'making strange.' From another quarter, Joseph Frank and his following have celebrated modernism's shift from temporal to so-called spatial form by means of similar disarrangements.[1] Biblical study shows the influence of these schools, though in a mixed chorus of voices where traditional source critics with a rather undefined ideal of wholeness, Aristotelian or otherwise, rub shoulders with some recent literary analysts infected by the modern rage against time in the name of spatial form or, most currently, none.

To be sure, nobody who has thought about narrative structure and interpretation is likely to deny that for narrative to make sense *as* narrative, it must make chronological sense. For if the events composing it do not fall into some line of time, however problematic their alignment and however appealing their alternative arrangement, then narrativity itself disappears. From early to late is not only the order of nature but also the order of causality, hence of plot coherence. Being chronological, the sequence of events is followable, intelligible, memorable, indeed chrono-logical. So much so, the critical approaches I have instanced might say, that it becomes too akin to the way of the world, too mimetic and transparent for art. To qualify for art, chronology needs to undergo such deformation in the telling as to be only gradually reformed or reconstructed in the reading, trial-and-error fashion, with appropriate delays and twists and surprises en route, if not pockets of darkness and ambiguity to the end.

In the light of this sweeping fiat, what are we to make of the Bible? And in the light of biblical practice, surely a leading test-case, what to make of narrative theory? In confrontation, one or the other must go down. For chronological sequence is the backbone of the Bible's narrative books, their most salient and continuous organizing principle. It figures not as a time-line that we reconstruct from some entangled discourse to make sense of what happens, if only in retrospect, but as an actual construction that we encounter all along: an unfolding of events from prior to posterior, from cause to effect. So for the Bible to communicate is to chronologize the surface itself, the narrative as well as the narrated sequence of events, rather than freely dechronologizing in narration what must be (re)chronologized in interpretation. The universal constraint on reading stories, else-where often left unsatisfied for long or recently even for good, operates here as a rule of storytelling. By and large, with certain provisos and latitudes built into the system, the order of presentation in the biblical text follows the order of occurrence in the biblical world.

In this the Bible contrasts with the entire tradition of large-scale temporal disordering, fathered by Homer's plunge *in medias res* and widely elevated ever since into the repository of artful arrangement. For better or worse, what could be more *ab ovo* than beginning with the very beginning of the world, hence of time, indeed with the word 'beginning' (*bereshit*) itself? What could make (and herald) a more orderly sequel than the march of Creation from the first day to the climactic sixth, then to the seventh with its sense of rest and arrest, fulfillment and closure? Beginning, middle, end – each finds its proper place and value in this paradigm of order.

Indeed, the books from Genesis to Kings, all likewise conceiving of story as divine history, follow suit both individually and in canonical series. Their variations in subject matter – from the primeval to the coeval, from the finished to the ongoing or suspended, from God's creation of nature to his affair with humanity and culture, from overt to hidden control of developments, from a single to a multiple line of action – do not in principle affect their adherence to the original model. By a loaded and thematic correspondence, the master of biblical discourse waits on the lord of biblical reality, as if the narrator's shaping must take its cue from God's forwarding of plot. Even the disorders made and suffered by the characters unroll in order; and however otherwise composed, the workings of time remain on the whole straightforwardly disposed.

Considering the bases and biases of different approaches to the Bible, it is not really surprising to find the consistency of this practice of arrangement challenged or on the contrary disparaged, or both, by voices that extend from source criticism to recent echoes of theoretical fashion. The wonder is rather that the principle itself has been denied, most notably in the Rabbinic school, which two thousand years ago codified the very opposite among the rules for expounding Scripture. 'There is no earlier and later in the Torah', the ancient sages lay down as an interpretative guideline. (They refer, of course, to the Torah's order of narration, not, Heaven forbid, to the possibility of our reshuffling the narrated events into historical sequence.) A latter-day follower goes so far as to oppose the disregard for chronology shown by Hebrew qua 'Oriental' literature and its observance in 'Greek and modern' writing.[2] One may well ask where such generalizations spring from, what exegetical interests and pressures they reflect, since the merest glance at Homer is enough to establish that, if anything, the contrast works the other way round.

But the Bible also contrasts with the tradition of ancient Oriental literature, in ostensibly adopting the norm of straight chronology while secretly breaking away to invent a unique double standard. It divides against itself, so to speak, through an internal divergence between levels within its composition: between the ordering of narratives (up to episode units) and of narrative (cycles, books, canonical history), blocks and architectonics, micro-plot and macro-plot if you will.

Historically novel, this biblical poetics of self-division also focuses an issue of much theoretical interest. In sequential arrangement, how does the part (phrase, sentence, scene, episode, or any other unit composed of linear subunits) stand to the whole? What are the relations between tactical and strategic, local and global ordering?

Most often, these relations fall into homology, against or along the chronological (and otherwise orderly) line. If anti-chronological, whether in the manner of Fielding, Sterne, Dostoevsky, James or the detective story, the disordering cuts across series and levels of the most various kinds. Such units as a book, a phase, a chapter, a dialogue, even a sentence, will then twist and turn to generate curiosity, surprise, suspense, to perform retrospection and prospection within their own limits, in harmony with the overall thrust of the narrative. At the opposite pole, chronological homology opts for orderliness and lucidity rather than ambiguity across levels. Its concordance goes as far back as ancient Oriental narrative, for example the Sumerian 'Inanna's Descent to the Nether World', the Akkadian *Gilgamesh Epic*, the Egyptian 'Story of Two Brothers,' the Canaanite 'Legend of King Keret'.[3] This is likewise the rule in historical writing throughout the ages, where the story of a battle and of the war that encloses it, say, will both follow the order of events. Either way, the part miniatures the whole in linear form and effect.

So far from invariably, let alone necessarily homologous, however, part and whole may as well conflict across levels. Vertically speaking, the extremes of arrangement then meet in the same discourse. That having it both ways is much less easy, and indeed less common, only renders the achieved polarity all the more notable. Thus, in modernism, the stream-of-consciousness novel. Parts scrambled out of continuity through the mind's opaque associative jumps, whole kept in lucid external order by appeal to the chronology of a single day: the divergence could hardly go any further than in *Ulysses*. And it is on this contrastive principle that the Bible operates over two and a half millennia earlier, by a very different combination of ends and means, local dechronologizing and grand chronology.

The individual episodes themselves exercise a rich and subtle art of temporal deformation, traced in my *Poetics of Biblical Narrative*.[4] Narrative interest, and with it the dynamics of meaning and effect, lives by such discontinuities, temporary and permanent. The episode often manipulates curiosity, for example, by perceptibly omitting some link in the chronology from its natural position, inviting conjecture about it, and closing the gap in retrospect alone or not at all: consider the pregnant silence about Eve's motives for eating the forbidden fruit, about Ehud's designs on Eglon, about Uriah's state of knowledge. Or the episode may opt for surprise tactics, as when Abimelech's plausible show of innocence regarding Sarah in Genesis 20 suddenly breaks down, to ironic effect, upon the (late, actually last-minute) disclosure of God's (early) intervention and the king's impotence ever since. Sarah having been restored to her husband untouched, 'God healed Abimelech and his wife and his female slaves, so that they could bear children. For the Lord had closed fast every womb in the house of Abimelech on account of Sarah' (20:17–18). In either case, the gaps in the sequence about character or event are repaired and the darkness lifted behind time, if ever.

But once the story of Abimelech or Ehud or Uriah is viewed not as a whole in itself but as part of a whole on a higher level – most clearly, a book – the compositional picture changes to the point of duality. For the arrangement of the episodes into (hi)story lines, though hardly simple, shows little of the delays and dislocations and reversals, far less of the total yet perceptible elisions, to which the episodes subject *their* components. While the narrative blocks specialize in such disorders, their own construction into larger sequences remains all along chronologically ordered: from early to late, from promise to fulfillment, from birth to death, from father to son, from primeval through patriarchal to national history, from Slavery to Exodus to Wilderness to Conquest to Judgeship to Monarchy to Exile. What follows in reading time also follows in world time; and the larger the unit, the more pronounced the shift in part–whole relations from the license of discontinuity to the rule of continuity.

On the narrative surface itself, this principle finds its expression in the Bible's language of time. The arrangement remains paratactic throughout, regardless of level; but the bigger the units arranged, the more vocal do the ordering implications behind and beyond parataxis grow. On top of the reticent series of coordinated verbs, there appear a variety of transitional time phrases. The most common of these markers baldly announce successiveness ('Then', 'After these things', but rarely 'Before these things') or specify an interval ('After x days/years'). Others locate an event in relation to some familiar antecedent, notably a landmark such as the Flood, the Exodus, the accession of a king. Still others build up the time-line not by directly ordering the episodes relative to each other but by placing each in turn within some reference span that covers the whole lot, for example the daily cycle (Gen. 18:1–19:1), the hero's life (1 Kings 1:1–2:1), travel along a route (the itinerary in Exodus and Numbers).[5] Whatever the form assumed, all these indicators spell out the correspondence of textual to temporal progress that lies buried (if not broken) in minimum co-ordination.

The distribution of time markers, verbal and otherwise, so foregrounds the rule of chronology that we are supposed to bring it to bear on the narrative's grand movement even in their absence, at least as an ordering hypothesis. The reader may indeed encounter directives to the contrary, whether notices of simultaneity ('At that time') or the meticulous dating that attends and controls the time-shifts in the overture to Numbers (1:1–7:1–9:1–9:15–10:11). From these time-shifts, predictably, the Rabbis have jumped to (or drawn support for) the interpretative principle that 'There is no earlier and later in the Torah'. But surely the care taken by Numbers to mark and advertise them combines with their exceptionality to demonstrate the very opposite. The absence of pointers either way, therefore, counts as an invitation to assimilate the paratactic members to the ongoing chronology – even where their continuity along the line, let alone the plot, is not immediately apparent or for that matter attractive.

A typical example would be the passage from I Samuel 8 to 9:

(19) The people refused to listen to the voice of Samuel, and said, No, but there shall be a king over us, (20) that we may also be like all the nations, and our king will judge us and go out before us and fight our battles. (21) Samuel heard all the words of the people and spoke them in the ears of the Lord. (22) And the Lord said to Samuel, Listen to their voice and make them a king. Then Samuel said to the people of Israel, Go every man to his city.

(1) There was a man from Benjamin, whose name was Kish, the son of Abiel, the son of Zeror, the son of Becorat, the son of Aphiah, a Benjaminite, a person of worth. (2) He had a son whose name was Saul, a good-looking young man. There was not a man among the people of Israel more good-looking than he; from his shoulder upward he was taller than any of the people. (3) Now the asses of Kish, Saul's father, were lost, and Kish said to Saul his son, Take with thee, pray, one of the servants, and arise, go and search for the asses. (8:19–9:3)

The one chapter ends with the Israelites' insistence on a monarchy in the face of dire warning and Samuel's dismissal of them, 'Go every man to his city', presumably a growl of assent. Instead of going on with Samuel as reluctant king-maker, however, the next chapter switches to new characters, Kish and Saul, engaged in activities that are completely unanchored in time – the search for the lost asses – nor otherwise related to what has gone before. Do the two episodes form a concurrence or a sequence, a loose juxtaposition or a straight if elliptical chain of cause and effect? This chrono-logical question gains point from the extent to which the answer makes a difference beyond the ordering of time itself. And I have in mind not only the genetic prehistory – the gap in the discourse has, predictably, been equated with a variance in source – but the poetic structure of meaning below the given story.

On the arrangement or reconstruction of the series into causal sequence, the prophet would appear to be dragging his feet again, as he has been doing ever since the people's first demand for a king to replace him and his corrupt sons. Samuel's obstructionism throughout chapter 8 having finally come up against the direct order to 'make them a king' – it now seems – he fobs off the assembly with equivocal words of dismissal and plays a waiting game for God knows how long. So God himself must take and make as well as announce the decisive action, intervening from behind the scenes to grant his people's wish and force his prophet's hand through the unknown youth. What on the simultaneous or otherwise juxtapositional reading is a mere coincidence – kingship and asses? – transforms on the successive into a typically coincidental-looking stage management on God's part, synchronization and all. The tighter the relation, in short, the more far-reaching the consequences for plot structure, character portrayal, thematics, judgment.

So how do the episodes link together in transition? How to map the given textual series onto the world? Out of Scripture's poetic context, in a nineteenth-century novel for instance, the two bridgeless chapters would suggest parallel plotting – that is, relations of simultaneity rather than successiveness, far less causality, and with a view to delaying rather than furthering, let alone settling the issue of kingship. Certain fine linkages to the contrary do lurk beneath the surface; but were it not for the Bible's rule of continuity, and hence the pressure for supplying it, the reader might miss them or their implications altogether. Thus the description of Saul's incomparable looks, with its twofold appeal to the people ('not a man among the people of Israel more good-looking than he . . . taller than any of the people') as point of reference. Thus his combining the peculiarities of bigness and smallness, towering above everyone else in height while ranking below most in origin ('from Benjamin . . . Benjaminite'; cf. 21:6), an auspicious sign within the Bible's reversed, because divine, logic of election. Thus also the asymmetry between the prophet's venal and rejected heirs (8:1–5) and Kish's engaging and obedient son, on top of the remoter but also more insistent symmetry with Samuel's own introduction via *his* father's genealogy (1:1ff); or between the people's eventual return *to* their towns by way of closure and Saul's present departure *from* his on a new quest. Each link implicitly projects analogy into chronology, uneasy relations of equivalence into plot sequence, Saul's distinctiveness (physical, tribal, actional, formal) into coming kingship. But how much interpretative weight will these bear?

Only gradually, in the interests of wonder and suspense, does the narrative actualize its early suggestions by drawing the national and the personal threads together. First comes the mention of 'a man of God' in residence, then his identification as 'Samuel', ultimately God's command to anoint Saul, whereby the poetic rule and our reading in its light find their dramatic vindication. Yes, the adjacent chapters are sequent and concatenated, the prophet obstructionist to the last, God in hidden control of developments. And yes, the narrator is likewise silently masterful and consistent within his own domain. Hovering between straight and parallel movement, he has traded on both along the tortuous, dilatory way to convergence with retrospective alignment. However long it may have taken the connection to reveal itself, the two episodes prove to follow in terms of world-time as well as text-time, of history along with history writing and reading.

So do many other episode series – even some whose order, critics of different persuasions would have us believe, has been left not just temporarily uncertain but reversed or scrambled in the writing and needs to be reversed back into proper chronology in the reading. Our reconstruction of events must, as it were, save biblical narrative from its own (mis)construction. A case in point is the sequence that extends from Rebekah's Wooing on behalf of Isaac (Gen. 24) to Abraham's taking Keturah to wife and raising a new family (25:1–6). The two marriage stories as given, it has been objected, can hardly make a chronological line, because Abraham would then be too old to procreate again.[6] How could he beget half a dozen children at an age of no less than 140 years, Isaac having been born in his hundredth year (21:5) and married at 40 (25:20)? For the order of events to accord with the natural order of things, therefore, the marriages must change places in history: first the father's, then the son's.

Unfortunately, however, such reordering has further consequences. It must also push Abraham's cohabitation with Keturah back to Sarah's lifetime, an embarrassment which in turn presses for assigning the affair to a source (P?) different from the Rebekah tale (J, J+E?) and branding the final editor with incompetence. This chain reaction is too high a price to pay for adjusting sequential to sexual proprieties – or the critic's idea of them – all the more so because the very point lies in the patriarch's exemption from such human reckoning by divine grace. To reverse the sequence, in the name of probabilities born of nature or culture, is to reverse its dominant logic and effect: that sexual potence waits on God's omnipotence, procreation on the Creator. By a telling irony, the hard-headedness of commentators since the midrash even rings a bell, having been anticipated by voices inside the Bible's own world. It has its precedent in the little faith and misplaced realism betrayed by Abraham and Sarah themselves forty years before – when each laughed in turn ('Shall a child be born to a hundred year old man?', then 'My husband is old') at God's promise of a son (17:15–21, 18:9–15) – and meets the same refutation from the event. Of the two pairs of newly-weds, appropriately, it is the 140-year-old father, rather than the 40-year-old son, whom God first blesses with children, and by a margin of decades too (25:20, 26). To judge from this crowning sequential twist, the narrative would appear to expect (not to say provoke) skepticism, with an eye to its discomfiture.

From initial surprise to parting shot, then, the disturbance to our sense of fitness is certainly there, but the composition invites us to refer it to heaven, not to bring it down to earth. Indeed, the ordering goes out of its way to highlight a strange-looking chronology *and* analogy in the service of ideology. Narrative order, event order, world order hang all together in proper hierarchy, each reflecting its superior to the gain of its own coherence and their joint impact.

These last examples raise a yet larger question in that they disturb, I hope, the old and strong prejudice against the rule itself. Whether in functionality or in artistry, they match their component units from the episode downward, which in turn accord with the persistent theoretical rage for so disordering the sequence of events in narration as to leave its reordering to interpretation. It is precisely against this dictate of 'chronology in reconstruction alone or at most' that the Bible's rule of grand construction offends, but only to show up the fiat itself as dogmatic, not to say arbitrary and confused. On top of all intrinsic claims to interest and novelty, the Bible's example may well provoke second thoughts about chronological narration as such, its ends and means, its limits and freedoms, not least its resources for artful maneuvering in or out of time behind the façade of artlessness. For now let me introduce, in telegraphic style, some of the principles to be traced at work throughout the argument.

To start with, the Bible's adherence to the arrow of time follows from its complex of strategic goals: the historical, the ideological, the artistic proper, along with the rhetorical or communicative pattern designed to bring them home. However distinct their thrust, all these teleologies pull the same way, so joining forces to enjoin the grand chronology that we can disentangle them only in analysis. Local effects and exigencies may vary, to the point of demanding an inversion of time tactics from one stage to another. (Consider how temporal means shift even in the service of a relatively uniform end, like the sense of wonder in the tales of Saul's anointment vs. Abraham's remarriage.) But this alliance of strategic directives remains essentially constant throughout, as do the underlying reasons.

Edward Gibbon said that the mind takes much higher delight in progressing from cause to effect than in regressing from effect to cause. But he generalizes as a historian wedded by occupation to the natural order, of course, and literary enthusiasts for disorder would, and in effect do invert the scale. Which suggests that the movement in either temporal direction – the progressive or the regressive – has its proper pleasure along with its proper role and logic. Nor do the two directions, with their respective goals, fall into generic polarity, except in the range of choice. If fiction may and often does opt for straightforward movement – a fact that narrative theorists tend to forget, shrug off, even deny – historiography must in principle go straight by the very terms of its case. Whatever its merits in storytelling, the progression from early to late and from origin to result is the norm in history telling, since it mimes the supposed order of occurrence and causation in reality itself. So given the Bible's truth claims, chronology imposes itself as the only viable strategy of arrangement. No matter whether the story narrated by it is in fact real or only realistic, historical or history-like, its narration must suit the means to the generic end.

All the more so considering the variety and magnitude of the Bible's ideological stakes in linear progress. What hangs in the balance is nothing less than the foundations of Hebrew monotheism. Thus the new doctrine of origins, First Cause included; God's purposive control over developments in nature and society, with particular regard to Israel; the relaxation of divine omnipotence in favor of humanity, free to make choices and held accountable for the results; the attack on the very notion of time as cyclical or reversible, of which the Myth of the Eternal Return[7] is paradigmatic throughout paganism; the entire sense made of the world, in short. For better or worse, this sense is still very much with us, not necessarily as a matter of religion – though to believers it has ever since become an article of faith – but as an image of reality, a model with or against which to pattern the world. Less obviously, however, it owes its power and persistence to a distinctive craft no less than to a body of writing, to a manner at the heart of the matter. Why does it take such an effort even nowadays to imagine God as other than a Creator, Prime Mover or Almighty, to divorce humanity or morality from the problematics of freedom, to reduce the movement of time to circularity – let alone seasonal and immutable, after the fashion of the mythological mind in its innocence of history? This is doubtless the heritage of the biblical revolution, and this revolution largely turns on the fore-grounding not only of new causes and new effects, nor simply of their interaction, but also of their straight, lawlike, irreversible, hence unmistakable enchainment under God.

The world-picture embodied in history therefore combines with the rise of historiography. The one order merges into the other: the represented ('real-life') into the communicative process, the memory and meaning of what happened in time into the arts of recording it in due sequence. Here, indeed, the Bible can serve as an object lesson to literary theory, which pays a heavy price for its blindness to history in either sense. Like the view of chronology as a naturally soft option, the tendency to privilege fictional over historical narrative betrays anachronistic thinking on top of parochialism. For moderns, if anything, it perhaps requires an even more energetic exercise of the historical imagination to appreciate the novelty and the challenge involved in the Israelite project of history writing, or indeed of so much as extended plot-making, at a juncture when most of what we take for granted as basic narrative conventions still needed to be forged by way of experiment and invention. In artistic as well as in ideological context, the Bible's line of time is far from being the line of least resistance.

For this reason, the set of three teleologies so far outlined also dovetails with the rhetorical enterprise. That discourse must communicate or else the whole effort has been in vain holds of course particularly true where a new ideology is built into the narrative fabric. But to a culture defined by its history, past, present and to come, the story of history must render itself intelligible to each and every member of the Israelite audience, 'men and women and little ones and the sojourner within thy gates' (Deut. 31:11–12; cf. Josh. 8:34–35, Neh. 8). Hence the directive of what I call *foolproof composition*, which leaves its mark on every choice made by biblical narrative on the strategic level. This imperative redoubles the pressure for chronological arrangement, exactly because it is the one most orderly, therefore most transparent-looking and accessible. The question of ordering presents quite a different face as an insurance policy for maximum inclusion and as a disregard, even (to judge from modern manifestos) a guarantee or conspiracy for the exclusion of the many to the delight of the few. How can a narrative privilege the chosen where the whole people it addresses have been chosen? So in terms of biblical inclusion, to put it at its plainest, readers unequal to the finer structure and detail may yet make sense of the chain of cause and effect; those incapable of working out the chain will at least manage to follow and remember the line; the happy few, to be sure, will read below the line, between the lines.

And there is a great deal to be read there. That the Bible pretends and provides for simplicity does not yet render it simple but, quite the contrary, all the more deceptive. For its foolproof composition puts the greatest distance between minimal and maximal reading, and very effectively so, if the record of interpretation speaks true. So far from needing any special allowances to be made for its exigencies –

doctrinal, rhetorical, artistic – it exposes our own preconceptions about literary structure and history.

Temporal in relation to spatial arrangement is a major case in point. Spatial form, one often hears, is an innovation of modernism, deriving from its ideal of simultaneous organization and apprehension according to equivalences among things. In fact, however, the Bible already deploys a whole range of such formations: from linkage by similarity to contrast, from thematic through dramatic to verbal analogy, from overt comparison to allusive intertextual art, from the tiniest echo to the largest recurrence and orchestration. Even considering the universality of this principle – a fact that still awaits due recognition – its mastery as well as its multiplicity in the ancient Hebrew writings yet remain outstanding and epoch-making by any standard, modernism included.

Or take the related slogan that temporal and spatial arrangement militate against each other, to the point of mutual exclusion, the one focusing on events in sequence and the other on patterns of meaning beyond sequence. Yet the Bible dismisses this either/or choice throughout, its composition making nonsense of the very idea along with the associated value scheme. While unfolding its history along the axis of time for all to see and plot as best they can, it secretly throws bridges of equivalence across time as a running commentary (interpretation, elaboration, judgment) on the course of history. How, then, to divorce one principle from the other in the finished composition? And why assign the sequential a low or even negative value relative to the suprasequential? An example as modest as the Keturah episode is enough to suggest the point, illustrating one of the many ways in which chronology (Abraham's potence in extreme old age) and analogy (the opposition with the young but childless Isaac) may not only live but work together.[8]

Finally, regarding time itself, the Bible's composition is not nearly so simple as it may appear. One reason has already been mentioned, namely the difference between strategic and episodic (or otherwise small-scale) temporality, whereby the manipulations and effects denied to the higher, chronological level gain almost free play on the lower. This vertical self-division enables the narrative to make the most of both deployments, which run not parallel but together (one within the other, as part and whole) along the text-continuum. It also establishes beyond doubt that the orderliness of macrotime, like the twisting of its components, has been devised for a purpose, not adopted or inherited for want of art. The art itself is twofold, in an unprecedented and systematic way. Moreover, considering how the teleology insists on chronology, the two theoretical alternatives turned partners could not even switch places. The assignment of each to its respective level perfectly accords with the master principle. For the smaller the unit, the less crucial the deformation of its elements as long as the overall plot and sense of direction hold or, in communicative terms, the more acceptable the dialogue with the knowing behind the back of the common or minimal reader.

A second reason or compensation bears on the strategic level itself. It is one thing to displace an entire material episode, let alone elide it beyond interpretative recovery; it is another to hide or ambiguate the causal links between episodes in canonical line or among character, destiny and event. For the latter form of silence, as open to the grand design as to its blocks, just recall the temporary but pivotal, far-flung and multifunctional gap about the linkage of I Samuel 8–9; or the permanent reticence about the world order behind the strange wedding order of Isaac and Abraham. Likewise, note that strategic figures (Joseph, Moses, Saul, David, Ahab), though carried over a series of episodes or even books, only grow more rather than less intricate and mysterious as their story unfolds with their life. Yet this is due to the absence, not of some particular key scene(s) from the chronology, but of a magic key to character from the Bible's psychology.

The third counter-artistry is the most interesting and instructive in that it bears on the latitudes, loopholes, licenses amidst the decorums of chronological arrangement proper. How to maneuver within the limits of the rule? How to achieve nonchronological, even nontemporal ends without becoming anti-chronological? How to combine the gains of different, if not opposed, arrangements to maximum effect? How, speaking in terms of artistic challenge, to dance in chains? Since this flexibility-in-constraint informs or subsumes all the other points just outlined, as well as focusing the play between surface and depth in general, I will build the argument round it.

Intermediate blanks: time as selection vs. combination

The rule that biblical episodes unroll in proper sequence has no other strings attached to it. Their unrolling need not fall into any predetermined (causal, thematic, far less transparent) pattern: the Bible does exhibit a set of marked choices and regularities, but nothing like a law, in the design superimposed on chronology for meaning and effect. Nor, within time itself, need the episodes so much as flow into one another to present a uniform continuum of happenings. This kind of package deal, whereby sequence goes with fullness in the manner of calendar and chronicle, is still made by Thucydides: note his double commitment to 'keeping to *the order of events* as they happened *by summers and winters*'.⁹ Practiced by later storytellers down through the ages, inside as well as outside literature, the automatism of keeping even pace with time has given rise to Fielding's attack on 'the painful and voluminous historian, who, to preserve the regularity of his series, thinks himself obliged to fill up as much paper with the detail of months and years in which nothing remarkable happened as he employs upon those notable eras when the greatest scenes have been transacted on the human stage', instead of imitating the wise traveller 'who always proportions his stay at any place to the beauties, elegancies, and curiosities which it affords'.¹⁰

Fielding himself twists as well as proportions his own event-series out of 'regularity'. Yet his attack bears on selectional (as distinct from combinatory or sequential) failures of art alone. And the Bible would therefore readily meet, if not beat, his standard. Here, the episodes rather follow than fill up the time-line. If anything, they tend to be separated by an interval of varying duration, which the narrative may bridge by way of summary from a phrase ('After x days/months/ years') upward or leave completely empty. Genesis 16 thus ends by fixing Abram's age as 'eighty six' at Ishmael's birth, while Genesis 17 greets us with the news that 'Abram was ninety-nine years old' when God appeared to enjoin circumcision and promise a son and heir by Sarah. Likewise, the bulk of three books having detailed the Exodus and the year or so following it, the passage from Numbers 19 to 20 buries in silence decades of wandering (according to the original text, without so much as a chapter break by way of marker) to resume with the last, fortieth year. No wonder that the Bible's history, like Fielding's, sometimes seems to stand still and sometimes to fly.

Whether bridged or unbridged, moreover, the intervals between episodes (let alone cycles or books) often diverge in perceptibility and role from their equivalents within a single episode. Along the *intra*episodic sequence, such discontinuities easily force open *gaps* – in plot structure, character, inner life – which demand closure from the reader on pain of incoherence and may obtain it from the narrative itself in later retrospect. Where the line of events tightens into a chain, as befits a well-formed episode, a temporal sequitur may double as a causal non sequitur, and require interpretation accordingly. What, for instance, has so changed Joseph's mind during the 'three days' (Gen. 42:18) that divide his first from his second interview with the brothers? Why does God approve Balaam's journey 'at night', only to have an armed angel waylay him 'in the morning' (Num. 22:20ff)? How come that David prays so fervently for the sick baby's recovery but will not spend a moment lamenting its death 'on the seventh day' (II Sam. 12:15–23)? All manifestly following in time, none of these event-series yet follow in sense and consequence – not at least unless (and until) the narrator thinks fit to supply the missing causal link. (Of the three examples, indeed, this happens only in the last, where the tale finally closes the incongruous gap by having the king disclose his mind to his servants and indirectly to the reader: 'While the child was still alive, I fasted and wept, because I said, Who knows, perhaps the Lord will be gracious to me and the child may live? But now he is dead, why should I fast? Can I bring him back again? I shall go to him, but he will not return to me.') Even where the temporal bridge is explicit – 'three days,' 'at night' and 'in the morning', or 'on the seventh day' – the causal is left to our inference; even where the suppression of the cause is to prove temporary, as with David, we do not know and cannot wait. Given the line, the reader must somehow fill in the gap in its middle to work out the secret plot.

Along the *inter*episodic sequence, on the other hand, the empty span between units grows in extent, just like the units themselves, but not in relevance and fillability. Here the discontinuities can hardly be temporary – the in-between episode(s) first entirely elided and then, like David's *volte-face*, repaired behind time – for such delay would incur a twofold distortion of chronology on a large scale. But nor are these discontinuities in the grand chronology left permanently open to secretive and suggestive effect, like the Joseph enigma, through a perceptible elision that challenges us to figure out some missing episode(s) for ourselves. As historians and busybodies, of course, we would give much to know how Abraham spent the thirteen years between Ishmael's birth and circumcision, or whether Moses brooded over his failure during the 'many days' (Ex. 2:23) of his exile in Midian, or what atmosphere prevailed in the Israelite camp throughout the decades of purposeless wandering, with nothing ahead but death, or what happened in the long interludes of peace separating the national crises in Judges. But here the text in no way goads us to speculate about the absent, by either threats of incoherence or promises of richer understanding, because speculation would divert notice from its own line and focus of interest. To go beyond or beneath the givens on either side of the discontinuity, with a view to fullness, is then to go against the rationale of narrative selection – for example, tempo, foregrounding and backgrounding, scaling of value, thematic continuity across time and plot – rather than to go through the twists of narrative combination.

Within the structure of time, therefore, we must always distinguish temporal *gaps*, created for their interest through disordering, from temporal *blanks*, left vacant for their lack of interest without any felt offense against order and to the advantage of the privileged givens and gaps. In principle, this distinction applies everywhere, clean across the boundaries of textual segmentation as well as of whole texts and genres. Within biblical structure, however, it also correlates to a significant degree with that between units of various sizes – or local vs. global composition – and thereby helps to delimit the episode unit as one framed, hence also focused, by blanks.

Simultaneities in narrative sequence

Sparse coverage or none with a view to selectiveness need not, and in the Bible does not, rule out multiple coverage in the name of inclusiveness. For actions may be simultaneous in occurrence as well as successive; and when they are, the period of time where they all unroll together fills up, gaining a plenitude denied to a single line of development, let alone one punctuated by blanks. But despite this contrast to blanking in rationale and effect, the rendering of simultaneity equally involves a manipulation of time, if only due to an inescapable discrepancy between world and medium, real and verbal temporality. Since language can render only one thing at a time, concurrence itself cannot but emerge in sequence. Even a narrative that favors the strictest chronology must at least mark time as it shifts or spreads out in space from one arena to another. Rather than hastening on the march of events in the world through ellipsis, blanking fashion, the discourse then suspends it along one line while tracing its parallel, often with constant interlinear movements backward and forward as a result. Why, then, subject history to forking and its stories to turn-taking?

World and discourse in simultaneity: from mimetic to artistic motivation

Even if we discount all free variables – local exigencies, special forms or deformities, refinements – the Bible displays an impressive complex of forces and pressures and motivations for simultaneity in occurrence. Of these, several are mimetic in that they belong to the represented world, to the field of reality itself, distinctive properties and all. One is the Bible's omnipresent structure of conflict, presupposing two sides for the narrative to shuttle between at will from outbreak to resolution. Another is the coexistence of the human with the divine: ideologically built into the action and running the gamut of interaction, from harmony to head-on clash, this may again require or repay parallel treatment at any moment. A two-level world makes a two-level scene and arena, without recourse to any contrivance like the balcony above the platform in the Elizabethan theater. Still other forces, no less charged with thematic value and distinctiveness, bear on the human world alone. If God is eternal, humans come and go. But in the meantime, as long as each struts and frets his hour upon the stage, they lead social lives that intersect at various points with their elders, coevals and successors. This further widens the repertoire of crosscutting options and permutations, within and/or between age groups, so as to generate some of the Bible's thematic plots from Genesis to Kings. Consider the partiality for dramas of sibling rivalry, often on top of intergenerational overlapping, whereby sons appear and compete on stage in their fathers' lifetime throughout the patriarchical era, just as each heir and pretender in Samuel rises while the outgoing (or, in Absalom's rebellion, ongoing) leader still clings to power. Similarly with such favorite frictions as between prophet and king or people, Northern and Southern tribes, Israelite and nonIsraelite, public and private life, externals and internals.

All coming from the Bible's world and world-view, these pressures for simultaneity join forces, often even dovetail. Conflict serves as their highest common denominator, their major point of interaction and interlinkage throughout the Bible. It equally marks, hence easily coordinates, the most various relations: the dealings of God with humanity, of brothers or generations or tribes or leagues or kingdoms quarrelling over some prize, from divine favor to earthly hegemony, even the pairing of inner thought and outer, social behavior. Observe the tensions – complete with transitions in the rendering of simultaneity – between God and his people from the Exodus to the Exile, between Joseph and his brothers, David and Absalom, North and South, Moses and Pharaoh, Hezekiah and Assyria, between Jephthah's military success and domestic catastrophe, or between Abraham's falling on his face in apparent gratitude for the promise of an heir and his secret incredulous laughter at the thought of a child born to a centenarian with a 90-year-old wife (Gen. 17:15–18). Like the forces for simultaneity themselves, accordingly, their meeting and central meeting ground are distinctive, precisely because they issue not so much from the nature of narrative as from the disharmonious make-up of reality in biblical narrative. Where harmony naturally brings together – in terms of peaceful coexistence, even oneness – disharmony tears reality apart into sides, which art must keep going abreast by sequential turns across space, until the time comes for (re)union. How much more so with multiply compounded disharmony, networks of interlinear (interpersonal, interfamilial, intergenerational, intersocial, international, intercultural, interexistential) friction. The Bible's is a world never at rest, always at strife, hence in constant need for synchronizing agents, camps, positions, movements, story lines.

Yet in the Bible as elsewhere, such world-logic (however potent and composite) does not yet go far enough, because there must be reasons for the features as well as for the facts of simultaneous plotting. The drives we have so far outlined motivate the range and rate of simultaneity in the action – as an image of life, a model of reality – not its enactment, still less its management, in the narration. They at most explain why the underlying (hi)story runs together various events, agents, lines, rather than why and how the finished narrative chooses to arrange these concurrences in sequence.

Chooses, because the narrative could always do otherwise, and often indeed does: this point, still more easily missed than the very need for motivation in the first place, is of the utmost importance. In principle there is always a difference between what we reconstruct from the given text and what we find constructed on the text's surface, between what happened in the world of (hi)story and what unfolds in the art of (hi)story telling. Even where the action in the world itself moves along two lines, for example towards a showdown, the composition may nevertheless avoid (and a fortiori minimize) all shuttlework between them – by anchoring the point of view in either and leaving the other off stage, implicit, reconstructible only as it impinges on the favored line. Thus the practice, indeed the rule, of gearing the entire world and plot to a single mind in restricted (*Lolita*) or self-restricted (*The Ambassadors*) narration. The more internalized the perspective and the closer the adherence to its workings and discoveries – as in modernism – the fuller the transformation of multi- into unilinearity: objective simultaneity (Strether in Europe, Mrs. Pocock in New England) into subjective continuity (Strether hears, talks, thinks about Mrs. Pocock), constructional and progressive into inferred and retrospective synchronism. Local equivalents abound throughout literature, drama, film, temporal art at large, including the Bible (e.g. Gen. 22:20–24). And it is only insofar as the text chooses to decline such one-track continuity in favor of simultaneity proper that it incurs and must face the constraint of linearizing multilinear activity by turns.

This goes to show that the questions with which I started, 'Why subject history to forking and its stories to turn-taking?', are essentially distinct or rather complementary. To answer the first, as we have done, is still to leave the second unanswered. And to answer why forking gets enacted at all – let alone to explain why in this of all possible forms of turn-taking, this or that frequency, this or that order, this or that juncture, this or that linkage – we must go deeper: from the way of the or *this* specific world to the arts of discourse that operate behind and through it for a purpose. As always in the face of representation, especially artistic, we are supposed to view reality itself as a means to an end, if only to infer that the seesawing of a conflict by turns (say) functions to sharpen our sense of conflict, that the shuttling between the divine and the human planes of action brings home the necessity or variety or point of their interaction, and the like. The world as mimesis answers, even bends, to the exigencies and strategies of the discourse as poesis. The rule is that the mimetic logic or principle of motivation overlies – indeed itself motivates in reality-like terms – the aesthetic, the rhetorical, the communicative. The two logics of composition fall into a means-end hierarchy even at their most accordant.

It now remains to see in what principled fashion the Bible's system of narrative implements this rule: how, above all, the mimetic forces for simultaneity combine not among themselves alone but also with others of a purely artistic nature. No less than four artistic motivations vibrate beneath the surface: crowding, perspectivizing, keying up, and analogizing the world's affairs. But they are not all of the same order of constancy or, the other way round, of distinctiveness. Roughly, the first two inhere in the pattern and change with its manifestations alone, while the second two may be excluded at will and need contriving to turn operative, let alone dominant and cooperative. So in inverting the scale of theoretical constants and variables, the discussion below follows the Bible's own priorities.

The sense of plenitude and panorama, with its reality-effect, has already been mentioned as a universal function behind multiplotting and imaging coexistence at large. So has the universal of diversifying point of view, even within the otherwise uniform framework of omniscient narration. A shift in story-line entails, and reflects, a shift of perspective, if only to bring into focus another agent or set with their peculiar range of knowledge, concerns, fears, hopes, judgments and value schemes. In the transition between protagonist and antagonist this tie-up leaps to the eye, but only as a special case of the rule, because every agent is also a subject: you cannot bring him into the action while keeping out his mind. Thus the cut from Abraham pleading for Sodom to the angels charged with its destruction, from the Israelites encamped at last on the Jordan in sight of the promised land to the Balaam menace arising and quashed behind their backs, from the jubilant Philistines to the blind Samson intent on revenge,

from Saul as hunter to David as prey. Even without overt inside-
views, multilinearity involves multi-subjectivity throughout. Apparently
far removed, in theory, plot and perspective closely interdepend –
which is why *The Ambassadors* will avoid or minimize both
discontinuities in its quest for maximum consistency of impression
and design. For better or (according to Jamesian modernism) for
worse, departures from unilinearity give a sense of a full world along
with a full registration of the world, a plurality of viewpoints on
existence, in coexistence.

The pair of universals thus go together. As constants, however,
their operation not only remains general in itself but also attaches and
adapts to the contextual thrust of other forces less built-in, hence
more distinctive. Two such variable roles take the lead: narrative
interest about the action and parallelism between strands of action, or
to bring out the difference in effect another way, uncertainty and
suspense through delay as against illumination through the coupling
of the delayed with the delaying occurrence.

Thus the very constraint of tracing only a single line at a time, so
that the progression of one is the suspension of the other, plays into
the Bible's hands in licensing the zigzags and benefits of suspense. All
suspension entails suspense in that it blocks the ongoing movement
towards the future that the text has promised (or, if fearful rather
than hoped-for, threatened) to complete. Of the various modes of
suspension, however, the interlinear enjoys a peculiar lifelike guise in
the form of co-temporality: the retardation intervenes not as an open,
arbitrary contrivance to play on our expectancy, but, as it were,
under the mimetic pressure of an activity with an equal claim to
treatment, because it runs parallel and has itself suffered retardation.
'Sorry to break off here', the narrator appears to be saying at each
turn, 'but our business calls us elsewhere for a while, otherwise we'll
never keep up with developments'.

Suspense strategy having been analyzed in *Poetics of Biblical
Narrative*, its implementation in simultaneity need not detain us
except for a few specifics. In effect, this particular resource may be
heightened, minimized, even neutralized. And as usual, the Bible
ranges over the spectrum of options, canalizing and integrating their
impact to suit its different needs. This is the case with all major
variable factors. Does the narrative break off and/or cut in at a
moment of suspense? And in either instance, does the suspense
concern the outcome or the process, the *what* or the *how* of
resolution? In turn, these polar choices lend themselves to anything
from gradation to inversion even in the dynamics of a single tale.

For an example of suspense reduced to the minimum through

timing and foreshadowing – both so crafty as to verge on deception – observe the junctures at which the narrative crosscuts between the Israelite and the Egyptian sides of Joseph's history. Once Joseph has been removed to Egypt, the narrative stays behind in Canaan just to enact the Tamar imbroglio before shifting the scene with him; and on good mimetic as well as artistic grounds. For the time being, at least, the family conflict has played itself out and come to a standstill, frozen though hardly resolved. There's nothing for it but to leave Jacob to his anguish, the brothers to their guilty satisfaction, with Tamar alone serving as a reminder that life still goes on and biblical life will not let matters rest there. Across distance, even against likelihood, the parallel lines will sooner or later meet again. In the meantime, however, we trace Joseph's checkered Egyptian career step by step up to the onset of the famine – three chapters or twenty years later – when 'the people cried to Pharaoh for bread' and Joseph feeds them (41:53–56). Here the scene turns worldwide for a moment ('all the earth came to Egypt to buy grain'), yet only to motivate and emphasize the transition back to the one family that matters: 'Jacob saw that there was a grain in Egypt' (41:57–42:1). With this (re)close-up, the family conflict indeed resumes to the exclusion of everything else and as a simultaneity within (or beside) a simultaneity with the developments in Egypt itself, to say nothing of the world. But then the Egyptian crisis has apparently been stabilized with the issue of emergency rations. All being well, there remains nothing to tell at the moment. Just as with the earlier reverse cut to the Egyptian line, no suspense arises from the narrator's dropping it in turn to shuttle among Jacob at home, Joseph abroad, and the brothers on the move. The family circle now provides all the suspense needed, or desired, without recourse to any felt suspension of outside activity.

It is only when these stresses have all been worked out through the prolonged testing, the denouement, the reunion, the settlement in Goshen – or so it looks till Jacob's death uncovers a bleaker reality – that the narrative reverts to the effects of the famine on Egypt (47:13–26). And then it suddenly transpires that the state of affairs there has been all this time far from well and uneventful – so far that a profound socioeconomic change, nothing less than an agrarian revolution, has taken place. The original account at the point of transition in chapter 41 was misleadingly rose-colored, we now discover, because the Egyptians obtained the grain from the royal stores only in exchange for 'all the money', then for 'all their livestock', then for 'all the land of Egypt', with its former owners relocated and according to nonMasoretic versions even enslaved. (Not to mention that neighbouring peoples, such as Canaanites, excluded from the livestock and the land barters, must have starved to death when their money had run out.) In suppressing all details apart from the bare sequence of crisis *and* resolution, the original coverage remains true to the facts but as distant from the whole truth sprung in playback as reassurance from anxiety, formal from operative suspension. Yet the discovery comes too late for the reader to do anything except appreciate in long retrospect how the narrator has manipulated us into the desired frame of mind. To prevent any distraction from the twists and torments of the national story about to be picked up, he has not just chosen but devised a tranquil cut-off point for the simultaneous foreign emergency. Nor does that tranquillity erupt into full-fledged drama even in playback. For by the time the whole truth begins to emerge we already know the resolution – Joseph will deliver the goods, because in the earlier round he *has* delivered the goods – and only wait to see and see out the gradually rising price. All real suspense about the outcome is first neutralized altogether, then modulated into surprise in reversion and played down to the how-why-when gaps of retardation. Two concerns of Joseph's, two scales of concern: the priorities of interest and value, here along national lines, operate amidst simultaneity of occurrence itself.

Elsewhere, the Bible's handling of concurrence gravitates toward the other extreme of suspenseful suspension, one in dynamic effect as well as mere temporal form. In the struggle over Dinah, once the two families have reached an agreement unpalatable to both, we cannot help wondering as they part ways again whether either will keep it; and the leisurely enactment of the Hivite violations, adding threat to past injury, then reloads the question concerning the Jacob party. Here the future remains opaque, the alternative outcomes equally possible, and the event itself the only reliable closure. Yet, instead of such free, end-directed play, the Bible favors some intermediate dynamics of suspense, especially at key junctures in its history.

This strategy is at work throughout the zigzagging between Saul and David from their first encounter to the Gilboa catastrophe and release. The one having been rejected, hence doomed, the other newly anointed and bound to prevail, the issue may seem a foregone conclusion by divine will. So it proves, but not without hitches en route – some mainly by way of actional delay, some grave enough to problematize the fulfillment of the scenario in affective or even moral terms. The foreclosure turns out to be a premise and incentive, rather than an obstacle, to the operations of suspense anchored in the narrator's double focus on God's antagonist and protagonist.

Take the concluding phase, where the intricate rhythm of meeting and parting, engagement and near-engagement, appears to resolve itself into final disengagement with David's flight to Gath in I Samuel 27. By a boomerang effect, this desperate bid for disengagement of forces soon comes to look anything but final, precipitating instead the most explosive engagement of all. The one chapter having put as much distance as possible between the rivals, seemingly for good, the next threatens to draw them together again, this time as parties to an international conflict with David on the wrong side. 'The Philistines gathered their forces for war, to fight against Israel, and Achish said to David, Thou must know that thou art to go out with me in the army, thou and thy men' (28:1). David's counsel of despair has led him from bad to worse – the stigma of Philistine vassalage – and from worse to the very worst. Once pressed into battle in the ranks of the enemy, he will have saved his skin twice (once from Saul's sword, once from Achish's) at the cost of his soul along with his eligibility, moral if not practical, for kingship. Whatever the oil of anointment might absorb, how can it mix with native blood?

Wordlessly leaving us (and David) in this hopeless quandary, the narrative shifts sides, not just to retard but to aggravate matters in the process, and along more than one line at that. First comes a public-operational long shot, recording the Israelite countermuster at Gilboa – no escape from hostilities – then a private-affective close-up, minutely dramatizing Saul's trials at Ein-dor. Even the one brighter vision amidst all this darkness arises in passing, on hitherto fallible authority, and without resolving the dilemma. The monarchy, Samuel's shade rubs into Saul, has been 'given to thy neighbor, to David' (28:17); but – supposing the throne to be still within David's reach – at what price, socially and ideologically speaking? If the worst comes to the worst, will God really overlook the blot, the people forgive, posterity ever forget?

By itself, then, the reaffirmation makes cold comfort, nor does the narrator hasten to warm it into reassurance. Having exploited the scene-shift to pile on the tension, he graduates its release in switchback. The two musters first receive another notice, again collocated within a single verse but no longer within a single arena: textual juxtaposition for maintaining the drama, geographical separation (from Shunem vs. Gilboa in 28:4 to Aphek vs. the Jezreel spring in 29:1) for lowering the sense of its imminence. Yet by way of compensation, as it were, the narrative at once goes on to tell how the Philistines advanced 'by hundreds and thousands', explicitly naming David among Achish's contingent. So the repetition introduces one brightening and one darkening variant, the first giving the hero a little more time, the second barring the door of escape. What is he going to do, with whom, against whom – we still wonder, perhaps he too – since do or die he apparently must? But if this touch improves the balance of hope and fear, the next reverses it from an unexpected quarter: none other than the enemy, and by implication God. The Philistine generals will not trust the former champion of the Hebrews; Achish regretfully bows to the majority veto, sending his vassal away despite his indignant (and safe) protestations of loyalty; and the narrator again puts maximum distance between the two rivals – one trapped in the North, the other hastening South – this time, for life.

When it does come, the relief from suspense goes quite a long way: all danger averted, predicament vanished, disengagement accomplished, the enemy's suspicion doubling as a testimonial, and David's pressure for the service that a moment before must have pressed on him like a nightmare even affording a comic catharsis of sorts. But this relief comes with a distressing slowness – and without warning at that – the narrator having taken two chapters to zigzag through a crisis that he might reduce to two verses or even omit in the first place. Instead of a false reassurance, as in the Joseph story, he contrives and prolongs a false alarm. The relief also comes after a painful journey through pity for the rejected king combined with fear for his successor, each caught in his own impossible situation. Always fortunate, David gets off with his image as whole as his skin, but not without a bad fright by way of memento, lesson, token retribution for an equivocal act putting immediate survival before national solidarity and divine providence. But for the grace of God, after all, the lesson might have been fatal and the suspense resolved by an end as tragic as Saul's. Indeed, this is also why the relief no more comes in full measure than quickly and easily. With the psycho-ideological dilemma sidestepped rather than worked out, the question remains, What *would* David do if put to the test that he was mercifully spared? Though the tension dissipates, the might-have-been scenarios persist to keep wonder and warning eternally alive. Their persistence even in retrospect, as gaps of character *vis-à-vis* destiny, does not undercut but complicates the sequential, temporary effects of plot retardation, which is understandably the Bible's staple of future-directed interest. The future's opacity concentrates less in *what's* (Will David, or Joseph, prevail?) than in *how's*: the ordering of simultaneity is no exception to this rule. In default of real suspense about the issue, which does not well agree with God's control over history, such retardatory suspense about the means and the route to unravelling is at a premium.

No less important, the very discontinuity that the story line must suffer in the interests of this effect promotes, and masks, interlinear continuity at a deeper level. With the onward chrono-logical march temporarily suspended and arenas more or less loosely juxtaposed, the contiguities of action (time, place, cause) weaken to benefit the workings of similarity. For the multiple lines unfolding in sequence naturally fall, and easily tighten, into relations of equivalence. Sides in a conflict are thematic as well as dramatic opposites, analogues as well as coexistents. So, in or out of collision course, are God and man; so are believer and nonbeliever, social and secret activity, brothers, leaders, generations; so may anyone and anything become in skillful linearization alongside a contemporary.

Such crosslinkage runs through all the examples of simultaneity glanced at so far. Abraham's incredulous state of mind belies the devout posture of his body; the unsuspecting people on the Jordan bank stand opposed to the designing Balak, the shifty Balaam, the omniscient and ever-vigilant God; the final temple scene juxtaposes Samson to the Philistines for maximum (sociocultural, thematic, perspectival, actional) contrast: Hebrew vs. foreigner, deliverer vs. oppressor, tricked vs. triumphant, eyeless yet knowing vs. seeing but ignorant, complete with the last role-reversal in the long series of variations on victim vs. victimizer. By a more intricate balance of likeness and unlikeness, the Israelite immunity from the plagues not only underscores the Egyptian affliction but also establishes the common, heavenly source of both. Again, the antithesis between Saul as rejected antagonist and David as elected hero takes on unsettling complexity in their last near-encounter under the pressure of other forms and relations of analogy: straight (e.g. both deadlocked), mixed (e.g. both facing the same enemy, the one openly and the other less than honorably), dynamic (the one making a heroic exit, the other extricated by the backstairs). More detailed instances of spatial bridging will appear below. But we have seen enough of the principle to generalize its scope, flexibility, interplay with such universals as point of view, and above all, its appropriateness in poetic context. To a secretive art like the Bible's, this affords a repertoire of silent commentary built into plot movement yet operating across it: linkage by (dis)similarity beneath contiguity, mutual mirroring in the guise of temporal coincidence, comparison for explanation and judgment – all artistic simultaneities of meaning or reading passed off as mimetic simultaneities of happening.

The opportunities for imposing such spatial-analogical design on the time flow are therefore no less rich and welcome than the extra loopholes for injecting suspense into our experience of time. The two opposed axes of structure, like the assorted features (conflict etc.) attaching to the reality-model, issue the same directive to the storyteller. They bow together to the rule of chronology, pull together against its will to arrow-like flight, work together to interpret and complicate and orchestrate the historical record, and all in the guise of mimesis: by appeal to the fact that history itself advances on more than a single front.

So if the world-oriented features chiefly explain why multilinear plotting recommends itself to the Bible, their artistic fellows and coordinators also indicate the kinds of sense actually made by its manipulation into the linear telling designed for the reader. What are the shapes assumed by or behind this fundamental tension between object and image, and to what purpose? Where does the medium's constraint of sequencing leave off and the text's art of sequence begin? Within linearizing choice, again, how to distinguish theoretical range from actual repertoire – potential from performance, what art in principle or sociocultural matrix enables from what each art (here, the Bible's) implements, favors, minimizes, avoids – and how to account for the distinction? Where, particularly, to draw the line between licensed and deviant ordering of simultaneities, between going across and against chronology, between suspending and snapping the thread of history? How do other rivals, likewise essential to the system of narrative simultaneity, interact in (con)text: dramatic vs. reading process, time vs. space as axes of the multiline world, temporal vs. spatial composition (or interpretation) brought to bear on that world, and, cutting across all, mimesis vs. poesis? These questions I want to pursue in a roughly ascending order of complexity, from basic forms to virtuoso, though still rule-governed, deformations.

Juxtaposition and alternation

To begin with the simplest form of simultaneity, *juxtaposition* arranges two or more contemporaneous events (acts, episodes, arenas, plots) in narrative sequence, often relating them through a formula like 'at that time'. The 'time' invoked as a common framework is extremely flexible in reference, and with it in juxta-positional range. Its extent thus varies widely: from a discriminated moment to an hour, a day, a year, even an entire era. A marked contrast, again, to the season as narrative unit and ceiling in Thucydides.

On the one hand, the time-span of juxtaposition may narrow down to a single point, a unique and transitory juncture. Thus the nice spatio-temporal coordination required to enact *or* prevent an encounter between agents on the move, or a convergence of progressive activities:

Before he [the Wooing Servant] had finished speaking, and behold, Rebekah coming out . . . with her pitcher upon her shoulder. (Gen. 24:15)

[Having assassinated Eglon king of Moab], Ehud went out into the vestibule, and closed the doors of the roof-chamber upon him and locked them. He had just gone out when his [Eglon's] servants came and saw, behold, the doors of the roof-chamber locked! And they said, He is only relieving himself. (Judg. 3:23–24)

Both the similarities and the differences among these cases of exact relative timing would normally make sense by appeal to universal functions of narrative – like plotting, dramaticness, suspense, wonder, relief. So they do in the Bible, yet with a peculiar and versatile ideological twist (or thrust) that I call the omnipotence effect. Whether the characters meet or miss each other, whether the happenings manage or just fail to coincide and intersect, depends on precision work that is not so much the narrator's as God's. The one, far from flaunting his own mastery and artifice, as fiction makers will do, only records in the narrative what the other performs in the world. It is the design to establish and glorify God's control over the plot that explains the features of juxtaposition here – from the drama itself to the discourse, from the very staging through the pinpoint synchronism to the language of these encounters or near-encounters.

'Before' the servant 'had finished speaking' his inward prayer, God silently grants it in the medium of action through 'Rebekah coming out', so that the double time-relation combines the persuasive benefits of linearity and simultaneity. Where a two-part sequence of request followed by advent would in itself imply marvellous causality but still leave an aperture for chance – *propter hoc* or just *post hoc*? fulfilment or good fortune? – the intersection of events stamps the coincidence as providential, as well as demonstrating God's insight into the requester's heart and his approval of the request. Poles apart, all this maneuvering, from the self-advertisement of fictional synchronizers or, what often serves as their mimetic front, the appeal to the mystery of things, benevolent, malign, cussed, indifferent. The Wooing Servant and Rebekah thus come together under auspices opposed to, say, Sterne's Sentimental Traveller and *his* fair lady, who happen to benefit from 'Fortune's whimsical doings: to take two utter strangers by their hands – of different sexes, and perhaps from different corners of the globe, and in one moment place them together in such a cordial situation, as Friendship herself could scarce have achieved for them, had she projected it for a month.[11] Even the universals of narrative interest – including the sense of wonder in coincidence – adjust and contribute to the model of reality.

Similarly with the maneuvering round the *non*coincidence of Ehud's departure and the Moabite retinue's arrival on the scene. Far from content to order the events into plain or indeterminate sequence, as with the people's exit and Saul's introduction in Samuel 8–9, this example aims for a sense of near-coincidence, hence of hairbreadth escape. Besides the immediate shifting from protagonist to antagonist, it generates this sense through bare repetition: having told how 'Ehud went out', it resumes with 'He had just gone when the servants came.' Again, the discourse sharpens the drama to bring home that the hero is almost caught in the act, the simultaneity-with-catastrophe being so narrowly averted as to bespeak a miracle and a miracleworker behind the human scenes. Whether bent on maximal coincidence or minimal noncoincidence, then, the split-second timing in juxtaposition promotes the rhetoric of God's omnipotence. The divine stage management, precisely because it remains otherwise invisible, must impress itself on the observers – present and to come – with the force of certitude. So the narrower and more dramatic the simultaneity, the more impressive the show of power.

On the other hand, the temporal common denominator may stretch so far as to accommodate events belonging to the same generation or period, or even millennium, as with the Sons of God episode (Gen. 6:1–4). The markers of simultaneity – 'when men began to multiply . . . In those days' – let us know only that this episode falls within primeval history, somewhere between Creation and Flood; and considering its enigmatic if not explosive implications, perhaps for good reason. Even as it is, these verses have become notorious for their incongruity with the Bible's world-view. *Sons* of God? Intermarriage with the daughters of *men*? In face of the blurred line between humanity and divinity, religious apologists in Judaism and Christianity have glossed over the embarrassment by humanizing the Sons of God into aristocrats, righteous men or, as in Milton's *Paradise Lost* XI, Sethites; others have detected traces of a mythological ontology and theology. But for the narrative to tighten the simultaneity with the fortunes of mankind, if only to say when miscegenation began, would be to heighten the ideological incongruity by concretizing those mysterious beings: anchoring them faster in that world, perhaps also betraying their nature and origin. The less pinpointed the episode, as well as the less said about it in general, the better.

A still more telling measure of flexibility is that the Bible's juxtaposition may neutralize and reshape our very sense of temporal difference and distance. It has the power not only to bring together under some umbrella-span events that are objectively remote in terms of chronology, but even to wrench their given sequentiality into simultaneity in retrospect. Take the two episodes that make up the so-called appendix to Judges (chs 17–21). Both clearly antedate most of what has gone before: the story of Micah and the Danites features Moses' grandson (18:30), and that of the Raped Concubine, Aaron's (20:28). Apparently, then, the book moves in canonical order, only to finish with a couple of retrospects on the distant past. In fact, however, it juxtaposes the two final to all the preceding episodes and to each other through the formula 'In those days there was no king in Israel, every man did what was right in his own eyes', repeated (with variations) at key points. It occurs at the outset of the 'appendix', twice for good retrospective measure (17:6; 18:1), recurs at its conclusion, which doubles as that of Judges (21:25), and also at the joint between its components (19:1). Beginning, middle, end: this loaded refrain calls for a repatterning of the whole Book of Judges. It seeks to replace nothing less than the book's principle of unity by effecting a switch in temporal framework and perspective, for example from the cycles of *post*Joshuite (1:1; 2:6–23) sin and deliverance to a bird's-eye view of the *pre*monarchical age, from a chaotic narrative past and present ('In those days') to a stable narrative future ('king in Israel'), from divine overlordship to human institutions of government, tribal as against royal.

Possibly an appendix in origin, the refrain instanced and dramatized by the final series of outrages does not behave like one, in that it would govern or at least reorient the body itself in the guise of juxtaposing with it. The anticipation works backward, as well as forward, to generate a levelling and enlarging effect of closure. Levelling, because in its light not only the two final retrospects but everything that precedes them in the discourse suddenly turns out to be juxtaposable, comparable, reducible to the same negative: absence of kingship. And enlarging, because the sense of difference no longer operates on particular agents, episodes, transitions, but on eras and books within canonical history. At whatever cost to the materials wrenched out of particularity, temporal and otherwise, the horizon widens as a prelude to the great divide. Where, then, do events belong in time? Apart along one sequence, or together within another that dwarfs it? The answer always varies with the scale or point of view – itself sensitive to juxtaposition – and here dynamically, even violently overturns in long-range review.

Alternation consists in recurrent juxtaposition, so that the narrative sequence moves to *and* fro between objective simultaneities. By one zigzag method or another, it goes forward along two plot lines, paths, routes, threads, which may intersect and usually converge to form a resolution. In Euclidean geometry, of course, parallel lines never meet; in the novel, especially of the modern age, they need not meet. In the Bible, the lines having for a while run parallel to each other, they finally run into each other: whether they come together to join or to oppose forces, the sequel turns unilinear. As with the juxtaposition of chapters 8 to 9 in I Samuel – the popular yearning for a monarchy and the search for the asses – so always with the rhythm of alternation. Thus the shuttling between two sides in a major conflict – Joseph vs. his brothers, Israelites vs. Egyptians or God and Moses vs. the people throughout Exodus, David vs. the rebels in the Absalom cycle – till the showdown brings the crisis to a happy or unhappy end.

In this regard, the Book of Kings deserves special mention, and less for its notoriously troubled than for its strategically doubled chronology. Once the kingdom has been divided for Solomon's sins, alternation expands into an overall principle of arrangement, complete with two well-defined geographical arenas – 'Judah' in the South, 'Israel' in the North – and the synchronism of the accession of a king in one line with the regnal year of his contemporary in the other. The strategy governs not only an entire book, minus the end points (I Kings 1–12; II Kings 18:30–25:30), but also a period of two centuries (922–722/21 BC), a nation-wide and often international stage with an ever-changing cast, and the tense relations along the God–Judah–Israel triangle.

Precisely because the Kings narrative branches out into two (or, counting God and his prophets, three) strands, nothing less than a double plot, the systematic shifting of focus points a general lesson about composition. In multilinear narrative, local or global, alternation operates as a force for unity, favourably contrasting with juxtaposition in this role, and not so much despite as due to its pulling against simple linear continuity. Imagine the results of a juxtaposing strategy designed to preserve that continuity by telling the whole of (say) the Judah story first – down to the fall of Jerusalem, the burning of the Temple, the exile, the two-edged, bittersweet finale of King Jehoiachin getting his daily bread at the king of Babylon's table – then going all the way back to the point of division in order to follow the Israel line to its no less violent end. Where such chronological tracing of either time-line from start to finish before the other is taken up would decompose the book into two sequences – concurrent in the action, consecutive in narration – the weaving in and out of them makes for their interweaving. It actually makes for economy as well as unity, because wherever the two lines meet, for better or worse, in peace or on the battlefield, the common stretches of (inter)action need telling once not twice. So intersection in history trims, tightens, thickens the story. As a clear gain, this interweaving also enables a range of subtler devices and effects under cover of alternation, notably the play of equivalence below sequence with an eye to anything from variety through perspective to ideological counterpoint.

Reconsidered in the light of the Bible's drives to simultaneity, therefore, Kings is not such a special case after all, except in terms of magnitude. Its alternation originates from conflict with God, always threatens and occasionally explodes into conflict between the sister kingdoms as well – a throwback to sibling rivalry on a national scale – and breaks off in conflict with foreign scourges that destroy both sides, yet the North first, to leave a unilinear finish (and the future) to the chosen line of David. Nor is there anything exceptional about the operations of suspense, thriving on conflict; also of analogy, if only those adhering to or straining against the book's 'deep' interlinear polarities of theme: South vs. North, Chosen vs. Inflicted, Dynastic vs. Disposable and Doomed, Temple vs. Calf, Eternity vs. Mutability. That even this much goes such a long way towards activating and orchestrating the rationales behind simultaneous drama is a measure of the Bible's systematicity. The forces that work for one-time juxtaposition do the same for intermittent or Kings-size alternation, only more so.

And no wonder, if their similarities in linear ordering and reading amidst multilinear happening are weighed against the differences. We can now doubtless see more clearly why in either form, juxtaposition or alternation, the mimesis of simultaneity is opposed to blanking as departures from an ideal norm of chronological narrative. If such a chronology would evenly and impartially cover all its time-units, then each blanking (or, less simply, gapping) of the action leaves some time-span uncovered, while each synchronism has one covered more than once. Blanking cuts or foreshortens the time-line, however quietly and innocuously, to speed up motion; synchronism doubles or multiplies it through widening strokes in space, which necessarily change the scene (rather than the date) and may slow down the tempo, to the point of freezing by turns. With each change of scene, indeed, a line must be dropped for its parallel to unfold. Yet here the breach remains in principle temporary, the Bible's return to close it assured, and the whole to and froing athwart time orderly, pleading the necessity of retardation for progression, not the freedom of omission. The one departure from ideal chronology, then, skimps the fullness of time, while the other celebrates it in staging a world so peopled and busy that the narrative sequence must arrange turns to keep up with its multifold activity.

Those arrangements, moreover, swell the discourse even in excess of the action. For in picking up the thread temporarily immobilized, the narrator often links its past to its coming development through resumptive summary by way of cohesion and mnemonic. A simple example: the Stolen Blessing narrative having brought Jacob to such a pass that he 'went to Paddan-aram to Laban' (Gen. 28:5) in fear for his life, it juxtaposes or intercalates Esau's baffled countermove (28:6–9), to resume with 'Jacob left Beer-Sheba and went to Haran'(28:10).[12] A kind of catch phrase, this, making for extra plot connexity and followability. With the result that not just the time-line but, in pullback, even the coverage of a single subline (e.g. the Jacob thread) gets doubled.

Likewise with rehearsals on a larger scale or across a wider stretch of text. In Genesis, the narrator having finished with Cain's genealogy, he paves the way for the shift to the line of Seth by retelling the story of humanity from its creation in God's image to Seth's own birth: the fuller and further back the review, the more privileged its beneficiary *vis-à-vis* his sibling (5:1–3). As within, so across books. Thus Exodus opens with a selective relisting of Jacob's descendants who left for Egypt, followed by an updating of the Genesis catalogue and account – the Joseph generation died out, the Israelites kept multiplying – before it crosscuts to the new Egyptian king who did not know Joseph (Ex. 1:1–7, Gen. 46:8ff). Again, the review gives such and so much detail as will prepare for the shift of focus from one side to another, and what is more, from one book to another: from intrafamilial to international and intercultural strife. In either example, then, the playback grows in reach, coverage and wordage along with significance, but without outgrowing the family resemblance to its analogues in microtime.

Nor is such doubling by way of catch phrase limited to the resumption of a hitherto suspended thread but applies to the entire pattern: to the summary recapitulation of its ongoing mate, or to their juxtaposition at the point of shift. Consider again the repeated mention of Ehud's timely exit, 'He had just gone out when his servants came' – with a view to heightening our sense of providential near-coincidence – itself soon repeated in switchback ('Ehud escaped while they delayed') for good ironic and ideological measure. Further, of the two sides to be locked in conflict, Exodus starts by providing a retrospect on the Israelite – the one never really dropped since Joseph's appearance – though less for dramatic as for pre-dramatic, expositional effect: to mark the resolution of the earlier family drama, to widen the scene into international panorama, to place the former associates and future combatants in battle stations. But it is still through the apparent rehearsal of the known, the gratuitous resumption of the ongoing, that the Bible effects this artful change in detail, scale, emphasis, perspective.

Nor, finally, does the linear tie-up by catch phrase form anything like a package deal with interlinear movement by crosscutting, because they relate to two distinct levels, even orders of composition. If the forked time-line enjoys the lifelike guise of 'Such is the story' – while X (Jacob, Ehud, Cain) was doing this, Y (Esau, the Moabites, Seth) did that – then the extra coverage of the subline(s) remains purely a matter of art: 'Such is discourse, the ways and exigencies of narrative.' All this compounding of (mimetic) alternation by (poetic) repetition, of multilinearity by multiconnexity, of (hi)story itself by the arts of (hi)story telling, therefore perfects the antithesis to the silence of the blank: overtreatment vs. undertreatment.

And yet, insofar as blanking omits inessentials while multiplicity interrupts the flow of the action itself – under the pressure or guise of the very rage for fullness – it is not the more cavalier treatment of time that manipulates it to more perceptible effect. And as the number of threads or at least of shifts rises, so do the demands and the opportunities for composing them. Compared with juxtaposing, indeed, the disarray into which chronology is thrown by alternation escalates by more than the simple arithmetic of turns.

For one thing, there is the cumulative impact of the 'go-stop-and-again' rhythm on the façade of artless registration. It progressively indicates the need to refer the simultaneous workings of time in the world both to the shape assumed by suspense in linear reading time and to patterns other than time, for example spatial, perspectival, thematic, rhetorical, linguistic.

For another thing, the more recurrent (and large-scale) the alternation, the harder it becomes to keep the time-lines exactly synchronized: to chop up the parallels into equal bits, spans, units of action. Reality or at least active life does not fall into natural subdivisions – even the 'summers and winters' in Thucydides delimit times of or for activity on both sides, not turns of activity – nor does such pedantry agree with the artistic imaging of reality. This is why, in resuming its threads, the Bible's alternation will rather repeat how things stand or stood last – suiting the language of retrospect to the occasion – than tie itself down to the ready-made juxtapositional form and formula 'At that time'. It is not without reason, for instance, that the narrative harks back to Jacob's flight to 'Paddan Aram to Laban' through the newly coined repetition 'Jacob left Beer-Sheba and went to Haran', rather than through a standard phrase that would synchronize the flight abroad with Esau's intervening action at home. For that action might indeed have started at the same point in time as the flight but then gone on and outrun it by days, weeks, months, if not years or decades. So why should the narrator commit himself by 'At that time' (say) to the strict simultaneity of the two brothers' doings, where a loose one will serve the purpose and requires no more than a catchphrase? In juxtaposition proper, of course, he may have no choice in the matter: if either party appears or the two run parallel only once – as with the Sons of God, Judges and Ruth in the Christian canon, and their numberless equivalents since – there will be no earlier event for the narrative to hook onto and every reason to synchronize lines through some reference-time. But why bother with interlinear synchronizing where, as always in alternation, linear tie-up will do?

This reasoning holds even in the absence of resumptive summary. Each line can in turn *run ahead* of the other, if only to arrive at some approriate point of rest and return. Here, then, it is the avoidance of symmetrical alternation for the sake of one-track unity – that is, the distance or delay between chronological and actual cutoff – that demands notice and explanation.

Running ahead

Such running ahead takes on a variety of functions, but they can be ultimately generalized into two. One is integrative and sequential, working for plot continuity. The other is cognitive and relational: the centering of interest, attention, judgment. In throwing parallel movements out of symmetry, both distinctively repair and adjust at need the logic of simultaneous narrative as a system whose juxtaposition or alternation of lines would otherwise produce *dis*continuity and *de*centering in the name of even-handed treatment. Here lies their family resemblance, possible cooperation included: to run ahead, whether for flow or focusing or both, is to prolong one line's turn beyond the due, objective chronological point of return to the other.

The more basic role is plot continuity, which in Genesis, say, leads to advance references to the demise of fathers at junctures where their lives in fact still run parallel to their offspring. And one pronounced dead by the narrative, never mind how far ahead of his earthly term, counts as dead for all the practical purposes of alternation, juxtaposition, even simple collocation with the living. Where a novel may anticipate a death and go on to unfold the life – or even first stage a death scene, as *Tristram Shandy* does Yorick's, then double back to the life in normal intersection with others – Genesis will as a rule anticipate, but without fanfare and without retrospect thereafter. The narrative departure would appear no less (and to judge by the conjuring up of Samuel's spirit, yet more) final than the event itself, a land from which no comer returns to pick up the threads of simultaneous existence alongside his kin, except between the lines.

This begins as early as 'the book of the generations of Adam':

Adam lived a hundred and thirty years and begot [a son] in his likeness, after his image, and named him Seth. The days of Adam after begetting Seth were eight hundred years, and he begot sons and daughters. All the days that Adam lived were nine hundred and thirty years, and he died. Seth lived a hundred and thirty years and begot Enoch (Gen. 5:3–6)

Actually, 'he died' precedes 'Seth lived' in the narration alone, by means of premature curtain-dropping or foreclosure. In the action itself, as a quick reckoning establishes, Adam with his lifespan of 'nine hundred and thirty years' lived to see not just his grandson Enoch but even his great-great-great-great-great-great-grandson Lemech, born 874 years after Creation and, in terms of textual sequence, as late as verse 25. This means that Adam nearly spans the entire genealogy called after him (or at least the series of births: having suffered one traumatic bereavement, in Abel's murder, he was mercifully spared the funeral of any other descendant). But the early notice of death serves to give each item along the list, as well as the list of items, its own continuity and wholeness: to reconcile the purely genealogical chronology of the line (from father to son down the generations) with the biographical chronology of the life ('lived' to 'died' within the limits of a single generation). The foreclosure works for the closure of units (Adam, Seth, Enoch, etc.) without arresting or breaking the onward march; the jump ahead of absolute time keeps two meaningful times in step; the disregard for synchronism does no real violence to the facts – all reconstructible – but enables the synchronizing of effects. So there is more even to genealogy than the genealogical imperative with its procession-like chronology; more to chronology itself than a single, uniform logic of temporality, let alone that of the clock or calendar purged of human time and teleology.

As with the miniatures of genealogical listing, so on the larger scale of narrative proper, from the very outset of patriarchal history. Between Terah's migration with his family from Ur of the Chaldeans to Haran and Abra(ha)m's call followed by his migration to Canaan, there intervenes the notice that 'The days of Terah were two hundred and five years, and Terah died in Haran' (11:31–12:5). How can the three events in this series reflect the order of occurrence, given that Terah 'begot Abram' at the age of 70 (11:26) and 'Abram was seventy-five years old when he left Haran' (12:4)? Impossible, unless one cuts this time knot in the manner of the Samaritan Pentateuch, which kills off Terah at the age of 145. Again, where the Samaritan version preserves or forces the correspondence of the narrative to the chronology through literal antedating, the Rabbis opt for figuration: 'Scripture calls him dead', *Bereshit Rabbah* argues, 'since the unrighteous are called dead even in their lives'. Of the two, this is the less thorough resolution, because the moralistic figure does not actually straighten out the numerical; also the more gratuitous in the first place, because its proponent could always appeal (as some medieval Rabbis in effect do) to 'There is no earlier and later in the Torah.' Yet both solutions resort to emergency measures – the one taking liberties with the text, the other with the sense in order to save the text – only due to an artificial isolation of the problem. They approach as a special case, requiring ad hoc treatment, what is in fact just another instance of a rule within the book and the Bible. Accordingly, as the Masoretic Text has it, Terah's death went after Abraham's migration from Haran – as well as his own from Ur – and by an interval of no less than sixty years (205 minus 70+75), easily covering the births of Ishmael and Isaac. Quite a jump ahead, this, but then where else to intercalate the obituary notice without breaking the thread of Abraham's drama? And how else, moreover, to adumbrate and in retrospect dynamize the sense of Abraham's heroic break with his family and past, which he leaves behind as if they were dead? Terah's premature exit is a matter neither of objective chronology nor figural homily but of narrative function, including subjective psychology. His main work done, the old father is buried alive, so to speak, that the son's life may start anew and run undisturbed.

Abraham himself, *his* work as patriarch done, receives the same treatment from the narrator. (Not from atomistic interpreters, though, who suffer the same embarrassment without recourse to the same remedy: the Samaritan Version leaves the numbers alone, nor dare the midrash repeat its twist of pejorative figuration. Terah is one thing, Abraham another, best passed over in silence – the usual hardships of piecemeal work.) The solemn closure, 'These are the days of the years of the life of Abraham that he lived, a hundred and seventy-five years. Abraham breathed his last and died in a good old age, an old man and full of years, and was gathered to his people' (25:7–8), makes it possible to open or reopen 'the history ['generations'] of Isaac' (25:19) as an independent sequel. So independent, in fact, that the narrator (re)starts it by harking back to retell that 'Abraham begot Isaac' and Isaac married Rebekah, then goes on to tell about the birth of Esau and Jacob when 'Isaac was sixty years old' (25:26) –

and, out of sight, Abraham still around at 160. Having got off the official record, he can and does make his presence felt alongside his heir only below it: through the valedictory chronology and, even after his real as well as his narrative departure, analogical comparison.

Predictably, the weak Isaac gets packed off yet earlier in favour of his strong son. Not that he is denied the formal beginning and end of biography within genealogy, through foreclosure at both cut-off points, but that the usual marking of limits highlights the unusual scantiness of the middle. Of all the patriarchs, Isaac's run is the shortest as well as the least distinguished and distinctive, as if to suggest that his is less a life in its own right than a link in the chosen line. Having virtually disappeared as soon as Jacob (and with him the narrative) leaves for Haran, he makes the briefest reappearance on Jacob's homecoming (25:27–29) in order to die in form ('The days of Isaac were a hundred and eighty years'), while invisibly lingering on almost to the descent into Egypt.

Jacob alone lives on stage to his last moment, fighting all comers for power and notice. In old age, we still observe him playing favorites, mourning, quarrelling, complaining, negotiating, rejoicing, migrating, reuniting his grown and acquiring new sons, making testamentary dispositions, short- and long-term, from arrangements for his own burial to the fortunes of the tribes to come, before he finally 'breathed his last and was gathered to his people' (50:1). Jacob thus imposes his will not only on elders, coevals, heirs, angels, but even on the narrator himself in a sense. He will never say die nor, as it were, let this be said of him a minute ahead of full time. Which is out of rule but splendidly in character. All the more so because the character involves such fusion of personal self with historical role – biography with genealogy – that they for once cannot be told apart and together resist foreclosure. Jacob transcends the Adam-old divergence between what I called the chronologies of the life and the line, because his life from birth to deathbed *is* (therefore coextends and merges with) the establishment of a line; or, if you will, because his is the elected line, all of it, so that no single descendant can replace him, only the entire family tree and nation, with which Exodus duly opens.

With the exception of this born survivor and lifelong history-maker, then, lifespan outreaches text-span, text-span shortchanges lifespan. The running ahead always privileges time over space values: the effect of continuity over simultaneity, of biographical units amidst genealogical movement over realistic plenitude or orderly symmetry, of the sequence over the coexistence of generations. Where, how, to what point the ongoing ('dying') generation overlaps with its progeny

– Adam with Seth to Lemech, Terah with Ishmael and Isaac, Abraham and Esau and Jacob, Isaac with his twins' families – is never stated, let alone enacted in the apparently unilinear construction, but left to the reconstruction of dates and spans into a multigenerational chronology. For all we know *from* the reconstruction, the dramatis personae may well have not just overlapped but rubbed shoulders and interacted across ages, even across lines, in the immemorial way of kinfolk. But there is not so much as a single real clue to all this – till we come to Jacob – though some intergenerational blanks and silences are more telling than others. On the narrative surface itself, Genesis unobtrusively ushers fathers out ahead of time in order to give their sons a clear run, as persons and inheritors, till their own turn comes to exit from history.

But a clear plot run also means, in cognitive terms like attention and perceptibility, a clear stage for either runner. Which begins to suggest the tie-up with more intricate run-ahead operations, notably the focusing of interest and viewpoint and attitude. These often use plot continuity as an excuse for their secret maneuvers, just as they bring into play the whole artistic complex and repertoire behind the mimesis of simultaneity. How else would it be possible to devise a focus for the reader – given a system living, and a surface crisscrossed, by shifts in focus?

As regards the focusing of interest, for example, observe how I Kings throws out of symmetry the contemporaneous reigns of Jehoshaphat in Judah (871–847 BC) and Ahab in Northern Israel (874–853 BC). Of the two, Jehoshaphat's accession actually appears first (15:24). But no sooner has it been recorded, just sufficiently to tie a knot in time, than the narrative performs a shift-cum-regression to Israel's line of kings. It goes back forty years to trace the divinely-forecast destruction of Jeroboam's house by Ba'asha, then of Ba'asha's by Zimri, then the countercoup leading to Zimri's suicide and Omri's rise to power, then the succession of his son Ahab (16:28). Now that the Judah dynasty has been more or less overtaken, the narrative might return to Jehoshaphat in the South. Instead, leaving the early time-knot untied or even untouched, it forges ahead on the Northern axis for the duration of about six chapters and twenty years packed with dramatic incident – from Ahab's first clash with Elijah to his mortal injury in the battle against the Arameans. It is as late as this battle (22:1–40) that the parallel lines meet in the common front presented by the two Hebrew kings against the enemy; but Jehoshaphat still reappears as Ahab's ally and foil, not in his own right and sequence. Indeed, so long has he been kept out of sight and mind that when he does eventually re-enter in an independent role, he needs *re*introducing, newcomer fashion. (Or, under Genesis's rule of *inter*generational overlapping, in the fashion of a son like Isaac, once he steps into his father's shoes.) Yet even Jehoshaphat's formal reintroduction comes only after Ahab's death, in belated and summary retrospect: resumptive glance back at accession, warm praise, burial (22:41–51).

Why, then, all this perceptible avoidance of orderly synchronization? It operates to establish a contextual hierarchy of importance, one sharpened by the double contrast in the two kings' rendering and ranking, whereby the scale of treatment (detail vs. outline, showing vs. telling) is in inverse proportion to the scale of merit (unrighteous vs. righteous).[13] It is precisely because the sinful royal line of Israel is again and again broken in the world (Jeroboam's dynasty cut off by Ba'asha, Ba'asha's by Zimri, Zimri by Omri, the Omride Ahab by the Arameans) that its breaches must run unbroken in the discourse to highlight the workings of divine retribution. The upheavals in Israel, making a fourfold chain of destruction, have more point and appeal than the ongoing reign of David's house, embodied in the descendant who frames and, as it were, runs parallel to the entire stormy cycle by way of contrast; thematic continuity with counterpoint takes precedence over temporal even-handedness; Ahab plays a bigger and more colourful role in the story of Kings than the nobler Jehoshaphat. Here, then, the order of ideological and characterological priorities in alternation outranks the merely chronological.

So does it throughout Genesis, in the steady alternation between the chosen and nonchosen line, but this time along rather than against the scale of merit. At every fork in the course of humanity toward Israel, from Adam to Isaac, the narrative sooner or later temporarily leaves behind the God-elected son to execute a *summative prospection* on the line of the rejected. It runs ahead with Cain's line (4:17–24), never to be revisited, before doubling back with fanfare to the birth of Seth (in Adam's 'own likeness, after his own image', itself 'in the likeness of God') and enumerating his 'generations' down to Noah and the Flood (4:25–9:29). Upon Noah's death, it catalogues the 'generations' of Japheth, Ham and Shem (10:1–32), but only to revert to Shem and trace the descent of Abraham (11:10–32). With Abraham himself, the suspension–prospection–reversion movement occurs twice. No sooner has Keturah borne him a handful of children than the narrator lists their progeny, as if to mime Abraham's own gesture in bestowing on them the gift of commemoration as a prelude to dismissal in favor of Isaac (25:1–5). And no sooner has Abraham breathed his last than the descendants of Ishmael unroll (25:12–18), again to clear the stage for Isaac (25:19ff). Likewise with those of

Esau, whose roster (36:1–43) precedes the history of Jacob's sons, all divinely if unequally chosen.

All this no doubt carries further than the Kings instance the extent and the impact of asymmetrical ordering: late before early, the distant future of one line before the present and the progress of the other. Still, due to the thematic antithesis between those left behind for the duration and those followed *seriatim* beyond their proper turn only to be abandoned forever, what the running ahead of time in Genesis foregrounds throughout is the suspended rather than the unfolded line of descent. It implies a need to glance down each bypath, for the record and goodbye, before returning to the highroad of history.[14] The more so since the bare genealogies accorded in prospection often look even barer upon the return to the norm of dramatic specificity in backtracking and overhauling. It is precisely in this extra resource of proportioning detail to importance, quantity to centrality, that the Genesis alternation outdoes its otherwise miniature rehearsal in I Chronicles 1, where either branch telescopes into a series of mere names and begot's. To such even-handed scaling in uneven-handed timing, contrast the verses allotted to the Keturites or Ishmaelites or Edomites as against the chapters (within the canon, even books) lavished on their opposite numbers, boasting scenic dialogue and action as well as the rest of biblical arts. This maximizes the dissonance between temporal and cognitive-hierarchical priorities in alternation, between the order and record of birth and the sense of chosenness. The objective facts of simultaneity compose in the discourse into a higher perspective of generational sequence.

As in the example from Kings, therefore, selection and temporal (dis)arrangement work together as a focusing system. They again build up a scale of interest, importance, priorities – with the difference that the continuous treatment of either line here reflects and promotes the logic of election. At some early juncture, if not right at the first crossroads, alternation between sons (Cain and Seth, Ishmael and Isaac, Esau and Jacob) must give place to summative dismissal of the older in favor of the younger, bilinearity must shrink into juxtaposition and then into unilinearity, because the human alternates do not constitute divine alternatives.

Let us now turn from the control of value-laden interest to that of judgment proper, from the rhetoric of focusing attention to the rhetoric of evaluation. Compare the run-ahead sequence in the Jephthah as against the David and Bathsheba cycle. In both the narrative ends, as it began, with a movement between two sides or strands of the leader's career – whereby his public business (involving, as it happens, a war against the Ammonites) comes late and last owing to the need to wind up an affair from his private life. Of the two simultaneous episodes, the public one suffers delay in the telling that the private one may enjoy unimpeded development and resolution.

With Jephthah, the order of alternation is as follows: 'prebattle vow of sacrifice – victory over Ammon – homecoming, daughter revealed as victim, her sacrifice two months later – Ephraim menacing and massacred' (Judg. 10:29–12:6). This construction evidently departs from the chronological order of occurrence, which we reconstruct as 'vow – victory – Ephraim crisis – homecoming – sacrifice' or, far more probably, '. . . homecoming – Ephraim crisis – sacrifice.' In terms of absolute time, the daughter's sacrifice at home (if not the father's homecoming itself) must go after the intertribal clash and round off the cycle, since the Ephraimites would not wait two full months (11:39) before picking a quarrel with Jephthah about his omission to summon them to the war. On the best simultaneous reconstruction of the plot, therefore, the national crisis did not actually conclude matters but intervened between stages in the domestic.

Likewise with David. As early as the exposition, the national and the private arenas are introduced in ironic juxtaposition: 'At the turn of the year, at the time when kings go forth to battle, David sent Joab and his servants with him and all Israel, and they ravaged the Ammonites and besieged Rabbah, and David stayed in Jerusalem' (II Sam. 11:1). The spheres of action having been established – place, agents, doings, incongruity and all – the narrator arranges a two-way traffic across the distance to meet the demands of the plot. David, hoping to cover up Bathsheba's pregnancy, 'sent word to Joab, Send me Uriah the Hittite' (11:6), and then, finding the soldier uncooperative, sends him back with a secret death-warrant in his hand (11:14–15). Joab in turn sends a messenger to report the execution (11:19–25). But once David learns about Uriah's death, all this shuttling between the Rabbah battlefield and the Jerusalem palace (11:1–25) modulates into a two-part sequence: first the drawn-out process of retribution and resolution at home, then the victory abroad (11:26–12:25; 12:26–31). Alternation gives way to juxtaposition. And if the initial alternation shifted in space to preserve the continuity of time – departing for Rabbah where the plot needed to have Uriah summoned, killed, reported dead – the final juxtaposition reverses these priorities of structure. It sacrifices time to space or rather the temporal continuity of the sequence as a whole to the spatio-temporal continuity of each sequence (line, thread) by itself, especially the developments in Jerusalem. The victory over

Ammon must have been held in suspension to let the palace drama run its course – Bathsheba's delivery, the confrontation with Nathan, the baby's death, another pregnancy, Solomon's birth – for the siege of Rabbah could hardly have lasted two years. Hence the same distinctive manipulation of chronology as in the Jephthah tale. Simultaneity in the happening becomes not just consecutiveness but uneven consecutiveness, deformed beyond the exigencies of alternation, in the telling. The national business that coincides with the middle of the private misfortune is kept for the end, enclosing what it should have been enclosed by.

As with the earlier pair of examples from Kings and Genesis, however, the similarity in temporal form only brings out the variety, indeed the contrast in rhetorical function and impact. Briefly, the disordered alternation in Judges works in Jephthah's favor or at least minimizes the disfavor he might otherwise incur. With this in view, it both likens beginning to end and opposes the hero's implicit perspective to his antagonists'. For the nonchronological closure – 'Ephraim menacing and massacred' – leaves us with the image of a strong leader forced again into war by an aggressor, now inside Israel, rather than with a father who stumbled into a domestic and moral nightmare. The narration of that father–daughter tragedy (or its macabre finale) ahead of time even explains and softens his ruthless dealing with Ephraim's belligerence. Apart from the sense of ingratitude and danger immediately produced by these troublemakers, the narrator quietly throws a bridge of analogy from one crisis to the other in order to suggest that they are playing with fire, in a real and terrible sense beyond their comprehension (or so one hopes). We can imagine the feelings evoked by the Ephraimite threat to 'burn thy house over thee with fire' in a man haunted by the prospect (and in narrative order, the memory) of sacrificing his daughter 'for a burnt offering' (12:1, 11:30–31). To make things even worse, 'thy house' (*beitkha*) both sounds like 'thy daughter' (*bitkha*) and assumes the same meaning in context. She being his only child, his house is already as good as burnt, and all for *their* sake.

In Samuel, however, David's nominal conquest of Rabbah (actually reduced by Joab's siege) is kept to the last, behind time, in order to heighten ironic judgment. It crowns the recent story of the wife-stealing man – just when it appears to have resolved itself – with the new story of the credit-grabbing king; and the suspension of chronology, whereby the concurrent arenas and events remain distinct, highlights the unflattering analogy. Even the play of sequence and equivalence here, even the meeting of the Jerusalem and the Rabbah viewpoints, generates distance rather than sympathy.

In each instance, of course, the delayed public climax would be awkward to narrate in its proper turn, because it would interrupt the leader's personal story. Yet the awkwardness of strict alternation is avoided to radically different effect, the innocent-looking running ahead with a view to continuity serving as a cover for two polar strategies of control.

Either way, finally, these two basic motivations for dislocating turns reappear in typical partnership, major–minor or means–end scaling included. No less typically, readers may miss with relative impunity the entire maneuver, that is, the covert rhetoric, the plot cover, and the plotted material itself: the sidewise, local, temporary fold in the grand chronology. This is not only because rhetoric often works best (or most insidiously) where least detected, but also because the sequencing of simultaneity by nature consists in ordering the unordered rather than, as with dechronologization proper, in disordering the ordered. Across the whole range between maximal and minimal reading, the thrust of the action holds. Jephthah assumed office, stood up to the enemy abroad and at home, paying with his daughter's life for a rash prebattle vow; David stayed behind in Jerusalem, fell into trouble and crime, extricated himself at the price of bereavement, immediate and impending, left for Rabbah to lead the conquest in person. This much history remains foolproof. The rest of it, and the best, lies hidden in the storyteller's art as a challenge to ours.

Between simultaneity and successiveness: ambiguities of alternative ordering

We have seen how and why even-handed synchronization would ill accord with a spectrum of desired ends, from plot continuity to focusing to shaping response. In view of the pressures against it, small wonder that the reader cannot always place events with certainty *vis-à-vis* one another, not even to the degree of establishing whether they are simultaneous or successive. Is their sequential arrangement (we then ask) due to the constraint of alternation in language, to the contrivance of some unequal or otherwise artful alternation in the narrative, or simply to a unilinear order of occurrence in the world? Nor, despite real-life logic, are these possibilities mutually exclusive in biblical composition and reading.

Take the Judah and Tamar episode. We find it inserted, as a chapter-length digression from the main narrative, between the selling of Joseph (Gen. 37) and his rise in Potiphar's house (39:1–2), ushered in by the juxtaposing formula 'It happened at that time' (38:1). But the interposed story of Tamar could *not* in fact have happened at that time, not all (or even most) of it at least. While the Joseph main plot creeps forward to and in Egypt, chapter 38 gallops over something like twenty years – from Judah's Canaanite marriage, through the deaths of his older sons and the delaying tactics by which he hopes to save the youngest, to the crisis precipitated by Tamar and the birth of his (grand)sons. Given the chapter's time-span, therefore, it is impossible to have its opening formula of synchronization cover the whole episode that follows. Rather, some part(s) must be earlier or later, and only some other(s) simultaneous with, the removal of Joseph to Egypt. Even so, the reader cannot tell for sure which is which.[15] Does the marker of simultaneity with the main plot bear on Judah's initial marriage alone, so that the entire sequel of the digression runs years and years ahead of Joseph's fate at the time? Or does it bear on the 'three months' (38:24) of final crisis and unravelling – Tamar's trickery, pregnancy, death sentence, last-minute disclosure and exposure – so that the earlier years antecede the whole Joseph cycle? Or does some in-between possibility match the twofold drama best?

We can leave aside both the weighing of these hypotheses and, for the moment, even the information that emerges later on. For in *immediate* context, not only does the question of what to synchronize and what to sequence defy closure but the answer does not greatly matter. The closure implied at this point works far more on analogical than chronological lines, privileging the continuity and development of theme between the two arenas over or across the time scheme. The thrust of the juxtaposition lies in the well-known ironic reversal of Judah's role between the Joseph and the Tamar stories – from trickster of his own father ('Recognize, pray, whether this is thy son's tunic or not') into tricked father with a vengeance ('Recognize, pray, whose these are, the signet and the cord and the staff'). In this light, the two trickery sequences would no doubt appear the best, because the most charged and meaningful, candidates for simultaneity: their thematic parallelism and wry causal ('tit for tat') alignment might benefit from such pinpoint coincidence. Still, the coincidence only sharpens rather than generates the effect of the interposed tale, either as the narrator's or as God's commentary on the main plot, as judgment by variation or by retaliation. Therefore any other temporal match will do just or almost as well. What matters is that Judah should have the tables turned upon him, not whether their turning occurs at once ('simultaneously') or much later ('successively'). In terms of narrative ordering and hence impact, after all, retribution in kind follows hard on the crime anyway; and in terms of poetic strategy, its elusiveness within the 'real' order of events helps to deliver the pattern from overneatness and transparence. What with the rest of the camouflage (the appearance of digression, the opening linkage to Judah's marriage, the detail and drama surrounding his role reversal), the casual reader may indeed miss the point altogether. At this juncture, unlike the time-puzzle ('When?') of Abraham's last union, analogy conspires with ideology against chronology, exploiting its show of paratactic vagueness and artlessness ('at that time') to keep their artful operations hidden.

But in principle, and often in practice too, especially with events drawn out to episode size, such two-facedness makes quite a difference. For if simultaneity in occurrence entails a double time-line, then ambiguity between simultaneous and successive occurrence triggers a double reading *of* the time-line. In one instance, we convert the inescapable sequentiality of discourse into *parallel (sub)plots*, movements, happenings. In the other, where the sequentiality of discourse will not readily cohere into either a sequence or a coincidence of events, we puzzle out *alternative plots*: unilinear vs. multilinear, multilinear at this vs. that point. And insofar as neither alternative establishes itself to the exclusion of its rival, gaining a monopoly over arrangement by its power to resolve and motivate all discourse features, temporal or otherwise, we hold both in tense interplay. The world of action itself cannot have it both ways, to be sure, but narrative art can and the Bible's does in rendering that world – against the decorums of naïve realism, epic or novelistic, and with implications for plot, sense-making, the limits of (hi)story telling, literary history, even methodology.

In a special sense, this is the case with many biblical doublets, traditionally regarded by source criticism as variants that have both survived through the reluctance of some editor to consign either version to oblivion by making a choice. Thus the two stories of Ishmael's expulsion by Sarah (Gen. 16, 21:9–21), of Esau's deprivation by his brother (Gen. 25:29–34, 27), of Saul's rejection by God (I Sam. 13:1–14, 15). What each 'twice-told tale' reflects or rather betrays, on this genetic, source-oriented view, is an original simultaneity in the sense of alternativity: each time-slot does not so much require and invite as preserve a double filling, each link in the chain benefits or suffers from parallel accounts. This would make every pair of versions simultaneous, alternative, parallel in much the same way as the two endings, the happy and the unhappy, which John Fowles imposes on *The French Lieutenant's Woman* in defiance of novelistic resolution. Except that the difference between the biblical versions lies not in the ending itself but in the route to it – not in the final effect of rejection, say, but in its cause – and the divergence in route supposedly arises from a divergence in origin. Accordingly, the simultaneity bears on the process of transmission rather than of action and communication; on the text's prehistory, not on the text as recorded history. Under the aegis and pressure of tradition, a structuralist would say, the either/or of the deep plot (where each variant might by itself lead to the historic result) assumed the surface form of both/and.

However that may be, once we switch from the genetic to the poetic perspective on these doublets, each compels (just as Fowles's resists) a successive reading. In the finished narrative they have all been linearized into stages within a well-plotted chronology. Ishmael gets expelled on two distinct occasions, first in the womb through his mother's impudence and then, irrevocably, for his own misconduct; Esau is deprived first of birthright, then of blessing; Saul rejected first as the founder of a dynasty, for his disobedience to the prophet in the Philistine war, and then, having broken God's command regarding Amalek, as a king in his own lifetime.

Thus ordered, the three doublets make ideological and persuasive as well as chronological sense. It is no accident that all three occur at some juncture in history where God makes a choice that humanity may well find arbitrary, if not unjust, because it runs counter to natural or social priorities. Thus the reversal of primogeniture, so that the younger son (Isaac, Jacob) comes to outrank and oust the first-born (Ishmael, Esau), or of royal status, whereby Saul gives place to David, with a loss of sanity and finally life itself as well as throne. Given the problematic but ideologically and historically inevitable outcome – the reversal must happen, indeed has happened – doubling the cause into seriality furthers in each instance the rhetoric of (dis)election. Its working is best seen, and generalized, against the background of the nonserial strategies open to the narrator as persuader.

Even in face of divine judgment, a single account is liable to leave the reader sympathetic to the loser (especially as superior turned underdog), antagonistic to the winner, and out of accord with God in both respects. Again, an either/or pairing of two accounts, *The French Lieutenant's Woman* fashion, would only confuse the issue, betraying authorial uncertainty about facts and reasons and justice alike. Normatively, it would also keep open the weakest and worst (as well as the best) possibility as the only true line of explanation: that Saul lost his place on his first offence – a minor lapse at that – Ishmael for no fault of his own, Esau by a conspiracy between Rebekah and Jacob. But a series of two enables the narrative to strengthen, diversify or balance the grounds for reversal and to draw out its execution. Ishmael could not help his mother's misbehavior, yet he must bear responsibility for his own. Esau was cheated of the blessing only after having sold his birthright to Jacob for a mess of pottage. Saul, having been warned once against disobedience, goes from bad to worse and suffers accordingly. Throughout, the doubling *along* time extends divine choice from act to process – second chance included – and softens the impact of the blow against the nonchosen by delivering it in installments, occasionally even in ascending order. And by the time the second round comes to actualize or finalize the demotion, the first has got us accustomed to the idea; hence also the care taken to interpose other matter between the rounds, so as to let duration do its habituating work in the meantime. Their discontinuity within continuity thus stretches from narrated to purely narrative temporality, combining the one's historical with the other's rhetorical process to have the best of both. In short, where a singleton or a variant pair would be enough to execute but not quite to justify the movement from cause to effect – forging the chain in terms of plot without rendering it morally or emotionally acceptable – the doublet operates to maximize assent and consensus.

Of course, the desired goal may widely differ. But it always trades on the dovetailing of patterns enabled by the 'twice-told' chronology: iteration with variation, sequence with equivalence, movement with increment, temporal with ascending or otherwise scalar order. What is possibly alternative in terms of the deep logic of action shows itself to be multiply progressive in the actual discourse along chronological, causal, hierarchical lines, and mutually supporting rather than exclusive in configurations above the line as well. No matter what the prehistory, at best conjectural, the plot of history falls into lucid yet intriguing shape – its dynamics unmistakable ('foolproof') in direction, complex in resonance and response.

Here, then, the rivalry between simultaneous and successive understanding remains a matter of methodological viewpoint, genesis vs. poetics (or within poetics, deep vs. surface construction). But such rivalry may also arise from the play of givens and gaps in the text itself to form an interpretive ambiguity proper – a double reading born of incoherence and seeking to establish coherence by appeal to a time-line that spreads both ways for a purpose. The reader who rises to this challenge will find it well worth his while, since the double composition or interpretation in despite of naturalism yields dividends over and above the game of art itself.

Such difficult coherence and sense-making, I have repeatedly argued elsewhere, is integral to the Bible's poetics of ambiguity. *Within* the episode unit, this particular variety of it can be seen at

work in the Rape of Dinah (Gen. 34). There the time-line is equivocal
not only at several junctures but even in several directions. Thus one
recalcitrant chronological duplicity, as to whether the brothers'
homecoming preceded or followed their learning of the rape, is
compounded by another as to whether their arrival followed or
paralleled the Hivites'. Just as the opening ensures temporal lucidity –
Shechem first 'took' Dinah by violence, then wanted to 'take' her in
marriage – so does the sequel go to the extreme of opacity:

(5) Jacob heard that he had defiled Dinah his daughter – his sons were with
his livestock in the field – and Jacob kept still until they came. (6) And
Hamor the father of Shechem went out to Jacob to speak to him. (7) And
Jacob's sons came in from the field when they heard it. The men were
grieved and very angry [*or*: When they heard it, the men were grieved and
very angry], because he had committed an outrage in Israel by lying with
Jacob's daughter, a thing not done. (8) Hamor spoke to them, saying, The
soul of my son Shechem longs for your daughter. Pray, give her to him for a
wife. (34:5–8)

Was the news withheld by Jacob till the brothers' return from the field
or dispatched to press for immediate return? The rapist and his father
having gone 'to Jacob to speak to him', did they find him
unresponsive and had to wait for the brothers to speak 'to them', or
did the movements so coextend and converge that they at once
addressed the family assembly?

Without rehearsing the details,[16] I want to emphasize two strategic
rules. First, however irresolvable in terms of 'real life' plot, each
temporal doubling here finds its resolution (and its coherence with the
other) in terms of character-portrayal and judgment and theme. Each
tells two stories at once, because both stories tell against the
patriarch, co-operating to expose Jacob's indifference to his, or rather
Leah's, unhappy daughter. For example, note the ascending order of
condemnation that lurks in the reversible sequence of news and
homecoming. Did Jacob 'keep still' only while and because 'his sons
were . . . in the field' – 'until they . . . came in from the field when they
heard it' – or did he keep so still as to sit on the news 'until they came'
at their usual hour? Did he fail to act or even to speak and
communicate? Note, likewise, the two-pronged attack behind the
unsynchronized movements in verses 6 and 7. If the Hivites 'went out
to Jacob' before the 'sons came in' – the order of verses mirroring the
order of events – then the variation from the intended 'speak to him'
to the actual 'spoke to them' casts Jacob in a new do-nothing-say-
nothing role. He will no more respond to another's speech than take
the initiative himself. And if the Hivite departure coincides with the
sons' arrival, then their simultaneity underlines and ironizes afresh

Jacob's passive attitude by giving a sense of busy activity on either side, except for the key figure on whom both converge. In short, as I put it elsewhere, 'the variant hypotheses achieve maximal effect through minimal disclosure: mutually exclusive in terms of reality, they are mutually supporting in terms of rhetoric.' The motivation for either double plot, along with its doubling, is purely poetic (functional, affective, rhetorical) instead of mimetic.

This brings us, second, to the variable balance between poesis and mimesis, especially to the license of ambiguity in storytelling *vis-à-vis* the constraints of lucidity in history telling. In the Bible, the balance markedly changes not only with the size of the unit gapped into multiple reading, but also with the kind of gap that triggers such reading. The smaller the narrative unit, the wider the freedom it enjoys to twist (out of order and surface coherence) what happened in history; the bigger the unit, the finer the distinctions it observes between permissible and prohibited dechronologizing.

For instance, the two Dinah gaps just outlined are very much akin in bearing as well as in working, far beyond minimal family likeness. Of course, all gaps are by definition children of time in that they arise from some discrepancy between the orders of occurrence and of presentation. But these two play havoc with time even as an order of occurrence – what happened *when?* – so as to become chronological gaps in the fullest possible sense of the term. Amidst all this kinship, though, there remains a difference. For the one gap is *unidimensional*, concerning the relations of early and late along the time sequence of events as they happened in the narrated world. (News followed by homecoming or, reversely, homecoming followed and greeted by news?) The other gap is *bi-* or *interdimensional*, throwing doubt on time–space relations in that world, hence on the distribution of events between sequence and simultaneity. (The Hivites' movement toward Jacob followed or paralleled by the sons'?)

However fine-looking, even more so than the distinction of chronological gaps proper from their standard mates, such difference makes a difference – and in narrative practice as well as in theory. Though equally and jointly operative within the (Dinah) episode, these two forms of chronological ambiguity do not have quite the same disordering effect on time and therefore are no longer equally viable as we move up the Bible's scale of units: from episode to cycle and book, from local to grand chronology, from microplot to macroplot. The ambiguity pitting the sequence of events against itself violates the Bible's logic of *inter*episodic relations – whether in its historical or its foolproof aspect – while the one equivocating between sequence and concurrence does boast large-scale examples.

Not that the alternative readings along one single dimension are more mutually exclusive than those between dimensions, but that they do more (and usually more perceptible) violence to the march of biblical history, its authority, its intelligibility. With this much at stake, it would be asking for trouble to entangle and disrupt the grand chronology to the point of reversibility; but it occasionally pays so to loosen that chronology as to have it extend in time and in space at once, going forward in a straight line while, impossibly, branching out into parallel lines.

This is surely the case where the hovering between dimensions remains temporary, as well as implicit, launched for some artistic reason along the way but brought to mimetic ('historical') rest and closure at last. We have in fact already glanced at a typical example in the passage from I Samuel 8 (the clash over the monarchy) to 9 (the quest for the lost asses). But though the play is rich and rewarding, its stretch perhaps looks a bit short. For a more sustained (and otherwise complementary) instance, we may return to the dynamics of the Judah and Tamar story.

Does the opening 'at that time' synchronize Joseph's removal with Judah's marriage or with his entrapment by Tamar decades later? How to order the juxtaposed events of the plot and the subplot into antecedence, concurrence, subsequence? The uncertainty between the rival orderings, we saw, signifies far less within the episode than the thematic pattern cutting across them: the inversion of Judah from unfilial victimizer by trickery into paternal victim. In immediate context, the pattern of equivalence-with-reversal so integrates the digression that the exact timing of its components appears a small matter – a blank rather than a gap – hardly troublesome, if indeed noticed at all. To make an ado about it at this point, as commentators have done by appeal to some future references to age and duration, amounts to what I call the hindsight fallacy: reading late disclosures and developments into an early stage where they have not yet come to light. Only too common in interpretive practice, such wisdom after the event goes clean against the step-by-step unfolding, twists and all, of narrative as a temporal medium and art.

But the time-question does (re)surge, suddenly clamouring for more and more notice, as the brothers resume their dealings with Joseph after an interval of twenty-two years (37:2; 41:46, 53; 45:6). For Judah, their leader, now acts and speaks after a fashion so inconsistent with his early self that his character is in danger of splitting apart. Is it credible (to mention only the climactic incongruity) that the brother who initiated the sale into slavery of the patriarch's favorite should now volunteer, even beg to substitute as slave for another Rachel-born favorite, Benjamin? 'Let thy servant, pray, remain instead of the lad as a slave to my lord, and let the lad return with his brothers. For how can I return to my father if the lad is not with me? I fear to see the evil that would overtake my father' (44:33–34). And the crucial repercussions of this offer on every level of the narrative, from action to value system, maximize the interpretive pressure exerted by the gap. The threat to the unity of Judah's character is a threat to overall coherence.

So, in turn, this new gap revives and upgrades the old blank in the chronology into full gaphood. The dormant trouble perceptibly springs to life, because the quest for resolution of ongoing develop-ments now pulls us back, with fresh interest and energy, to the Tamar story as the only intervening drama that focuses on Judah. Here, if anywhere, the clue to his secret must lurk. In retrospect, indeed, the old thematic analogy with Jacob not only comes to the fore but takes on psychic and causal force as well, sufficient to bridge the apparent discontinuity between the past and the present Judah. Before confronting Joseph again and offering to take Benjamin's place for the sake of Jacob, we infer, Judah had gone through an experience that forced him to consider and reconsider family tangles from the paternal viewpoint. It has opened his eyes and his heart to the predicament of fatherhood – trials, injustices, suffering, and all. Nor is Judah, the role-reversal imposed by his conflict with Tamar behind him, now allowed to forget that chastening and enlarging experience. On the contrary, as the main action thickens and rises to a climax, so does the analogy with Jacob, far beyond the initial trickery equivalences of chapter 38. Thus, confronted with Jacob's outcry that two of his sons are 'gone' and he will not expose his youngest (Benjamin) to the same fate by surrendering him to dangerous relatives, how can Judah fail to identify the reenactment of his own unwillingness to deliver his own youngest son (Shela) into Tamar's arms, where the two older brothers have found their death? Family history repeats itself once more before Judah's eyes, with the tables again ironically turned on him. The lesson Judah learns the hard way, by 'real life' analogy with the Tamar affair, is multifold and cumulative, indeed developing. This hard-earned lesson now explains the newly-revealed empathy with his own father, including the very appeal to paternal favoritism as a ground for self-sacrifice: its effects an 'evil' no longer to be resented but to be prevented from 'overtaking my father' at any cost, perhaps by way of atonement for past evil.

The analogy in parenthood thus extends from thematics to dramatics – from hidden commentary on the plot to the workings of the hidden plot itself, from heavenly judgment to self-judgment, from punitive to redemptive irony, from the reader's eyes to Judah's. But this extension of scope or level presupposes in turn coherence with the temporal limits of the drama: with the plot as well as the character, or indeed with the character qua agent as well as qua moral and psychological being. So the analogy no longer freely cuts across the chronology. Once Judah's change of personality and approach comes to depend for its very sense on his role-reversal in the meantime at Tamar's hands, the time element also assumes new importance, because that reversal *must* intervene between the confrontations with Joseph in Canaan and in Egypt.

Fortunately, the distributed pointers reveal, it could so intervene on either arrangement of chronology. If we synchronize the brothers' trickery with Tamar's, Judah has learned his lesson decades ago; and if with Judah's marriage, then the passage of twenty-two years before the descent into Egypt allows the long sequel to the marriage (three sons born, two dying in wedlock, youngest withheld from the widow) just enough time for the Tamar crisis to break out and resolve itself at the eleventh hour. However wide the divergence in the linearization of events from sale to reunion, then, the analogy fits into the given chronological limits, hence qualifies for psycho-dramatic life as a presence and a force in Judah's own mind. The simultaneity may go either way, with little effect on essentials.

But in the characters' world, as in any historical or history-like world, things must have gone one way *or* the other. All the stranger, then, that the Bible should waste its own energy and the reader's on juggling with dates, only to leave that world suspended between incompatible time-patterns. Why tamper with story and history for nothing or less? The apparent pointlessness of such a complication urges us to weigh the alternatives more attentively, with the result that their divergence sharpens even further. In terms of one pattern, Judah went through his ordeal over twenty years ago and arrives in Egypt a long-changed man, his earlier self outgrown or at least ripe for treatment at Joseph's hands; in terms of the other pattern, he has only recently been subjected to Tamar's trickery and appears before Joseph with the lesson still fresh in his mind. The reconstruction of simultaneity vs. successiveness, then, makes quite a difference to the common denominator itself – Judah's intervening growth. And by leaving us suspended between the scenarios, the Bible as usual turns the difference to account: it enjoys the benefits of both Judah figures, the old and the new convert, long-term and short-term memory, in the teeth of time. Mimetic either/or composes into poetic both/and, not just to good psychological effect, such as complexity, but even to higher realistic effect. For the montage of the two Judah's renders his admirable conduct throughout the present, Egyptian ordeal more likely than would either portrait by itself. Indeed, within realism itself, the loss of surface history-likeness in the action is the gain of character and motivation.

Yet even this loss proves temporary. The brothers having passed the test, and the drama come to a happy end by recognition and peripety, Jacob himself leaves for Egypt with his whole clan. The list of seventy emigrants includes 'the sons of Judah: Er, Onan, Shela, Perez, and Zerah. Er and Onan died in the land of Canaan, and the sons of Perez were Hezron and Hamul' (46:12). By the decorums of genealogy, the reference to the dead Er and Onan among 'the descendants of Israel who came into Egypt' is incongruous; and so is the mention of the fourth, if not fifth, generation ('Hezron and Hamul') in a catalog that as a rule goes down only to the third. But the genealogical oddities powerfully redirect attention to the Judah and Tamar episode. The opening of the item ('Er, Onan, Shela, Perez, and Zerah') retells the story by nominal shorthand; the bare series then fills out a little by a reminder ('Er and Onan died in the land of Canaan') veiled as a pedantic corrective; while the conclusion ('the sons of Perez were Hezron and Hamul') updates the story with a twist, to the effect of disambiguating its chronology at long last. The surprising thing is not so much that the children of Judah's (grand)son by Tamar ('Perez') should receive mention as that he should by this time have children himself. (By a typical irony, the same Speiser who disputed the sequence of Genesis 24–25 on the grounds that Abraham was too old to procreate, now complains, source-critical scissors in hand again, that Perez was much too young.) To accommodate this disclosure, Tamar's trickery must have been simultaneous with the brothers', more or less, both occurring twenty-two years or so prior to the family reunion in Egypt.

One of the incompatible orderings establishes itself, after all.[17] But then the rival ordering has already accomplished its work, which nothing will take away, and may now bow out with honour in response to a new demand. The narrator having so far darkened and deformed the chronology in the interests of character, with related pleasures and profits, he now throws retrospective light on it to keep the historical record straight. A milestone like the descent into Egypt has its own priorities and proprieties, whether the realism of exact placement within a credible, let alone followable action or the magic attached to the full complement of seventy.

The new function, in short, calls for a new (or rather, newly dominant) form to stablize the play of chronology at last. From blank through gap to closure, from vagueness within the digressive episode through ambiguity in the main plot to lucidity in the genealogy: this is the route marked out here for the relations between simultaneity and successiveness among events, each stage in the shaping and dynamics of plot time correlated with one in our reading experience along time.

But the Bible may also leave such relations in permanent ambiguity. An example that has become notorious, though more for its problematics than for its point,[18] is the twofold story of David's debut: as an accomplished musician summoned to ease Saul's mania (I Sam. 16:14–23) and as a zealous shepherd boy volunteering to humble Goliath's pride (17:12–58). In form and role as well as origin, this may seem just another doublet of the type instanced earlier, with a shift in focus from the rejected (Ishmael, Esau, Saul) to the elected. Except that this doublet, far from compelling, no longer lends itself to smooth linearization into a process. Nor will it click into a formation of deep plot or 'simultaneous' alternativity, in the manner of the either/or endings in *The French Lieutenant's Woman*. Instead, it marks and elaborates a third theoretical strategy by combining those unidimensional arrangements (one in time, the other in space) into interdimensional traffic, that is, by pulling two different ways at once.

On the one hand, the doublet does pay homage to the Bible's chronological rule and doubling subrule by presenting the analogous tales as consecutive in history as well as in discourse. We even find the second tale prefaced by a comment that assumes the first, namely that David shuttled back and forth between his duties at court and at home (17:15). On the other hand, the first tale's premises and developments are at such odds with the second – for example, David's characterization as 'a man of war' (16:8) with his being 'unused' to weaponry (17:38–40), Saul's need and love for David (16:21–23) with his failure to identify him (17:55–28) – as to undercut their alignment.

Carried thus far, the havoc played with the continuity of character and interpersonal relations will not be domesticated into an ongoing plot. And once the analogy between the tales conflicts (instead of easily harmonizing) with chronology and variance with recurrence, their discontinuity goes to the limit of disjunction. We are left, that is, with the logical impossibility of two *first* encounters between David and Saul. Compared with the Tamar story, this means that the gap about time here is far more salient and disturbing, wider in scope, permanent not temporary, an obstacle rather than aid to interepisodic coherence in or out of sequence. This also makes the doublet a parade example of the simultaneity (co-presence, co-availability) in tradition that others camouflage as successiveness in the action.

However, if from the genetic angle this surface rupture apparently betrays the common source of doublets, then from the poetic it flaunts a limit case to the rule of alignment-before-everything, with constructive ambiguity in view. A limit case, because it pushes alignment in time to the halfway extreme of equality or alternativity with concurrence, but still well short of blocking plot alignment altogether, much less of darkening and loosening it into free reversibility. No more focused on space than on time by themselves, the ambiguity about what-happened-when remains hovering between dimensions.

Hence this twice-telling marks a contextual extreme, rather than a norm in the Bible's genesis or a freak in the poetics. As such, its deliberateness has by now acquired firm support. The smooth linear transition devised for its counterparts (e.g. Saul's dismissal) even within the same book, and feasible here as well through nothing more than cutting, points this way.[19] So does the recurrent, though usually muffled and sooner or later arrested, play among dimensions of ordering, as throughout the Judah and Tamar dynamics. And so, most powerfully, does the Bible's master strategy of gaps, forced on our notice by tensions or non sequiturs and leading to multiple gap-filling: divergent closures, equivocal or forked movements, dual portraits, yoking together of opposites, logical and psychological and chronological. Beyond doubt, our plot ambiguity between simultaneous and successive arrangement keeps the best biblical company. The question is not whether but why the narrator opts for burdening the simple order of events with a contradiction in terms, by which David emerges from obscurity twice for the first time. As the hero could so easily go from strength to strength, why push him forward with one hand while pulling him back to the starting point with the other hand? And the answer implied likewise follows established principles of biblical composition that I can only outline here.

It all begins, I would argue, with the strategic need to throw behind David the combined benefits of divine and social approval, both conditions of kingship in Samuel, while keeping them in their proper hierarchy. The solution is provided by the ambiguity imposed on time. According to one arrangement, David's rise marks a straight and ascending line under God's guidance: first divine choice and anointment at home, then (and, evidently, therefore) royal favor among courtiers, then popular acclaim in victory with quick promotion. Suggestively – if we recall the Bible's alignment norm in doublets as elsewhere – this thematic plotting enjoys the power of first impressions, and for quite a while at that. It not only arises first in the reading but also long develops, to gain momentum and hold, without any warning or pull to the contrary. Apart from its own recommendations, there is nothing at all to disturb it at the joint between the tales in 17:1ff, nothing really to threaten it before 17:39 recounts David's abandonment of traditional weapons, nothing to shake and rival it before 17:55–58, where Saul makes the overdue inquiries about him towards the end of the episode. Such distribution of materials along the reading process, whereby one hypothesis (and in poetic context, the right one) modulates into two, again shows a composer at work. And the common neglect to trace the emergence of the hypotheses is another manifestation of the hindsight fallacy, behaving as if the events and clues were all presented in the discourse at the same time, rather than one at a time and some even behind time. Why, if not to give this sequential reading the longest and best possible run, does the narrator delay to the last possible moment Saul's failure to recognize David – the strongest argument against its monopoly and for an alternative (re)arrangement?

According to the alternative, as soon as David has been secretly anointed, his public career launches itself on all fronts *at once*. He thereby bursts into the action both in peacetime at court and in wartime on the battlefield, both as a healer by music and giantkiller by slingshot, both on the initiative of others devoted to Saul and on his own, his charisma attested by a polyphony of social voices (the tribute from the royal servant, Saul's and later Jonathan's love, Goliath's left-handed compliment, the women's victory song, the admiration of the entire people) as well as by the Almighty whom he invokes against the Philistine and glorifies through his very success.

And yet, however far apart in the discourse (the one surfacing early, the other in late retrospect), however incompatible in reality (the one plotting the doublet onto time, the other counterplotting it across space), the alternative orderings dovetail in their impact. For the simultaneous pattern confers on David the stamp of approval all around – from the most various quarters, as if by unanimous election – while the successive controls the temporal along with the causal and normative priorities. Throughout, the hero's change of fortune refers to his hidden entrance: the emphasis shifts backward from the (gapped) relations between the two public debuts to the (certain) priority of the anointment scene to both. In its light, putting God first in every sense, we know whence, where and why all the rest goes. So the sequel concerning the worldly rise of God's anointed may equivocate not just with impunity but with profit; history bends but does not break under the pressures of ideology and rhetoric; the line suffers duplicity that the *point* may gain maximum convergence and energy.

Unlinear distortion

The most drastic tampering with chronology is also, for reasons already given, the most restrained and much the least common in the grand chronology: deformation along a *single* time-line, especially a plot-line, such as the reversible causal relations between homecoming and news in the Rape of Dinah episode. A staple, indeed a glory of the Bible's microline and microplot, the gap in time – disorder, rupture, secrecy, ambiguity – comes into little demand on higher levels of sequence. It may freely persist beyond the episode, as with the enigmas of character, but not extend into anything like episode-length itself, giving a sense of global omission or even deferral. On this scale, there are various measures of its going against the grain in the Bible's narrative architechtonics, increasingly so as we ascend from cycles to book-units to the main body of canonical history.

First, such displacement never bears on the overall beginning and end, so that the two temporal boundaries and, perceptually, strong points remain beyond its operations. An episode may at will plunge *in medias res*, devising a non-coincidence between temporal and textual starting point to be repaired later on in the narrative, through retrospection, if ever. An episode may also finish *in medias res*, so to speak, through a parallel noncoincidence in cut-off point, whereby the actional terminus or closure is followed by a retrospective *dis*closure and restructuring. (The story of the lost asses, its divine causality gradually released, exemplifies the former procedure; Abimelech's abduction of Sarah, with his motive for restoring her sprung in the final verse, illustrates the latter; Samson's Philistine marriage in Judges 14:1–4 combines both, since God's designs on the enemy come first in the happening but last in the telling.) Within the episode unit, then, the beginning and ending are as subject to displacement as any element in between. By contrast, each book (even Judges in the sense explained) starts and finishes with the appropriate occasion along its chronology, often a memorable episode or landmark at that – for example, Creation and Joseph's death in Genesis – so as to establish the clearest limits for the period under its jurisdiction.

Between those limits, second, the only book that scrambles the grand chronology of the middle is Deuteronomy. I refer of course to Moses's retrospect on forty years of thankless leadership, duly flanked by a placement of his address to the nation (1:1–5) and his death within sight of the promised land (34:1–12). Moses begins *in medias res* with the Horeb turning point (1:6), to which he later reverts again and again (e.g. 4:10, 33, 36; 5:1–28; 9:8–21, 25–29; 10:1–5; 18:16). He partly closes the huge *in medias res* gap by glancing back at the descent into Egypt (10:22) and harping on the miracles of the exodus (e.g. 4:34; 7:8, 15, 18–19; 8:14; 11:3–4), but in no systematic fashion. He interpolates into the Golden Calf tale a series of references to Tab'erah, Massah, Kibroth-hata'avah, Kadesh-barne'a, all locations where the Israelites have likewise 'provoked the Lord to wrath' (9:22–25). He abruptly recalls individual episodes such as God's turning against him on the people's account (4:21–22; 31:2), or the Korah rebellion (11:6), or Miriam's leprosy (24:9). And so on, not excluding forecasts of more or less possible events and speech-events to come. None of this global shuffling has either precedent or sequel in the Bible's own tradition, or for that matter any real equivalent in Homer's or elsewhere before the precursors of modernism. But then the Bible not merely owes Moses a valedictory story, it can well afford to let him tell it his own way.[20] After all, he does not so much tell as retell. Given the sequence of the Bible's narrative canon, by the time we reach Deuteronomy the historical path Moses erratically retraces is as familiar to ourselves as to his dramatic audience, and as followable, hence foolproof; the matter is not essentially new, only the manner. And as for the manner itself, the novelty of time structure goes with that of perspective, the narration being exceptionally delegated to a figure inside the world and one that could hardly show more involvement. So the one divergence from the compositional norm finds its rationale or motivation in the other: the order of (re)telling turns associative, oratorical, thematic, prophetic, persuasive and subjective, rather than objective.

Outside Deuteronomy, third, books as a rule confine their departures from chronology to one of the two possible directions. The episode line may give an early glimpse of the future (as when God foretells the descent into Egypt in Genesis, say, or the ascent in Exodus) but hardly ever twist into a belated unfolding of the past. Hence another contrast with the episode unit, its order of telling free to range between prospection, where the narrative looks ahead of developments with a view to suspense, and retrospection, which entails a gap in time and then a closure behind time (as with Saul's election, Abimelech's impotence, Samson's Philistine marriage) in the interests of curiosity or surprise. This makes an enormous difference in temporal options and resources. For suspense as I define it is a condition and shorthand for all the effects attached to reading with the future half- or end-illuminated, while curiosity and surprise embrace all those adhering to a past half-illuminated and misilluminated respectively.

This opposition of the overall to the tactical management grows yet sharper (and more restrictive) seeing that the Bible grants no compensation to the level directed to the future alone. Biblical suspense, that is, enjoys no greater latitude across than within episodes, but equally arises in the least disordering manner. It never derives, modernism fashion, from the scrambling of episodes out of their continuous time-line; seldom even from an overt flashforward in the narrator's own voice, and then usually by way of what I called summative prospection. Rather, the staple means are dramatic (forecast by characters, human and, more reliably, divine), thematic (e.g. sin pressing for retribution), compositional (as when a precedent augurs well or ill for an ongoing analogue), all forcefully predictive yet built into the action itself. However versatile in form and effect, therefore, the order of interepisodic suspense goes in step with the order of history.

Fourth, the rare flagrant infringements are exceptional with a vengeance, offending against sense along with time and suffering the penalty, as if to bring home the lesson by way of negative example. They betray some infelicity, confusion or, what amounts to the same thing, overtransparence. Once the doting Solomon has strayed into idolatry, we learn how God 'raised an adversary against him' by having Hadad the Edomite return from his asylum in Egypt to throw off Israel's yoke (I Kings 11:14–22). Not only does this story largely consist in an exposition that harks back to David's crushing of Edom and Hadad's flight; even the most recent part of it belongs to the time of Solomon's accession, not his old age, for Hadad returns to plague him as soon as the news of David's death reaches Egypt. So the episode is doubly mistimed, the initial attempt to put it forward in the action clashing with its subsequent emergence as a delay and a retrospect in the narration. Obviously, and abortively, the narrator seeks to give the impression that Solomon's harassment followed hard upon his sin: just as his youthful piety had been rewarded with 'no adversary' (5:18), so was his senile idolatry punished with 'an adversary'. The trouble is that the punishment actually *antedates* the crime, and by so long as to produce a boomerang effect that reflects upon God's justice. The Hadad affair indeed appears out of sequence, or in reversible sequence, but hardly to the gain of the book's ideology of retribution.

Or consider the hole in the sequence of Hezekiah's fight for independence. His defiance of Assyria in II Kings 18:13–16 is met by a punitive campaign that reduces him to abject submission and tribute payment. But the listing of that tribute runs straight into the account of the high-powered delegation sent by the king of Assyria to bring Jerusalem to her senses (18:17ff), which presupposes yet another bid for freedom on Hezekiah's part. A whole intermediate episode lurks between the adjacent verses, then, and we gather from the sequel that it concerned some understanding with 'the broken reed' of Egypt. An extensive surprise gap? No, because neither the silent discontinuity nor its retrospective emergence and casual closure show anything like the Bible's mastery of shocks of recognition. So little so that one suspects a textual misadventure, a lacuna in the genesis rather than a gap or a blank in the poesis.

This is even more obviously the case with a pair of books, or rather, significantly perhaps, booklets: Ezra and Nehemiah. Their chronology has likewise provoked endless dispute among historians and text critics, with the most wide-ranging consequences for that key period.[21] We find the book of Ezra placed before Nehemiah in the Bible, yet which of the two rebuilders of Judah and Judaism came first in the order of biblical time, by how long, and to what effect on his world and his successor? The internal dating, filled out by external evidence, would seem to establish only that Nehemiah's work ran from the twentieth to sometime beyond the thirty-second year of the Persian Artaxerxes I (Neh. 1:1; 2:1; 13:6; 445–433 BC). By contrast, the very anchorage of Ezra's debut (Ezra 7:7) in 'the seventh [?] year of King Artaxerxes [I? II?]' remains indeterminate and otherwise perplexing. So, did Ezra's arrival and career in Jerusalem precede or follow Nehemiah's, or maybe their terms partly overlapped? Accordingly, does the narrative reflect the order of events, reverse it for some anti-chronological purpose, or bow to the constraint of linearizing the simultaneous, and if so, in innocence or cunning: why put Ezra first? How, in short, does construction within and especially across these books stand to reconstruction? It is as impossible to tell, with anything like confidence, as to figure out a reason other than genetic for the impossibility. No play of gaps, this, because the elisions and incoherencies have run out of control: we can neither infer what happened, nor pattern the happening into well-defined ambiguity, nor refer the darkness of facts to its effects. Given the close links between the places, times, enterprises, if not between the two persons themselves, something must have gone wrong in the telling or the transmission. Whatever it was, the violence done to intelligibility on the simplest level of who-when-what assumes such proportions, textual and historical, as to find no precedent in biblical storytelling. And little wonder, because a precedent on this scale would leave us in doubt about the order (if any) of patriarchs, of Moses vis-à-vis Joshua, of major judges or kings.[22] The very absurdity of the thought underscores an important fact, perhaps a clue: the two books are not just late but also sharply discontinuous (in narrated time, in narrative posture and style, even in length) with the body of canonical history from Genesis to Kings.

The counterexamples widely vary, then, but the principle remains constant. As with the temporary delay of the Hadad trouble, so with the permanent loss of Hezekiah's Egyptian gamble and the irrecoverable Ezra–Nehemiah relations. As with forward jump, so with reversible sequence and its compounding by possible concurrence. As with episode series, so with entire books or booklets. Throughout, the failure to conform to the Bible's art of interepisodic composition betrays a fall below art. Considering modern prejudices – to finish where I began – it is ironic that this fall invariably attends not the march but the exceptional breach of the grand chronology.

NOTES

1 For references and critical discussion see my *Expositional Modes and Temporal Ordering in Fiction* (Johns Hopkins University Press, Baltimore and London, 1978); 'Time and reader', in *The Uses of Adversity: Failure and Accommodation in Reader Response*, ed. Ellen Spolsky (Bucknell University Press, Lewisburg, Pa., 1989); and 'Telling in time (I): chronology and narrative theory', forthcoming in *Poetics Today* 10 (1990). See also nn. 4 and 8 below.

2 Umberto Cassuto, e.g. in *A Commentary on the Book of Exodus* (Magnes Press, Jerusalem, 1952), pp. 54–5, 129–30.

3 Collected in *Ancient Near Eastern Texts*, ed. James B. Pritchard (Princeton University Press, Princeton, 1969), pp. 52–7, 72–99, 23–5, 142–9 respectively.

4 Meir Sternberg, *The Poetics of Biblical Narrative: Ideological Literature and the Drama of Reading* (Indiana University Press, Bloomington, 1985), esp. chs 6–13. The same, moreover, holds true for yet smaller units, down to phrases or even words in coordination, hence in more or less formal and unordered-looking parallelism. For a general theory of the dynamics on this level – the sequencing forces and patterns behind coordination – see my 'Ordering the unordered: time, space, and descriptive coherence', *Yale French Studies*, 61 (1981), pp. 60–88, and 'Deictic sequence: world, language and convention', in *Essays on Deixis*, ed. Gisa Rauh (Gunter Narr, Tübingen, 1983), pp. 277–316, both with biblical material. From these I can only extrapolate here, for future reference and comparison, the set of linear mechanisms available to the Bible and operative below its surface: the chrono-logical, the hierarchical, the perspectival, the deictic. All dynamic, in that they convert and tighten unordered equivalence into ordered sequence, each mechanism still

preserves its own rationale. The *chrono-logical* projects a series of items (nouns and adjectives as well as verbs) onto time, so as to unfold a line of events or, where causality also beckons, even a mini-plot. The rest of the set, in contrast, work across and often against chronology, their miniature dynamics no less subtle than the episode's but more implicit and various. The *hierarchical* mechanism thus assimilates a coordinate series to a scale of some kind, whether in ascending (I Sam. 22:9, 13) or in descending (I Sam. 15:9) order or both (Gen. 12:1). The *perspectival* transforms a given coordination into a subject's order of experience, perception or discovery (e.g. Judg. 4:22 vs. 21). And the *deictic* makes linear sense of parallel members by appeal to the situation-bound order of reference: from first through second to third person (e.g. I Kings 1:12, 21). For further examples and discussion, see also the index in *Poetics of Biblical Narrative*, under word order.

5 For some further details, interspersed with somewhat hasty conclusions, see Gershon Brin, 'Studies in biblical phrases indicating time', *Te'udah IV*, ed. Mordechai A. Friedman and Moshe Gil (Tel-Aviv University, University Publishing Project, 1986), pp. 37–54. The topic still requires investigation, in a poetic and comparative as well as a microlinguistic light. It even needs to be studied how much of the notorious problematics of the Bible's chronology derives from its relative positioning of events in immediate sequence, how much from its own dating of them, especially across long stretches of narrative, how much again from scholarly attempts to confirm or disconfirm either internal datum by reference to independent witnesses, often foreign in every sense. It is revealing, for instance, that the first and least problematic resource makes the staple of the chronology, whether grand, episodic or miniature. But, apart from hints scattered throughout the argument below, I must reserve these questions for separate treatment.

6 For example, E. A. Speiser in the Anchor Bible's *Genesis* (Doubleday, Garden City, NY, 1964), p. 189; likewise the traditionalist Benno Jacob: 'Der [Abraham] Abschnitt liegt also zeitlich vor c. 23 und selbt c. 17 oder schon c. 14' (*Das erste Buch der Tora: Genesis*, Schocken, Berlin, 1934). Some have opted for solutions other, but no less suggestive, than temporal reversal. Speaking in genetic terms, Gerhard von Rad is thus prepared to let the text stand on the hypothesis that 'the ancients' did not pay much attention to 'biographical consistency' in redacting their sources (*Genesis*, tr. John H. Marks, SCM Press, London, 1970, p. 256). Along midrashic lines, *Bereshit Rabbah* (with a following among later rabbinic exegetes, e.g. Rashi and Sforno) identifies Keturah as Hagar, who, having married, bred *and* divorced since her expulsion, was now conveniently free to return with a half-dozen children for Abraham to bring up. That this fantasy does not accord with so much as the Bible's language – e.g. the plural of 'concubines' (25:6) – reveals what a difficulty Abraham's age presents even to interpreters who do not usually shy at miracles.

7 For a critical survey of this and related notions, see Arnaldo Momigliano,

'Time in ancient historiography', *Essays in Ancient and Modern Historiography* (Blackwell, Oxford, 1977), who argues in effect that the immense body of work on the subject is in inverse proportion to the light it throws on the realities (mentalities, writings, antitheses, developments) of ancient culture.

8 More complex examples of this interworking appear below as well as, along a wider front, throughout *Poetics of Biblical Narrative*. For theoretical background, see my *Expositional Modes and Temporal Ordering*, pp. 69ff; 'Spatiotemporal art and the other Henry James: the case of *The Tragic Muse*,' *Poetics Today*, 5 (1984), pp. 775–830; 'Time and reader', esp. the final section. The argument against the reductionist or isolationist theories cited there equally applies to the practice and underlying assumptions of much biblical exegesis over the centuries: from the Rabbis or the Church Fathers as anachronistic typologists to, say, Joel Rosenberg's analysis of the Garden story and others in *King and Kin: Political Allegory in the Hebrew Bible* (Indiana University Press, Bloomington, 1986), which carries the opposition to an extreme, in principle at least, if not always in actual and more intuitive reading.

9 *The Peleponnesian War*, tr. Rex Warner (Penguin, Harmondsworth, 1962).

10 Henry Fielding, *Tom Jones* (Signet, New York, 1963), pp. 64–5.

11 Laurence Sterne, *A Sentimental Journey* (Oxford University Press, London, 1963 [1768]), p. 29.

12 To this familiar device, alas, Shemaryahu Talmon reduces 'The presentation of synchroneity and simultaneity in biblical narrative', in *Scripta Hierosolymitana*, 27 (Magnes Press, Jerusalem, 1978), pp. 9–26. Even so, the reduction leaves a good deal to be desired. On the one hand, resumptive summary belongs not to the presentation of simultaneity as such but as a form of discontinuity, which equally requires bridging in the most unilinear narrative (miniatures like II Samuel 22:2–3 included). Far from confined to a particular object, whether multiple or simple action, resumptive summary extends to the medium and the discourse at large, answering to the exigency of resuming whatever needs resumption. On the other hand, just as its principled scope is much wider, so is its actual scope much narrower than the narration of simultaneity: it need not appear there at all, because the resumptive function may be performed through means other than summary, for example dating or time formulas. Neither sufficient nor necessary, then, resumptive summary is one of the devices available to the narrative in retrospection – though for uses and effects, again, considerably more versatile than Talmon and his predecessors believe. Some illustration immediately ensues.

13 This springs into yet bolder relief against the opposed, morally proportioned hierarchy that governs the parallel account in II Chronicles (17:1–21:1): it spotlights Jehoshaphat, on his own merits as well as David's, to the extent that Ahab and their alliance enter only in relation to him, as a deplorable lapse from virtue on the hero's part. The two

versions reflect, as usual, the larger variance between ideological (Genesis to Kings) and near-didactic (Chronicles) narrative.

14 Or in the midrashic parable that Rashi applies to 37:1, a man looking for a jewel must first sift out the sand around it.

15 'At that time', like 'after these things' (e.g. I Kings 21:1), relates some event or event-series located before the formula to another that comes after it, but not perforce immediately after. Correspondingly, as the so-called appendix to Judges shows, the backward glance through this formula need not be to the event that immediately precedes it. Rather than limiting itself to pinpoint linkage, the Bible typically exploits the flexibility of reference in either direction to vary the shape and sense of time, ambiguity included. It would take too long to go properly into these and related niceties of biblical usage. Let me just mention in passing that the very large-scale principle with which we are now concerned has at least two microcosmic equivalents (as well as supporters) on the level of language. One is grammatical, lying in the ambiguity of the so-called perfective form of the verb between (*inter alia*) retrospection and crosscutting: shift backward in time or sideward in space, topic, line? The other is lexical, such as the common duplicity of 'then' (*'az*) between sequencing and synchronizing the events in question: linear or lateral? Combined, the bare hints in this note may yet give an idea how closely, here as elsewhere, the Bible's linguistic system dovetails with the poetic. (See also nn. 4 and 5 above.)

16 See Meir Sternberg, 'Delicate balance in the Rape of Dinah: biblical narrative and the rhetoric of narrative', *Hasifrut*, 4 (1973), pp. 193–231; *Poetics of Biblical Narrative*, esp. 448–53.

17 Unless one takes the mention of Hezron and Hamul not as a retrospect on intervening births but as a prospection on the development of Judah's line. Umberto Cassuto thus infers from the variant reference to the two – 'the sons of Perez *were* Hezron and Hamul', with explicit and unnecessary copula – that they were not yet born at the time of Jacob's migration ('The story of Tamar and Judah', *Biblical Literature and Canaanite Literature I*, Magnes Press, Jerusalem, 1972, pp. 112ff.). To my mind, this reading and the approach behind it go against the plain sense of the genealogy, hence cannot really maintain the ambiguity under the pressure of the new information, still less validate the alternative reconstruction. (E.g. if Hezron and Hamul are still unborn, then the long-buried Er and Onan have to be numbered in their place among the 'seventy' emigrants. A grotesque in the manner of Gogol's *Dead Souls*, who exist on census paper alone? Better living grandchildren than dead children.) But the linguistic clue in favour of this hypothesis combined with its earlier rise and operation may give it a lease of life: nothing like the monopoly that Cassuto claims for it, but perhaps a loophole for survival, as a question mark within the otherwise untwisted ordering.

18 But see the welcome attempts at interpretation in recent years, starting from the portrait drawn by Kenneth R. R. Gros Louis, 'The difficulty of ruling well: King David of Israel', *Semeia*, 8 (1977), pp. 15–33.

19 In fact, such cutting need not go nearly so far as the Septuagint's Codex Vaticanum, LXX[B], which lacks almost half of the Masoretic Text: the entire scene of David's arrival at the battlefield in 17:12–31, on top of the real obstacle to surface continuity, Saul's nonrecognition of him after the victory in 17:55–8. (For a recent analysis of the variants see Emanuel Tov, 'The composition of I Samuel 16–18 in the Light of the Septuagint Version', *Empirical Models for Biblical Criticism*, ed. Jeffrey H. Tigay, Philadelphia, 1985, pp. 97–130.) Even for one of his reputation among source analysts, the Masoretic redactor would have to be abnormally obtuse and heavy-handed in splicing to have mismanaged the bare minimum; and his performance elsewhere argues that he was nothing of the sort, but had in mind something quite different from easy coherence.

20 His own, of course, in the dramatic rather than the authorial sense: that idiosyncratic way still remains under the control of the primary narrator in the textual-temporal frame, who officially quotes and silently manipulates Moses's address for his overall ends. On their relations see Robert Polzin, *Moses and the Deuteronomist* (The Seabury Press, New York, 1980), pp. 25–72.

21 For Hezekiah, see the review of problems in John Bright, *A History of Israel* (SCM Press, London, 1972), pp. 296–308; for Ezra and Nehemiah, pp. 392–403.

22 That is also why to biblical ears, like those of the Jews in the Temple, Jesus's time-reversal cum tense-paradox 'Before Abraham was, I am' (John 8:58) sounds so outrageous: an offence against sense, history and faith rolled into one.

5

Sodom as Nexus: The Web of Design in Biblical Narrative

Robert Alter

The very terms we habitually use to designate the sundry biblical narratives reflect an uncertainty as to whether the stories taken in sequence have something that could be called a structure, and as to what sort of larger configurations they might form. The first eleven chapters of Genesis are usually called the Primeval History, as though they constituted a continuous historical narrative, despite the repeated scholarly arguments that they are in fact an uneven stitching-together of the most heterogeneous materials. On the other hand, we often speak of the Patriarchal Tales or the Wilderness Tales, a designation that suggests something vaguely anthological. Or again, it is common practice to invoke with a certain ring of academic authority the Abraham cycle, the Jacob cycle, the Elijah cycle; but if that term has a precise application for Norse sagas or Wagnerian opera, it seems chiefly an evasion in the case of biblical narrative. We do, of course, talk about the Joseph story and the David story, but this is only because these are rare exceptions in which the ancient Hebrew writers have given us a relatively lengthy, continuous narrative – apart from a few seeming interpolations – that follows the chronological movement of a central figure's life.

If one's standard of unitary narrative is drawn from self-consciously artful novels like *Madame Bovary*, Ford Madox Ford's *The Good Soldier*, or even, on a more ambitiously panoramic scale, *Anna Karenina*, it goes without saying that biblical narrative is far from unitary. Scholarly opinion has by and large jumped to the conclusion that if biblical narrative is not unitary, it must be episodic. Episodic structure, as Aristotle first observed, means no necessary sequence among the incidents told. In the case of a single author, episodic structure may be quite intentional and often expresses a rejection of hierarchies, an enchantment with the teeming heterogeneity of experience, as in *Don Quixote*, Lesage's *Gil Blas* or *Huckleberry*

Finn. By contrast, the episodic character of biblical narrative, as it is usually represented in scholarly analysis, is the result of editorial inadvertence rather than authorial intention: the anonymous redactors, working under the constraints of authoritative ancient traditions in ways we can no longer gauge, are imagined patching together swatches of very different materials, sometimes splicing two or more versions of the same story, sometimes inserting extraneous stories that originated in radically different contexts.

It may be helpful in trying to think about the larger configurations of biblical narrative to keep in mind that only a minority of long narratives anywhere, whether pre-novelistic or novelistic, are consistently unitary. Dickens, for example, often used the devices of tightly sustained suspense of the detective-novel plot, and modern criticism has celebrated the symmetries of his symbolic structures, yet the typical Dickens novel is studded with anecdotal digressions and, in the earlier phase of his career, with interpolated tales. Fielding is justly praised as one of the most architectonic of English novelists – Coleridge rated the plot of *Tom Jones*, along with that of *Oedipus Rex* and Ben Jonson's *The Alchemist*, as one of the three most perfect in world literature – yet both *Tom Jones* and *Joseph Andrews* include long interpolated tales that are different from the surrounding narrative in style, tone, genre and personages. The instance of Fielding is particularly instructive because it suggests that even a writer so supremely conscious of unified artifice – in *Tom Jones* one might mention the structural symmetry of six books in the country, six on the road, six in town, or the tonal unity conferred by the ubiquitous ironic narrator – might for his own good reasons introduce materials whose chief connection with the main narrative was a matter of shared theme or mere analogy.

Let me propose that something quite similar repeatedly occurs in biblical narrative in the juxtaposition of disparate materials that are purposefully linked by motif, theme, analogy and, sometimes, by a character who serves as a bridge between two different narrative blocks otherwise separated in regard to plot and often in regard to style and perspective or even genre. Obviously, in the Bible the proportion of such insertions is quite unlike what one finds in Fielding, who makes only occasional use of them. Indeed, it may be inaccurate to speak at all of 'insertions' in the case of the Bible, for the artful juxtaposition of seemingly disparate episodes is more like a basic structuring procedure, a feature especially evident in Numbers, Joshua, Kings and, above all, in the Book of Judges, but also discernible elsewhere. This would appear to be the expression of an activity that in recent years has come to be called redactional art, but in what follows I shall speak of the writer rather than the redactor in the interests of accuracy as well as of simplicity, for we need to remind ourselves that the redactor, however enshrined in modern biblical scholarship, remains a conjectural entity, and the more one scrutinizes his supposed work, the more the line between redactor and writer blurs.

Rather than try to describe the overarching design of a whole book or sequence of books, a project that would require a great deal of space for persuasive execution, I would like to demonstrate the general principle by following the biblical text at a point where there seems to be a break in narrative continuity. In fact, the example I have chosen involves what looks like a triple break from the surrounding narrative, but I shall try to show that all three stages of the break are firmly linked together and locked into both the immediate narrative context and into the larger thematic design of Genesis and subsequent books in a way that complicates the thread of meaning.

In Genesis 17, God appears before the 99-year-old Abram, changes his name to Abraham and Sarai's to Sarah as an affirmation of the covenant, and resonantly announces a future of progeny through Sarah – a promise so improbable that it causes Abraham to laugh in disbelief. In the first half of the next chapter, we have the story of the three mysterious visitors who come to Abraham (from what one can make out, they are God himself and two of his messengers), one of whom brings the good tidings that within the year Sarah will bear a son. This time, it is she, overhearing the promise from the tent-opening, who laughs in disbelief, perhaps even sarcastically. Documentary critics have been quick to identify these two sequenced stories as a duplication from two different sources, P and then J. Whether in fact scholarly analysis has succeeded in 'unscrambling the omelette' here, to borrow a telling phrase from Sir Edmund Leach, is something I shall not presume to judge. More essential to our purposes is that the writer wants a double version of the promise of progeny, partly for the sheer effect of grand emphasis, but also because he needs first a patriarchal version and then a matriarchal one. In chapter 17, Abraham alone is present before God; the plight of the 90-year-old barren Sarah is mentioned only in passing and in secondary syntactic position after Abraham (verse 17); and male biology is very much at issue in the stress on the newly enjoined commandment of circumcision (though Abraham undertakes it for himself and all his future sons, its placement in the narrative sequence makes it look like a precondition to the begetting of the son, as, analogously, in Exodus 4, the tale of the Bridegroom of the Blood, the circumcision of the son is the necessary means for his survival). In the first half of chapter 18, we encounter the inaugural instance of the annunciation type-scene. As a conventional tale, it is pre-eminently matriarchal, for the good news always comes to the wife, often in the absence of the husband. Here, however, perhaps because of the force of the idea of Abraham as founding father, there is a partial displacement from matriarchal to patriarchal emphasis, the angel speaking to Abraham while Sarah eavesdrops on her own annunciation. In any case, it is she who laughs, and it is her biology – the twice-stated fact of her post-menopausal condition – that is at issue. This shift, even if it is a somewhat qualified one, from patriarch to matriarch in the second version of the promise is crucial, for in what follows women and sexuality, women and propagation, will be central.

Now, in all other occurrences of the annunciation type-scene,[1] the first two motifs of the conventional sequence – (a) the woman's condition of barrenness; (b) the annunciation – are immediately followed by the third motif of fulfillment (c), the birth of the son (cf. Gen. 25:19–25; Judg. 13; I Sam. 1; II Kings 4:8–17). Here, however, there is a long interruption before the birth of Isaac at the beginning of Genesis 21. First, God announces to Abraham his intention to destroy Sodom and Gomorrah, and Abraham launches upon his memorable effort to bargain with God over the survival of the doomed cities, starting with the possibility of fifty righteous souls therein and working down to ten (18:17–33). The first half of chapter 19 tells the story of the destruction of Sodom, concluding with what looks like an etiological tale (to explain a geological oddity in the Dead Sea region) about Lot's wife turning into a pillar of salt. The second half of the chapter is a very different kind of etiological tale, accounting for the origins of two trans-Jordanian peoples, the Moabites and the Ammonites, in the incestuous copulation of Lot and his daughters. The whole of chapter 20 is then taken up with the second of three versions of the sister–wife story: the patriarch in a southern kingdom (here, Abraham in Gerar) who proclaims that his wife is his sister, in consequence almost loses her to the local potentate, but in the end departs with wife intact and heaped with riches by the would-be interloper. Since nowhere else are there such interruptions of the annunciation's fulfillment, we are surely entitled to ask what all this has to do with the promise of seed to Abraham. Let me suggest that in the view of the biblical writer, progeny for the first father of the future Israelites involved a whole tangle of far-reaching complications for the adumbration of which these three intervening episodes were necessary, and that Sodom, far from being an interruption of the saga of the seed of Abraham, is a major thematic nexus of the larger story.[2]

We should observe, to begin with, that the dialogue between Abraham and God in the second half of Genesis 18 sets up a connection between the covenantal promise and the story of Sodom by adding a new essential theme to the covenantal idea. The two previous enunciations of the covenant, which take up all of chapters 15 and 17, are ringing promises of progeny and little more: your seed, God assures the doubting Abraham, will be as innumerable as the stars in the heavens. The only condition hinted at is that Abraham remain a faithful party to the covenant, but remarkably, no *content* is given to this faithfulness. It looks almost as if a trap were set for the audience, encouraging them at first to think that the divine promise was a free gift, entered into through a solemn ritual (the sacrificial animal parts of ch. 15) and perpetually confirmed by still another ritual (the circumcision of ch. 17). Now, however, when God reaffirms the language of blessing and the future of nationhood in chapter 18, he adds this stipulation about Abraham and his posterity: 'For I have singled him out [new JPS] so that he might instruct his sons and his family after him, that they should keep the way of the Lord *to do righteousness and justice*' (Gen. 18:19, my emphasis). Survival and propagation, then, depend on the creation of a just society. This idea is immediately picked up as God goes on to warn Abraham of his intention to destroy the Cities of the Plain because of their pervasive wickedness. Abraham, aghast at the possibility that the righteous might be wiped out with the wicked, tosses back the very phrase God has just used about human ethical obligations: 'Will the judge of all the earth not *do justice?*' (18:25). The echo of *shofet*, judge, and *mishpat*, justice, will then sound loudly in a jibe about Lot made by the citizens of Sodom, whom he has implored to desist from their violent intentions: 'This fellow came to sojourn, and now he presumes to judge, yes, to judge' (19:9). The verb *shofet* also means 'to rule', which may be its primary sense here, but the play with 'doing justice' of the previous chapter is quite pointed: Sodom is a society without judge or justice, and a latecomer resident alien will hardly be allowed to act as *shofet* in any sense of the word.

As many commentators have noted, the hospitality scene between Abraham and the divine visitors at the beginning of Genesis 18 is paralleled by the hospitality scene between Lot and the two angels at the beginning of Genesis 19 – paralleled with a nuance of difference, for Lot's language to the angels is more urgent, in a string of imperative verbs, less deferentially ceremonious than Abraham's language, and here the narrator gives us nothing like the details of the menu and the flurry of preparations for the feast that we are offered in the pastoral setting of the previous chapter. Lot's rather breathless hospitality – is he already scared by what could happen to strangers in his town? – is of course the single exception to the rule in Sodom. This story of the doomed city is crucial not only to Genesis but to the moral thematics of the Bible as a whole (compare the use of Sodom in Isaiah 1 and Judges 19) because it is the biblical version of anti-civilization, rather like Homer's islands of the Cyclops monsters where the inhabitants eat strangers instead of welcoming them. If we wondered momentarily what God had in mind when he told Abraham that the outrages of Sodom – literally, its 'crying out' – were so great that they reached the very heavens, we now see all the male inhabitants of Sodom, from adolescent to dodderer, banging on Lot's door and demanding the right to gang-rape the two strangers. The narrator offers no comment on the homosexual aspect of the threatened act of violence, though it is safe to assume he expects us to consider that, too, abhorrent, but in regard to this episode's place in the larger story of progeny for Abraham, it is surely important that homosexuality is a necessarily sterile form of sexual intercourse, as though the proclivities of the Sodomites answered biologically to their utter indifference to the moral prerequisites for survival.

At this ominous point, in one of the most scandalous statements uttered by any character in ancient literature, Lot's daughters, not previously mentioned, are brought into the story. 'Look', Lot tells the assailants, 'I have two daughters who have not known a man. Let me bring them out to you, and do to them whatever you want. But to these men do nothing, for they have come under the shadow of my roof-beam' (19:7). Some have sought to naturalize this outrageous offer by contending that in the ancient Near East the host–guest bond (someone coming under the shadow of your roof-beam) was sacred, conferring obligations that exceeded those of a man to his virgin daughters. The impassive narrator, as is his wont, offers no guidance on this question, but the unfolding of the story, and its contrastive connections with the surrounding narrative, cast doubt on this proposition that Lot was simply playing the perfect ancient Near Eastern host in rather trying circumstances. It is important for what happens at the end of the chapter that the two girls should be virgins, and Lot clearly imagines he is offering the rapists a special treat in proclaiming their virginity. What we are not told, in a shrewd maneuver of delayed exposition, is that both the girls are betrothed. This information is not divulged until verse 14, when Lot, at the angels' insistence, entreats his prospective sons-in-law to save themselves from the imminent destruction. Their response is to think Lot must be joking, *metsaḥeq*, the same verb of laughter that designates Abraham's and Sarah's response to the promise of progeny, and that here, in polar contrast, becomes a mechanism of skepticism that seals the doom of the two men. Now, at least according to later biblical law, the rape of a betrothed woman is a crime punishable by death (cf. Deut. 22:23–27), and it is reasonable to infer that Lot evinces a disquieting readiness here to serve as accomplice in the multiple enactment of a capital crime directed against his own daughters. The implicit judgment against Lot is then confirmed in the incest at the end of the chapter, to which we shall turn momentarily.

Let me first add a brief comment on the motif of sight and blindness, which helps structure the story thematically and also links it with the surrounding narrative. The transition to Sodom was first signalled visually when Abraham escorted the two visitors out on their way and they 'looked down' on Sodom, far below in the Dead Sea plain (18:16). The conclusion of the destruction is symmetrically marked at 19:28 when the next morning Abraham, in the equivalent of a cinematic long shot, 'looks down' (the same verb) on the Cities of the Plain and is able to discern columns of smoke rising from the distant ruins. In the Sodom story proper, the angels smite the assailants with blindness so that they are unable to find the door of Lot's house. Then, before carrying out the terrible devastation, the angels warn Lot not to look back; and, most famously, when his wife does just that, she is turned to a pillar of salt. I don't pretend to know precisely what this taboo – also attested to elsewhere – of looking back, or looking on the destruction, meant in the imagination of the ancient folk. I would observe, however, that the taboo against seeing has regular sexual associations in the Bible (as, of course, it also does in psychoanalytic terms). To 'see the nakedness' of someone is the standard biblical euphemism for incest. Genesis 19 does not use that idiom, but this rampant mob struck with blindness at a closed door is, after all, seeking forbidden sexual congress, and the story ends with a tale of incest.

That episode (19:29–38) is presented in an unsettling manner of impassive factuality, the narrator providing no indication whether the double incest should in any way be condemned. It would sadly reduce the story to think of it simply as a satiric representation of the dubious origins of two enemy peoples, the Moabites and the Ammonites, for its more important function is to tie together several thematically significant connections with the immediate and larger context of biblical narrative. Lot, we recall, has fled with his two daughters to the city of Zoar, which, as a special dispensation for his sake, has alone been saved from destruction among the Cities of the Plain. But Lot is afraid to stay in Zoar, whether because he fears still another wave of cataclysm or Sodom-like behavior on the part of the Zoarites, and so he flees once more with his daughters, this time to the rocky hill-country above the Dead Sea plain, where they take refuge in a cave. The despairing daughters – who, we should remember, enjoyed prenuptial status when we first encountered them – conclude that the whole country, or rather the whole earth (*'erets*), has been laid waste, and that there is no man left to lie with them. On two successive nights, then, they get their father drunk, and, the first-born going first, each takes a turn in bed with him and is impregnated by him. Twice we are told that 'he knew not when she lay down and got up', a wry play on the sexual meaning of the verb, for he knows his daughters well enough in the other sense, knows them without 'seeing' them. Thus the man who precipitously offered his betrothed daughters to gang-rape now is tricked into deflowering them himself.

This strange story alludes to the aftermath of the Deluge, and that connection in turn may help us see why it is placed precisely here in the Abraham narrative. The destruction of the Cities of the Plain is a second Deluge: there, iniquitous humanity was destroyed by water; here, by fire. A concrete link between the two is probably suggested by the writer's choice of a graphic verb, 'The Lord *rained down* on Sodom and Gomorrah brimstone and fire from the Lord, from the heavens' (19:24). The framing of the sentence by repeating 'the Lord' at both ends, and the odd syntactic obtrusion of 'from the heavens' at the very end, reinforce this sense of catacylsm showering from heaven to earth (no earthquake this), like the earlier devastation when the floodgates of the heavens were flung open. After the Deluge, Noah plants a vineyard and forthwith gets drunk. It is precisely in his state of inebriation that Ham his son 'sees his nakedness' (the idiom implicit in the alluding text is explicit in the text alluded to) and incurs his father's curse when Noah wakes from his drunken stupor and discovers what has happened. (There is a long tradition of exegetical opinion, whether right or wrong, that more than mere seeing has happened: many say, a sexual act, and in the opinion of some medieval exegetes, castration, which readily reminds us of analogues in Greek myth.) Interestingly, Ham's two brothers then cover their naked father with a cloak by walking backwards with it into the tent, taking care never to look behind them, in symmetrical contrast to the unfortunate Mrs Lot (see Gen. 9:20–27).

The Noah–Lot conjunction brings us back to the notion of the physical survival of group or species made conditional on moral performance. Abraham, the man who has in this very sequence demonstrated his sense of justice by daring to call God himself to the standard of justice, has one son, by his concubine, and will soon have a second son by his legitimate wife. Against these, Lot has two daughters, who as daughters figure, alas, in ancient Near Eastern imagination more as conduits for male seed than as the true progeny itself. Beginning with the son to be born within the year, from Abraham's loins a great people will spring, destined to be a blessing, as God has repeatedly promised, to all the nations of the earth. Lot's daughters, imagining that a second cataclysm has laid waste all the earth, desperately conclude that the only way to 'keep the seed alive' (19:32, 34) is by turning back to him who begot them. The propagation is carried out, but the two peoples that derive from it will carry the shadow of their incestuous origins in the (folk-) etymology of their names, Moab, from-the-father, and Benei Ammon, sons-of-kin; and perhaps we are encouraged to infer that in their historical destiny these peoples will be somehow trapped in their own inward circuit, a curse and not a blessing to the nations of the earth, in consonance with their first begetting.

At this point, it might seem logical for the narrative to revert to the fulfillment of the promise of offspring to Abraham. Instead, still another episode, taking up a whole chapter, intervenes. For the second time, Abraham goes to a southern kingdom, in this case Gerar in the Negev rather than Egypt and, as before, having announced that Sarah is his sister, finds she is taken into the harem of the local ruler. Now, it seems to me a piece of modern simple-mindedness to say, as is conventionally done, that since Abraham would appear to have learned nothing from the previous near-disaster in Egypt (Gen. 12:10–20), we must conclude that this is a duplication of sources, and a particularly clumsy one, at that. I do not think the biblical writers were concerned with consistent narrative verisimilitude in quite this way, or in any case such concerns could be overridden by the requirements of what I shall call compositional logic. Let me stress that I am not addressing myself to the issue of whether this thrice-told tale originated in different sources but rather to the compositional effect the writer achieves in retelling it as he does. (I will set aside the third occurrence of the story in the Isaac narrative, Genesis 26, as beyond the scope of the present discussion.) For our purposes, it is important to note that the story of Abraham and Sarah in Gerar is strikingly different from the story of Abraham and Sarah in Egypt in regard to both details and expositional strategy. Most of these differences, as we shall see, flow directly from the placement of the Gerar story directly after the destruction of Sodom and before the birth of Isaac.

In Genesis 20 no mention is made of a famine as the reason for the patriarch's temporary sojourn in the south. And, indeed, a famine at this point, just after Abraham has been promised the imminent birth of a son and after the destruction of the Cities of the Plain, would throw the narrative out of balance, introducing still another catastrophe at the moment before the great fulfillment. Sarah's beauty, much stressed in Genesis 12 in conjunction with the clearly implied concupiscence of the Egyptians, is not referred to here. Perhaps that may be because of her advanced age at this point in the narrative, though I'm not sure this is a consideration that troubled the writer. In any case, there seems to be a desire to shift the emphasis from Sarah's sexual attractiveness to the mere fact that the future mother of Isaac is evidently appropriate to take into a harem. In this version, Abraham offers no explanation at the beginning for his odd strategem of passing Sarah off as his sister ('lest they kill me for my wife'); that comes only at a late point in the story in his nervous attempt at self-exculpation to the offended Abimelech. Abimelech, in turn, is assigned a much more elaborate role than Pharaoh in the earlier version, and the terms of that role have a great deal to do, I think, with the immediately preceding story of Sodom.

When God appears to Abimelech in a dream to threaten him with death for taking a married woman (this, too, a contrast to Pharaoh, whose only communication from the Lord is through physical affliction), the Gerarite king responds in moral indignation: 'Will you slay even innocent people?' (20:4). The Hebrew here is a little peculiar, for strategic reasons having to do with the two previous chapters. The word for innocent, *tsadiq*, also means righteous, and is the very term Abraham used when he challenged God: 'Far be it from you to do such a thing, to put to death the righteous with the wicked so that the righteous would be like the wicked. Far be it from you. Will not the judge of all the earth do justice?' (18:25). It is for this reason that death is threatened to Abimelech but not to Pharaoh, so that Abimelech can be made, in a brilliant ironic turn, to take up Abraham's own recently stated moral theme. Abimelech cries out against the possibility that God might slay a righteous 'people' (*goy*), apparently referring to himself. As an idiom, this is anomalous enough in biblical Hebrew to have encouraged emendations of the text, but it is a word-choice that makes perfect sense against the backdrop of Sodom, where an entirely wicked people was destroyed. The Gerar story presents an initial parallel with the Sodom story that immediately swerves into sharp contrast. Here also, two strangers come into a town, and one of them is promptly seized for the purpose of sexual enjoyment – but then she has been passed off as an unmarried woman. The moment Abimelech discovers Sarah's actual status, he speaks as a model of conscience, and he scrupulously avoids touching her. God identifies Abraham as a 'prophet' with powers of intercession, which seems appropriate just after Abraham has made his great effort to intercede on behalf of Sodom. The punctilious Abimelech nevertheless feels, with some justice, that Abraham has behaved badly: 'Things that should not be done you have done to me' (20:9). When Abraham finally responds (to the king's first challenge he remains silent, as though at a loss for words), he spells out his fears in the following language: 'For I thought, surely there is no fear of God in this place, and they will kill me for my wife' (20:11). Abraham, in other words, assumes that Gerar is another Sodom, while Abimelech's behavior demonstrates that the contrary is true. The issue of judge and justice first raised in chapter 18 is here seen to involve a shifting interplay of peoples and performance, with by no means all instances of justice set up on the side of Abraham and his seed. For this reason, the livestock and slaves that Abraham acquires in Egypt seem to accrue to him almost without an agency except the divine one (Gen. 12:16), whereas here we witness Abimelech both performing and announcing acts of munificence, and adding, to boot, a thousand pieces of silver to the livestock and slaves.

There is one final way in which the Gerar story diverges from the Egypt story that most vividly illustrates how carefully the latter episode has been placed in the surrounding narrative configuration. Of Pharaoh we are told that the Lord afflicted him and his household with 'great plagues' (*nega'im*). The nature of these plagues is not specified, but surely the term is used to heighten the effect of foreshadowing in Genesis 12, which looks forward far more directly than does Genesis 20 to a time when Abraham's descendants, once more threatened with starvation, will sojourn in Egypt and will need God to heap plagues on Pharaoh and his people in order to obtain their release from enslavement. In Gerar, on the other hand, we are first told not of plagues but only of a death-threat by God – significantly, a threat not only to Abimelech but to his entire household, or perhaps his entire people – which, as I have indicated, aligns the story with the destruction of Sodom. Then, at the very end of the episode, it is revealed that Abimelech and his whole palace have in fact also been suffering from an affliction ever since Sarah entered the harem, an affliction of a specified character: 'For the Lord had closed fast every womb in the household of Abimelech because of Sarah, Abraham's wife' (20:18). The very next words in the text – we should keep in mind that in the ancient scroll there would have been no indication of the chapter-break introduced by a much later tradition – are, 'and the Lord remembered Sarah as he had promised'. Indeed, given the perfect tense of the verb and the reversal of the usual predicate–subject order, the actual implication of the statement, within the paratactic constraints of biblical Hebrew, is something like: But in contrast, God remembered Sarah as he had promised.

Propagation appears at the beginning of Genesis as a divinely ordained imperative for humanity. But as the moral plot of human history rapidly thickens into the most terrible twists of violence and perversion, it becomes progressively clear that propagation and survival are precarious matters, conditional, in the view of the Hebrew writers, on moral behavior. This idea is first manifested on a global scale in the Deluge story, and we have seen why the writer feels it is important to invoke the Deluge in his representation of the aftermath of Sodom. Precisely because of the biblical writer's sense of history as an arena fraught with danger, it would be too simple, too smooth, for the narrative of the founding father to proceed uninterrupted from divine promise to the initiation of the covenanted people through the birth of a son. Unusual shadows must be cast over the way to fulfillment. The first of these is biological: the extreme old age of the patriarch and, especially, of the matriarch, which has no equivalent in any of the other annunciation type-scenes. Beyond that, the three intervening episodes of the destruction of Sodom, the act of incest between Lot and his daughters, and the sojourn in Gerar convey to us an urgent new sense of perilous history which is the thematically needed prelude to the birth of Abraham's son. As the biblical imagination conceives it, neither national existence nor the physical act of propagation itself can be taken for granted. A society that rejects the moral bonds of civilization for the instant gratification of dark urges can be swept away in a moment; the elemental desire for survival in a seemingly desolate world may drive people to desperate means, to a kind of grim parody of the primeval command to be fruitful and multiply; the very danger of illicit sexuality may blight a kingdom with sterility, until the favored man intercedes, the near violation of the stranger woman is transformed into princely reparation, and the innocent intentions of the afflicted man are publicly recognized. The historical scene Isaac is about to enter is indeed a checkered one, and he and his offspring will have troubles enough of their own, in regard to both moral performance and physical survival.

As to the larger unfolding design of biblical literature, Sodom, firmly lodged between the enunciation of the covenantal promise and its fulfillment, becomes the great monitory model, the myth of a terrible collective destiny antithetical to Israel's. The biblical writers will rarely lose sight of the ghastly possibility that Israel can turn itself into Sodom. When Isaiah, having begun his prophecy by mordantly referring to Israel as 'sons' who have betrayed their father, goes on to liken the people to Sodom and Gomorrah, we are meant, I think, to recall the full tension of interplay between Genesis 19 and Genesis 17–18. Still more shockingly, when the author of Judges 19 wants to represent in the Benjaminites at Gibeah a wholly depraved society, he adopts a strategy of elaborate allusion, borrowing not only the narrative predicament of two strangers taken in by the only hospitable inhabitant of a violently hostile town but also reproducing nearly verbatim whole sequences of narratorial phrases and dialogue from Genesis 19. Here the host has but one virgin daughter to offer to the mob in place of the demanded male visitor, and so he makes up the tally of two proffered women by adding the visitor's concubine. This being a version of Sodom without divine intervention, the denouement is grimmer. The visitor is no angel in any sense of the term, and instead of striking the assailants with blindness, he thrusts his concubine out into the street where she is gang-raped all night long. At daybreak he finds her expiring on the threshold, and compounding the real act of mayhem with a symbolic one, he hacks her body into twelve pieces, which he sends to the tribes of Israel in order to rally them against Benjamin. As we might expect, the writer has drawn from the Sodom story not only the grisly plot but also its principal thematic ramifications. The Gibeah story, like that of Sodom[3] is prefaced by two hospitality episodes; the lavish and finally importunate hospitality of the concubine's father to the estranged couple, and then the ill-fated hospitality of the old man – like Lot, not a native of the place but a resident alien – at Gibeah. The depravity of the town results in its destruction, not through supernatural means but in a bloody civil war (Judg. 20). And here, too, what is finally at issue is the survival of the group. Thus we have the peculiar story in Judges 21 of the tribes of Israel taking a vow not to give their daughters in marriage to the Benjaminites, which places the latter in the male equivalent of the plight of Lot's daughters, who fear 'there is no man on earth to lie with us'. The tribes then regret their vow, fearing that 'a tribe of Israel will be cut off', and so they are compelled to devise two rather bizarre stratagems, the first a violent one, for providing the Benjaminites brides. One is not sure whether the very end of the Lot story, in which taboo copulation produces ambiguous offspring, is meant to be part of the pattern of allusion. In any case, this extraordinary instance of Sodom *redux*, where pervasive vicious-ness triggers an upheaval that calls a people's futurity into question, provides a fitting conclusion to the Book of Judges as an account of the chaotic period when 'there was no king in Israel, each man did what was right in his own eyes'.

What may be inferred from the example of Sodom about the way the various pieces, small and large, of biblical narrative fit together? The tendency of more than a century of scholarly analysis has been powerfully atomistic, encouraging us to imagine the Bible as a grand jumble of the most disparate and often contradictory materials. In strictly literary terms, this is a conclusion that simply does not hold up under a close inspection of the sundry texts and their interconnections. There are, of course, elements of overlap and incongruity between different texts; but one should not mistake every allusion or recurrence of a convention for a stammer of ancient transmission, and what is often called a 'contradiction' may prove to be either the imposition of provincially modern norms of consistency or, as in the case of the sister-bride story, may be an inconsistency deemed secondary by the writer to the primary concern of thematic composition. In the foregoing discussion, I have edged away from the term 'structure' because it may suggest an architectural solidity and symmetry not entirely characteristic of biblical narrative. *Tom Jones* is a book that pre-eminently has a structure; I doubt if one could say the same of the Book of Genesis, not to speak of the larger narrative sequence that runs from Genesis to the end of Kings. Nevertheless, the way the Sodom episode reaches back multifariously into the Abraham narrative, and further still to the Deluge and ultimately the creation story, and forward to the future history of Israel, suggests that there is elaborate if irregular design in this large complex of stories. It might be better to think of it less as structure than as finely patterned texture, in which seemingly disparate pieces are woven together, with juxtaposed segments producing among them a pattern that will be repeated elsewhere with complicated variations.

Perhaps it could not have been otherwise for the Hebrew writers. Historical and moral reality was in their sense of it too untidy, too quirky, too precipitously changeable, to lend itself to the schematism of a highly defined structure. At the same time, there was nothing purely fortuitous, nothing intrinsically episodic, in reality: everything, however perplexing, was ultimately linked to everything else in the large movement of God's purpose through the difficult medium of history. Let me suggest that this tension between the baffling untidiness of the surface and deep design is worked out formally in the very texture of biblical narrative in the way each of its seemingly discrete units is tied in to what goes before and after. It is easy enough to admire the artistry of biblical narrative within the limits of an episode, and much keen analysis in recent years has been devoted to just that task. But it is equally important to see how the episode is purposefully woven into larger patterns of motifs, symbols, and themes, keywords, key phrases, and plots, for otherwise we are likely to under-read the individual episodes and grasp at best imperfectly the broader horizon of meaning towards which the biblical writers mean to lead us.

SUMMARY: THE SODOM NEXUS IN GENESIS

Chapter 17	Covenantal promise of seed to Abraham (patriarchal)
	Abraham laughs
	Commandment of circumcision
Chapter 18	(a) Annunciation type-scene-promise of seed (matriarchal)
	Sarah laughs
	Sarah after menopause
	bridge: 'looking down' on Sodom
	(b) Covenantal promise to Abraham with moral stipulation ('to do what is right and just')
	(c) Abraham bargains over Sodom and Gomorrah, expecting God to 'do what is just'.
Chapter 19	(a) The destruction of the Cities of the Plain
	closure: Abraham 'looks down' on Sodom
	(b) Incest between Lot and his daughters
Chapter 20	Abraham and Sarah in Gerar
Chapter 21:1–7	The birth of Isaac

NOTES

1 I have followed out this particular type-scene in 'How Convention Helps Us Read: The Case of the Bible's Annunciation Type-Scene', *Prooftexts*, 3/2 (May 1983), pp. 115–30. I first proposed the concept of type-scenes as a component of biblical narrative in *The Art of Biblical Narrative* (Basic Books, New York, 1981), ch. 3.

2 J. P. Fokkelman provides an excellent discussion on progeny and survival as organizing themes of Genesis in his article on that book in *The Harvard Literary Guide to the Bible*, ed. Robert Alter and Frank Kermode (Harvard University Press, Cambridge, Mass., 1987).

3 I was first alerted to the fact that the hospitality episode of Genesis 18 is part of the pattern of allusion through an astute seminar paper by Nitza Kreichman.

6

The Keeping of Nahor: The Etiology of Biblical Election

James Norhnberg

In the beginning was the end: the beginning with which Genesis ends is the death of Patriarch, who has just become Ephraim's godfather. Conversely, the end with which Genesis begins is the spiritualizing of the forefather as the forefather's god, and the forefather's god as the creator of fathers. The blessing of the son by his father confirms the original paternal donation of being to the son, through the mother's insemination. But blessed in having sons, the blessing upon the parents is again from God. And from the sons: for sons can bless the father when they invoke God's blessing on the father for his having been their father. 'Thank God for the iron in the blood of our fathers,' said Teddy Roosevelt. The sons of Abraham, Abraham is promised, will thank Abraham for the Abraham in the blood of their fathers. Abraham can count his chickens before they are hatched, because when they are they will thank their lucky stars that it all started with Abraham.

In blessing Isaac, God honors his promises to Abraham, and Abraham's faith in the promises. God also honors his blessing of the creation, for Abraham is blessed with the original blessing of fertility. Echoes of this blessing are heard upon the departing of Rebekah for her marriage, and at the contracting of Boaz for Ruth. Thanks to this blessing Terah through Rebekah can become Perez in Ruth's blessing, and Salmon can become Solomon through Ruth. Ruth's blessing also invokes Rachel, the strongest biblical example of God's will to greatly multiply pain in childbirth and difficulty in conception. Population explosions and the attempt to contain them also revert to curses in the Bible: the cursing of fertility in the story of Noah's Flood and the plaguing of fertility at the beginning of the Exodus show that the generative beginning is dialectically entailed with a genocidal beginning. As a result, the pedigree of survival generally begins with interruption or sterility.

By the time Genesis ends, the family of Jacob is delivered out of the evil of their not being able to keep each other, but is delivered into the evil of their being a people in the midst of another people. Thus the Joseph-*roman* begins from the setting apart of a people genealogically, but the story does not properly end until that people is set apart ethnographically, as the people who celebrate the Passover. The question is, how is this end present in the beginning? In the beginning, the human subject is portrayed as acting somewhat in the dark. Laban, for example, gives Jacob his bride in the dark: come the dawn, she is not Rachel, but Leah. Laban explains that where he comes from the older daughter is given in marriage before the younger, and thus he convicts Jacob of a certain ignorance as to where he is, and where his future lies. Jacob's kidnap attempt upon the principles of primogeniture has apparently not gone unnoticed in more conservative family circles. God sees where man does not, yet the sense that one has been seen by a transcendental observer allows one to see better. That insight will prevail appears from the beginning: both Genesis and Exodus begin with a furtive human subject coming to this incriminating knowledge of having been seen at the outset.

Jacob is kept in the dark on a general principle of Genesis. The same principle imposes drunkenness on Lot when his daughters recruit his seed in a cave; imposes disbelief on Abraham and Sarah at the annunciation of Isaac; imposes a veil on Rebekah as she approaches Isaac; imposes a disguise on Tamar when she recruits the seed of Judah as a prostitute. Jacob's services as a husband are bought by Laban for his older daughter, and Jacob's services as an inseminator are bought by Leah and sold by Rachel behind his back. Jacob is deprived of his favorite sons by other sons with whom terrible things seem to happen away from home; these sons in turn become hostages to Joseph's secret knowledge of them. Only when Jacob blesses Ephraim is the Patriarchal transactor of a vital transaction able to assert that he knows, in his blindness, what he is doing. The seed of bequeathal is passed in the dark, and so are the bequeathals themselves. Abraham must commission and trust his servant to arrange Isaac's marriage. Isaac can hear but cannot see that he is blessing Jacob in place of Esau: he consents not to know, and in this consent we may discern an inferior kind of Abrahamic faith that God will provide the sacrifice – the sacrifices that Abraham has already made of Ishmael, and that Isaac is now making of Esau.

Nonetheless, if Genesis is a revelation, it is the revelation of kinship. God is the author of all knowledge, and so we may ask what knowledge is it which God authorizes in the knowledge inscribed in the genealogies in Genesis.

Adam takes as his wife a woman who is, ontogenetically speaking, his daughter; consanguineously speaking, she is his sister; nominally speaking, she is the mother of all living. When Adam and his wife see as the immortal gods see, with their eyes open, what they see is their nakedness before each other. If the nakedness is that of kin, the thing telling them they are naked is the incest taboo. In cohabiting with his wife, Adam has been cohabiting with his kin – not only his kind, but his own flesh. The embarrassment of the sexual relation is that its intimacy is otherwise familial; vice versa, the embarrassment of the familial relation is that its intimacy is otherwise sexual. Joseph accuses his brothers of being outlanders spying on the nakedness of Egypt, but it is Joseph in the disguise of an Egyptian who is spying on the nakedness of his brothers. The indecency of doubled intimacy attaches to the second Adam too: Noah's nakedness is looked upon by a kinsman whose name makes him a distinct race, so Ham's encounter with his father's nakedness suggests a violation of the incest taboo as a violation of the miscegenation taboo. The same thing is suggested when Lot is slept with by his two daughters, who conceive sons named for two racially distinct peoples.

Within the Patriarchal saga itself, Abraham twice alleges his wife to be his sister, and his son Isaac does this once again. Isaac also marries his cousin, or his cousin's daughter, and Jacob does this twice again. In the next generation, Reuben sleeps with his father's second wife's maid, and thus symbolically violates intra-tribal cohesion, while insulting the handmaid tribes, as the Shechemites insult the sons of Jacob in the rape of Dinah. Tamar sleeps with her father-in-law to preserve this same intra-tribal genetic cohesion that Reuben violates. Figure 6.1 shows the yin and yang of intimacy and relatedness as distributed across the text, and as centered on endogamous relations. Is there a theme here?

Man's first recorded words in the Bible affirm his kinship with the first woman, and man's first question is a smart answer to God's question about the whereabouts of his kin. 'I am looking for my brothers,' Joseph will explain to an anonymous interlocutor at the outset of an ordeal that will ultimately vindicate a search for the relations that Cain initially sacrificed. While genealogical research may not be what the narrator who planted the speech has in mind, just such research is wished upon Abraham's ambassador at the heart of the tale I have to tell.

The genealogical imperative has two sides: the imperative to increase and multiply, to marry and give in marriage; and the

Table 6.1 Familial and sexual intimacy and integrity across Genesis

	Pre-patriarchal	Abraham period	Isaac period	Jacob period	Post-patriarchal
Incestuous congress or exposure	Adam/Eve	Lot/Daughters			Reuben/Bilah
	Noah/Ham				Joseph/Brothers
Wife alleged to be spouse's sister		Abram/Sarah			
		Abram/Sara	Isaac/Rebekah		
Parallel cousin marriage			Isaac/Rebekah	Jacob/Leah	
				Jacob/Rachel	
Family's genetic integrity kept	Adamic Sethites Noachic Shemites	Nahorites (1): Milcah/Nahor	Terahites	Nahorites (II)	Israelites Dinah/Brothers Judahites: Tamar/Judah

imperative to divide and incorporate and become genetically distinct. Patriarchal endogamy and polygamy express the same imperatives, even while they form a double mean between extremes of incest and promiscuity, or exclusive and inclusive unions. Thus Rebekah is defined as both a near and distant relative of Isaac's, owing to his marriage being both conservative, from his point of view, and innovative, from hers. Again, Adam found no mate among the beasts, and avoided sodomy; he married his own flesh only after God had set it apart, and avoided incest. He adopts Eve as his honorary kinswoman, without knowing anything about sisters and daughters. He is like the Abraham of modern scholarship, who invokes the Hurrian code allowing brother–sister marriages without knowing anything about it. How could he? His lie would not be very useful, if it continued to expose him as a man with a dangerously attractive wife, rather than an eligible sister.

Abraham's election brackets the fate of Sodom, precisely because he is elected as a Patriarch. Incest and sodomy, the two extremes pulling on the life of Lot, presume the same indistinction in sexual partnering. The fertility of incest and of promiscuity alike destroy the knowledge of relations, of who is who. As a father, Lot has not arranged his daughter's marriages, as Abraham has arranged Isaac's. Abraham protects Lot, but he cannot do for him what Nahor has done for Milcah – he has no marriage to offer Lot. Lot has chosen only Sodomites for his daughters, infertile by custom and by such a custom foreign and unadoptable. The sons-in-law do not survive Sodom's fate. Lot offers his women, the Sodomites refuse: both act toward extinction.

Lot's daughters lie with Lot in a cave, the place where one sleeps with one's father. But you only sleep with your closest kin in accouchement with the unmarriageable Hittites, even while he is arranging for his son's *non*-Hittite marriage. The episode that ends when Isaac goes to bed with Rebekah in his tent begins when Abraham buries Sarah in his cave: here is where father and son will lie together when they are dead. When you are sleeping with your kin, they've become your kind. In Lot's case, the process is condensed, so Lot's daughters bear the tribes Moab and Ammon. Lot has been assimilated no less than if he had stayed in Sodom – he is as bereft of paternity as his wife is of fertility. Abraham's story begins with a dislocated father and a barren wife, which is where Lot's story ends. Lot chose a place to live like the Garden for fertility, but his wife becomes, like Milton's displaced paradise, a stranded island, salt and bare.

The incest of Lot's daughters issues in tribes without patrilinearity: the tribal group in which the father is unknown. The Moabites and Ammonites know Moab and Ammon, not Lot. Ham's voyeurism also violates the primal scene of his own begetting, in effect, in that Ham thereby begets the ethnicity of the Canaanite who lacks the inhibitions in question and is thereby cursed. In Sodom, it is not even the father who is not known, but the sex itself – anyone will do, strangers are desirable.

The alternative choice of marriage begins in Adam. Adam is endowed with the power of appraisal exercised in giving things names. Man thus begins not so much the master of language, as the master of taxonomy. He recognizes his own flesh. All flesh is not the same flesh, the ox is forbidden to plow with the ass. The wife, however, shares with man cognate flesh, and the man embraces the wife with an affirmation of their kinship – 'flesh of my flesh'. This affirmation is directly insulated from its incestuous consequences by the non-sequitur, 'Thus does a man leave his father and mother and cleave unto his woman.' Marriage is thus said to be fleshly, but not shameful. Adam and Eve's nakedness before each other does not shame them, so their being one flesh does not constitute an unlawful or impure intimacy between kin that confuses spouse and blood. But since no fit partner was found for man among the beasts, his marriage is endogamous with respect to the species. It is not a miscegenous compounding of two kinds of flesh, unlike the 'one flesh' of Sodom, where anal is confounded with genital.

Though 'bone of my bone' sounds traditional – as if the story were invented to explain the utterance aetiologically – it is really the other way round: the phrases reconstruct the traditional context, which is an appeal to clan loyalty. The text transforms a kinship formula into a betrothal formula, as must happen whenever a man finds his mate outside his immediate family. Adam is an exception, but his sleep has been deep enough for him not to know this entirely. It is less like the deep sleep of Abraham than the drunkenness of Lot.

The phrasing 'These are the generations of . . .' indicates a general historiographic purpose of Genesis, that of recording lineage that either claims such-and-such a descendant for a given ancestor, or such-and-such an ancestor for a given descendant. Genealogies lead up to the stories of important characters, and issue from them. The stories exist to introduce the genealogies, as much as the genealogies to introduce the stories. An example inspired by this precedent is the genealogy of Elkanah that begins I Samuel, where the barrenness of Elkanah's first-named wife brings six generations of Ephraimite history to a halt. Thus the list reaching back to Ephraim has been generated out of the very rebukes to Hannah's infertility which are the initiatory grievance of the story proper. The subsequent annunciation to Hannah sounds in the ignorant priest's very question, 'How long?' The genealogist wants to know, how long is Elkanah's line; the priest wants to know how long the woman will be in disgrace; the woman wants to know how long she will be barren; and the kind of prophecy born with the kingship inaugurated by her son wants to know how long God will delay his visitation. The priest calls the woman a daughter of Belial; the narrator calls the degenerate priesthood the sons of Belial. The question is, how long will the sons of Belial occupy the priestly office, and the answer is, until the newly elected son of Hannah is installed in their place. This is an example of how the genealogy stretches into the story, and the story out of the genealogy.

Election is choice, and in choosing Sarah, Abraham has chosen the right son. In getting born so late, Isaac has chosen the right father, in that only Abraham, with God's help, can have been that father. Pharaoh and sheik might have slept with Sarah once, but not by the time Isaac is being sired. The scorn the parents conceive for the notion of their parenthood provides the derivation of their son's name. Rachel weeps over her children who were not, Sarah laughs, but it is the same dissent against barrenness. Anything is possible with God, Sarah is warned; it is *nothing* that is apparently impossible with him. Thus the genealogy from Abraham also leads back to the creation: because anything is possible with God, and nothing is not.

The unfairness of election can be reduced to our objections to our contingent, filial status: our parent may choose to sacrifice parenting to some other dictate, as Abraham is about to do on Mount Moriah;

our parent may be chosen for us, as Abraham chooses Rebekah to the ultimate diselection of Esau; our sibling may be chosen over us, as Joseph is chosen over his brothers, even though his brothers did not choose not to have Rachel for their mother. The narrative privileges choice, especially marriage-choice, even while disallowing much of it to the individual. Families make choices, and when the Israelite looks at his Edomite twin, he necessarily says, 'There but for the grace of God go *we*.' Yet Jacob clearly succeeds in choosing himself, against the odds, and thus he stands for the Deuteronomistic idea of conversion, the choice one can make to help one's self to favor. But the election of life is seldom simple. Choosing the life of obedience causes Abraham to hazard the life of Isaac. Seeking merely to survive causes Esau to give up the right to the life he was heir to.

Since a given place in a genealogy depends on either a distinguished ancestor or descendant, the most important place in the Patriarchal genealogy belongs to Isaac, since the most important places in the Patriarchal narrative are occupied by his father and his son. The human election of Isaac particularly appears when Abraham selects to breed his stock with his brother Nahor's. Abraham has pre-chosen the uniqueness of his son by abiding with the barren Sarah, and he pre-chooses his descendants when he commissions his servant to seek out his relatives. When Isaac at his sacrifice called upon his father, he bespoke or chose his father *as* his father, recalling him to the name with which Abraham has been renamed, when formerly choosing for Ishmael. Through circumcision Abraham chooses an ethnological election for Ishmael; but, in circumcising himself as well, out of ethnic solidarity with Ishmael, Abraham procures a genetic election for the unborn Isaac. Ishmael is circumcised so that his genetic election can be sacrificed for that of Isaac.

Isaac's claim upon his father is also put into the mouth of both the distraught Esau and the dissembling Jacob. But Jacob uses one father (Isaac), to claim another – Abraham. Esau has as much right to the patrilineal identity as Jacob, but Jacob claims the *Patriarchal* identity by acquiring its established ethnographic feature, the vocation of shepherding, and its established dynastic feature, the favor of the mother. Choosing the one Rebekah has chosen, Jacob repeats Rebekah's choice of Abraham for a father-in-law, when she elected to remove from Mesopotamia and so to follow in her father-in-law's own footsteps.

Isaac's own identity-in-trust is compounded from the fatherhood of Abraham and the sonship of Jacob and Esau. Having Abraham as his father means that Isaac is not blessed or chosen in his own right, and having Jacob as his son means that Isaac will not be able to bless or choose in his own right. Isaac is a means for Abraham to recover the people he has lost in his remove from Mesopotamia. And Isaac is a means for Jacob to recover whatever of Abraham that he has lost to Esau, just as Laban is a means for Jacob to recover whatever of Nahor I Abraham has left with Nahor II. Isaac is the weak link between a strong father and a strong son: through Isaac passes the identity of those widely distributed peoples who call Abraham their father, into the identity of those who call themselves the sons of Jacob. 'These are the generations of Isaac', the text says, by which it means Abraham and Jacob.

Typically, 'These are the generations of . . .' produces the generations from a human progenitor. This is not the case in the first instance, the generations of the heavens and earth. But the creation is anything but a spontaneous natural generation, a *genesis*. The Bible takes huge exception to the pagan creation myth, the myth of genesis, where the congress of heaven and earth generates the gods, or where the gods generate monsters. ('Let us make monsters,' Tiamat says; but she doesn't make them, she generates them.) The miscegenous sons of god who come unto the daughters of men provoke the Flood in which the waters below and the waters above merge not only two texts, but confound what the original creation distinguished and drown the species. (In Milton these waters seem to generate monsters.) The pagan or ontogenetic explanation for the creation is fossilized in the single expression in question. Otherwise, the heavens and earth are the virtual antithesis of the darkness and the deep facing it – the barreness or nothing that is the one thing impossible with the creator. God's intervention in the barrenness of Sarah has the most awesome precedent in God's original mercy to non-entity.

The phrase recapitulating God's creation is paralleled by a re-beginning of the narration:

> These are the generations of the heaven and earth when
> they were created
> In the day Yhwh God made earth and heavens . . . (Gen. 2:4)

Similarly:

> When Terah was seventy years old he became the father of
> Abram, Nahor and Haran.
> These are Terah's descendants: Terah became the father of
> Abram, Nahor and Haran. (Gen. 11:26–27)

Again:

> This is the story of Isaac son of Abraham.
> Abraham was the father of Isaac. (Gen. 25:19)

Thus the phrase is like a genealogy itself, for it bridges a hiatus, between terminus and origin, or origin and derivative, between the Israel that dies with one generation in the wilderness and the Israel that is born with another generation in the wilderness, between fatherhood in Abraham and sonship in Jacob. In this way every genealogy is an abridgement of barrenness, while barrenness is the resisting medium in which the growth of genealogy takes place. Biblical story-telling begins by establishing its characters and their names genealogically, from circumstances of birth, habitus, fatherland or ancestry. And the story that typically begins from an interrupted genealogy or succession typically ends upon a restored one. The genealogies tell the rest of the story, the stories tell the rest of the genealogy. Story and generations are the same Hebrew word in these contexts. Placed in an initial or terminal position, the word is neither wholly initiatory nor conclusive: it is interconnective, like shifting gears. As Fig 6.1 shows, the phrase usually bridges a more serial, chronographic, patrilineal accounting and a more ethnographic, parabolic, sociological, aetiological account. These accountings prove to be two ways of accounting for inherited or adopted identity.

Figure 6.1 'These are the generations of . . .'

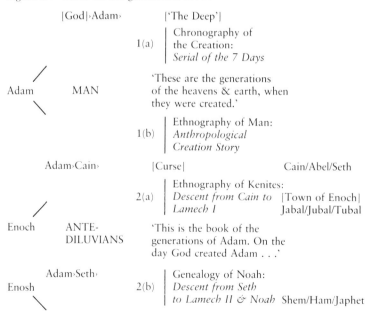

Figure 6.1 'These are the generations of . . .'

cont.

Fig. 6.1 cont.

```
. . . Lamech Il›Noah›      'These are the
                           heroes of old, the
                           men of renown.

                               |Flood|

                               'These are the clans of Noah's
                               sons, according to their
                               generations.'

                                       |   Ethnography of the Nations:
                                 3(a)  |   Table of Nations
                                       |   Semites/Hamites/Javanites   |Town: Babel|
        /      POST-              |Tower of Babel|
Heber          DILUVIANS         'These are the generations
        \                        of Shem . . .'

                                       |   Genealogy of Terah:
                                 3(b)  |   Descent from Shem
                                       |   to Nahor & Terah     |Towns: Ur, Haran|

. . . Nahor›Terah›         'These are the generations
Nahor                      of Terah: Terah became
                           the father of Abram . . .'

                               |Emigration to Canaan|

                                       |   Ethnography/Genealogy of Abram's Issue:
                                 4(a)  |   The Story of Abram
                                       |   and his Wives and Sons
                                       |                    Ishmael/Isaac/Keturahites
        /                        'This is the story of Isaac son of
Isaac        PATRIARCHS          Abraham; Abraham was
        \                        the father of Isaac . . .'

                                       |   Ethnography/Genealogy of Nahorites:
                                 4(b)  |   The Story of Jacob        Leah/Rachel/Handmaid
                                       |   and Esau and Laban        Tribes

                               |Sojourn in the East|

                           'These are the generations of Jacob.
. . . Esau}/               Joseph was 17 years old.'
Jacob}/›Judah›/{Perez ›
›{/Zerah                               |  'Roman morale' of Jacob's Issue:
                                 5(a)  |   The Story of Joseph
                                       |   and his Brothers

                               |Immigration into Egypt|

        /                        'These are the names of
Joseph,      EGYPTIANIZED     the sons of Israel who went with
Remains      ISRAELITES       Jacob into Egypt, each with his family. . .'
of
        \                              |   Census/Chronology/Liturgy of Israel:
                                 5(b)  |   Story of the Calling
                                       |   of Israel from Egypt

. . . Jacob›12 sons›'Israel'   |Exodus|
```

The gear-change comes between two kinds of genealogy, which issue in two kinds of identity: patrilineal, and ethnic. 'This is the account of the generations of Adam' comes between the descent from Cain to Lamech I and the descent from Seth to Lamech II. Lamech I issues in three sons with three different vocations: this is ethnographic. Lamech II issues in Noah, who is defined genealogically, for he is announced, born, and named prophetically. Noah in turn issues in Shem, Ham, and Japheth, and so fathers the subsequent table of nations, which is again ethnographic. The Cain-ite Lamech becomes the father of clans; hence we learn the names of Lamech's wives, who are catechized in the clan policy regarding vengeance. Lamech is descended from Cain, who was both obliged to avenge a brother's murder, and to live in fear of his life for want of a brother to avenge his own. The mark God gives Cain confers on him the benefits of clan-membership, and gives him an invisible clansman. Cain foregoes territorial identifications only intermittently: having been a sedentary farmer, he becomes a borderlands wanderer, yet his list begins from his city-founding in the name of his son. The Cain-ite list, ending on itinerant vocations, observes Cain's own pattern, going from settlement to nomadism, and from genetic affiliation to ethnological incorporation.

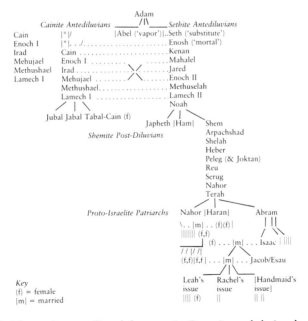

Figure 6.2 The major patrilineal descents in Genesis, and their ethnographic tripartition at the locus of epochal displacement and re-origination.

The patrilineal Sethite genealogy is introduced by the generation of Seth and Enosh – as Chronicles starts out, 'Adam Seth Enosh'. Calling on the name of Yhwh, Enosh calls on a greater kinsman than Adah and Zillah can invoke, and in Seth a new man is substituted for a mortal one – the Sethite list ends in the new man Noah and his three sons being substituted for Lamech I and his three. The second list answers to a prayer of the second Lamech for a deliverer, rather than an avenger. Noah is one who might raise up seed to the mortalized and bereaved race itself.

In both lists the issue is survival. God favors Abel, and hears his blood crying from the ground as a loyal kinsman might be expected to do. God does not kill Cain, however; he protects the remaining member of Abel's family. He becomes Cain's adoptive kinsman, and protects Cain from the vengeance he's owed. With God's protection, Cain can carry out half his obligations to Abel, to raise up sons to Abel's remaining family. Cain's line produces cattle-keepers, who may be named after Cain, but who take after Abel. Seth, likewise, preserves Adam's image but substitutes for Abel. His descendant Noah reverts to dressing gardens and thus takes after Cain. The intervention of God and the quasi-adoptive switch from one brother to another have preserved the life of both lines. The archival impulse is to preserve the evidence that has survived, but the genealogical impulse is to preserve the evidence of *having* survived.

Ethnographic diversification tends to be terminal for patrilineal descent. A line ends and must be rebegun when it is fissioned into three. Adam has three sons, and one dies. Noah has three sons, and one sins and is cursed. Jacob has twelve sons, and one third of them are handmaid tribes. From such triformation ethnographic identity emerges and appears in the ethnographic lists: the three Cain-ite tribes of Lamech I; the Semetic, Hamitic and Ionian strands from Noah; and the Ishmaelite, Hebrew and Keturahite strands from Abraham. The ethnographic refrain is the geographical dispersal and linguistic and tribal differentiation of the peoples. The patrilineal refrain is 'After the birth of heir Y, father X lived n years, and became the father of nameless sons and daughters.' Once the names of the sons are multiplied, patrilinearity divides and is subsequently refocused on one of the sons. This brings the second patrilineal list to Terah's issue Abram, Nahor and Haran. Like Abel, one of Terah's three sons dies, and like Cain and Seth, the lines of the two survivors run mysteriously parallel, yet with one line seeming to be more ethnic, conservative, clannish and territorial than the other.

The localizations in the ethnographic genealogies contrast with the narrower, patrilineal pedigree of survival, which mentions a native land only terminally. The only land Abraham owns is his grave. The diselect typically settle or are settled before their elect counterparts. The narrative supplementing the Shemite genealogy of Terah comes up against the death of Haran in the presence of his father in the city of Ur. Terah's remove from here implies his dividing from the hegemonic minded Babelians of a preceding narrative. There seem to be two ways to preserve the patrilineal identity from absorption into a national one: emigration, and in-house marriage – endogamy. Neither works alone. Endogamy by itself leads to an extended tribal family that dissolves patrilinearity. Removal from this family, by itself, leads to alone-ness, rootlessness, dependency and loss of identity in another nation's cities – the deracination of the rootless cosmopolitan and the sterilization of the displaced person: Lot's wife outside Sodom. Where biblical election favors one genetic sharer over the other, the less elect are fissioned off from the genetic stock, and settled down or pensioned off with an ethnographic identity that may be racial, vocational or territorial, but is not cultic or ideological.

The narrative shows Abraham escaping the fates of Lot and his wife, and achieving patrilineal election, through the emergence of that great sustainer of narrative, the family. We know the family is suddenly present, because there are two families there that work to define it. For the first time daughters are named as well as sons: they are *marriageable* daughters, for there can be no family without another family – wives in one are sisters in the other. The exception proves the rule, for Adam's family contains both the old consanguineous family of which Eve is the daughter, and the new nuclear family formed when he takes Eve for his wife. Nahor's and Abraham's families are each 90 degrees from Adam's endogamous nuclear family, but 180 degrees from each other. Nahor's extended family is endogamous, Abraham's nuclear family is exogamous. (An extended exogamous family belongs to the Jesus who tells his mother that his disciples are his family.)

Abraham keeps his family together by keeping it small; Nahor keeps his family together by keeping it consanguineous. The two kinds of family coherence are united by the marriage of Isaac, but not before they are divided by the migration of Terah. For election to pass from those who call Abraham their father, to those who call themselves the sons of Jacob, there must be an intermediate stage whereby the mechanism for generating filial relations is itself privileged. Through marriage, family, and the genealogy of the family network, election is transferred from the patrilineal to the ethnographic pole of genealogy. Hence the paradox that in Genesis family members share blood, genetically, but divide occupations, ethnographically.

The stories make relatives out of farmer and herdsman, settler and sojourner, nomad and migrant, hunter and rancher, trader and local, shepherd and agriculturalist. These relations seem symbiotic, since the relatives may depend on each other to survive. There is not a particular, elect occupation, yet there may be a more successful or reliable one at a given time. Farming is less successful for Cain than herding for Abel, hunting less successful for Esau than ranching for Jacob. With the dialectic of vocations also goes a dialectic of abroadness and landedness. The result is an elect mean between extremes, between pure nomadism and pure territorial conquest, or between occupational extremes. Noah makes farming successful, but he also pens animals in the ark and becomes a meat-eater; he is forbidden blood, even while the appetite for vengeance is rationalized and sanctioned, and wine is added to his diet. Abel's herding seems a mean between Cain's farming, nomadism, and city-building. Abraham's highland flock-keeping seems a mean between Lot's lowland settlement and his subsequent status as a refugee in a cave. Isaac's pastoral occupation seems a mean between hunting in the wilderness and bedouin federations – both linked to Ishmael. Jacob's stock-breeding and domesticity seem a mean between Esau's hunting in the field and his lordship in Edom.

While the ethnographic genealogies lateralize descent over space, the patrilineal genealogies elongate it over time. Ethnographic lists divide descent among siblings, while the patrilineal pedigrees prioritize it according to first-bornness. The second-born on the patrilineal lists seem to be born ages later – they are an afterthought like the sons of Abraham by Keturah. In the opposite case, the first-born would be twins, and first-bornness would be up for grabs. This development signals the shift towards a predominantly ethnographic identity, which is otherwise announced by the shift from the name Jacob to that of Israel. Esau's defeat is understood ethnographically. He surrenders his pedigree or birthright because of economic constraint: the hunter who finds no game must have recourse to the stock-breeder. The red pottage Esau consumes may be an agricultural product, for all I know, but it might also have been made with the red blood that Noahide law already forbade eating – the almost magical revival of the famished Esau looks suspicious, and hunting implies a taste for bloodshed. Jacob wins the blessing from Isaac in exchange for wild meat that will generally be deemed inedible in Israel, even if it is typical that the herder, unlike the hunter, can procure meat upon demand. The climactic example of patrilineal identity being exchanged for ethnographic identity also involves dietary differentiation. Jacob's wrestling partner at Peniel blesses Jacob with the new name Israel in exchange for wholeness. With the new name comes the single-most ethnographic aetiology in all of Genesis:

So Jacob called the place Peniel, saying, 'It is because I saw God face to face, and yet my life was spared.' The sun rose above him as he passed Peniel, and he was limping because of his hip. Therefore to this day the Israelites do not eat the tendon attached to the socket of the hip, because the socket of Jacob's hip was touched near the tendon. (Gen. 32:30–32)

For whatever reason Jacob was spared, Israel survives because the Israelite has preserved his cultural identity by such means as are recorded here. The apparently supplemental gloss on the story proves to be the very thing that makes the telling of it possible, for there must first be an Israel to tell it.

As the parallel with the nocturnal attack on Moses suggests, the lameness of Jacob glosses his twinship in somewhat the way that the circumcision of Abraham glosses his fatherhood. The taboo suggests that if you eat the sinew in question, you lame Jacob. You deprive Jacob of a member by not doing as others in Jacob or Israel do. You accede to the lameness of a member of the flock that ought to be whole before its creator. One expresses identity with Jacob in sparing him, in differing from what would lame him or his flock, for if everyone differs from him, they become one through the group observance – they become Israel itself by virtue of incorporation. Differing from Jacob's difference makes whole, because Jacob himself is bent on differentiation – otherwise Jacob is a twin. But if Jacob limps, he becomes more singular and identifiable, different from all the others. If he loses symmetry with himself, he also loses it with his twin. Thus Jacob becomes singular just when he acquires his other side, Israel, as opposed to his former patrilineal identity as Jacob. We might also see here Israel's cultural identity as the favorer of the lame or disadvantaged. In accepting and making the most out of the particolored offspring of Laban's pure flock, Jacob also accepts Leah, a blemished but sturdy breeder. Jacob, in the third generation, puts the question as to who is this god of the fathers so careful to renew this identification upon his visitation – Jacob divines that communications within the Patriarchal circle of immediacy cannot be relied upon forever. The god of Jacob will need to become the god of Israel, who will rescue the lame and gather the strays (Zeph. 3:19), and gather his flock that halts into Zion (Micah 4:6f).

Membership in Abraham is primarily got by being in the loins of Abraham. Membership in Israel is primarily got by doing as the

Hebrews do, even if that mainly means marrying Hebrews: which Esau does not do. Being in the womb with Jacob proves a positive disqualification, unless you are also in the bed with Leah and Rachel. Isaac's sons are two in number, but being sired only once, there seems to be only one blessing for them. One son is disinherited twice, the other endowed twice, as if he were being adopted as both sons.

Jacob seems to stick his relatives with diselect eating habits at the moments of election – they will be what they eat, and he will not. The means to election are both genetic and cultural, and it is not surprising that Jacob avails himself of all the means, both heritable and appropriable. He is especially on the scene where the means overlap, at the legal assigning of inheritance at the deathbed, and at the legal appropriation of genetics, in the marriage bed. The ethnic claim upon Abrahamic identity can be made by circumcision, but neither Ishmael in the preceding generation, nor the Schechemites in the succeeding one, marry right. Their marriages threaten to assimilate rather than preserve Patriarchal identity. As a result of following the example of Isaac, Jacob gets marriage right. Owing to Isaac's marriage, Jacob is genetically 'Terah' on both his parents' sides – he has been dosed with a double portion of patrilinearity. As a result of his own marriages, his son's are more Terah than those of Abraham, and more ethnic than their forefather Isaac.

While the succession of Abraham, Isaac and Jacob thickens Hebrew blood, the linearity of patrilinearity is increasingly attenuated, since each son is less securely first-born than his predecessor. This increasing pressure upon primogeniture causes it to yield in the fourth generation, when the patrilineal inheritance is finally distributed among the sons of Jacob: each becomes the eponymous ancestor of his own tribe. Hence the appearance in the narrative of the ethnic terminology with corporate overtones: Reubenite, Horite, Ishmaelite. Jacob's first and last sons are both *ben* – Jacob is getting himself a house, the sons of Jacob.

Those calling Abraham their father have a common patrilineal identity, and a differentiated ethnographic identity. Those calling themselves the sons of Jacob have a common ethnographic identity, and a differentiated patrilineal identity. The tribes are exogamous, so the unity of federated Israel is not genetic but ideological. Thus the national genealogies of Exodus 6 and Numbers are neither patrilineal nor ethnographic; they are inventorial and connect to narratives about plagues and offices and conscription. They are really a census or muster of Israel as survivors, office and land holders, and recruits.

It is through Rebekah that the blessing crosses from the genetically elected line of Isaac and Esau, to the culturally and historically elected line of Jacob and Ephraim. The latecomers in the prequel prove to be the early birds in the sequel. Time is on the side of the younger, the Bible seems to say. Isaac favored Esau as the expression of his manhood, Rebekah favored Jacob as the expression of her womanhood: her homemaking and fertility. To see the disguised Jacob's claim on patrilineal identity magnified, we can compare the suit of the disguised Gibeonites, who get themselves included in Israel during the Conquest: the Gibeonites board the Mayflower at Ellis Island. What is sworn cannot be unsworn, and the Gibeonites are in, blessed, as Jacob was, with the name Israel.

Election is choice, and four successive choices lead to the election of Jacob/Israel. There is the choice of Terah to divide his family, the choice of Abraham to marry his son to his family's other half, the choice of Rebekah to marry Isaac, and the choice of Jacob to re-appropriate the family identity from both sides of the dual family. This family is repeatedly elected, but what family is it that is being elected?

We do not know why Terah moves from Ur, but one suspects he refuses to assimilate with the melting pot that immigration makes of the city. The early cities of the Bible figure as places where patrilineal identity is transformed into something else, whether the city is that of Cain, Nimrod or the Babelians. Perhaps a sort of inveterate itinerancy in the Hebrew family blood has kept it blood. Terah, at any rate, divides his lineage and favors the nuclear family over the extended one, the exogamous over the endogamous one, the potential over the actual one. And Terah has favored the more spiritual family, the one reconstituted around those who are initially strangers to it. Here are the origins of Abrahamic hospitality. Terah distinguishes between the marriages of his two sons, and the more consanguineous family is the one of which he takes his leave. The one he leaves with is the more adoptive half.

Any attempt to connect the idea of election theology and covenant theology needs an idea of adoption. 'I will be your God' is election by God; 'you will be my people' is adoption by God. 'I will be your God and you will be my people' is their covenant only when it is rejoined responsively and adoptively by the other party, 'you will be our God and we will be your people'. There are two adoption prototypes inherent in family structures: one is the taking of the spouse outside of one's own bloodlines, and the other is identifying one's self as the offspring of the less immediate party to one's begetting – originally, the father. But before anyone can identify anyone else with the father, one has to identify the father as the father. The legal basis for the father's inclusion is the discovery that the father is the father, and that there are such things as fathers. There is only one way to discover the facts of paternity and that is for the mother to have been adopted by the husband – or vice versa – to the exclusion of other male mates or partners. This mate and protector becomes the spiritual father, adopted over her original father, which is only the collective father provided by the elders of the tribe. Thus the spiritual family and the exclusive, nuclear family have their destinies intertwined originally, and so do the physical and inclusively consanguinous families. 'Hail wedded love . . . by thee/Relations . . . Of father, son, and brother first were known.' The process has two parts. The physical father Terah adopts the family of the spiritual father Abram, whose wife is barren and who will be spoken to by Yhwh. But in segregating himself from his clan by his marriage and migration, Abram re-establishes himself as the physical father, eventually of Sarah's child. But he has become the spiritual father Abraham, in adopting Ishmael, since Sarah is barren.

Sarai is introduced as barren: she is the potential gap in the patrilineal genealogy. Dynastically speaking, a barren Princess is a contradiction in terms, so Sarai is renamed by her name, when she is able to be a princess in fact as well as in name. Insofar as Abraham has had to believe in God for the child's begetting, Isaac's father is the god of Abraham as much as Abraham himself. Spiritual fatherhood is fatherhood at one remove from genetic fatherhood, just as fatherhood is one remove from motherhood – this is what creates the contrast between spiritual and physical parenthood in the first place.

Spiritual or adoptive parenthood enjoys priority, because the spiritual family must be formed for the literal one to follow. The breeding unit must be segregated and named for it to be known at all – otherwise the breeding unit is the committee of the whole. The facts of paternity, the annunciation to Sarai might tell us, are revealed by God. The incest taboo can scarcely be relied on to reveal them, if you do not know who it is you cannot know sexually. The biblical language for carnal knowledge becomes crucial here: Rebekah at her engagement had not known man. Tamar, on the other hand, seems to have played the harlot: God only knows whom she has known. The incest taboo cannot exist – and you cannot avoid sleeping with kin – unless you know who they are; and you cannot know that unless you are distinguishing between the ones you are sleeping with and not sleeping with, in accordance with the taboo. Terah helps advance this knowledge, in the sense that his action suggests the division of the All-family into two exogamous phratries with sexual partners for each phratry being adopted from the other. Only at this point is marriage made visible. But who reveals the rules, when the phratries cannot exist without them, and the rules cannot be applied without the phratries? Who imposes the distinction between kin and in-laws, siblings and spouses, between knowing a partner and acknowledging a relative? It seems obvious that an outsider could manifest these distinctions, an outsider who found sanctuary with one particular insider; or an insider who cleaved unto only those originally closest to her: either a strange woman taken as a wife from beyond the tribe, or a daughter kept as a virgin by her mother and sisters. The scenario requires this woman be held back from possession by the tribe.

The contrast between spiritual and physical family depends on that between insider and outsider. The spiritual family is the one in which the outsider finds sanctuary otherwise enjoyed by the insiders in the physical family. With respect to the womb, even the father is an outsider originally, a kind of in-law. Consider the two families of Terah. Behind him Terah leaves his son Nahor and his granddaughter Milcah. If Haran died in the presence of his father and left him the care of his surviving children, Milcah has been taken care of by means of an endogamous marriage to one of Terah's sons, her uncle Nahor. They will raise up grandsons to Haran, or grandsons and great-grandsons to Terah. The marriage Terah throws in his own lot with, however, is not made up of Abram and the other orphaned girl Iscah. She drops out – like Haran, like Abel, like Ham, like the tribes cursed with assimilation in Jacob's blessing for resisting assimilating with Shechem. Abram is the host to outsiders: the bereaved Terah, the barren Sarai, and the orphaned Lot, his ward. Abram's family history as a whole will seem like a tissue of adoptions – Eliezer, Hagar, Ishmael, Isaac's guardian, Isaac's wife, a Hittite grave-site, and a father-god.

The text records no act of faith on Terah's part, but one infers his faith in the viability of Abram's marriage, which begins in the adoption of Sarai. Nahor could well embrace Milcah with 'This is bone of my bone', and Laban says as much to Abraham's grandson Jacob, anticipating Jacob's betrothal to his kinswomen. The Nahorites are like the Adam who used the solidarity formula physically and literally, while Abram would have to be like the Adam who used it figuratively and adoptively. The two marital archetypes combine in subsequent Patriarchal marriages. Isaac marries conservatively, but Rebekah marries innovatively, for Rebekah leaves home to marry. Jacob marries conservatively when Laban marries him to Leah, innovatively when he espouses Rachel. (Leah conserves kin through fertility; Rachel dies upon yielding up the unconservable household gods.)

The patrilineal pedigree of survival from Seth and Shem re-records itself in the further survival of the physical fathers through the generations of Nahor, Bethuel and Laban, but also in the spiritual fathers indicated by the barrenness of their wives Sarah, Rebekah, and Rachel – wives who would be barren in the course of nature, except for the god who giveth the increase. (Even Leah is one whose prayer has been heard.) When the pedigree is appropriated for the future, at the calling of Israel out of Egypt as God's adopted son, it appears as *God's* pedigree, the god of Abraham, Isaac, and Jacob. Without God's intervention the genetic linkage would not be: the imperiled and reaffirmed paternity of the Fathers is the evidence that this god may be called upon, as it were, yet once more.

But how did he become the god of Abraham in the first place? What was the family religion? Terah was fixed on relocation, and if you are on the move, the need for a spiritual kinsman could be paramount. Unless your kinsmen dislocate with you, you will have no allies in the new neighbourhood except such allies as you can make; the way to make them is to assimilate, but assimilation extinguishes the patrilineal pedigree that Lot's inclusion in the removers suggests Terah honors. Maintenance of the pedigree seems a part of the family religion too. Thus Abram and Isaac pretend their wives are their sisters, to keep themselves from being murdered for possession of these wives. They are true to the honorific or adoptive identities of their wives, even if they falsify their genetic identities. Since the wives are vital to the survival of the distinct line anticipated by Terah and Abraham in relation to their daughters-in-law, God must intervene to insure the wife's survival along with the husband's. This intervention is directly associated with the comparable intervention in the barrenness of Abimelech. Jacob's attempt to assimilate the potential assimilator by circumcision – in the case of his threatened daughter Dinah – cannot overcome the ingrained desire of his sons to retain Dinah's dignity or status as their inviolable sister. She is what the Patriarchal wives are alleged to be, the genetic not the adopted sister. Her brothers are what God had to be, the jealous kinsman. If reverence for the natural kinsman originally brings you to awareness of the spiritual one, the spiritual one protects you long enough for you to generate the natural one. In the fourth generation the sons of Jacob are strong enough to take protection into their own hands; what they protect is the genetic purity of the line their sister is part of. The daughters are strong enough also, since Tamar secures the genetic continuity of her tribe from the same generation, where before God would have intervened unaided. The barrenness of the Patriarchal wife, the virginity of the post-Patriarchal sister, and the bereavement of the post-Patriarchal daughter, all point to a distinction between the woman's identity as a breeder and her identity as a blood relation, even if each story breaches that distinction in the cause of preserving it: preserves the wife Sarai as a wife by calling her a sister, preserves the sister Dinah as a sister by dissimilated agreement to her being forced, and preserves the wife Tamar as a mother in Israel by her serving as a prostitute to her husband's blood relation.

If this is a religion, it is the religion of family autarchy, which Terah breached for purposes of re-creating it. Terah in effect throws Abram upon his spiritual kinsman God, and God tells Abram to relocate, to divide from the unity formed by country, district, family and father's house – and all for the purpose of re-finding or re-founding these same three things abroad: land, nation, and name as a father of nations. This family is set apart in its spiritual apprehension of its future as another family. Yhwh and the future speak to its leader in one voice. Melchizedek greets Abram in the name of the creator, and God declares thereupon that God, not Terah, brought Abram out of Ur. The God Who Intervenes is the God Who Innovated in the creation, and the saving of Lot by Abram is one with the numbering of the stars and the numbering of the peoples.

How does the Bible distinguish between the claims upon God's patronage, between family candidates for election? Isaac's claim on Abraham at Mount Moriah is not more compelling than Ishmael's claim on Hagar in the wilderness – both earn God's intervention. Why then does Yhwh suddenly switch to calling Isaac Abraham's only son? Because Ishmael's mother has chosen her son an Egyptian bride. She has not made the wrong choice, any more than Orpah will make it in Ruth; but Hagar has turned her back to her own people, favoring consanguineous relations over adoptive ones. The future is with adoptive relations, since man's relation to God is itself such a relation. Sarah forces Hagar back to her own people, and Abraham himself reverts to his, in sending off to Mesopotamia for Rebekah. Yet here is the act of conversion that aligns God's choice with that of the human chooser. The choice of Isaac is not merely that of Sarah, but also Rebekah's choice of Abraham. Innovatively, Abram chose Sarai; conservatively, he chooses Rebekah, in favor of conserving 'Nahor'. But *Rebekah* chooses innovatively, to leave 'Nahor' and migrate to Abraham. Isaac's marriage is spiritualized by having Rebekah keep faith with the future and with strangers. Adoptive relations dignify choice, as in Rebekah's consenting 'I will go', or Ruth's 'where you go I will go'. These words imply the marriage vow, but also conversion to Yhwh in the motion towards adoption into the genealogical stock that belongs to those Yhwh has already chosen.

Rebekah's place in the genealogy is more secure than Ruth's – Ruth has no genealogy of her own, while Rebekah has a surplus. Ruth will be adopted into a genealogy not her own, while Rebekah will depart from a genealogy that culminates in her. Ruth will depart from the Moabites, the incestuous tribe that cannot give you a genealogy. Rebekah departs from something analogous, the consanguineous group (seven uncles), but she is restored to the other half of this group, just as Abraham has been divided from a homeland to be endowed with one.

Rebekah's story begins with Abraham being informed of a store of relatives back home. Milcah has borne sons to Nahor, among whom there is found a daughter. As Nahor married Milcah, so Abraham makes a Nahor-like choice for Isaac. As Haran was *not* around to provide and arrange for Iskah, so Laban *is* around to provide and arrange for *both* of his daughters, as Isaac cannot do for both of his sons. But it is Laban's sons who drop out, like Iskah and Esau, for there is nobody for them to marry as conservative of lineage as Laban's daughters. The sons of Nahor are similarly deprived of Rebekah. How is this story of genetic conscription told? Everybody knows that the Patriarchs married girls from the Old Country. To this tradition corresponds the foreknowledge of Abraham's servant, who knows that Isaac must be married to such a girl. Everybody knows that Isaac's wife was named Rebekah, but the servant cannot know the content of this name, Rebekah's personal identity or mind. The story tells us more about her mind and more about her genealogy, in the memorable form of the servant's inquiry after them.

Nowadays a genealogy can be acquired by mail, and those who send off to Europe for this purpose do so precisely because of their removal from Europe. Abraham's servant doubles as this ambassador and genealogist, seeking out the bride but moreover the bride's antecedents. She will become the mother of Israel, and insofar as the audience identifies with him, he is somewhat in the role of the protagonist of the movie *Back to the Future*, arranging for the date that will get the future inquirer born, while seeing what it was like back then or back there. Mom was fairly forward, we learn; that is where *Jacob* at the well got it from.

The language of genealogical inquiry is 'who's whose what?' and identity depends on the possession of relations and connections. At the outset, the servant is sworn not to return his ward to Mesopotamia. From an internal point of view, the message is, 'Remember Lot's wife.' The servant will not let Rebekah tarry a week in the same place where Jacob gets trapped almost three weeks of years: Remember Laban's wiles.

Abraham's own guardian, God, took him from *his father's house* and *his kindred's land*. God promised an angel would be sent before him, and told him to take Isaac's wife from back there. The angel starts to slide from being Abraham's to being the ambassador's. The servant goes unto the city of Nahor, the place where the Nahorite half of the patrilineal pedigree has come to rest. Somehow he has penetrated to virtually Abraham's father's house, Nahor being the name of Abraham's grandfather as well as that of his brother. Beyond the city, and at a well at the right hour for encounters there, he prays to *the god of his master*, virtually the god of my father. Lo and behold, the daughters of the city's men appear, and he prays that the girl he asks for water will make him the doubly hospitable answer, and that she will be the girl God has appointed, and that God will reveal his choice in this way, and behold Rebekah herself, trailing her tri-generational genealogy behind her, with her beauty and virginity scarcely less discernible than the pitcher on her shoulder. One can see that no man has known her, and so we are informed of her genealogy, since her chastity and bloodlines go hand in hand, as we have said they must. No man has known her, which is why her family can be known: her kin have not been her sexual partners.

The narrator *has* known her, but his disclosure does not violate her mystery but introduces it – characters in the Bible are not introduced into a story in which they will survive genealogically without their names and genealogies being introduced as well. The information about Rebekah being already before us, we are in a good position to see the servant acquiring it, as David seeks the identity of Bathsheba that he might know her. But can the servant learn the information? The daughter serves the servant, and his camels also; he begins to think he's home free. She has proven her worth in the terms he set for it; she has as good as divined those terms. He brings forth a kind of engagement ring – we did not know he was so well prepared – and he asks for room in the *girl's father's house* (the place he's zeroed in on, without its having been made quite explicit that this is what Abraham meant, in addition to his country and kindred). The girl does not immediately say 'yes, there's room', but instead reverts to the question of whose house hers might be, giving a second recital of her genealogical identity, minus the connection to Abraham, whom she may well never have heard of. (Her father's long-lost Uncle Abe.) Then she affirms the house's sufficiency to accommodate the servant's entourage, and the servant worships *his master's god*, the master who has been favored by the leading of the servant to *his master's brethren's house*. He must say all of this aloud, and she must hear it all, for she returns to tell *her mother's house*: she invokes the more immediate and physical bond, because she is in fact retreating from her calling, even as she is also approaching it. Seeing the wealth bestowed upon his sister, Laban comes forth to the well and addresses the servant as one might address Abraham himself, as blessed of Yhwh. Laban insists he has already readied a suitable reception, but the servant – not less intent on his purpose than Laban is upon his (ingratiating himself with the source of wealth) – insists upon not eating until he has made his pitch. He affirms his identity as the servant of Abraham, who is indeed blessed of God, with wealth and household and with the child of his wife and old age, whom even now he makes the heir. *My master's wife*, he says, introducing the critical affiliation with the double genitive that the dual narration keeps forcing him into, and explaining his vow to go to *Abraham's father's house* and kindred, to take a wife for the son. But the servant reports that he objected to his master that he might not be successful with the woman, and thereupon Abraham promised the Lord would send an angel with him, to take a wife for his son, of his kindred and of *his father's house*. The servant has commandeered the services of Abraham's angel and also Abraham's phraseology about the house Abraham came from. He wants to insist that his mission has been anything but a shot-in-the-dark: more like a hole-in-one. The servant asserts that he established Rebekah's genealogy *before* he engaged her with the rings – not so: thereupon he worshiped Yhwh God of his master Abraham, that is who all this is thanks to, that is who led him the way to take *his master's brother's daughter* to his master's son. It is not so much Abraham's idea as God's, just as it's not the servant's idea, but Abraham's – the servant is two removes from the source, like Aaron the mouthpiece of Moses the spokesman for God.

The kinsmen of Rebekah can scarcely deny that this motion is of Yhwh, for the servant has been at such evident pains to portray it so. They *are* a bit dumbfounded, perhaps because the servant, for all his pretense to participate in God's omniscience, has finally got Rebekah's genealogy wrong. Even though Rebekah has told it him correctly, and even though the servant has just repeated her version of it verbatim, his final report of his prayer of thanksgiving contracts the genealogy by one generation, or else uses the word daughter to mean granddaughter. The servant has mastered double genitive after double genitive, and more still with the triple genitive of *his master's brother's daughter*. To ask the servant to achieve this quadruple genitive might be a little like extending biblical vengeance to the proverbial fourth generation. And the abridgement in question is not unique: God tells Jacob he is the god of his father Abraham, the god of Isaac (Gen. 28:13): if the physical grandfather can be the spiritual father, then the physical granddaughter can be the spiritual daughter.

The climax of the servant's speech, the culmination of his hopes, is the connecting of Rebekah to her relations at home and abroad. Perhaps his eagerness causes him to mess up and skip over a generation, in his desire to refer his object in the daughter back to her antecedents in Abraham's closest relative. The servant keeps trying to say it is destiny that they have met, given the nearness of their relations, while his mistake suggests he is more of a stranger than he might like to admit. Nonetheless, genealogy is a kind of destiny; Rebekah's retreat to her mother's house might throw her upon Milcah's example of in-house marriage, but this is not the model for marriage to the future. For if Rebekah were to marry entirely as her mother did, she would marry one of the eight sons of Nahor, her uncles. It is in the servant's interests to make Rebekah *her uncles' sister, and thus unmarriageable by them*. Rebekah and the servant may be of one mind about this, for Rebekah may well want to leave home. She is engaged by the servant with his rings *before* she has told him who she is, and before he has told her who he is. For all she knows, he is himself the eligible suitor who owns the camels and gold; and for all he knows, she is only a ready woman eager to please strangers with her aptness and goodwill. Thus she is pre-contracted before she is known to anyone but God, the narrator and the reader. In responding to the servant, she is already responding to his forthcoming proposal, and to the candidate from afar. He does not quite know who she is, and she does not quite know who he is, and out of this their match is made – some mutual instinct recognizes eligibility and opportunity. The reasons for the marriage are aristocratic and dynastic, but the chances of it are like the chances of a blind date: from Yhwh.

Marriage requires leaving the more consanguineous house for the more adoptive one: one surrenders intimacy with one's own bloodlines, but one has to have bloodlines specific enough to surrender intimacy with. The cross-country, cross-cousin marriages of Isaac and Jacob show this. The exclusive pole appears in closeness of genetic origin, the polygamous pole in remoteness of territorial origin. In Jacob's double marriage exclusive choice is symbolically maintained while it is literally suspended. The same two poles create the mystery of Rebekah at the well: is she Nahor's daughter, or his grand-daughter; Haran's granddaughter, or his great-granddaughter? Is she Rebekah or Rebekah's niece? Is she the answer to the servant's prayer, or an acceptable substitute-order? Is the servant the answer to an unmarried girl's prayer, or is the servant the servant of that answer? Is it Rachel or is it Leah? Every blind date poses the same questions, and on the wedding night one stands on the threshold of a blind date for life.

By means of the contradiction of the servant by himself, or at least an ambiguity in his use of the word daughter, the narrator must be showing that the servant is relying on a general persuasion of genealogical appropriateness that he does not himself quite grasp. The servant comes to rest on a cousin–cousin symmetry, which Providence must be providing for. But if Isaac were actually to marry one of his cousins, he would have to marry children of a bond-woman, Nahor's *concubine*. The only choice, really, is the sole daughter of the last-born son of Nahor's wife: Rebekah-come-lately. Sarah dies upon the revelation of this genealogical possibility; that is, when there is only one candidate for dynastic marriage from each side. The sons of Keturah are only born after election for Isaac has been pre-secured by making him the husband of the only wife available from the narrower stock of Terah. Keturah's sons will find no such wife, even though they are sent away in the eastward direction the servant takes – the direction Rebekah takes in reverse.

The servant's researches show that Isaac marries across three generations. Had he not arrived so late, Isaac could conceivably have married Milcah, his actual wife's grandmother. Isaac's wife has been preparing over three generations – God works while man sleeps, as Adam might have observed. The backward Isaac delays in the loins of Abraham, while Rebekah makes haste, as if she had to cover all three of the Patriarchal generations to confirm her eligibility to become the sponsor of the late-born Jacob's claim on Abraham, the Jacob whom she will rush into Esau's place.

Isaac's marriage is a dynastic one that secures his claim to patrilinearity – to Terah – over that of any other relative to Nahor, Laban only excepted. The marriage of Jacob to both of Laban's daughters has the same dynastic significance: Laban's sons cannot marry as well as Jacob without marrying their sisters – Abraham has no daughters to exchange. Terah has divided one family from the other so that one can produce daughters to engage the other's sons at the wells where there is marrying and giving in marriage.

Like the servant, Jacob succeeds in the genetic recoupement of patrilinearity. But he does not conserve it so much as appropriate it, and just as clearly he distributes it. Having accumulated through three generations, it is divided among the twelve tribes (in preceding generations it accumulated through three and seven generations, and was divided among three sons). Jacob's talent for alienating others' inheritances to himself suggests the shift through Jacob of patrilineal bequeathal to ethnic bequeathal. As a type of racial shrewdness,

Jacob has his originals in Rebekah and Laban. His four means to be the heir – Esau, Isaac, Leah, and Rachel – require of him extortion, imposture, servitude and bill collection. His flock is almost gotten by the usury he has earned on an interest-free loan. The division of his gift to Esau show how he has increased and multiplied, and that he has arrived at the place where Abraham separated from Lot. The only alternative to ethnographic division at this point is political incorporation or confederation. The advent of this inevitability appears in the altar at Bethel, and in Joseph's dream of the twelve stars, symbolizing the unionization of a sovereign Israel, as they do in Betsy Ross's American flag.

Siring all his children, Jacob becomes Israel. Upon the completion of their birth, and after the cultic burial of foreign gods has exposed Rachel to death, three further reports mark the shift from patrilineal to ethnic identity: Reuben's incest, Isaac's burial and Esau's fathering of the kingdom of Edom.

The passing of the Patriarchal marriage saga into its status as a historical prefix to the Exodus first appears in Reuben's sin against his father: a sin unthinkable in a Patriarch, as a sin against his own status. The sin reflects the escalation of sibling rivalry over three generations, each mother's intervention seeming more 'Oedipal' than the last, and the parents of the children being that much closer in relation. The ultimate expression of this internecine anger is Reuben's contempt for his father's relation to the rival mother: in sleeping with Bilah a Leahite violates a Rachelite, and so anticipates the violence that will be directed against Joseph, probably for telling tales about just this sin. This sin is terminal for the marriage-saga because when patrilinearity is distributed out among the twelve tribes, they will not intermarry. They will conserve the history, not the genetics, of the forefathers' relations. Marriage across tribal lines threatens the tribe with assimilation, disinheritance and extinction. Reuben violates past patriarchiality, but also future patrilineality, which is intra-tribal.

Bilhah's incest contrasts with the story of Tamar, one of the two obvious extensions of the Patriarchal saga into what follows, namely the Joseph-*roman* and the genesis of the Exodus. Joseph's story is not at the patrilineal but at the ethnographic pole of obligations to kin. Answerability for the whereabouts or safety or preservation of one's brother remains crucial, but only in Judah's case is it answerability for genealogy. Joseph has obligations to kin as his stalking-horse, but his real object is the obligations of the just to victims of injustice. On the horizons are the obligations of the strong to the weak, and the advantaged to the oppressed. Thus the story's recognition-scenes promote the recognition of something more than a kinsman – guilt between accomplices, victimage, conspiracy and treachery. The exception is the story of Tamar, where the recognition of patrilinearity within a *gens* is promoted. The story is at the genealogical pole of our discourse, yet it shows the introversion of the tribe into a genealogically self-sufficient unit. The phrase 'House of Joseph' implies something similar – sort of like being a New Yorker. This tribal independence opens the way for political and idealogical affiliation.

The ethnographic pole is similarly transformed in the story of Moses at the well. At such a site and in terms of precedent, we might expect a 'genealogical' transaction; but in terms of the well-betrothal scene in John 4: 3–42, we might expect an 'ideological' transaction. Moses joins with the family of the priest of Midian not because they are his flesh, but because they provide Moses with sanctuary. The claims made at the well are not upon the future genetic vehicle, but upon mutual protection, the claim of the widow and the orphan and the manslaughter. Moses will live in the Midian until the men who seek his life are dead, which anticipates the appointment of the cities of refuge, where the shedder of blood is safe for the life of the city's high priest. Thus Moses is not the long-lost kinsman repatriated, but the stranger naturalized and the fugitive harboured and rehabilitated. Despite his immersion in the Patriarchal past, the innovative feature is prevailing over the conservative one. Judah was answerable to Tamar for not insuring that her brother-in-law raise up seed to his brother's widow: this is the genealogical keeping of Nahor that was originally the keeping of Abel entrusted to Seth. But the protection of Moses and the daughters at the well is at the other pole of our discourse, the ethnographic pole. Within Genesis, the redress for injuries is entrusted by Lamech to Lamech and otherwise to Noahide law. In Exodus, the most complete enunciation of the law of retaliation attaches to the penalties for the abuse of the pregnant woman. Within Genesis, the abused pregnant woman at the well gives birth to Ishmael, whose hand will be raised against every other. We are speaking, then, of the keeping of Hagar and the keeping of Cain. This was entrusted directly to God.

NOTE

I am deeply and gratefully indebted to Meir Sternberg, *The Poetics of Biblical Narrative: Ideological Literature and the Drama of Reading* (Indiana University Press, 1985), pp. 131–52, 'The Wooing of Rebekah', for much of my reading of the details of the ambassador's performance: the reversal of the order of events, the jumping of the gun regarding Isaac's inheritance, and so forth.

7

The Hermeneutics of Midrash

Gerald L. Bruns

The words of Torah are fruitful and multiply.

Talmud, Hagigah, 3b

In this chapter I want to examine in some detail a midrashic text that, from a hermeneutical standpoint, seems to articulate most fully the ancient rabbinical conception of what it means to interpret the Bible. But in order to forestall some typical misunderstandings, both of midrash and of hermeneutics, I want to begin by asking about the nature of the theoretical interest that hermeneutics takes in midrash (or in any interpretive practice).

This is not an easy question to formulate in our current intellectual situation. We live in a culture that likes to define its intellectual tasks methodologically, or in terms of the production of techniques of analysis that overcome one another in regular cycles of obsolescence and advancement. In fact, in our 'postmodern condition' hermeneutics is one of the things we are said to have advanced beyond. As Vincent Leitch says, hermeneutics has never amounted to much because it can't be converted into a research program that produces recognizable analytical results, that is, distinctive, competitive readings of great works and their cultural environments.[1] There is some truth in this. Hermeneutics won't give you a new angle on Shakespeare. It is not a method but a critique of method – or, more accurately, a critique of what Karl-Otto Apel calls 'methodical solipsism' and its obsession with the hardware of instrumental and procedural rationality.[2] Hermeneutics is thus not interested in midrash in order to promote a new form of criticism, say a New Midrash.[3] The task of hermeneutics, as Gadamer has explained at some length, is not to develop new procedures of understanding but to clarify the conditions in which understanding occurs, whatever the method that claims to produce it.[4] These conditions, moreover, are social and historical rather than 'logical conditions of possibility'. So a hermeneutics of midrash would not be an attempt to raise midrash to methodological self-consciousness by showing how it works; it would not try to produce a theory of it that would lay bare its logic or deep structure or tacit rules. The hermeneutical interest in midrash proceeds from the principle of historicality or the finitude of all interpretation. Interpretation is a social practice, not a logical (or methodological) process, so that in order to know what it is to understand and interpret anything, having a method is not enough; one must study the history of interpretive traditions – bizarre, irrational, useless or even exploitable as these practices may sometimes appear in terms of the strategic goals of current theory. Indeed, interpretation as something culturally embedded is untheorizable; it cannot be reduced to a deep structure but must be studied in all of its bewildering heterogeneity. I take this study to be one of the tasks of hermeneutics.

Within the history of interpretation midrash looms very large, yet it remains haphazardly and often disdainfully studied, and certainly poorly understood. It is certainly not clear that midrash is made up of what we call methods, rules, strategies or techniques.[5] In general 'midrash' is simply the ancient Hebrew word for interpretation. It is the word for the relationship of Judaism to its sacred texts (Torah), and one could say that it covers the relationship of one sacred text to another as well. Midrash is a rabbinical concept, or practice, but it is certainly as old as writing itself. The word derives from *darash*, meaning 'to study' or 'to tread', as if interpretation had as much to do with walking as with reading. Hence 'midrash' also includes the sense of 'to search', 'to investigate', 'to go in quest of'. Midrash is preoccupied with wisdom, where wisdom is not just what is contained in the head. More loosely, 'midrash' can be taken to mean 'account', that is, giving an account of what is written, where 'giving an account' could mean simply 'telling' but also 'accounting for', where the task of the account is to address whatever becomes an issue when the Torah is studied or recited, or whenever the understanding of Torah is called for. Insofar as there is never, in Jewish tradition, a situation in human life in which such understanding is not called for, midrash can be said to have a great range of application.

'This book of the law must ever be on your lips; you must keep it in mind day and night so that you may diligently observe all that is written in it' (Josh. 1:8 [New English Bible]). This text summarizes very well the midrashic incentive. At all events, my argument would be that we ought to think of midrash as a form of life (in Wittgenstein's sense) rather than simply as a form of exegesis (in the technical sense); that is, midrash is concerned with practice and action as well as with (what we think of as) the form and meaning of texts. There is a venerable distinction between midrash *halakhah* and midrash *aggadah*, that is, between an account given of a legal text and an account of every other sort of text – narratives (on rare occasions), verses, words, letters of the alphabet, as well as textual or diacritical embellishments like the tagin and te-amim that adorn words and letters. However, it is not obvious that this distinction covers actual practice, because the Torah is everywhere a binding text.[6] That is, midrash is concerned to tell about the force of the text as well as to address its problems of form and meaning. The sense of Torah is the sense in which it applies to the life and conduct of those who live under its power, and this principle of application applies to homiletic *aggadah* as well as to the explicitly legal constructions of *halakhah*. Indeed, this was the upshot of Joseph Heinemann's study of *aggadah*:

while the rabbinic creators of the Aggadah looked back into Scripture to uncover the full latent meaning of the Bible and its wording, at the same time they looked forward into the present and the future. They sought to give direction to their own generation, to resolve their religious problems, to answer their theological questions, and to guide them out of their spiritual complexities. . . . The aggadists do not mean so much to clarify difficult passages in the biblical texts as to take a stand on the burning questions of the day, to guide the people and to strengthen their faith.[7]

And as we shall see, this emphasis on application entails the political meaning of midrash as well as its spiritual purpose.

So what matters in midrash is not only what lies behind the text in the form of an originating intention but what is in front of the text where the text is put into play. The text is always contemporary with its readers or listeners, that is, always oriented towards the time and circumstances of the interpreter. It lays open paths to the future. 'Let the Torah never be for you an antiquated decree, but rather like a decree freshly issued, no more than two or three days old. . . . [Indeed,] Ben Azzai said: not even as old as a decree issued two or three days ago, but as a decree issued this very day.'[8] Moreover, this orientation towards the present and future helps at least in part to explain the legendary extravagance of midrash, where typically a single verse or word or letter will be given not a single, settled, official construction but a series of often conflicting and disputed expositions. This hermeneutical openness to the conflict of interpretation cannot be accommodated within modernist doctrines of romantic hermeneutics or Husserlian concepts of the primacy of intentional experience where understanding a text means understanding its author at least as

well as he understood himself, if himself is the word. Interpretation
on the Husserlian view means reconstruction of intentional experience
as this is reflected in the formal properties and historical background
of the text. Here interpretation is a working backward rather than a
taking forward. Yet we know that it is never enough to construe texts
just in this way, that is as historical documents and formal objects. A
legal text, to take the obvious example, cannot simply be construed in
relation to itself but must be understood in relation to the situations
in which it is applied if it is to be understood at all.[9] These situations
are always different in their particular ways from the one in which the
text was originally handed down. Each situation will command its
own sense of how the text has to be taken, which is why a legal text
has to be open, loosely textured, not indeterminate but not a calculus
of rules, either. Midrash applies roughly this same textual principle to
the scriptures and so presupposes that interpretation cannot mean
simply giving uniform representations of a text that is sealed off from
the heterogeneity of human situations. Midrash understands that if a
text is to have any force it must remain open to more than the context
of its composition.

Something like this idea underwrites the rabbinical gloss on I Kings
4:32 (I Kings 5:12 in the Hebrew Bible). 'And he spoke three
thousand proverbs, and his songs were a thousand and five': 'This
teaches,' the Talmud says, 'that Solomon uttered three thousand
proverbs for every single word of the Torah and one thousand and
five reasons for every single word of the Scribes.'[10] This reading
shows how the Rabbis conceived the spirit of midrash. To get into
this spirit we need to understand that midrashic interpretation is not
just something going on between a reader and a text with a view
towards intellectual agreement between them. We need to get out
from under the model of methodical solipsism that pictures a solitary
reader exercising strategic power over a text. Certainly the ancient
midrashists are not pictured this way. The midrashic collections that
come down to us (say from the fifth through the tenth centuries CE)
figure interpretation as something social and dialogical. Indeed, on
this social point the Talmud is very clear: 'Make yourselves into
groups [*kittoth*] to study the Torah, since the knowledge of the Torah
can be acquired only in association with others'.[11] The idea is that
Torah speaks to a public, communal situation, not to the solitary,
single-minded, private reader. Under these conditions – conditions
very different from those produced by the printing press and which
led Luther to restructure hermeneutics around the individual reading
subject – interpretation is bound to be many-sided and open-ended,
as in the following example, which concerns Ecclesiastes 12:11: *The*

words of the wise are as goads, and as nails well fastened (literally, 'planted') are those that are composed in collections: they are given from one shepherd:

Once R. Joḥanan b. Beroḳa and R. Eleazar Ḥisma went to welcome R. Joshua at Peḳi'im, and he asked them: 'What new thing has been said in college [the beit midrash or house of study] to-day? They replied: 'We are your disciples and it is your water that we drink' [i.e. we follow your interpretations]. Said he to them: 'Nevertheless one cannot imagine a college where something new has not been said. Whose Sabbath was it?' 'The Sabbath of R. Eleazar son of 'Azariah,' they replied. 'And on what topic was the exposition to-day?' They told him: 'On the section, "*Assemble.*"' [Deut. 21:12]. . . . He also opened a discourse on the text, '*The words of the wise are as goads.*' Why were the words of the Torah likened to a goad? To tell you that as a goad directs the cow along the furrows, in order to bring life to the world, so the words of the Torah direct the heart of those who study them away from the paths of death and along the paths of life. Should you assume that as the goad is shifted about so the words of the Torah can be shifted about, Scripture states: '*And as nails well fastened.*' Should you assume that as a nail contracts but does not expand, Scripture states, '*fastened (lit. 'planted')*'; to signify that as a plant is fruitful and increases, so the words of the Torah bear fruit and multiply. '*Those that are composed in collections*' (ba'ale asufoth).' '*Ba'ale asufoth*' applies to the scholars, who sit in groups and study the Torah, some of them declaring a thing unclean, others declaring it clean; some pronouncing a thing to be forbidden, others pronouncing it to be permitted; some disqualifying an object, others declaring it fit. Lest a man should say, Since some scholars declare a thing unclean and others declare it clean; some pronounce a thing to be forbidden, others declaring it clean; some pronouncing a thing to be forbidden, others uphold its fitness, how can I study Torah in such circumstances? Scripture states, '*They are given from one shepherd*': One God has given them, one leader (Moses) has uttered them at the command of the Lord of all creation, blessed be He; as it says, *And God spoke all these words* (Ex. XX. 1). Do you then on your part make your ear like a grain-receiver and acquire a heart that can understand the words of the scholars who declare a thing unclean as well as of those who declare it clean; the words of those who declare a thing forbidden as well as those who declare it permitted; the words of those who disqualify an object as well as those who uphold its fitness.[12]

There is considerably more to this text, as we shall see, but we might rest here a moment to place it in hermeneutical context.[13] What we have here is a midrash on the conflict (and not just the plurality) of midrashes. The text is a narrative report of a Sabbath performance by Rabbi Eleazar son of 'Azariah, a master of the beit midrash (the house of study where the rabbis and their students gather to expound and dispute concerning the Torah), and it is important to notice that the report is given by disciples of Rabbi Joshua, who was not present on this particular Sabbath. The allusion here is to a historic controversy that resulted in a revolt of a number of rabbis against the Patriarch, Rabban Gamaliel II (d. 110 CE), who had tried to bring halakhic interpretation under a central administrative authority.[14] The beit midrash is not to be imagined as a preserve of serene logic where a liberal pluralism neutralizes the force of disagreement; it is a place where power flows in multiple directions, and the struggle for control between the Patriarch and the Rabbis, as well as among schools and factions (and not infrequently between masters and disciples), is fierce and sometimes laced with insult.[15] Significantly, the focus of Rabbi Eleazar's midrash is on an outsider or newcomer who finds this conflicted environment bewildering and intolerable: 'how can I study the Torah in such circumstances?' How indeed? What is it to do such a thing? And what is the point of Rabbi Eleazer's reply, which counsels the study not just of the scriptural texts but of their competing interpretations as well? In order to be able to cope with these questions, we need to read further. The midrash continues as follows:

Another exposition of the text, '*The words of the wise are as goads.*' R. Tanḥuma b. Abba said: As the goad directs the cow how to plough in the proper furrow, so do the words of the wise direct a man in the ways of the Holy One, blessed be He. The Mishnah, observed R. Tanḥuma, calls the goad *mardea'*, while the Scripture calls it *darban* and *malmad*, as may be inferred from the text, *With an ox-goad* – bemalmad (Judg. II, 31), and also from, *To set the goads* – haddarban (I Sam. XIII, 21). R. Nathan asked: Why was it called '*mardea'* '? Because it teaches the cow knowledge (*moreh dea'*). Why was it called by the name of *darban*? Because it causes understanding to take up its abode (*dar binah*) in the cow. And why was it called *malmad*? Because it instructs (*melammed*) the cow how to plough in the proper furrow. It is so with the words of the wise. They implant understanding in the minds of men, they teach them knowledge and instruct them in the ways of the Holy One, blessed be He. '*And as nails* (masmerim) *well fastened* (netu'im).' They are implanted (*netu'im*) in man when he observes them (*meshammerem*). Why were they compared to a planting? Because in the same way that the roots of a tree penetrate in all directions, so the words of the wise enter and penetrate into the whole body.[16]

This midrash gives, one might say, the 'theory' of midrash – gives its 'formal operations' (shows us how it works). As the Rabbis themselves put it, midrash works by 'linking up words of Torah with one another'.[17] 'Linking', however, means several things, beginning with the common philological practice of tracking the words of the scriptures, counting them, noting how each one turns up – that is, how often, in what contexts and with what internal differences.

Scripture is one, but it is also a non-linear text whose letters and words can be discovered in heterogeneous combinations. 'Linking' also means using one text (a letter, a word, a phrase, a verse, a piece of narrative, in principle a whole book like the Song of Songs) to elucidate another. Indeed, the Rabbis treated the scriptures as a self-interpreting text, on the (again) ordinary philological principle that what is plain (i.e. understood) in one place can be used to clarify what is obscure or in question in another. 'Words of Torah need each other. What one passage locks up, the other discloses'.[18] In most cases this means using later texts to comment on earlier ones. In principle, one needs nothing but scripture to interpret scripture, as both Augustine and Luther would later argue (asserting, however, as Christians do, that one needs only the New Testament to interpret the Old). But the Rabbis also read the scriptures as being already hermeneutical, that is as works of interpretation as well as scripture: the prophetic books and wisdom writings, for example, are characterized as texts composed specifically for the elucidation of the first five books of Moses. The Rabbis seem not to have distinguished as we do between literary and hermeneutical categories of writing (did not, as we try to do, filter out the hermeneutical in order to keep literature pure). A midrash on the Ḥazita, or Song of Songs, says of Solomon that 'He pondered the words of the Torah and investigated the words of the Torah. He made handles to the Torah' – where 'handles' means parables and sayings, basic forms of rabbinical exegesis (ways of coming to grips with Torah).[19] 'So till Solomon arose,' the midrash says, 'no one was able to understand properly the words of the Torah, but as soon as Solomon arose all began to comprehend the Torah'.[20] What this comes down to, however, is the rabbinical version of the principle of the hermeneutical circle: 'linking up the words of the Pentateuch with those of the prophets and the prophets with the Writings' simply means making sense of the whole by construing relations among the parts, if not exactly vice versa.[21] Exactly what the 'whole' amounts to, however, is a question the Rabbis seem deliberately to leave open.

Indeed, what seems to distinguish a scribal from a print culture is how narrow the analytical distance between text and exegete remains when the text exists in memory instead of in a small, portable book. We probably don't have a very good idea of what the rabbinical textual imagination looks like. Certainly it is far from clear what sort of concept of parts-and-whole a reader of scrolls (v. codices, not to say printed books) might have. Anyhow midrashic interpretation is mediated by painstaking attention to the smallest details of the text and to the intricacies of their combination; taking a view of 'the whole' – using it as a hermeneutic standpoint – just doesn't seem to be part of midrashic practice.[22] What counts as a context in midrash? There is no firm or ready answer. What we would call 'the sense of the whole' seems to be highly fluid and variable, and it is this fluidity – this lack of fixed views as to where the hermeneutical circle should be drawn – that makes multiple, open-ended interpretation possible.

In the long midrashic text from which I have been quoting, for example, 'linking up words of Torah with one another' also means vigorous punning (*mardea*ʿ: *moreh dea*ʿ), that is picking up on the way the words of the scriptures are filled with echoes of other words (a practice underwritten by the fact that a consonantal text like the Hebrew Bible can be sounded or vocalized in multiple ways). Openness to the pun allows words of the text to be taken now one way, now another, so that the working-out of a hermeneutical question ('Why are the words of the wise as goads?') can be carried on at considerable length, or in several directions, and to no determinate end. This open-endedness suggests that the Rabbis did not think of interpretation as problem-solving, settling things once for all, or working towards a final agreement as to how the text is to be taken. Agreement or universal consensus does not appear to be the goal of argument (as it is for John Stuart Mill, for example). Midrash is more reflective than demonstrative, divergent rather than convergent. Indeed, the text is treated as something moving rather than fixed, something that is always a step ahead of the interpreter, always opening onto new ground, and ('Lest you assume' that now you finally have a handle on it) always calling for interpretation to be started up anew. And so, characteristically, our midrash continues:

Another exposition of the text, '*The words of the wise are like goads* (kedarbanoth).' R. Berekiah the priest explains the metaphor to mean '*kaddur shel banoth*,' 'like a little children's ball,' which they pick up and throw about, this way and that. It is the same with the words of the wise: One Sage gives his view and another gives his. Lest it be imagined that since one gives one opinion and another gives another their words merely fly about in the air, Scripture states, '*And as nails well fastened* (netuʿim: planted).' It does not say, 'As nails well fixed (kebuʿim)' but '*As nails well fastened* (netuʿim).' Why? Because Scripture compares the Sages' words to nails, and a nail that has a head is easy to draw out. Accordingly, it says, '*As nails* netuʿim,' for the roots of a tree that are implanted (*netuʿim*) are hard to pull out. Why were their words compared to a nail? Because an iron nail that has a head, although hard, can be easily pulled out, while the roots of a tree that are implanted, even though they are hard to pull out, have not the same strength as the iron has. For this reason it says, '*And as* nails *well* planted,' thus giving the words of the Torah the strength of iron and the resistance of the well-planted roots of a tree.

The midrash continues for several more pages, turning the words of the text (and words that sound like words of the text) this way and that, going backward and forward over the text again and again, each time picking up on some element or inflection not sounded before – all according to no discernible plot that would bring the whole to a close. Midrashic interpretations stop but do not end.

But this simply means that midrash is not linear exposition – not a species of monological reasoning but exegesis that presupposes or starts out from alternative readings and anticipates and, indeed, encourages or provokes them in turn. The text from which I have been quoting gives us an excellent insight into the dialogical nature of midrash. Midrash is not the work of the isolated reader but an endless give and take between the text and its exegetes and above all among the Rabbis who gather together to expound and dispute. Thus the pun in the text above which turns a goad into a ball that children play with opens the way to the characterization of midrash as multiple, heterogeneous and conflicting. The version of this midrash preserved in the *Pesikta Rabbati* puts it this way: 'so words fly back and forth when the wise come into a house of study and discuss Torah, one stating his view, and another stating his view, still another stating another view, and another stating a different view'.[23]

The main question, of course, is: how is this stratified, open-ended form of contested interpretation to be understood?

Customarily we understand the conflict of interpretation as a defect of interpretation itself, part of the logical weakness of hermeneutics. It is what prompts the desire to get 'beyond interpretation' to the meaning itself, settling things once for all. This appears to be the desire of the bewildered fellow who asks, 'How can I study Torah in such circumstances?' How can one know for sure what the Torah says when what it says is constantly in the air, endlessly open to dispute (open, indeed, to radical and not often friendly disagreement)? My thought is that this very question implies a transcendental outlook that has, in Western culture, never been able to accept the finite, situated, dialogical, indeed political character of human understanding, and which even now finds midrash to be irrational and wild. Our ideal is an uncontested grasp of the text. We want to say: all interpretation aside, what does the text really mean? The transcendental desire is unsatisfiable with respect to the historicality and social heterogeneity of understanding. It is a desire that seems always to end in a contempt for interpretation and a suspicion concerning the whole idea of dialogue as relativistic and empty, or what analytic philosophers refer to as 'just talk'. One can read the history of interpretation as a history of hermeneutical conflict highlighted by repeated efforts to get 'beyond hermeneutics' – that is, to bring the history of interpretation to an end or to regard it as a history of error from which we must emancipate ourselves before knowledge can begin. Our current desire to get 'beyond hermeneutics', for example, is very much a part of our Cartesian heritage (recall Descartes' contempt for controversy and his effort to seal thinking off from whatever is not itself).

What is especially interesting about our midrashic text is that its subject appears to be just this overarching and irresolvable conflict between transcendental and dialogical attitudes and the break-down that always threatens the institution of midrash (or any institution of interpretation) as a consequence. It would not be too much to say that interpretation generally is always in crisis; this is part of what its historicality means. In the case at hand the question seems to be (very roughly) whether the beit midrash should be structured as a dogmatic system in which certain interpretations will be formally instituted while others are ruled out beforehand, or as an agonistic forum in which argument and dispute constitute exactly the medium in which interpretations are to be developed and preserved. As we have seen, our midrash is framed by a narrative that situates the midrashic conversation in a highly conflicted social environment. In this context the heterogeneous glosses on Ecclesiastes 12:11 add up to an argument for open-ended dialogue and the need to study midrash in *all* of its multiple and contested cases. This seems directed against the dogmatic attitude implied in the line, 'We are your disciples and it is your water that we drink.' So even Rabbi Joshua directs his disciples' attention away from himself and his own teachings back to the house of study. The antidogmatic principle is that 'the words of these and of the other Sages, all of them' – that is, all the heterogeneous and even contradictory things said about these texts – 'were given by Moses the shepherd from what he received from the Unique One of the Universe'.[24] This is, in effect, an argument against collapsing the conflict of interpretation into a conflict of authority. There is (so the argument goes) no conflict of authority in midrash because in midrash authority is social rather than methodological and thus is holistic rather than atomic or subject-centred: the whole dialogue, that is the institution of midrash itself – rabbinic practice – is authoritative, and what counts is conformity with this practice rather than correspondence to some external rule or theory concerning the content of interpretation as such. Here the question is: what does this practice call for or allow for? What if puns and parables and open-ended dispute are the rule rather than systematic closure or even decision by majority rule?[25] Here one's own individual commentary is forceful by being part of the ongoing dialogue rather than by connecting up with something outside of it. No interpretation can be isolated from the whole and set up on its own ground, not without (in effect) setting up a new conversation or new community – or new Torah.[26] At the basis of Rabbi Eleazar's thinking on this score is almost certainly a midrash on Deuteronomy 14:1 ('You are the sons of the Lord your God: you shall not cut yourselves [*titgodedu*]'); that is, 'Do not split yourselves into factions [*'aguddot*] but rather be one faction, as it is said, *It is He that buildeth His upper chambers in the heaven, and hath founded His (single) vault* [aguddato] *upon the earth* (Amos 9:6)'.[27]

To be sure, one can understand the outsider's puzzlement and reluctance to join the argument. From a transcendental standpoint, this theory of authority is paradoxical because it is seen to hang on the heteroglossia of dialogue, on speaking with many voices, rather than on the logical principle of univocity, or speaking with one mind. Instead, the idea of speaking with one mind ('it is your waters that we drink') is explicitly rejected; single-mindedness produces factionalism. The dialogical point seems (like the hermeneutical circle) logically weak, but it is hermeneutically sound, because it is hard to see how one could make any sense at all of an individual midrash, with its scrupulous and sometimes exotic attention to detail, except by situating it in the context of an ongoing discussion in which just such attention is called for – in which details of the text are endlessly disseminated as if in the absence of established contexts. Context, in other words, is social rather than logical, and is therefore alterable and variable, as in the case of a conversation, where no statement is likely to make much sense when taken in isolation from the whole, even though the whole is not an internally coherent system superior to its parts but a chaotic system in perpetual transition back-and-forth between order and turbulence. In such a system parts tend to be more random than constitutive of a settled whole. Hence the principle that the conversation itself is the true author of all that is said in it; no one participant in the conversation can claim original authorship or final authority, because what one says derives from the give and take of the conversation itself, not from one's own subjective intention. This principle surely guided the compilers of the midrashic texts, but it also seems basic to the midrashic tradition itself. Each rabbi's interpretation is, strictly speaking, ungrounded: it derives its meaning and authority, not from its own separate correspondence – at a distance – to a piece of original textual evidence, but from its participation *in* the original, that is from its place in the dialogue inaugurated on Sinai when God addressed the Torah to

Moses. Midrash presupposes not ultimate ground (*Letztbegrundung*) but common ground; it presupposes belonging and participation rather than logical foundation.[28] Midrash is not method but form of life.

This line of thought tempers somewhat the seeming indifference of midrashists to the principle of non-contradiction ('some scholars declare a thing unclean and others declare it clean'). Interpretations are not to be figured on the propositional model as (mono-)logical assertions seeking their own separate validity; rather, they are the mode of participation in dialogue with Torah itself. Midrash is not a method for resolving hermeneutical disputes (even the principle of majority rule was rejected by many rabbis as alien to the whole idea of midrash); it is the place where disputes are meant to go on, where there is always room for another interpretation, or for more dialogue, where interpretation is more a condition of being than an act of consciousness. We need to shake the idea that midrash is (just) a mental process. The point is not to try to hold its multiple interpretations simultaneously in mind as if they constituted a logical system, a canon of internally consistent teachings to be held true for all time or tested against a rule or deposit of faith. On the contrary, to say that midrash is dialogical rather than systematic is to say that it is closer to the rhetorical inventory than to the logical organon; it is to say that it is structured discursively according to the principle of 'now one, now another', as within the open indeterminacy of the question rather than in the closure of the proposition. Indeed, if the task of midrash is to speak to concrete human situations in which something needs to be decided – situations which are themselves discursively structured ('now one thing, now another', in no predictable order, open-ended) – then midrash must always seek to nourish the conflict of interpretation, not to shut it down. Hence the danger of factionalism, or the dogmatism of schools: 'We are your disciples, and it is your water that we drink', is a scholastic motto whose subtext is, 'There is no more to be said'. Closing down the dialogue by means of a final interpretation, a last word or final appeal to a rule of faith, would be to close interpretation off from human life. It would turn Torah into a dead letter, a museum piece, a monument to what people used to believe. If the Torah is to have any force as a text, it must always be situated in a culture of argument. One imagines that this would be true of any text.

Earlier I remarked that it is difficult to know what sort of concept of part-and-whole guides midrashic interpretation; the Rabbis seemed not to have any recognizable sense of wholeness. Now we see that they imagined themselves as *part* of the whole, participating in

Torah rather than operating on it at an analytic distance. A participatory point of view undermines any formal sense of wholeness. And if participation replaces foundation in this way, it follows that the words of interpretation cannot be isolated in any rigorously analytical way from the words of Torah itself. This is consistent with the fact that the Rabbis do not possess (beyond a few formulas like the *Ketib-qere'*) a technical interpretative vocabulary but apply to the text the words of the text itself, using one verse as commentary upon another. It is this dialogical principle that underlies the picture of Solomon as an interpreter as well as author of sacred writings like the Psalms. It is this principle that underlies the rabbinical claim concerning the unity of written and oral Torah, which is not so much a formal, logical or aesthetic unity as a continuity of authority – the sort of unity entailed in speaking in another's name, which is how the Rabbis regularly characterize their own discourse. Both written and oral Torah are given from one shepherd, meaning that everything (including unheard-of ideas and spontaneous puns) is spoken in the name of God and Moses and the lines of interpreters descending from them. The idea is *not* that midrash is repetition or a postal service. The word Torah, and therefore its power and authority, extends itself to include not only the original books of Moses but also the Mishnah, the Talmuds and Aggadot as well. In other words, the Torah is constituted as an open canon. To be sure, the letters of the original scriptures are fixed, but they are not dead. Openness here has to be construed as the openness of what is written; that is, its applicability to the time of its interpretation, its need for actualization. What is important is that interpretation not be fixed – an idea that is reflected in the controversy (extending from at least the quarrel between the Pharisees and Sadducees to the beginnings of the midrashic collections) over whether the words of the Sages should be written down. 'Of the making of books there is no end' (Eccl. 12:12). Openness in this respect means openness of the written word to the spoken (an indispensable principle in the interpretation of a consonantal text).

Perhaps now we are in a position to situate properly the question, 'How can I study Torah in such circumstances?' To study Torah is clearly not to study a text independently of the interpretations through which it is handed down from the past. Study is not the activity of a private, sealed-off, monological subject. When Rabbi Eleazar tells the bewildered fellow to 'make your ear like a grain receiver and acquire a heart that understands the words of the scholars who declare a thing clean as well as of those who declare it unclean', he is saying, in effect, get into the spirit of dialogue. One understands by getting into the game, not by applying techniques.

Don't think of yourself as situated outside the text as an analytical spectator; think of yourself as belonging to the text. Only now you must picture the text not as a formal object (so many fixed letters) but as an open canon whose boundaries are shaped and reshaped by the give and take of midrashic argument. This means studying not just an original text but also midrash itself, for the words of the Sages constitute Torah, make it what it is and, above all, open it to the present and future. The words of the wise are not added to the text; they are the text as well, linking its words together to form, not an integrated, hierarchical system, but an ongoing tradition, a structure of mutual belonging. The Torah emerges as what it is, it comes into its own, only in the dialogue it generates; and only by entering into the dialogue can one enter the Torah. To belong to the dialogue is to belong to Judaism. This is why the Rabbis insist that the words of the wise, which are as goads, include not only the words of Rabbi Akiba and his colleagues but also the words of Solomon and of Moses, and not of Moses only but of God himself, who is frequently pictured studying his own texts.

However, where exactly does the line of power and authority get drawn? Who has the right to interpret? Who has access to the discourse of midrash? One view is that the Torah is not the exclusive possession of an interpretative community defined as those who come into the beit midrash, together with the whole ancestry of official midrashists extending from Solomon to Moses to God. Torah belongs to all, and all to Torah. A midrash on the text from Ecclesiastes we have been studying pictures it as follows:

When are the words of Torah spoken in their most correct form? When they who are versed in them hear them in assemblies. Whence do we know that if one heard (a teaching) from the mouth of an ordinary Israelite, he must regard it as though he heard it from the mouth of a Sage? There is a text, *Which I command thee this day* (Deut. vi,6); and not only as though he heard if from the mouth of one Sage but as though from the mouth of (many) Sages, as it is said, THE WORDS OF THE WISE ARE AS GOADS: and not only as though he heard it from the mouth of (many) Sages but as though from the mouth of the Sanhedrin, (as it is said), *Gather unto Me seventy men* (Num. xi,6); and not only as though he heard it from the mouth of a Sanhedrin, but as though from the mouth of Moses, as it is said, THEY ARE GIVEN FROM ONE SHEPHERD (XII.11), i.e., Moses; and not only as though he heard it from the shepherd Moses but as though from the mouth of the Holy One, blessed be He, as it is said, FROM ONE SHEPHERD, and SHEPHERD denotes none other than the Holy One, blessed be He, as it is said, *Give ear, O Shepherd of Israel* (Ps. lxxx,2), and ONE denotes none other than the Holy One, blessed be He, as it is said, *Hear, O Israel, the Lord our God, the Lord is One* (Deut. vi,4).[29]

Here is a text that sets itself squarely against the scholastic or dogmatic outlook. It is, in effect, a further extension of the rule of *lo titgodedu*: 'Do not cut yourselves into factions.' The interpretative community is nothing less than Israel herself, and all who belong to Israel belong to the ongoing dialogue in which the Torah is understood. No one, in other words, not even the 'ordinary Israelite', is without authority to say what the text means. So it is by no means just metaphorical to call midrash a form of life rather than a technique of exegesis. Midrash is the mode of identity of Torah and Israel. In rabbinic terms, it is the form of God's convenant with his people. 'Even though Israel be in exile among the nations, if they occupy themselves with Torah, it is as though they were not in exile.'[30]

Adopting Wittgenstein's phrase 'form of life', provides a short way of explaining why midrash, like interpretation generally, is irreducible to a logic of validation. Or, as Stanley Cavell says, the search for criteria always ends up being a search for society.[31] This means figuring the question of what counts as a good interpretation in terms of what Charles Taylor calls 'mattering'.[32] Say that interpretation is an act performed by a person to whom things matter, not by a consciousness primed to produce pictures of how things are in the world or in the text or in whatever state of affairs is put before it for analysis. The Torah is a text that makes things matter; it preserves the smallest details of life from inconsequence and triviality. Mattering at all events is what the midrashic text I have been quoting from presupposes with respect to interpretation. Midrash is not a formal operation but a form of life lived with a text that makes claims on people. A text that makes claims upon people turns them into respondents: they are answerable to the text in a way that is qualitatively different from the answerability of disengaged observers to the scenes they wish to depict. This is why, as in legal hermeneutics, you find in the foreground of midrash the idea that interpretation is inseparable from application to a situation that calls for action.

In the midrashic texts themselves this idea takes the form of a relentless preoccupation with the *force* of interpretation. The text from Ecclesiastes – 'The words of the wise are like goads', and so on – is a favourite of the rabbis because it concerns the point of midrash, its practical as against merely academic context. Midrash is not just talk. In the *Pesikta Rabbati* version, Rabbi Berechiah asks: 'Now since one states one view and one states another view, do their words merely fly aimlessly in the air? Indeed not!'[33] The words of the wise are *situated*; their meaning is embedded in their situation. This comes out in the careful unpacking of the mixed metaphor that has nails being planted like trees in the bodies of those who understand. The words of the wise 'impart sense' (*moreh de'ah*).[34] But imparting sense does not mean producing concepts in someone's mind. It is more like getting under someone's skin. The task of imparting sense cannot be separated from the task of getting someone (oneself or another) off his or her feet; imparting sense means moving the one who understands along a certain path. Moreover, understanding means moving in just this wise. Understanding is not a form of mental agreement with a textual object but a mode of being that can only show itself in action – call such action, in this context, walking in 'the ways of the Holy One, blessed be He'. Midrash on this theory is wisdom rather than know-how with respect to what the Torah says, knowing how to take it rather than just knowing how its words work. Midrash is *phronēsis* as well as *technē* because what matters in midrash is our responsiveness to the claims of the text, where responsiveness means knowing not only how the words of the text work but also how they are to be applied in this or that situation, how they are to be internalized and put into practice: 'the purpose is *to do it*'.[35] This is what it means to say that the concern of midrash is to make every jot and tittle of the Torah *matter* to human life, every moment of it. Nothing in the text is without consequence; nothing is to be overlooked or brushed aside. The whole point of midrash is to embed the sacred text in human life, and so to alter it, or channel it, or indeed define it in a certain utterly distinctive way. What midrash finally concerns itself with is the question of what it is to be a Jew. In the political and cultural turmoil and heterogeneity of the Diaspora, to say that understanding is a mode of being is no longer an abstract principle. Call it the criterion of a form of life.

One can take this point in a slightly different direction, of course, because a form of life is always a capillary system through which power circulates in potentially disruptive ways. Imparting sense means taking hold of this power, using it. I mentioned earlier that Rabbi Eleazar's midrash tries to keep the conflict of interpretation from collapsing, or erupting, into a conflict of authority. Hence the broad principle that every Jew has the right to interpret the text. But the framing narrative of our midrash suggests how controversial this question of authority is. Indeed, insofar as what matters in midrash is the *force* of interpretation, authority is the whole issue. It is what is always (tacitly, and sometimes explicitly) in dispute. Our midrash seems concerned to sort out the several strata of this issue in order to affirm rabbinical power, and to affirm it absolutely, as in the following:

R. Johanan used to recite on the first day of the Tabernacles festival the benediction, 'Blessed art Thou, O Lord our God, the King of the Universe, who hath sanctified us with His commandments and hath commanded us concerning the taking of the *lulab*,' while during all the remaining days he ended with, 'Concerning the commandment of the elders.' R. Joshua recited each day the blessing 'Concerning the taking of the *lulab*.' R. Joshua does not admit R. Johanan's contention that according to the Torah the *lulab* is obligatory only on the first day of the festival, since it says, *And ye shall take you on the first day*, etc. (Lev. XXIII, 40), but that on all the remaining days the obligation has only the force of Rabbinic authority. R. Simeon bn. Halafta in the name of R. Aha said that R. Joshua actually held the same view as R. Johanan, and the reason why he acted differently was because it is written, '*The words of the wise are as goads. . . . They are given from one shepherd*'; that is, the words of the Torah and the words of the Sages have been given from the same shepherd. *And more than of them, my son, be careful; of making many books there is no end; and much study is a weariness of the flesh* (Eccl. XII, 12). '*And more than of them, my son, be careful*,' means: More than of the words of the Torah be careful of the words of the Scribes. In the same strain it says, *For thy beloved ones are better than wine* (S. S., I, 2), which means: The words of the beloved ones (the Sages) are better than the wine of the Torah? Why? Because one cannot give a proper decision from the words of the Torah, since the Torah is shut up and consists entirely of headings. . . . From the words of the Sages, however, one can derive the proper law, because they explain the Torah. And the reason why the words of the Sages are compared to goads (*darbanoth*) is because they cause understanding to dwell (*medayerin binah*) in men.

The dispute here between Rabbis Johanan and Joshua is over the force of rabbinical authority *vis-à-vis* the force of Torah. Rabbi Joshua contends – this is certainly what put him in contention with the Patriarch, Rabban Gamaliel – is that there is no difference of power and authority between Torah and Sage. This (he argues) is what the Torah itself says when it compares the words of the wise to goads. The difference between Torah and Sage is that the words of the one are dark and powerless by themselves, whereas the words of the other are as goads: there is no mistaking them, nor escaping their import. And to underscore this the midrash construes a text from the Song of Songs as saying, 'The words of the beloved ones (the Sages) are better than the wine of Torah.' This is a powerful claim, and a trenchantly political one. The relation between Torah and Sage, text and interpretation, is one of *appropriation*; that is, the claim of the one is answered by the other in the form of an appropriation of what is written, a taking of it that amounts to taking it over, bringing its power under one's own control, putting it into play, inscribing it within one's self-understanding so that text and interpretation are constituted as a single political entity.

It would be a mistake, however, to reduce the political nature of midrash to power criteria, or to characterize power purely in terms of domination and control, because it remains the case that midrash is constitutive of rabbinical Judaism – that is, culturally constitutive of Judaism itself in the period following the destruction of Jerusalem and extending at least until the time of Maimonides and even, in some circumstances, to the present time. The politics of interpretation are not exhausted by the theme of coercion. At all events, a hermeneutics of midrash needs to take into account the full range of social and political consequences of interpretation and cannot simply map onto midrash the categories of instrumental reason. The argument here has been that midrash is not simply a technique of polysemic exegesis. Nor, for the same reason, is it enough to characterize midrash as simply an instrument of social control exercised by a particular class within Judaism; it is also a powerful medium of cultural and religious difference, a cultural practice that enables Judaism to set itself apart and articulate its identity against traditionally hostile cultural forms that have their own strategic (and frequently single-minded) picture of what the consequences of interpretation should be. Here the task for study would be the ways in which midrash itself constitutes a form of resistance within larger and more violent conflicts of interpretation. In this case the irreducibility of midrash to single-mindedness and logical rule, its unpredictability and uncontainability within dogmatic frameworks, its bewildering playfulness ('how can I study Torah in such circumstances?'), becomes an allegory of the resistance to dominant cultures that characterizes the history of Judaism itself.[36]

APPENDIX: From the Talmud, Berakoth, 27b–28a

THE EVENING PRAYER HAS NO FIXED LIMIT. What is the meaning of NO FIXED LIMIT? Shall I say it means that if a man wants he can say the *Tefillah* in the night? Then let it state, 'The time for the evening *Tefillah* is the whole night'! – But what in fact is the meaning of HAS NO FIXED LIMIT? It is equivalent to saying, The evening *Tefillah* is optional. For Rab Judah said in the name of Samuel: With regard to the evening *Tefillah*, Rabban Gamaliel says it is compulsory, whereas R. Joshua says it is optional. Abaye says: The *halachah* is stated by the one who says it is compulsory; Raba says the *halachah* follows the one who says it is optional.

It is related that a certain disciple came before R. Joshua and asked him, Is the evening *Tefillah* compulsory or optional? He replied: It is optional. He [the disciple] then presented himself before Rabban Gamaliel and asked him: Is the evening *Tefillah* compulsory or optional? He replied: It is compulsory. But, he said, did not R. Joshua tell me that it is optional? He said: Wait till the champions enter the Beth ha-Midrash. When the champions came in, someone rose and inquired, Is the evening *Tefillah* compulsory or optional? Rabban Gamaliel replied: It is compulsory. Said Rabban Gamaliel to the Sages: Is there anyone who disputes this? R. Joshua replied to him: No. He said to him: Did they not report you to me as saying that it is optional? He then went on: Joshua, stand up and let them testify against you! R. Joshua stood up and said: Were I alive and he [the witness] dead, the living could contradict the dead. But now that he is alive and I am alive, how can the living contradict the living? Rabban Gamaliel remained sitting and expounding and R. Joshua remained standing, until all the people there began to shout and say to Huzpith the *turgeman*, Stop! and he stopped. They then said: How long is he [Rabban Gamaliel] to go on insulting him [R. Joshua]? On New Year last year he insulted him; he insulted him in the matter of the firstborn in the affair of R. Zadok; now he insults him again! Come, let us depose him! Whom shall we appoint instead? We can hardly appoint R. Joshua, because he is one of the parties involved. We can hardly appoint R. Akiba because perhaps Rabban Gamaliel will bring a curse on him because he has no ancestral merit. Let us then appoint R. Eleazar b. Azariah, who is wise and rich and the tenth in descent from Ezra. He is wise, so that if anyone puts a question to him he will be able to answer it. He is rich, so that if occasion arises for paying court to Caesar he will be able to do so. He is tenth in descent from Ezra, so that he has ancestral merit and he [Rabban Gamaliel] cannot bring a curse on him. They went and said to him: I will go and consult the members of my family. He went and consulted his wife. She said to him: [28a] Perhaps they will depose you later on. He replied to her: [There is a proverb:] Let a man use a cup of honour for one day even if it be broken the next. She said to him: You have no white hair. He was eighteen years old that day, and a miracle was wrought for him and eighteen rows of hair [on his beard] turned white. That is why R. Eleazar b. Azariah said: 'behold I am *about* seventy years old, and he did not say [simply] seventy years old. A Tanna taught: On that day the doorkeeper was removed and permission was given to the disciples to enter. For Rabban Gamaliel had issued a proclamation [saying], No disciple whose character does not correspond to his exterior may enter the Beth ha-Midrash. On that day many stools were added. R. Joḥanan said: There is a difference of opinion on this matter between Abba Joseph b. Dosethai and the Rabbis: one [authority] says that four hundred stools were added, and the other says seven hundred. Rabban Gamaliel became alarmed and said: Perhaps, God forbid, I withheld Torah from Israel! He was shown in his dream white casks full of ashes. This, however, really meant nothing; he was only shown this to appease him. . . .

[There follows a dispute in the beit midrash between Rabban Gamaliel and R. Joshua in which R. Joshua proves to have the better argument.] Rabban Gamaliel thereupon said: This being the case, I will go and apologize to R. Joshua. When he reached his house he saw that the walls were black. He said to him: From the walls of your house it is apparent that you are a charcoal-burner [a blacksmith]. He replied: Alas for the generation of which you are the leader, seeing that you know nothing of the troubles of the scholars, their struggles to support and sustain themselves! He said to him: I apologize, forgive me. He paid no attention to him. Do it, he said, out of respect for my father. He then became reconciled to him. They said: Who will go and tell the Rabbis? A certain fuller said to them: I will go. R. Joshua sent a message to the Beth ha-Midrash saying: Let him who is accustomed to wear the robe wear it [let Rabban Gamaliel be master of the house of study]; shall he who is not accustomed to wear the robe say to him who is accustomed to wear it, Take off your robe and I will put it on? Said R. Akiba to the Rabbis: Lock the doors so that the servants of Rabban Gamaliel should not come and upset the Rabbis. Said R. Joshua: I had better get up and go to them. He came and knocked at the door. He said to them: Let the sprinkler son of a sprinkler sprinkle [let the priest, son of a priest, sprinkle the water of purification]; shall he who is neither a sprinkler nor the son of a sprinkler say to a sprinkler son of a sprinkler, Your water is cave water and your ashes are oven ashes? Said R. Akiba to him: R. Joshua, you have received your apology, have we done anything except out of regard for your honour? Tomorrow morning you and I will wait on him. They said: How shall we do? Shall we depose him [R. Eleazar b. Azariah]? We have a rule that we may raise an object to a higher grade of sanctity but must not degrade it to a lower. If we let one Master preach on one Sabbath and one on the next, this will cause jealousy. Let therefore Rabban Gamaliel preach three Sabbaths and R. Eleazar b. Azariah one Sabbath. And it is in reference to this that a Master said: 'Whose Sabbath was it? It was the Sabbath of R. Eleazar b. Azariah.'

NOTES

1 See Vincent B. Leitch, *American Literary Criticism from the Thirties to the Eighties* (Columbia University Press, New York, 1988), p. 208. Just so, hermeneutics is without a store in the shopping-mall of critical methods represented in *Textual Analysis: Some Readers Reading*, ed. Mary Ann Caws (Modern Language Association, New York, 1985) – which is in fact a superb showcase of the analytical sophistication and technical virtuosity that contemporary literary study has achieved. For similar reasons, namely the reduction of theory to method, hermeneutics doesn't really count as a theory, either. There's not a word about it, for example, in the most recent comprehensive anthology of studies in literary theory, *Contemporary Literary Criticism*, ed. Robert Con Davis and Ronald Schleifer (Longman, White Plains, NY, 1989).

2 Karl-Otto Apel, 'The A Priori of Communication and the Foundation of the Humanities', in *Man and World*, 5 (1972), pp. 3–37. Why is contemporary literary criticism so dominated by the vocabulary of strategies, techniques, projects, approaches, operations, paradigms, deep structures, tacit rules and the systematic production of effects? Whatever the answer, this is the language in which new developments in criticism explain and assert themselves. A case in point is the New Historicism. In Stephen Greenblatt's words, what makes the New Historicism 'new', what sets it apart or updates it from all that has preceded it, is just its 'methodological self-consciousness'. See Greenblatt's introduction to *The Forms of Power and the Power of Forms in the Renaissance*, a special number of *Genre*, 15 (1982), pp. 3–6.

3 A common mistake – Leitch makes it, and so do most midrashologists and students of early Judaism – is to confuse hermeneutics with Susan Handelman's project in *The Slayers of Moses: The Emergence of Rabbinic Interpretation in Modern Literary Theory* (SUNY Press, Albany, 1982), whose 'methodological preface' contains the following paragraph: 'I should like here to clarify and emphasize this description of my method. It is not, by any means, an orthodox "structuralist" approach – moreover, we are now in a post-structuralist era; nor am I a Lacanian, Derridean, or member of any of the contemporary "hermeneutical mafias." In the broadest sense, this book is itself a kind of midrash, a search for hidden elements and correspondences, a tropism or "wandering of meaning," which proceeds as much by analogy and association as by linear logic. Perhaps it should be called a "structuralist midrash." This method, though, has its own philosophic rigor, as I will show when I discuss the use to which it is put in Freud, Derrida, and Bloom' (p. xv).

It is not my purpose here is to link rabbinical interpretation with deconstruction or any recent school of criticism or theory.

4 See Hans-Georg Gadamer, *Truth and Method*, second, revised ed., trans. Joel Weinsheimer and Donald G. Marshall (Crossroad Publishing, New

York, 1989), p. 295. This does not mean that Gadamer is against method in the sense of a disciplined study of texts. On the contrary, in his own readings (whether of Plato or Paul Celan) he always shows the rigorous scruples of a classical philologist.

5 A longstanding scholarly tradition does try to defend midrash against the charge of irrationality by arguing that it is, despite its chaotic or non-linear surface structure, basically a rule-governed activity, and therefore rational after all. This view sometimes emphasizes the importance of the *middoth* of Hillel, Ishmael and Eleazar b. Jose Ha-gelili. See Hermann L. Strack, *Introduction to the Talmud and Midrash* (first published 1931; rpt. Atheneum, New York, 1983), pp. 93–8. However, it is not clear that *middoth* are rules in our sense, nor are we really clear about the context in which the *middoth* that come down to us are to be understood. (They don't seem to have been formulated systematically or intended to hang together as a manual for exegesis.) For many scholars, many of the *middoth* themselves are offensive to reason. See Saul Lieberman, 'Rabbinic Interpretation of Scripture', in *Hellenism in Jewish Palestine* (Jewish Theological Seminary, New York, 1950), pp. 47–82. J. Weingreen, in *From Bible to Mishna: The Continuity of Tradition* (Manchester University Press, Manchester, and Holmes and Meier, New York, 1976), esp. pp. 1–33, remarks on the strange incongruity between the analytical rigour of the Rabbis as textual critics and their bizarre extravagance as exegetes. Jacob Neusner tries to penetrate this extravagance to lay bare the deep structure or 'syllogism' of a midrashic compilation in *Judaism and Scripture: The Evidence of Leviticus Rabbah* (University of Chicago Press, Chicago and London, 1986). But this is not to defend midrash as interpretation. Neusner's view is that midrash is a perfect example of 'the ubiquitous datum of Western Biblical interpretation: it is that people make of Scripture anything they wish.' So there is nothing for it but to take midrash as a form of literature, not as hermeneutics. See Neusner, *Midrash as Literature: The Primacy of Documentary Discourse* (University Press of America, Lanham, New York, London, 1987), p. 20. My view is that, on any hermeneutically informed study of the evidence, midrash is not just eisigesis but a hermeneutical practice that tells us a good deal about what it is to understand a text. Unfortunately, mainline research on midrash is just hermeneutically naïve.

6 See Gerald L. Bruns, 'Canon and Power in the Hebrew Scriptures', *Critical Inquiry*, 10 (March 1984), pp. 462–80; rpt. in *Canons*, ed. Robert von Hallberg (University of Chicago Press, Chicago, 1983), pp. 65–83.

7 'The Nature of Aggadah', tr. Marc Bergman, in *Midrash and Literature*, ed. Geoffrey Hartman and Sanford Budick (Yale University Press, New Haven, 1986), pp. 48–9.

8 References to midrashic texts in this essay are to *Pěsiḳta dě-Rab Kahăna: R. Kahana's Compilation of Discourses for Sabbaths and Feast Days*, tr. William G. (Gershon Zev) Braude and Israel J. Epstein (Jewish Publication Society, Philadelphia, 1975); *Pesikta Rabbati: Discourses for*

Feasts, Fasts, and Special Sabbaths, tr. William Braude (Yale University Press, New Haven, 1968, 2 vols; *Midrash Rabbah*, tr. Harry Freedman and Maurice Simon (Soncinco Press, London, 1938), 10 vols; and *Sifre: A Tannaitic Commentary on the Book of Deuteronomy*, tr. Reuven Hammer (Yale University Press, New Haven and London, 1986). The quotation above is from the *Pĕsiḳta dĕ-Rab Kahăna*, 12.12.

9 See E. D. Hirsch, Jr, 'Meaning and Significance Reinterpreted', *Critical Inquiry*, 11 (December 1984), pp. 202–25.

10 'Erubin, 21b. *The Babylonian Talmud*, tr. Rabbi Dr I. Epstein (Soncino Press, London, 1938), hereafter referred to simply as *Talmud*.

11 Berekoth, 63b. The Talmud continues: 'R. Jose b Ḥanina said: What is the meaning of the text, *A sword is upon the boasters* [baddim] *and they shall become fools?* [Jer. 50:36]. A sword is upon the enemies of the disciples of the wise who sit separately [*bad bebad*] and study the Torah. What is more, they become stupid.'

12 *Midrash Rabbah*, Naso [Numbers], XIV.4. See also *Talmud*, Hagigah, 3a–b. A slightly different version of this midrash appears in the *Pesikta Rabbati*, Piska 3.2. I discuss this version in 'Allegory and Midrash: The Beginnings of Scriptural Interpretation', in *The Literary Guide to the Bible*, ed. Robert Alter and Frank Kermode (Harvard University Press, Cambridge, 1987), pp. 630–4. The present essay was substantially written in 1983 and formed the basis for the five pages on midrash in my contribution to *The Literary Guide*; it has been slightly revised for this volume.

13 See Richard S. Sarason, 'Toward a New Agendum for the Study of Rabbinic Midrashic Literature', in *Studies in Aggadah, Targum, and Jewish Liturgy in Memory of Joseph Heinemann*, ed. Jakob J. Petuchowski and Ezra Fleischer (Magnes Press, Jerusalem, 1981), pp. 55–71. Sarason warns, quite rightly, against conflating and confusing two separate questions with respect to midrash: 'The first deals with the nature, social setting, and function of the various midrashic compilations as they have come down to us and of the constituent materials in their current literary contexts. The second asks about the nature, social setting, and function of the midrashic activity in general and about the form and nature of the midrashic materials before literary encapsulation in their present contexts' (p. 62). He calls for an approach that gets us 'back *onto* the page' of the midrashic text as this comes down to us in the compilations that we have. What picture of midrash as a hermeneutical practice emerges from *these* pages? This is my concern in this chapter.

14 There is an account of the deposition and restoration of Gamaliel in *Talmud*, Berakoth, 27b–28a, reproduced in the Appendix to this chapter.

15 A good account of this state of affairs is given by Ephraim E. Urbach in *The Sages: Their Concepts and Beliefs* (Magnes Press, Jerusalem, 1979), vol. I, pp. 593–603 ('The Regime of the Sages after the Destruction of the Temple'), and esp. pp. 620–30 ('The Internal Relations in the Academies of the Sages'). Despite the fierce competition among the Rabbis, however,

Urbach explains that the Sages remained a fairly well-integrated class with a sharp sense of its privileges with respect to the community as a whole (pp. 625–8). We shall see below that we can read this midrash as an appeal to maintain this social and political integrity despite the internal conflicts that threaten to disrupt it. See also Gedalia Alon, *Jews, Judaism, and The Classical World: Studies in Jewish History in the Times of the Second Temple and Talmud* (Magnes Press, Jerusalem, 1977), pp. 314–33, for an account of the political antagonism between the Patriarch and the Sages during the early history of rabbinic Judaism.

16 *Midrash Rabbah*, Naso (Numbers), XIV,4.
17 Ibid., Hazita (Song of Songs), I, 10.2.
18 Ibid., Bemidbar, XIX, 7.
19 See Gerald L. Bruns, *Inventions: Writing, Textuality, and Understanding in Literary History* (Yale University Press, New Haven and London, 1982), pp. 30–1.
20 *Midrash Rabbah*, Hazita (Song of Songs), I, 1.8.
21 Ibid., I, 10.2.
22 See James L. Kugel, 'Two Introductions to Midrash', in Hartman and Budick (eds), pp. 77–104; rpt. from *Prooftexts*, 3 (1983), pp. 141–55. Jacob Neusner aims to dispute a verse-centered view of midrash in the studies cited above (n. 6) which seek to recover the unifying logic underlying such 'documents' as the *Leviticus Rabbah*, a midrashic compilation, but Neusner's argument is not very clear, and as developed in his *Midrash as Literature* it seems misdirected, or at least at cross-purposes with Kugel's account, which seems to me very far from controversial. Kugel is surely correct in suggesting that the verse-centered character of midrashic interpretation reflects the economy of a culture whose mnemonics are (however graphic) still oral rather than textual. The text in a scribal culture is still housed in the oral–aural library of memory. See Kugel, 'Two Introductions', p. 94. David Stern seems to me to penetrate to the heart of the matter when he locates midrash in the extraordinary intimacy that exists between God and exegete. The language of exegesis, he says, is a 'language of ḥavivut', of intimacy and familiarity; it is not the language of the prophetic sublime or of voices thundering from a great distance. So playful attention to detail is not pedantry or low seriousness but represents a new form of religious language. See 'Midrash and the Language of Exegesis', in Hartman and Budick (eds), pp. 105–24.
23 *Pesikta Rabbati*, Piska, 3.2.
24 Ibid., 3.2.
25 The Talmud speaks of 'the warfare of the Torah', which only means that fierce, free-wheeling argument is the medium of Torah-study. See Hagigah, 14a.
26 Hence the threat of 'two Torahs'. See Urbach, *The Sages*, I, p. 618. But in practice Torah is plural, as, for example, between Babylonian and Palestinian traditions, but also throughout the Diaspora, where halakhic decisions must be able to address diverse cultural conditions.

27 *Sifre on Deuteronomy*, Piska, 96. See Urbach, *The Sages*, pp. 618–20, on the rule of *titgodĕdu*.

28 On the distinction between foundation and participation, see Hans-Georg Gadamer, 'The Hermeneutics of Suspicion', in *Hermeneutics: Questions and Prospects*, ed. Gary Shapiro and Alan Sica (University of Massachusetts Press, Amherst, 1981), p. 84.

29 *Midrash Rabbah*, Ecclesiastes, XII. 11.1.

30 *Tanna de Be Eliyyahu*, ed. M. Friedmann (Vienna, 1902), p. 148; quoted in *The Rabbinic Anthology*, ed. C. G. Montefiore and H. Loewe (Schocken Books, New York, 1974), p. 132.

31 See Stanley Cavell, *The Claim of Reason: Wittgenstein, Skepticism, Morality, and Tragedy* (Oxford University Press, New York, 1971), pp. 3–36.

32 See Charles Taylor, 'The Concept of a Person', in *Philosophical Papers, I: Human Agency and Language* (Cambridge University Press, Cambridge, 1985), pp. 97–114.

33 *Pesikta Rabbati*, Piska, 3.2.

34 Ibid.

35 *Sifre on Deuteronomy*, Piska, 48.

36 While the present essay was in press, David Stern has published a fine essay, 'Midrash and Indeterminacy', *Critical Inquiry*, 15 (autumn 1988), pp. 132–61. Stern argues, quite rightly, that recent critical concepts such as textual indeterminacy cannot be mapped onto midrashic interpretation, where multiple interpretations frequently derive from serious political conflicts within the rabbinical community.

8

The Song of Songs: Lock or Key? Intertextuality, Allegory and Midrash

Daniel Boyarin

Pseudo-Sa'adya, an anonymous Jewish commentator of the tenth century, characterized the Song of Songs as a 'lock to which the key has been lost'.[1] Some few centuries earlier the rabbis of the midrash regarded the holy song as a hermeneutic key to the unlocking of the Torah. *Both interpreted the Song of Songs itself in essentially the same fashion* as a poem on the love between God and Israel. The question immediately rises: how can it be that opposite theories can lead to the same interpretation? What is the meaning of this opposition of theory? What happened, historically, to generate this difference in understanding? These are the questions I would like to explore in this text with a particular view towards achieving greater understanding of midrash and of rabbinic thought about interpretation and meaning.

This chapter will be divided into three parts. In the first, I will analyze the passage from the introduction to the midrash *Song of Songs Rabbah* to which I have just alluded, arguing that it is an important example of that rare bird, an explicit reflection by the Rabbis on their hermeneutic method. In the second part, I will try to show by actual examples that the theory I have posited was actually applied and explains the way midrashic interpretations work. In the third part, I will come back to the questions asked in the last paragraph.

I

Since the text is relatively unknown, I shall translate it here in its entirety and comment on it section by section:

Another word: 'Song of Songs', This is what Scripture has said: 'And not only that Kohelet was wise' (Eccl. 12:9). Had another man said them, you

would have had to bend your ears and hear these words; 'and not only that' –
it was Solomon who said them. Had he said them on his own authority, you
would have had to bend your ear and hear them; 'and not only that' – he said
them by the Holy Spirit. 'And not only that Kohelet was wise, he moreover
taught knowledge to the people, and proved and researched, and formulated
many *meshalim*.' – 'and proved' words of Torah; 'and researched' words of
Torah; he made handles[2] for the Torah. You will find that until Solomon
existed, there was no figure (Hebrew *dugma* ex Greek *deigma*).[3]

Kohelet is, of course, Solomon. According to biblical tradition, that
wise king wrote three books – Song of Songs in his youth, Proverbs in
his maturity, and Ecclesiastes (Kohelet) in his old age. Therefore, the
verse of Ecclesiastes which tells us of his intellectual activity in general
is appropriately referred to all three of his works. Now this activity is
characterized as 'teaching knowledge to the people', which for the
Rabbis means ineluctably teaching Torah. It follows that he 'proved
and researched' the words of Torah. And this interpretive activity is
designated by the verse itself as 'making of many *meshalim*', this last
glossed by the midrash as *dugma*, that is figure, simile, or paradigm.
The interpretive activity which Solomon engaged in was the making
of figurative stories which are 'handles to the Torah', that is, as I shall
argue, which render the axiological meaning of the narratives of the
Torah accessible.[4] Song of Songs, Proverbs and Ecclesiastes are
collections of figures made by Solomon to enable the reading of
Torah.

In the sequel to the above passage, the Rabbis give us no less than
six *meshalim*, through which we can get a double handle – through
the content and the form – on the meaning of Solomon's interpretive
work. I shall quote here only the last three:

Said Rabbi Yose: it is like a basket full of fruits, which had no handle, and it
couldn't be carried, and someone wise came and made for it handles, and it
began to be carried by its handles. So until Solomon came, no one could
understand the words of Torah, but once Solomon had been, everyone began
to comprehend Torah. R. Shila said: it is like a pot full of boiling water,
which had no handle to carry it, and someone came and made it a handle,
and it began to be carried by its handle. R. Hanina said: it is like a deep well
full of water, and its waters were cold and sweet and good, but no one could
drink of them. Someone came and provided a rope [tied to] a rope, a cord
[tied to] a cord, and he drew from it and he drank. Then all began to draw
and drink. So from word to word, from *mashal* to *mashal*, Solomon
comprehended the secret of Torah, as is written, 'The *meshalim* [We
translate 'proverbs' D.B.] of Solomon the son of David, King of Israel
(Proverbs 1:1) – by virtue of his *meshalim*. Solomon comprehended the
words of Torah.

These little narratives are themselves *meshalim* of the *mashal* and give us accordingly a first insight into the meaning of this term. The *mashal* is a story whose meaning by itself is perfectly clear and simple, and because of its simplicity enables one to interpret by analogy a more complex, difficult or hermetic text. This point should be amplified here, for it will be of some importance in our whole argument: the *mashal* is not a text which is itself enigmatic; it is a text whose declared function is to interpret.[5] Gerald Bruns has pointed out:

a commonplace distinction between light and dark sayings, or between proverbs and enigmas, where the one is a truth which circulates widely and which everyone can recognize, whereas the other requires study, reflection, investigation, and the assistance of the sorts of special insight possessed by unique individuals such as Tiresias or even Oedipus: people who are required to cope (often as a matter of life or death) with riddles and prophecies.[6]

This distinction is certainly relevant here, and the rabbis are clearly placing Solomon's works, including Song of Songs, into the category of light sayings, indeed light sayings whose very function is to illumine the dark sayings of Torah. By reading Song of Songs, Proverbs and Ecclesiastes as *meshalim*, then, the midrash is claiming that they are not hermetic texts, 'locks to which the key has been lost', but hermeneutic keys to the unlocking of the hermetic Torah, or in the words of the midrash itself, of 'the secret of Torah'. This is particularly important for reading the midrash on Song of Songs.

Our introduction to Song of Songs ends with a sort of *peroratio*, again making use of the *mashal*, in which we are urged to take this interpretive activity of Solomon's very seriously, and by implication to take the study of Song of Songs as seriously as we do the study of Torah itself:

The rabbis say: Do not let this *mashal* be light in your eyes, for by means of this *mashal* one comes to comprehend the words of Torah. A *mashal* to a king who has lost a golden coin from his house or a precious pearl – does he not find it by means of a wick worth a penny? Similarly, let not this *mashal* be light in your eyes, for by means of this *mashal* one comes to comprehend the words of Torah. Know that this is so, for Solomon, by means of this *mashal*[7] understood the exact meaning of the Torah. Rabbi Judah says: It is to teach you that everyone who teaches words of Torah to the many is privileged to have the Holy Spirit descend upon him. From whom do we learn this? From Solomon, who because he taught words of Torah to the many was privileged to have the Holy Spirit descend upon him and uttered three books, Proverbs, Ecclesiastes, and Song of Songs.[8]

Of recent writers, it seems that only Gerald Bruns has realized the crucial import of this text for the theory of midrash.[9] The three books that Solomon wrote were written as interpretations of the books of Moses. Indeed, all of the later books of the Bible are readings of the earlier ones. Midrash is thus a laying bare of the intertextual relationships of scripture itself. Bruns writes that midrash is founded on the

ancient hermeneutical insight [that] as the Rabbis, Augustine, and Luther knew, the Bible, despite its textual heterogeneity, can be read as a self-glossing book. One learns to study it by following the ways in which one portion of the text illumines another. The generations of scribes who shaped and reshaped the Scriptures appear to have designed them to be studied in just this way. Thus Brevard S. Childs speaks of 'the interpretive structure which the biblical text has received from those who formed and used it as sacred scripture.' This does not mean that redaction produced a unified text (or what we would think of as unified: a holistic text, free of self-contradiction, a systematic or organic whole: the Bible is everything but *that*); rather it means that the parts are made to relate to one another reflexively, with later texts, for example, throwing light on the earlier, even as they themselves always stand in the light of what precedes and follows them.[10]

The importance of Bruns's paper, in this passage, and throughout, is that he takes midrash seriously as hermeneutic[11] and realizes what I too consider to be its central defining characteristic – the creative reading of the ways in which scripture reads its own writing, earlier texts the later and later the earlier, what the midrash itself refers to as 'stringing [like beads or pearls D.B.] the words of Torah together and from the Torah to the Prophets and from the Prophets to the Writings.'[12] In what follows I would like to apply this concept of midrash to specific midrashic passages, initially having to do with the Song of Songs and then extending to other texts. I would like to take on three tasks which Bruns does not attempt in his essay: to exemplify in some detail the method of midrashic intertextual reading, to consider the importance of the *mashal* and its specific nature in this context, and to consider the relation of midrashic reading to allegory – particularly with regard to that classic of allegoresis, the common tradition of Song of Songs interpretation.[13]

II

The first text I will analyze illustrates very nicely the way in which Song of Songs can be read as a *mashal* which interprets the Torah.

The text is found in *Song of Songs Rabbah* on the verse, 'My dove in the clefts of the rock, let me hear thy voice (Song of Songs 2:14)':

The one of the house of R. Ishmael teaches: In the hour in which Israel went out from Egypt, to what were they similar? To a dove which ran away from a hawk, and entered the cleft of a rock and found there a nesting snake. She entered within, but could not go in, because of the snake; she could not go back, because of the hawk which was waiting outside. What did the dove do? She began to cry out and beat her wings, in order that the owner of the dovecote would hear and come save her. That is how Israel appeared at the Sea. They could not go down into the Sea, for the Sea had not yet been split for them. They could not go back, for Pharaoh was coming near. What did they do? 'They were mightily afraid, and the Children of Israel cried out unto the Lord (Ex. 14:10)' and immediately 'The Lord saved them on that day. (Ex. 14:30)'.[14]

What is going on in this text? First of all, the clearly figurative utterance, 'My dove in the clefts of the rock, let me hear thy voice', is being expanded into a full narrative, or rather it is being provided with a narrative context in which it can be read. What is the dove doing in the clefts of the rock? Who is addressing her? Why does he want to hear her voice, or why is it necessary that she make a sound? All of these questions are being answered by a simple method of narrative gap filling. The dove is in the rock because she is afraid. The rock is not a sufficient protection for her. The speaker is her master, and she must cry out so that he will save her. However, the claim is being made that this figure refers to a concrete situation in Israel's history, the crisis situation at the shore of the Red Sea. In order that we experience fully what the situation was there, what was the nature of the predicament of the People, why they cried out unto the Lord and why He answered them, the verse of Song of Songs is associated with it by means of the *mashal* or narrative figure. In other words, what I am claiming is that we do not truly have an interpretation here of a verse of Song of Songs, but rather of a verse of Exodus, or perhaps we might best say, a claim that the two verses, the earlier and the belated mutually illumine each other. The assumption having been made that Solomon wrote his poem as a key to the reading of the Torah, that poem is then read by reading it into (literally) a narrative context in the Torah. Its figures are made concrete by being identified with particular situations and characters from the Torah history. Those situations are rendered axiologically and emotionally sharper by the figures of the poetic text.

As evidence for this claim, I would like to offer another text, a parallel version, indeed, of the same text, from the midrash on

Exodus which originates in the same 'School of R. Ishmael', to wit the *Mekilta*:

'They were mightily afraid, and the Children of Israel cried out unto the Lord' . . . 'Stand still and see the salvation of the Lord' . . . To what were the Israelites at that moment like? To a dove fleeing from a hawk, and about to enter a cleft in the rock where there is a hissing serpent. If she enters there is the serpent! If she stays out there is the hawk! In such a plight were the Israelites at that moment, the sea forming a bar and the enemy pursuing. Immediately they set their mind upon prayer. Of them it is explicitly said (or interpreted!) in the Tradition:[15] 'O my dove that art in the clefts of the rock, let me hear thy voice.'[16]

Now we can see clearly what I would claim is probably the original context of this *mashal*. The interpreter, in order to render the situation of the Children of Israel with the Sea at their front and the enemy at their back sharp and tangible adopted the figure of a dove fleeing from an eagle and a snake, a figure which brings the pathos of the situation home very poignantly. However, that figure is not drawn from the imagination of the midrashist but taken from the stock of figures given in the Tradition, in the Sacred Writings, that is in the *mashal* which was 'formulated' by Solomon to enable us to understand the words of Torah. Note well, that – neither as interpretation of the verse of Song of Songs, nor as interpretation of the verse in Exodus, do we have a translation of the verse to another level of signification, or to use a different metaphor, in neither case do we have a pairing of a signifier with a signified; we have, rather, the establishment of an intertextual connection between two signifiers which mutually read each other. The narrative-*mashal* here is not a literary form but a hermeneutic figure (to use Bruns's apt formulation); it is a *dugma*, pattern or figure, which is used by the midrashist to enable the two verses to speak to each other.

Admittedly, there is nothing in the verse of Song of Songs here which explicitly directs our attention to the situation and the verse of Exodus.[17] In that sense we might feel that the midrashist has gone beyond what we would call reading in 'chaining the words of Torah to the Writings'. It will be instructive, therefore, to see cases in which precisely the same technique is used, where, I submit, we would freely grant that the Writings are indeed interpreting a verse from the Torah. We do not have far to look. We can find an excellent example in the same section of the same midrash on Exodus:

And Moses stretched out his hand over the sea (Ex. 14:21). The Sea began to stand against him. Moses said: In the Name of the Holiness. But it did not yield. The Holiness Blessed be He, revealed Himself; the Sea began to flee, as it says, 'The Sea saw and fled (Ps. 114:3)'. Its *mashal*; to what is the matter similar? To a king of flesh and blood, who had two gardens, one inside the other. He sold the inner one, and the purchaser came to enter, but the guard did not allow him. He said to him: In the name of the King. But he did not yield. He showed him the signet, but he did not yield until the king came. Once the king came, the guard began to flee. He said: All day long I have been speaking to you in the name of the king and you did not yield. Now, why are you fleeing? He said: Not from you am I fleeing, but from the king am I fleeing.

   Similarly, Moses came and stood at the sea. He said to him: In the name of the Holiness. And it did not yield, until the Holiness, Blessed be He, revealed Himself in His glory. The sea began to flee, as it is said, 'The sea began to flee (Ps. 114)'. Moses said to him: All day long I have been speaking to you in the name of the Holiness, Blessed be He, and you did not submit. Now, 'what ails you, O sea that you flee? (Ps. 114)' He answered him: Not from before you do I flee, son of Amram, but 'from before the Lord, tremble Earth, from before the God of Jacob (Ps. 114)'.

This text is a commentary on the verse, 'And Moses stretched out his hand over the Sea, and the Lord moved the Sea with a strong wind (Ex. 14:21). The question that the interpreter is tacitly asking is what is the meaning of this sequence of events? Why did Moses stretch out his hand over the sea if it is God who is doing the moving? The answer to these hermeneutic problems is given by reading the text of Psalm 114 as a commentary on this passage. It is important that we have a look at the whole text of this small poem to appreciate the moves of the midrash.

When Israel went out from Egypt; the House of Jacob from a foreign nation. Judah became His holy one; Israel His dominion. The Sea saw and fled; the Jordan turned back. The mountains danced like rams; the hills like lambs. What has happened to you, O Sea, that you flee; O Jordan that you turn back? O mountains that you dance like rams; O hills like lambs? From before the Master, tremble Earth, from before the God of Jacob.

The rhetorical question of the psalm is turned in the midrashic text into an actual colloquy between Moses and the Sea. That is to say, the figurative usage of the poem, the personification of the Sea, is contextualized historically and dramatized. This mini-drama is then correlated with the verse in Exodus, which is the subject of the midrash, and that verse is situated dramatically as well. Out of the two texts is created a third, a new text, which has qualities, both semantic and aesthetic, which neither had alone. The verse in Exodus is now motivated. The answer has been given to the question why Moses stretched out his hand, but then God was the motivating force behind the movement of the sea. The text of the psalm has been sharpened. Instead of a vague 'When Israel went out from Egypt', we have a specific moment. Instead of the somewhat enigmatic 'What has happened to you O Sea?' we have a specific, why did you not flee till now, or rather, why now and not before? Note that this interpretive move is very similar to those modes of interpretation that take the Song of Songs as dramatic dialogues, assigning the different parts to a king, a shepherd and a maiden. The function of the *mashal* here is to provide a narrative structure or pattern, a *dugma*, within which the text from Exodus and the text from Psalms can be read together and provide mutual inter-illumination.[18]

Now, what is significant here for us to note is that the text in Psalms *does* indicate explicitly that it refers to the narrative situation of the Exodus. In other words, here we have a case where the surface form of the later poetic text is manifestly a reference to the earlier prose narrative – a situation which is, of course, very common in the Bible and particularly in Psalms. The hermeneutic move which the midrash makes in order to specifically relate the two texts in this case is precisely the same as the one used above to relate the text of Song of Songs with that of Exodus. In both cases, a figurative dialogue, a poetic personification of somewhat vague reference is given a historical context which illumines and sharpens the motivations and events of the prose text. The vehicle of the narrative creation in both cases is the *mashal*, which is seen to be a formal function (providing the morphology, as it were, of the tale) ancillary to the hermeneutic function of the co-reading of the two texts. The claim I am making is that this method of reading the Song of Songs, placing its dialogues into the historical context of the Exodus (which is the primary mode of *Song of Songs Rabbah*), was inspired by such textual situations as the explicit relationship of Psalms 114 to Exodus 14. This is what the Rabbis meant when they said that Song of Songs is a *mashal*, and 'Let not this *mashal* be light in your eyes, for it is by means of the *mashal* that one can understand the words of Torah.'

This insight, if I may be permitted to call it such, will enable us to open up another text. The passage is again from the midrash on Exodus, and although it does not use the rhetorical structure of *mashal*, it nevertheless uses Song of Songs as a hermeneutic key to the Torah in the same way as the above texts:

This is my God and I will beautify Him (Exodus 15:2): Rabbi Aqiba says, I will speak the beauties[19] and the praise of the Holiness-Blessed-Be-He before all the Nations-of-the-World. For behold the Nations-of-the-World ask: 'What distinguishes your lover from all others, O most beautiful of women' (Song of Songs 5:9), that you are ready to die for Him, that you are ready to be killed for him?, for it says, 'Therefore do the maidens (*'alamoth*) love thee'

(Song of Songs 1:3) – We have loved You until death ('*al moth*), 'For Thy sake we are killed all the day' (Psalms 44:23). Behold you are comely. Behold you are heroes. Come and intermingle with us.

But Israel says to the Nations-of-the-World: Do you know Him? We will recite some of His praise, 'My lover is white and ruddy, braver than ten thousand. His head is pure gold; his hair curls as black as a raven. His eyes are like doves by the springs of water bathing in milk. . . . This is my lover and this is my friend, O daughters of Jerusalem' (Song of Songs 5:10–16).

Once the Nations-of-the-World hear all of this praise, they say to them: Israel! We will go with you, 'Where has your lover gone, O most beautiful of women? Where has your lover turned; we will seek Him with you'. (Song of Songs 6:1).

But Israel says to the Nations-of-the-World: You have no part in Him, but 'I am my lover's and He is mine, Who feedeth among the lilies' (Song of Songs 6:3); 'My lover is mine and I am His, Who feedeth among the lilies' (Song of Songs 2:16).

This passage is the crux for understanding R. Aqiba's reading of the Song of Songs, the reading which led him to say that 'All of the Writings are Holy, but the Song of Songs is Holy-of-Holies'.[20] R. Aqiba is providing commentary for the difficult verse in the Song of Moses: 'This is my God, and I will beautify Him.' How can man beautify God? The Rabbis have various answers to this hermeneutic problem. R. Aqiba's is that to beautify Him means to sing His praises, to describe His beauty. However, it is not necessary to stop merely with this bare paraphrase of the verse, for we have a concrete example, a *mashal* of *how* Israel sings the beauty of her God. In Song of Songs (5:9–6:3), there is a dialogue between the loving maiden and the Daughters of Jerusalem, a dialogue moreover with its own hermeneutic problems – how is 'I am my lover's and He is mine' a response to 'We will seek him with you?' R. Aqiba situates this dialogue textually-historically in the encounter between Israel and the Nations-of-the-World. In effect, he merely assigns the roles in the dialogue; no other interpretation is required. The text of Song of Songs is illuminated, but even more significantly, it illuminates the text of Exodus. Again, I would like to emphasize that there is no translation employed in R. Aqiba's interpretation of Song of Songs here and elsewhere, but only a situating of the poem in a given historical or, more to the point,[21] textual context[22] – that is, as above, reading it into a space in the Torah text. Moreover, the situating of Song of Songs in the narrative context of the splitting of the Red Sea *does have a surface justification within the Song of Songs.* I am referring to the verse, 'Like unto my mare in the chariots of Pharaoh have I compared thee, my beloved' (Song of Songs 1:9), a verse which becomes a key to the whole midrashic reading of the song. What the midrashist has done here is therefore precisely the same as what we have already seen in the above two examples. He has read the later text as a commentary on the earlier. Midrash is reading that joins signifier to signifier, not signifier to signified – midrashic reading is indeed 'stringing the words of Torah to each other and to the words of the Prophets and the Writings'.[23]

As remarked in the citation from Bruns above, midrash is best understood as a continuation of the literary activity which engendered the very scriptures themselves. Because of this literary history, the Bible is characterized already by a degree of self-reflexivity, self-citation and self-interpretation which is perhaps more evident than in literatures which have had a different kind of history. The Rabbis as assiduous readers of the Bible developed an acute awareness of these intertextual relations within the Holy Books, and consequently their own hermeneutic work consisted of a creative process of further combining and recombining biblical verses into new texts, exposing the interpretive relations already in the text, as it were, as well as creating new ones by revealing linguistic connections hitherto unfelt. As we have seen in the above examples, what characterizes midrash is an understanding of interpretation not as the translating of a text to a higher or deeper level of signification, or, to use a different metaphor, the pairing of a signifier with a signified, but rather, as the laying bare of an intertextual connection between two signifiers which mutually read each other. It is not, nor can it be, decided which signifier is the interpreter and which the interpreted; the verse from Exodus is interpreted, as it were, by the figure of the dove in the rock, but of course, the figure in turn is interpreted by its juxtaposition with the verses about the Jews at the Sea. The midrash on the Song of Songs is seen on this reading to be no different in quality from the midrash on any prophetic or wisdom text, although perhaps the quantity of intertextual readings generated by its rhetorical richness is greater.

III

This characterization of the midrashic interpretation of the Song is not the generally accepted one. The most often encountered approach understands the midrash on Song of Songs to be an allegorical reading similar in kind to the later Jewish interpretations of the poem as well as the Christian readings. The claim is made, in effect, that the hermeneutic method is the same; only the specific allegorical identifications are different, with God and Israel the male and female protagonists, rather than Christ and the Church. One finds this view in nearly every hand-commentary or introduction to the Song of Songs.[24]

However, it seems to me that we must clearly distinguish the midrashic reading of the Song from that of allegorists such as Origen. Aphoristically, we might say that the direction of Origen's reading is from the concrete to the abstract, while the direction of midrash is from abstract to concrete. Or, using Jakobsonian terminology, at least heuristically, we could say that allegorical reading involves the projection of the syntagmatic plane (metonymy) of the text onto a paradigmatic plane of meaning, while midrash projects paradigms (metaphor) into a syntagmatic plane of narrative-history. Thus, while seemingly similar strategies of reading (and often genetically connected ones),[25] Origen's allegory and midrash are really quite different from each other.[26]

Let us consider this difference by examining Origen's reflections on his method. In the third book of his great commentary on the Song of Songs,[27] the Alexandrian Father has discussed in detail the theory behind his allegory. It is explicitly founded on a Platonic-Pauline theory of correspondence between the visible things of this world and the invisible things of God.[28] Origen goes on to say:

So, as we said at the beginning, all the things in the visible category can be related to the invisible, the corporeal to the incorporeal, and the manifest to those that are hidden; so that the creation of the world itself, fashioned in this wise as it is, can be understood through the divine wisdom, which from actual things and copies teaches us things unseen by means of those that are seen, and carries us over from earthly things to heavenly. But this relationship does not obtain only with creatures; the Divine Scripture itself is written with wisdom of a rather similar sort. Because of certain mystical and hidden things the people is visibly led forth from the terrestrial Egypt and journeys through the desert, where there was a biting serpent, and a scorpion,[29] and thirst, and where all the other happenings took place that are recorded. All these events, as we have said, have the aspects and likenesses of certain hidden things. And you will find this correspondence not only in the Old Testament Scriptures, but also in the actions of Our Lord and Saviour that are related in the Gospels. If, therefore, in accordance with the principles that we have now established all things that are in the open stand in some sort of relations to others that are hidden, it undoubtedly follows that the visible hart and roe mentioned in the Song of Songs are related to some patterns of incorporeal realities, in accordance with the character borne by their bodily nature. And this must be in such wise that we ought to be able to furnish a fitting interpretation of what is said about the Lord perfecting the harts, by reference to those harts that are unseen and hidden.[30]

We see accordingly the metaphysical grounding of the allegorical method used by Origen, and indeed by Philo as well. In order for the scripture to have an 'inner meaning', there must be an ontological structure that allows for inner meaning. Allegoresis is thus explicitly founded in a Platonic Universe. Indeed, it is no accident that for Origen, the *Song of Songs* has three meanings, a corporeal one, a pneumatic one and a psychic one, for we have here the 'Platonic tripartite man – body–soul–spirit – applied to the Word of God, in which Origen sees an incarnation of the Holy Spirit.'[31] Moreover, 'If the Logos in His Incarnation is God-Man, so, too, in the mind of Origen the incarnation of the Pneuma in Holy Scripture is divine-human.'[32] All this is very far from the description of hermeneutic activity which the midrash offers:

Ben-Azzai was sitting and interpreting (making midrash), and fire was all around him. They went and told Rabbi Aqiba: Rabbi, Ben-Azzai is sitting and interpreting, and fire is burning all around him. He went to him and said to him: I heard that you were interpreting, and the fire burning all around you. He said: Indeed. He said: Perhaps you were engaged in the inner-rooms of the Chariot [theosophical speculation]. He said: *No. I was sitting and stringing the words of Torah* [to each other], *and the Torah to the Prophets and the Prophets to the Writings, and the words were as radiant/joyful as when they were given from Sinai, and they were as sweet as at their original giving.* Were they not originally given in fire, as it is written, 'And the mountain was burning with fire' (Deut. 4:11)?[33]

Ben-Azzai does not speak of having achieved the original meaning or inner meaning or hidden meaning of Torah, but only of having read in such a way that he reconstituted the original *experience* of revelation.[34] He did what he did, not by linking texts with their meanings but by linking texts with texts. For the midrash the correspondences are not between things seen and their hidden or inner meanings, but between texts and events,[35] or texts and other texts, between signifiers and signifiers, not between signifiers and signifieds, and meaning, that is emotional and axiological content, is released in the process of generating new strings of language out of the beads of the old. Indeed, if Origen is correct in his description of his own, and it would seem, *mutatis mutandis*, of Philo's hermeneutics, his type of allegory is only possible in a Platonic world of ideal forms, for which there is precious little evidence in early rabbinic thought. In midrash, the Written Text is not read by recovering the Oral Event of its original speaking as in a logos theology, but neither is the process of reading it characterized by absence as in some contemporary theories of meaning; rather it is re-citing the Written Torah, as in Ben-Azzai's wonderful experience, recreating a new event of revelation, the Oral Torah or midrash.

We can now suggest answers to the questions with which we began this essay. The Rabbis of the midrash who understood that the Writings as a whole are a reading of the Torah did not perceive the Song of Songs as being at all like a lock to which the key has been lost. They understood it rather as an hermeneutic key to the interpretation of Torah. The way in which the Writings were comprehended as interpretation was by relating the more or less vague situations of various poetic texts to specific parts of the Torah. The reading method is accordingly not allegorical – relating signifier to signified – but intertextual-relating signifier to signifier. But it is indeed possible for midrashic-intertextual readings to be substantially the same thematically as allegorical readings, since the Torah-texts to which the Song of Songs was understood to refer describe the relationship of Israel to God. Thus the very same thematic material could be transposed, as it were, from the midrashic mode of the earlier Rabbis to the allegorical mode of the later ones. This should not obscure for us, however, the fundamental differences between the two types of reading. For the Rabbis of the midrash, the highest reality, other than God Himself, of course, is the Torah – that is, a text, not an abstract idea. No wonder, then, that reading on the highest level in midrash is intertextual reading, the connecting of texts to the ultimate Text, and not allegory, the connecting of texts to abstract ideas. Only in those rabbinic circles – that is, the Hellenistic Judaism of Philo in the midrashic period, or the later Platonically influenced Judaism which became dominant from the time of R. Sa‘dya Gaon on, could allegorical reading methods replace the earlier midrash of the Rabbis.

The crucial concept for understanding how the midrash relates the texts of the Writings to the text of the Torah is the concept of *dugma* or *mashal* – a rhetorical term designating generally figures of likeness or type and token. The text of the Writings is itself understood as a *mashal*, that is as a series of readings in figurative language of the text of the Torah which provides through these figures powerful emotional and axiological realizations of the narrative situations described mimetically in the Torah itself. Moreover, the formal device of *mashal*, the metaphorical story, is often used self-consciously by the midrash as a tool for 'stringing together the verses of the Torah and the Writings'. Thus the common prophetically used *mashal* of Israel to a bride and the Covenant to a wedding provided for the Rabbis sufficient motivation for reading the Song of Songs as they did, as a figurative poem interpreting the *text* of Israel and God's love for each other at the moment of their nuptials – the Exodus and its sequels. Jeremiah's, 'I have remembered for you the grace of your youth, the love of your honeymoon, your following after Me in the wilderness' (Jer. 2:2) or Isaiah's, 'as the groom rejoices over his bride, so shall your God rejoice over you' (Isa. 62:5); these were the models for application of the *mashal*, Song of Songs to the love of bride and bridegroom at the Red Sea and at Sinai.[36]

NOTES

Earlier versions of this chapter were read at a colloquium of the Lechter Institute of Literary Research at Bar Ilan University and at the Modern Language Association meeting in December 1986. I would like to thank all those who by their comments helped me to improve my work. I would also like to thank Meir Sternberg for having read a draft of this paper and helping me blur some overly sharp distinctions, as well as making other very useful comments. Responsibility for all errors and opinions remains my own.

1 *The Five Scrolls with Various Commentaries*, ed. and tr. (from Arabic into Hebrew), Joseph Kafah (ha-Agudah le-hatsalat Ginze Teman, Jerusalem, 1962), p. 26. Unless otherwise noted all translations from Hebrew/Aramaic in this paper are my own.

2 The word for 'handles' and the word 'proved' come from the same root in Hebrew. 'Handles' is being used in a sense very similar to that of the modern English colloquial phrase, 'I can't get a handle on that idea', i.e. a place of access. Cf. Bruns's work cited n. 6 below.

3 *Song of Songs Rabbah*, ed. and interpreted by Samson Dunsky (Devir, Tel Aviv, 1980), p. 5. Compare the following use of the term *dugma* from the same midrash, 'Your eyes are doves – like doves, your figure [*dugma*] is similar to a dove' (*Song of Songs Rabbah*, p. 100.) *Dugma* is accordingly practically an etymological equivalent of *figura*.

4 Compare David Stern, 'Rhetoric and Midrash: The Case of the Mashal', *Prooftexts*, 1 (1981), pp. 261–91.

5 Cf. the following description of our text by Gerald Bruns: 'The passage is essentially a litany of parables giving the theory of the parable as a hermeneutic rather than (as we would figure it) a literary form: the parable is a vehicle of instruction in the meaning of Scripture – but notice that it is a vehicle of a special kind. It does not convey a meaning to an audience, rather it conveys the audience to the meaning. The meaning of the Torah is, after all, a hidden meaning and is meant to remain so: it is not to be carried out of the Torah, that is, its hiddenness is not to be dispelled by understanding but requires to be preserved, for hiddenness is an essential part of that which is to be understood.' (Gerald L. Bruns, *Inventions: Writing, Textuality, and Understanding in Literary History* (Yale University Press, New Haven, 1982, p. 31).

6 In Gerald L. Bruns, 'Midrash and Allegory: The Beginnings of Scriptural Interpretation', in *Harvard Literary Guide to the Bible*, ed. Frank Kermode and Robert Alter (Harvard University Press, Cambridge, Mass., 1987.)

7 That is, the Song of Songs.

8 The order deviates from both the chronological and canonical ones because this passage is an introduction to the midrash on Song of Songs, and its author wishes therefore to end his discourse mentioning that book.

9 Initially in Bruns, *Inventions*, and more recently in Bruns, 'Midrash and Allegory'.

10 Bruns, 'Midrash and Allegory'.

11 As opposed to those scholars who regard midrash as being homiletical exploitation of the biblical text for purposes quite other than its interpretation. Cf. for example the following statement of Joseph Heinemann: 'Much of aggadic exegesis is, therefore, a kind of parable or allegory. The aggadists do not mean so much to clarify difficult passages in the biblical text as to take a stand on the burning questions of the day, to guide the people and strengthen their faith. But since they addressed themselves to a wide audience – including simple folk and children – they could not readily formulate the problems in an abstract way, nor could they give involved theoretical answers. In order to present their ideas in a more comprehensible and engaging fashion, the sages cast them in a narrative format and employed parables and other familiar literary means which appeal to all.' 'The Nature of the Aggadah', in *Midrash and Literature*, ed. Geoffrey H. Hartman and Sanford Budick (Yale University Press, New Haven, 1986, p. 49). To be fair to Heinemann, I should say that his description of *aggadah* is somewhat more nuanced than this citation would suggest.

12 *Song of Songs Rabbah*, p. 42. See below for the full context of this citation.

13 In spite of the title of Bruns's essay, he does not discuss the relationship of midrash to allegory, but rather discusses the midrashic and allegorical methods separately as early hermeneutic techniques. Bruns's discussion of allegoresis is as insightful and sympathetic as his discussion of midrash.

14 *Song of Songs Rabbah*, pp. 72–3.

15 In this sort of context, this term always means the Prophets and Writings.

16 *Mekilta de-Rabbi Ishmael*, ed. Jacob Z. Lauterbach (The Jewish Publication Society of America, Philadelphia, 1933; rpt. 1961) vol. 1, p. 211. I have followed Lauterbach's translation with minor variation.

17 But see below, that there *is* such a clue in the Song of Songs itself.

18 For another version of this argument, see Daniel Boyarin, 'Rhetoric and Interpretation: The Case of the Nimshal', *Prooftexts*, 5 (1985), pp. 269–76.

19 Lauterbach's reading 'prophecies' (*Mekilta*, p. 26) makes both R. Aqiba's interpretation of the verse, as well as of the following narrative extremely difficult to understand. The whole point of the latter is to provide the context in which Israel describes the beauty of her lover. The better reading, 'beauties' was already available to Lauterbach as his apparatus will show.

20 *Song of Songs Rabbah*, p. 11.

21 More to the point, because R. Aqiba is offering interpretation of precisely that other text.
22 Cf. Marvin, *Song of Songs: Anchor Bible* (Doubleday, Garden City, NY, 1977) and quote below in n. 24. See also nn. 33–5, below.
23 It goes without saying that neither Bruns nor, *a fortiori*, I are the first to point out the interconnecting of texts as a distinguishing feature of midrash. Thus James Kugel writes: 'The second fundamental point, still more basic, is that midrash is an exegesis of biblical verses, not of books. The basic unit of the Bible, for the midrashist, is the verse: this is what he seeks to expound, and it might be said that there simply is no boundary encountered beyond that of the verse until one comes to the borders of the canon itself. . . . One of the things this means is that each verse of the Bible is in principle as connected to its most distant fellow as the one next door; in seeking to illuminate a verse from Genesis, the midrashist is as likely to have reference (if to anything) to a verse from the Psalter as to another verse in the immediate context – indeed, he sometimes delights in the remoter source' (James Kugel, 'Two Introductions to Midrash', in Hartman and Budick [eds.], p. 93). However, I believe that Bruns's insight goes beyond this in several ways. First of all, this way of reading is understood (correctly in my opinion) as the *sine qua non* of midrash, or rather, as that which makes midrash midrash. Second, the prime issue is not, in my view, the lack of borders between the verse and the canon, which would translate as an insensitivity to the fact that Song of Songs or the book of Jeremiah, for example, are works with a certain literary and thematic integrity, but rather, as Bruns has put it, that the Bible can be read as a constantly self-glossing work. Indeed, it must be emphasized *contra* Kugel here that the midrash often does present consistent readings of biblical texts larger than the verse. See Daniel Boyarin, 'Voices in the Text', *Revue Biblique*, 93–4 (1986), pp. 581–97.
24 See, for example, 'It is clear that Aqiba must have understood the Song allegorically'. (Pope, *Song of Songs*, Anchor Bible, p. 19).
25 See E. E. Urbach, 'The Homiletical Interpretations of the Sages and the Expositions of Origen on Canticles, and the Jewish-Christian Disputation', *Scripta Hierosolymitana*, XXII (1971), pp. 247–75.
26 I would like to add two clarifications at this point. The first is that the category of 'allegory', both as a genre(?) of text production and as a reading practice is a notoriously slippery one. 'Each of those acceptances looks blurry under scrutiny' (Carolynn Van Dyke, *The Fiction of Truth*, Cornell University Press, Ithaca and London, 1985, p. 18). It should be clear that when I say allegory in this text I mean allegorical reading of the Philonic-Origenal type, which has a fairly clear structure as well as explicit theoretical underpinnings. The other point that I wish to make here is that I am **not** contrasting Jewish with Christian modes of reading. The Gospels themselves, Paul and even much later Christian literature contain much which is midrashic in hermeneutic structure (more, in my opinion, than is currently recognized, e.g. *Piers Plowman*, a subject which I have lectured on and which I hope to return to soon in writing).

Moreover, much authentic Jewish hermeneutic is allegorical or otherwise 'logocentric' in structure. Nor am I trying to valorize midrash over against Alexandrian allegory; I wish only to clarify the two modes of reading as different in order to understand midrash better.

27 I am using the English translation of R. P. Lawson, *Origen, The Song of Songs: Commentary and Homilies* (Newman Press, Westminster, Md, and London, 1957). The citations below are to this edition.

28 Ibid., p. 218.

29 A reference to Deuteronomy 8:15. For a midrashic reading of this verse which points up by contrast precisely the difference between the midrashic and allegorical methods, see my, 'Old Wine in New Bottles', forthcoming in *Poetics Today*.

30 Lawson, *Origen*, p. 223.

31 Lawson, *Origen*, Introduction, p. 9.

32 Ibid.

33 *Song of Songs Rabbah*, p. 42.

34 'Revelation is never something over and done with or gone for good or in danger of slipping away into the past; it is ongoing, and its medium is midrash, which makes the words of Torah rejoice "as when they were delivered from Sinai" and "as sweet as at their original utterance".' Bruns, 'Midrash and Allegory'.

35 This is not to deny metaphorical transfer in much rabbinic reading, including, of course, that of the Song. Metaphor, even extended metaphor, is not necessarily allegory – by the Origenal definition and understanding of that term. Whitman's 'O Captain My Captain' comes to mind as a metaphorical poem, even an extended metaphor, which is nevertheless not allegorical in this restricted sense. Moreover, it should be noted that the dean of modern midrashic scholars, the late Saul Lieberman, went even further in his concretization of the midrash on Song of Songs. He regarded it as founded on a reading of the Song as actually having been recited at the time of the Exodus; that would make it approximately as if Whitman's elegy had been recited at the funeral of Lincoln. Saul Lieberman, 'Mishnath Shir ha-Shirim', in Gershom Scholem, *Jewish Gnosticism, Merkabah Mysticism, and Talmudic Tradition*, (Jewish Theological Seminary of America, New York, 1960, pp. 118–27.) In a Hebrew paper on this subject, I intend to discuss Lieberman's position and its implications more fully. Here I will only say that I believe that it does not take account of how similar the midrash on this book is to other midrash, where such claims are certainly excluded. What it does do, however, is point up the historicization of midrashic reading as opposed to allegorization.

36 The last point was already made by the medieval commentator, R. A. Ibn Ezra in the introduction to his commentary on the Song of Songs.

9

J. L. Austin and the Book of Jonah

Terry Eagleton

The surrealist farce known as the Book of Jonah is easily summarized. God commands Jonah to go and cry doom on Nineveh, a city whose viciousness has just come to his attention, but Jonah doesn't reckon much to this mission and takes off instead for Tarshish. A divinely engineered storm threatens his ship, and he requests the crew with remarkable *sang-froid* to pitch him overboard. God sends a fish to swallow Jonah up and spew him out again three days later, whereupon Jonah does manage to get himself to Nineveh and wanders the city proclaiming imminent catastrophe. Unusually enough, the inhabitants of the city, prodded a bit by their king, take Jonah's prophecy to heart and repent, which infuriates Jonah so much that he goes and sulks outside the city hoping to die. God fools around with him briefly, sending a plant to shade him, then a worm to devour the plant, then a sultry wind to make him faint from heat, and finally treats him to a short homily about his mercy.

Why was Jonah so reluctant to go to Nineveh in the first place? Perhaps because hectoring a seedy bunch of strangers about their vices isn't the best guarantee of a long life. But in the storm scene Jonah shows scant regard for his own safety, and indeed by the end of the text is betraying a powerful death wish. The fact is that he refused to obey God because he thought there was no point, and tells God as much after he has spared Nineveh. God is a spineless liberal given to hollow authoritarian threats, who would never have the guts to perform what he promises. Jonah understands divine psychology far too well to take such tetchy bumblings seriously, and is loath to embark on the tiresome, complicated business of getting himself to Nineveh (it takes three days just to cross the city) when he knows that there is no impending disaster to be averted. He is angry with God because he can foresee all this from the outset and feels that God, who after all is supposed to be omniscient, would foresee it too if only he wasn't so mystified by his own macho image of himself. The point of Jonah's getting himself thrown overboard is to force God to save him, thus dramatically demonstrating to him that he's too soft-hearted to punish those who disobey him. If God wheels up a fish to rescue Jonah, won't he do something equivalent for Nineveh? Jonah is of course taking a fairly hair-raising risk here, but he calculates that if God rates him as important enough to play the prophet in Nineveh, it would be perverse of him to let him drown. In any case, Jonah's disobedience is a kind of subtle flattery of God, a bit of emotional blackmail which God would be churlish to respond to by letting him go under: he reminds God later, after the Nineveh debacle, that he had told him at the outset that he was too loving and merciful to live up to his bloodthirsty intentions. Disobeying God is a crafty way of telling him what a nice chap he is, and thus – so Jonah hopes – may be done with impunity. Fleeing to Tarshish is just a flamboyant way of trying to bring God to his senses, induce a little self-knowledge in him; but God obtusely fails to take the point, and Jonah, perhaps despairing of the Almighty's capacity for self-enlightenment, sets out for Nineveh after all with a deepening sense of existential absurdity.

Once in the city, Jonah shambles around playing at being a prophet, no doubt pretty perfunctorily, and is disgusted to find that his clichéd denunciations actually work. Disgusted, because of course Jonah doesn't believe for a moment that Nineveh's suspiciously sudden repentance is anything of his own doing: it has been brought about by God, to save himself the mess, unpleasantness and damage to his credibility as a nice chap consequent on having to put his threats into practice. Jonah is enraged because God is simply using him as a fall guy to let himself off the hook of his own soft-bellied liberalism. What has happened is what Jonah knew would happen all along: he has been used as cover for a massive climb-down on God's part, and God can now carry on persuading himself that he's a tough guy underneath. Jonah has merely been used as an instrument in the perpetuation of divine false consciousness. God would have spared the city even if Jonah had stayed at home; it's just that he needs some excuse to do so, and has maneuvred Jonah, against his own better judgment, into providing him with one. Even if God *was* toying with the idea of blasting Nineveh, or at least thought he was, there would still have been no point as Jonah sees it in leaving home; for since God is omniscient he presumably knew when he asked Jonah to set out either that the city would be destroyed, in which case Jonah's journey was supremely unnecessary, or that it wouldn't be, in which case his journey was also unnecessary. Jonah doesn't know the outcome himself, but he knows that God does, and suspects that either way this renders his own part in the narrative ridiculously superfluous.

What happens in Nineveh is exactly what Jonah feared all along: that God's own chronic self-deception would drag him into its own wake and leave him looking a complete idiot. He has stomped around Nineveh proclaiming that its end is nigh, and now it isn't. God's view of the matter, of course, is that it's *because* Jonah has cried doom that the doom hasn't come. The only successful prophet is an ineffectual one, one whose warnings fail to materialize. All good prophets are false prophets, undoing their own utterances in the very act of producing them. In the terms of J. L. Austin's *How to Do Things with Words*,[1] prophetic utterances of Jonah's sort are 'constative' (descriptive of some real or possible state of affairs) only in what one might call their surface grammar; as far as their 'deep structure' goes they actually belong to Austin's class of 'performatives', linguistic acts which get something done. What they get done is to produce a state of affairs in which the state of affairs they describe won't be the case. Effective declarations of imminent catastrophe cancel themselves out, containing as they do a contradiction between what they say and what they do. In this sense they exactly fit the prototype of what the deconstructionist critic Paul de Man in his *Allegories of Reading* calls a 'literary' enunciation.[2] The literary, for de Man, is the kind of speech-act within which the grammatical and the rhetorical are somehow at odds, and which thereby either subvert what they say by what they do or undo what they do by what they say. Yeats's celebrated line 'How can we know the dancer from the dance?' inquires, grammatically speaking, about how we can distinguish the dancer from the dance, perhaps with the implication that it's somehow important to do so; but as a performative or rhetorical utterance the line of course powerfully suggests that we neither can nor should. Literary language for de Man founders in a kind of fissure between its grammatical and rhetorical dimensions, and so do Jonah's prophecies of doom. All such prophets are self-deconstructing fools.

This, however, isn't exactly why Jonah is so furious. He is angry, as we've seen, because he feels he has been shamelessly used as a pawn in God's self-mystifying game; and it is this which plunges him into the existential *angst* and nausea we find overwhelming him at the end of the narrative. If Jonah wants to curl up and die, it is because he can no longer stomach a history struck utterly pointless by God's self-blindness and self-indulgence. If the Creator himself is stupid enough not to know that he's the helpless victim of his own over-sanguine temperament, what hope for human self-insight? And if God just goes around forgiving everybody all the time, what's the point of doing anything? If disobedience on the scale of a Nineveh goes cavalierly unpunished, then the idea of obedience also ceases to have meaning. God's mercy simply makes a mockery of human effort, which is why Jonah ends up in the grip of *Thanatos* or the death drive.

There is another way of accounting for Jonah's final depression and melancholia, his resolute 'decathecting' of reality and withdrawal of libido back into himself. Paul de Man, as we have seen, speaks of the discrepancy or aporetic relationship between the grammatical and the rhetorical (or performative) in literary discourse; but, drawing on Nietzsche's notions of rhetoric, he also strives to deconstruct the very idea of performativity itself. For if performance is caught up in language, and if language is irreducibly figurative or tropological, then there may come a point, so de Man argues, when *we cannot know whether we are doing anything or not.*[3] 'Rhetorical' discourse, in the sense of language intended to have definite public effects, is marred and insidiously undone by 'rhetoric' in the sense of verbal figuration. Something like this, I would suggest, is the abyss or aporia, the vertiginous collapse of meaning, in which Jonah is finally embroiled. For even if he could console himself by surmising that his journey really *was* necessary, that his crying doom was performatively effective rather than farcically redundant, there is no way in which he can ever know this for certain, no way in which he can ever know whether he was doing anything or not. There is no means of precisely determining the hair-thin line between describing and getting something done, being a spectator and being a participant. You can never know how far a particular narrative has always already included you in, because to do so would require an impossible kind of meta-move. Johah thinks he occupies such a metal-position in respect of God, outdoing God's own omniscience in his superior insight into divine psychology; but it could just be that God had one over Jonah all along. For what if God's narrative had always already reckoned Jonah's into it, and the whole point of this pantomime was to bring Jonah to the point where he knew that he did not know whether he was doing anything or not? Jonah's initial presumption implies that action isn't important, and his subsequent despair implies the same; indeed, these two conditions aren't in the least opposites for him, since the source of his despair is precisely his presumptuous belief that human initiatives are struck superfluous by God's mercy. But there is also a more subtle kind of despair, which springs from a 'deconstructive' insight into the ambiguous, problematical nature of action as such. To assume that human practice isn't necessary is to assume you know what it is, and it's perhaps this ground which is now crumbling from beneath Jonah's feet.

To view action as problematical and ambiguous is not necessarily a recipe for quietism, though some such implication might indeed be detected in the work of de Man and some of his colleagues. If action is a *text*, it is not necessarily an illegible one. What the Book of Jonah can be read as calling into question is less action as such than a particular ideological model of it: the assumption that at the source of all practice lies a well-defined, autonomous subject whose behavior lies entirely within its affirmative mastery. The damage which Marx and Freud have inflicted on this model in our own day is inflicted in the case of Jonah by that unmasterable otherness known as 'God', the condition of possibility of all practice. The over-rigorous distinction made by Jonah between what he himself knows or does, and what God knows and does, returns in our own time as a liberal humanist dichotomy between the agent and his or her enabling conditions. To trouble this tenacious opposition is to fall at first into what seems like nihilism, a despair as to the potential effectivity of action; and Jonah shares this syndrome with Paul de Man and J. Hillis Miller. What he, and they, apparently do not see is that in order to be able to act efficaciously at all you must have somehow gone all the way through this shaking of the foundations and emerged somewhere on the other side. Neither the old-style humanistic agent, nor the ecstastically decentered and disseminated subject, offer adequate models of human practice, and are indeed to a great extent the mere flipsides of one another. Any profound process of political transformation calls, paradoxically, for human agents who are on the one hand a good deal more centred, resolute and affirmative than the subjects of quotidian life, and on the other hand will shake such affirmative identity to its roots. To act effectively at all, you must have some positive sense of who you are; but if oppressed groups and peoples were able to have such a sense they would not need to act in the first place. Political action consists not primarily in expressing an already well-founded identity, but in creating the social conditions in which it might just become possible to say who one was, or to discover what one would like to be. It is the rulers, not the oppressed, who are happily dispensed from worrying about who they are. The Book of Jonah leaves its protagonist caught in a transitional stage between false consciousness and some new, currently unnamable style of identity; and to this extent we have made little advance upon it. Nobody to my knowledge has yet produced a satisfactory paradigm of a form of subjectivity which would be at once affirmative and self-interrogative, centered enough to act decisively yet constituted to its core by the

sense of some ineradicable otherness. If we are currently caught
between two prototypes of subjectivity, the one dying and discredited
and the other powerless to be properly born, it is not because
researchers in the field are remarkable for their low intelligence but
because of the nature of our political and historical conditions.

The book ends with a small Dadaist drama in which God conjures
up a plant, worm and wind in rapid succession, like a magician on a
ropy night at the Hammersmith Palais. This bizarre sadistic taunting
is presumably meant among other things to show Jonah that God
isn't such a nice chap as he seemed; if he can indulge in this sort of
nasty insensitive trifling then he might just have blasted Nineveh after
all. There's a darkly malevolent humor about this divine tomfoolery,
which suggests in quick symbolic notation that God can either save
Jonah or scupper him as the fancy takes him. If he can clown around
as aggressively as this, setting Jonah solicitously on his feet one
moment only to kick his legs from under him the next, God isn't
perhaps quite the patsy Jonah thought he was. What seems
particularly callous about God is that his flashy, second-rate
conjuring act is a kind of grisly parody of Jonah's black despair;
God's gratuitous cavortings, pulling worms and winds from his sleeve
like so many rabbits, writes cruelly large Jonah's own nauseated sense
of the gratuitousness of all meaning under God's libertarian regime.
It's in that sheer unfounded gratuitousness of meaning, that abyss of
all signification, that God brutally, therapeutically, rubs Jonah's nose.
God's mercy is indeed a kind of absurdity, but there's no need for
Jonah to make a song and dance of it, which is why God makes a
mocking song and dance of it. Jonah just has to find some way of
living with the fact that he can never know whether he is doing
anything or not, which was perhaps the point of the whole futile
narrative after all.

NOTES

1 J. L. Austin, *How to Do Things with Words* (Harvard University Press,
 Cambridge, Mass., 1975).
2 Paul de Man, *Allegories of Reading* (Yale University Press, New Haven,
 1979).
3 Ibid., pp. 121ff.

10

Interpretative Narrative

Paul Ricoeur (translated by David Pellauer)

This chapter is devoted to a category of narratives that we may call interpretative narratives. These are narratives in which the ideological interpretation these narratives wish to convey is not superimposed on the narrative by the narrator but is, instead, incorporated into the very strategy of the narrative. I shall take as an example of such narratives the passion narratives in the synoptic gospels, which seem to me particularly apt for illustrating this specific literary category. In them, the kerygmatic proclamation makes specific what, a moment ago, I called, in a neutral sense, an ideological interpretation, because this interpretation results directly from the narrative configuration. Indeed, as one literary critic, Frank Kermode, has pointed out, a noteworthy feature of the gospel of Mark is that it functions like a midrash; that is, simply as a narrative it exercises an interpretative function.[1] It is this idea that a narrative can have an interpretative function in relation to its own kerygmatic intention that will serve as a guideline for my analysis. Having developed this directing idea in the first part of my remarks, I shall then subordinate it in the second part to an inventory of the procedures and strategies brought to light by contemporary theory of narrative.

From kerygma to narrative

Let me begin by indicating again the guiding idea behind my remarks, namely that the juncture between exegesis and theology, before being a work of interpretation applied *to* the text, already functions *in* the text if this text is a narrative with an interpretative function.

This type of narrative is not just limited to the gospels. In his *The Art of Biblical Narrative*, Robert Alter has applied a strictly literary approach, which places between parentheses the historical-critical method and any attempt to sort the text into sources, strata, borrowings and so on, to a number of narratives taken from the Hebrew Bible, in order to set into relief the art of literary composition that presides over the redaction of the text as we now read it.[2] He notes in this regard that if literary analysis cannot ignore the history of tradition and of redaction, in return it must hold that this work of identifying sources (J, E, D, P) itself rests upon unacknowledged, and generally naïve, literary criteria. For example, that the oldest text must be the shortest one, the one that presents no interruption or doubling, the one that is clearly delimited and coherent. However, these criteria slight the rich resources of what he calls 'historicized prose fiction',[3] resources that the modern novel has made us more aware of, and resources that a purely literary study of the Bible shows its astounding mastery of. The most important lesson to be gained from Alter's work – a lesson that had already been formulated with much power by Eric Auerbach in his *Mimesis*[4] – is that it is precisely the narrative composition, the organizing of the events in the narrative, that is the vehicle for or, better, that foments the theological interpretation. He adds that it is the fullest grasping of this literary art that proceeds to the sharpest perception of the theological intention.[5] What struck Alter in the more dramatic of these narratives is the fact that the text aims at communicating the conviction that the divine plan, although ineluctable, only gets realized by means of what he calls 'the refractory nature of man'.[6] These are not pious stories, they are stories of cunning and murder, stories where the right of primogeniture is scoffed at, where the election of the hero depends on the oblique maneuvers of an ambitious young man such as David. Taking this problem up from the other end, we might say that a theology that confronts the inevitability of the divine plan with the refractory nature of human actions and passions, is a theology that engenders narrative; better, it is a theology that calls for the narrative mode as its major hermeneutical mode, and it does so in virtue of the paradoxical and – why not? – the aporetic character of such a theology which pays no attention to speculative dialectic. Thus the closing words of Alter's book are relevant to our investigation: 'it is in the stubbornness of human individuality that each man and woman encounters God or ignores Him, responds to or resists Him' in 'the perilously momentous realm of history'.[7]

We have yet to see what narrative constraints of prose fiction these ingenious writers treated both as conventions to be respected and norms to transgress, within the very process of figurizing these constraints. This is what Alter undertakes to discover in his book, where he emphasizes the art of reticence, the roles of the interior monologue and indirect discourse, and above all, the position of the omniscient narrator. However, the most important thing is the appropriate character of these narrative techniques as regards the hermeneutical problem of the collusion between the inevitable divine plan and the unpredictability of human contingency.

My question is whether the passion narratives have a comparable function, as regards the close imbrication of theology within the narrative, and whether the problem is not to bring into relation the theological function and the narrative structure, whether it be a deep or a surface structure, so as to evaluate appreciatively the appropriateness of this structure for this function. Indeed, it seems to me that the most striking feature of the gospel narrative lies in the indissociable union of the kerygmatic and the narrative aspects. But it is not sufficient just to assert this, we have also to show by what literary procedure the form of the gospel narrative is obtained, that is, the form of a kerygmatized narrative or a narrativized kerygma.

Let me say something first, though, about the term 'kerygmatic' and about its relation to the term 'theological', applied by both Auerbach and Alter to some of the Hebraic narratives. Three features of the gospel narratives, which I will order in terms of an increasing difference, indicate the resemblances and the differences between these two terms.

First, the Christian kerygma prolongs the biblical message insofar as it too confronts the inevitability of the divine plan and the contingency of human action. Later, we shall see that the core of the passion narratives may be summed up in the phrase: 'the Son of man had to be betrayed'. This formula, which underscores the inevitability of a certain course of events, also depends upon a narrative about treason, denial, abandonment and flight, which testifies to the refractory nature of human beings, the privileged pathway for the inevitable plan. Thus, in the passion narratives, a narrative mediation similar to the one described by Alter gets inserted between the statement that 'the Son of Man had to be betrayed into the hands of sinners', and the contingency of 'and Judas drew near to him'. The verb 'betrayed' has the double sense of something inevitable and of recalcitrance. Through this first trait, the passion narratives are inscribed within the larger biblical orbit insofar as, in the absence of any speculative mediation in a Hegelian fashion, the narrative mediation brings about the unity of the supratemporal and the intratemporal.

A second feature completes the first one at the same time that it corrects it. What is at issue is not a theology but a christology – or, rather, a number of christologies. In this regard, it is the history of forms – and its residues, the history of traditions and the history of redaction – that makes us attentive to the difference between the respective christological projects of the four gospels. However, only literary analysis shows that it is across the specificity of the narrative composition of each gospel that its corresponding christological project can be discerned, no matter what was its polemical or apologetic aspect in relation to the ecclesiastical disputes of the day. This tie between the narrative and its *Sitz im Leben* is surely the concern of the historical-critical method, but the way in which this polemic or apologetic project is brought to discourse is a matter for a literary analysis bearing on the narrativization of the kerygma. Only then does what we might call the *Sitz im Wort* of the reported events make sense.

If the narrative mediation characteristic of the gospel in general and of each gospel in particular prolongs the Hebraic theologoumen of a divine plan carried through in spite of . . . or thanks to . . . our human refractory nature (our first trait), and if, furthermore, this mediation specifies the theological project as a christological one (our second trait), we may ask in the third place where there is not something in the christological kerygma that calls for narrative, in an absolutely specific way. Ernst Kaseman has emphasized this point with much force. The most primitive kerygma that the historical-critical method can reconstitute does not oppose the Christ of faith to the Jesus of history, but rather bears witness to their identity. The Christ who speaks to the enthusiastic believers, the charismatics of the primitive assemblies is held to be identical with the Jesus about whom there circulate narratives having to do with his teaching, his miracles, his confrontations with this or that group, including his own disciples. In producing a narrative with a kerygmatic weight, the project of narrativizing the kerygma seems well anchored in the Christian kerygma in its most definite specificity. Do we not have one indication of this in the least narrativized proclamations, such as in I Corinthians 15:3–8, where we read 'that Christ died for our sins in accordance with the scriptures, that he was buried, that he was raised on the third day in accordance with the scriptures, and that he appeared to Cephas, then to the twelve'. That this is the same kerygma that we discern in the filigree of the gospel of Mark, for example, is a disputed question. But that the kerygma of I Corinthians 15 contains a minimum of narrativization is what matters to our investigation. Let us looks closer at this passage. We find four verbs in the aorist of narration, constituting the beginning of a narrative chain and punctuating the proclamation. We may see in this a call for narrative, which, without being the only provocation to narration, can be taken at least as a condition *sine qua non* of narrativization. The equation we are seeking to reconstruct between a narrativized kerygma and a kerygmatized narrative seems indeed to have its rationale in the identity proclaimed between the Christ of faith and the Jesus of history. Starting from his core, it is comprehensible that other factors of narrativization may have played a role or been drawn into the same gravitational space. I will mention a few of them.

In the first place, there is the question that Hans Frei's book about the identity of Jesus Christ centers upon: 'Who do you say that I am?'[8] (After all, the Old Testament can also be summed up in the question, who is the Lord?) It is one of the functions of the narrative art, through the combined interplay of plot and character development (as has been well known since Henry James's reflections on *The Art of Fiction*), to answer the question 'who?' by indicating what we may call the narrative identity of the character, that is the identity produced by the narrative itself. Now, it is a fact that the identity of Jesus remains an acute question throughout the gospels. And, as I shall indicate further in a moment, it is perhaps the function of some narratives to deepen the enigma of the character, while clarifying the arrangement of the plot. This identity of Jesus is essential to the equation between the Jesus of history and the Christ of faith. To say who Jesus is, is also to say who the Christ is. And this is what the gospels do, especially the passion narratives. If it is true, for example, that Mark wanted to polemicize against a christology of glory that wanted to do away with the humiliation of the cross, and if it is true that, through his narrative, he wanted to illustrate a christology of the Son of Man that retains the features of the Suffering Servant from the 'songs' of second Isaiah, as well as those of the persecuted righteous person of the Psalms, it is no less true that it is through narrative means that he carries out this apologetics for his christology. It is in narrating that he interprets the identity of Jesus. Correlatively, it is in composing his narrative with a literary art that is in no way maladroit – as has been said for a long time now – that he signifies his christology of a suffering Son of Man.

Here is another corollary: I mentioned brief narratives about the life of Jesus that might have been drawn into the gravitational sphere of the kerygma looking for a narrative and in the course of narrativization. Some of these already indicate a trajectory capable of ending up in a passion narrative. On this point, it seems to me that Joachim Jeremias, along with my late colleague Norman Perrin in his *Rediscovering the Teaching of Jesus*[9] was correct in discerning a deep-lying affinity between the theme of Jesus betrayed, taken in its double theological and narrative signification, and those narratives that depict Jesus sharing the table of tax collectors, sinners and prostitutes, and in giving discourses – parables and other forms – that generated confrontation. Between preaching, confronting, sharing sinners' food and being betrayed, there is, if not a completely given narrative connection, at least what the Russian structuralists call a *fabula* or, let us say, occasions for narrative, which present a sort of homology among themselves, a mutual fittingness, surpassing any pure chronological arrangement. It is these occasions for narrative that must have served as a basis for the rule-governed composition of a large narrative in which the Passion would be both an ineluctable continuation of earlier events and a distinct core, more narrativized than the other portions, yet capable of extending its narrative cohesion to what went before, so that the gospel appears to us today, in the words of Martin Kähler, as a passion narrative proceeded by a long introduction.

I would like to add two narrative-effects to these different aspects of the call for narrative, which, when considered in themselves, give rise to a certain autonomy of the process of narrativization, to such an extent that it escapes the control of the christological intention and, in a way, begins to amplify itself on its own terms. These two effects are, moreover, in many ways the opposite of each other. What we too quickly call an embellishment has a more complex function that is a source of perplexity. If it is true that narrative interprets, one of its ways of doing so is to explain in a plausible manner, on the basis of what is reasonable, following Aristotle's rule in the *Poetics*. Every narrative explains, as soon as it tells why some character did something. As has been said, there is no narrative if one simply reports the king died, the queen died. There is a narrative, if one says, the king died, the queen died of grief. By introducing a motive, the narrative invites us to explore a whole set of connections with the resources and conventions of what is reasonable. Thus, to cite an example, the role of Judas swells, becomes more precise and more anecdotal from one gospel to the next.[10] Thanks to this amplification subordinated to the rules of what is reasonable, the narrative is clothed with an aspect of what Hans Frei in his *The Eclipse of Biblical Narrative* has called being 'history-like'.[11] With Matthew, and especially with John, this effect of quasi-historical verisimilitude is confined to material positivity, most likely owing to a polemical intent.

However, the increasing autonomy of the narrative can also aim at a strictly opposite effect. The systematic usage of reticence, as the inverse of amplification, a usage that Robert Alter sees at work in many narratives in the Hebrew Bible – for example, Abraham and Isaac are silent on the route to the place of sacrifice – can guide a perfectly opaque narrative that augments the enigma by strictly narrative means. Perhaps the distinctive feature of the gospel of Mark is that he narratively produces more opacity than clarification. This feature, better than the inverse one of amplification, can be set in relation with the type of christology that constitutes the kerygmatic intention of his narrative. A narrative that obscures things, as Mark's may in fact do, may have a profound affinity with the christology of the suffering Son of man that he presents. But whatever the variety of modes of narrativization, it is the task of hermeneutics to track down these homologies between narrative technique and kerygmatic function. In a moment, I shall give a few examples of this.

Narrative articulation

In the second part of my remarks, I would like to refer to some of the narrative techniques put in service of a kerygmatic narrative. I shall do so briefly, but I do want to indicate how I see the articulation of the narrative and the kerygmatic, if we limit ourselves to a literary analysis of the text that deals with it as a prose-fiction.

Three levels of analysis seem to me to provide a place for forms of literary analysis distinct from those of the historical-critical method.

1. The first level is that of a semiotics of narrative, illustrated by the methods of Vladimir Propp and A.-J. Greimas, where the analysis is carried out in terms of 'functions' (or abstract segments of action) or 'actants' (or typical characters). This method is especially pertinent for texts close to the traditional folk-tale, in which a certain order is initially upset by a misdeed or a lack, then reestablished through a series of qualifying tests that glorify a hero, who encounters the aid of helpers and the hostility of opponents. Use of this perspective is not out of place inasmuch as the popular tale illustrates logical universals of narrative that function at a depth concealed by their being invested in individual figures (Jesus, Peter, Judas, etc.). What I have called the narrativization of the kerygma implies just such a passage through the semiotic constraints on narrativity and its most universal features. The benefit of this approach results, furthermore, from its immense respect for the text, whose details, at end of the analysis, are justified through a mutual adjusting of the general rules of narrativity and their individual instantiations.

So I will not reproach this method for imposing too rigid a grid on its texts. Those who have practiced it are well aware of the half-steps and rectifications required by any investigation into the details of a semic reconstruction, whether discursive or figurative. Nor will I reproach it for missing the link between the narrative and the kerygmatic aspects – which would be a mortal reproach. By setting on stage of the receivers, through whom comes about the contract that qualifies the hero, we have in effect a semiotic equivalent of the kerygma of election. What is more, semiotic analysis should be praised for including, among the numerous codes and isotopies it considers, an ideological code, under which may be placed the christological titles.

Instead, I will say that the semiotics of narrative is constrained in the case of the passion narratives to working at its limits, and this calls for two complements I will discuss in a moment. It must do so for three reasons. First, its codified roles are largely subverted by their figurativization in the passion narratives. It is not correct to say that Judas alone is the only opponent. We shall see in a moment that everyone betrays, denies, flees, up to and including the women at the tomb. And what are we to make of the pair Judas/Peter? Here any semiotic analysis runs into a real test. This subversion of roles, I believe, is the narrative expression of the kerygmatic project; for example, Mark's christology. The subversion is double in the sense that the helper Peter becomes an opponent, while the opponent Judas becomes, as do the recalcitrant characters of the Hebrew Bible, the instrument of the hero's triumph. Yet perhaps it is the equation between glory and humiliation in the figure of the hero that most drives semiotic analysis to work at its limits. And this leads to my second reservation. Speaking precisely of figures and figurization, Louis Marin has shown in a convincing fashion, in his 'semiotics of the traitor', that the figurative level is far from being just a plane where structured roles from a deeper level are given some specification.[12] This is the level where initiatives get taken, which not only introduces contingency into the narrative, it also governs the transformations that take place on the deeper levels. Here working at the limit leads to subversion of the model in question itself. Marin, for example, uses the occurrence of the dynamics of the narrative on its surface level to ask whether it is not this dynamism, reported on the surface plane, that engenders the transformations on the semiotic and discursive planes. What is at issue here is the question of the passage from the paradigmatic to the syntagmatic in a model where the transformation rules are themselves atemporal (e.g. conjunction, disjunction, etc.). In other words, the important question that Marin raises – which has not been sufficiently noted – is whether it is not from the figurative level, the level of figuratization itself, that that semiotic model receives, through a kind of recoil-effect, its capacity for syntagmatization. With this, the distinction between depths and surface wavers, particularly if it is in fact from the figural contingency that the model draws its power for narrativization. Indeed, what we have here is the question of the functioning of the Aristotelian peripeteia, which a careful literary analysis can discern beneath the heavy weight of semiotic apparatus, but which we are better able to recognize when we come to the limits of such semiotic analysis. In my own investigations concerning narrative, I relate this aspect of concordance and discordance in narrative to a first-order understanding of narrative, and I expect the second-order rationality of semiotics to provide an ever finer, less intuitive reconstruction of the accidents in any narrative.[13] My own belief here is that, as in historiography, to explain more is to understand better what has already been pre-understood.

This brings me to my second reason for saying that the semiotics of narrative touches its limits in the case of the passion narratives. Let us return again to the question of contingency: Jesus betrayed. This puts it on the figurative level. But 'to betray' also works on a second plane, which is not one that semiotics calls the deep level, that is, the level of the codified roles on the plane of a logic of narrative. The Son of Man betrayed is both a theological statement and an event at the same time. In the first instance, the statement is transhistorical, even gnomic: the Son of Man had to be betrayed. . . . The time of this being-betrayed is that time signified by the 'hour' ('and he prayed that, if it were possible, the hour might pass from him' – Mark 14:35, at Gethsemane). In the second case, the event gets inscribed in the chronology that Mark indicates through the series of the three hours of the watch: 'It is enough; the hour has come; the Son of Man is betrayed into the hands of sinners. Rise, let us be going; see, my betrayer is at hand' (Mark 14:41–42). The hour in the first sense of the term, the one in which the man of sorrows prays to the Father that he might be removed, and the hour in the second sense, where the one who will betray him approaches, form a pair that stem from the figure in the text, but this is no longer a question of the figurativization of codified roles, but rather something more in the sense of *Figura*, so admirably exposed by Eric Auerbach in his well-known article with this same title.[14] This *Figura* assures the unity of the kerygmatic and the event-like by giving the figure another kind of depth than that dealt with by semiotics, a typological depth, which subsequently will be articulated in terms of the theory of the four senses of scripture.

Can narrative semiotics make sense of all this? Yes, but only up to a certain point. I have said that semiotic analysis has at its disposal a whole conceptual arsenal with its categories of sender and receiver, and its notion of an ideological isotopy. Its limit, however, lies in the fact that both the sender and the receiver and the isotopy constitute structural entities deprived of the plurivocity that allows for the symbolic transferences at work in the two expressions 'to be betrayed' and 'hour'.

   2. Here I see a second relay station, which, by the way, is not alien to semiotics. Do we not make better sense of the kerygmatic meaning of being-betrayed and the term 'hour' by assigning them to a speaker, that is, to someone who speaks the narrative and who interprets it while recounting it? The distinction here between uttering and utterance is an extremely important one, for it allows us to make sense of an 'instance of discourse' which the notion of an ideological code is not able to account for. Indeed, a code is a pre-existing virtual system of discourse that prescribes the inscription of appropriate isotopies in a narrative. An instance of discourse, on the contrary, is a singular operation, like *parole* or speaking in relation to *langue* or the atemporal language system. I would not deny that narrative semiotics might be developed in this direction. And it has its successes, as shown by Greimas's *Maupassant* and his essays collected in *Sens II*.[15] Yet it seems to me that there is something in this notion of an instance of discourse that destabilizes the actantial model. Evidence for this is the fact that the theory of utterance, or of speech-acts, has undergone considerable development, without making use of either Greimas's semiotic square or the whole weighty apparatus of semiotics in general. I have in mind not only the work of Gérard Genette and his distinction between utterance and statement (or narrative properly speaking and the told story, the recounted events, the *fabula*), but also all the works devoted to the relation between the narrator's discourse and that of the character, an excellent example of which may be found in Dorrit Cohn's *Transparent Minds*.[16] To this work should be linked the work of the second generation of Russian structuralists, Bakhtin, Lotman, Ouspensky, who have developed a theory of 'point of view' as the principle of narrative composition.[17] For literary analysis, there can be no doubt that the christological qualification given to the characters and events in the passion narratives stems from that dialogical principle of literary composition. And when Lotman and Ouspensky deal with point of view, they draw upon this work, which needs to be applied in detail to the passion narratives.

   3. I would like to indicate one last development in literary theory that will give us another tool even more appropriate to the problem of

the narrativization of the kerygma, or of narrative with a kerygmatic intention, which we may call confessional narrative. This is the notion of narrative voice. In one sense, it is close to that of point of view, since, for Bakhtin, point of view and voice are interchangeable terms, as may be seen in his notion of a polyphonic narrative. But, however much it may be possible to depersonalize point of view, as, for instance, Genette proposes to do when he substitutes focalization for point of view in his recent *Nouveau Discours du Recit*, it is impossible to do so for the narrative voice. Someone speaks, someone speaks to me in the text, someone addresses himself or herself to me, a voice, which is of course an instance of the text, but which tells me, like the voice to which Augustine attributes the origin of his conversion, *tolle! lege!*, take and read. In this sense, if there is an *écriture*, a writing, in all speech, as Jacques Derrida puts it, there is also a speaking in the writing. This speaking in the writing is the narrative voice, the narration of the narrative, for which all the fictive or real events are in the past, in the preterit of narration.

These are some of the resources for a literary analysis of the passion narratives that allow us, if not completely to capture or, even less, to exhaust them, at least to get closer to this unique literary genre: a narrative constructed as interpreting a kerygma, which it brings to language by articulating it on the level of narrative.

Outlines of a literary analysis of the passion narratives in the gospel of Mark

To conclude I would like to attempt to outline a literary analysis of the passion narratives in Mark, which, following Robert Alter's approach to Hebraic narrative, will show how the christological component is signified on the narrative plane by the arranging of the events, by the interplay between utterance and statement, and finally, by the intervention of point of view and the narrative voice.[18] Jesus betrayed is the major peripeteia. This theologoumen of Jesus betrayed is given a history that, in each of its episodes, is a story of treason, denial, abandonment and flight, oriented towards the disappearance of Jesus' body, to the point of positing the equivalence between Jesus 'risen' (elsewhere) and Jesus absent: 'he is not here' (Mark 16:6). We may, of course, reduce the narrative component to the benefit of the work of the concept. This is what happens in the Hegelian reinscriptions of the theology of the cross into the negativity of the absolute Spirit's return to itself. But the gospel of Mark never goes so far as to formulate this separate theology, even in its confessions of faith, sealed by the centurion's confession in response to the dying Jesus' cry of dereliction. This confession is narrativized by the bias of a 'quoted monologue', to use one of Dorrit Cohn's categories: he said, 'Truly this man was the Son of God' (15:39). Beyond this procedure of using quotation, the monologue is also narrativized by the motivation the omniscient narrator assigns to him: 'And when the centurion, who stood facing him, *saw that he thus breathed his last,* he said. . . .' This clause constitutes an extraordinary example of a narrative having to do with the intimate thoughts of a third person, which themselves belong to the order of interpretation. The same thing must be said of Jesus's double confession before the high priest ('Are you the Christ, the Son of the Blessed?' and Jesus said, 'I am' [14:61−62]) and before Pilate ('Are you the King of the Jews?' asks the Roman. 'You have said so,' answers Jesus [15:2]).

What the direct confession about Jesus or of Jesus cannot produce, on either the kerygmatic or the narrative plane of signification, is the series of antagonistic relations − treason, denial, flight, abandonment − that stakes out the theme: Jesus betrayed into the hands of sinners, in other words, the more and more violent dialogical structure that ends in the situation of dereliction. Nor is the monologual confession capable of correcting the misunderstanding that is not just confined to the relations between antagonists, but that transpires throughout the whole narrative, to the point of making such an opaque narrative that the reader is finally led to identifying with the women at the empty tomb, concerning whom the narrative tells us: 'And they went out and fled from the tomb; for trembling and astonishment had come upon them; and they said nothing to any one, for they were afraid.' Flight, silence, fear, this is how the Gospel of Mark terminates in 16:8 according to the majority of exegetes.

If such is the case, to explicate this gospel means looking for the indications of the equation it posits between its christology of a suffering Son of Man and the story of the betrayed Jesus. The chain that these indications constitute makes the passion narrative into a literary unit, whatever may be the history of its tradition or of its redaction, as well as for any conjectural relation between a primitive narrative, or a shorter and a longer version.

1. Let us begin with the 'Anointing at Bethany' (14:3−9). In Mark and Matthew it comes immediately after the announcement of the chief priests' and scribes' plot against Jesus − in Luke and John it is not at this point, Luke having an anointing narrative at 7:36, while John places it six days before Easter, in the context of the resurrection of Lazarus. Why does this anointing occupy this place in Mark? Perhaps because so embedded (by 14:1−2) in the passion and

resurrection narrative, it refers us in a symmetrical way to the anointing that does not take place on Easter morning. In it, the moment of absence is already indicated (cf. 14:7–8: 'but you will not always have me. She has done what she could; she has anointed my body beforehand for burying'). The anticipated anointing thus counts as a burial anointing. Let us further note the interlacing of the themes developed in what follows. First, the indignation of 'some' in 14:4 (who in Matthew will become the 'disciples' and in John, 'Judas Iscariot, one of his disciples') announces Jesus's being abandoned by his own followers, among whom Judas is just one of these followers. If the start of Judas's treason in 14:10–11 immediately follows the pericope of the anointing at Bethany and precedes the preparation of the Passover meal, is this not so as to establish the equation between the theologoumen 'the Son of Man had to be betrayed' and the event of Jesus betrayed? There is still another significant indication. By calling Judas 'one of the twelve' in 14:10, the narrative underscores his belonging to the group of disciples – Matthew will retain this point, as will Luke with even greater emphasis; as for John, like Luke, he would prefer to satanize Judas. We need also to ask what the exchange of Jesus' body for money signifies. It is a derisory exchange if the true exchange, the final one is the one that exchanges the body for the word in 16:8. But let us not lose hold of our guideline, Jesus betrayed, which connects the two registers of theological necessity and narrative contingency.

2. Let us move on to the narrative of the last supper, which tradition history and redaction history tell us is an independent pericope. Clearly we are to take the preparation, the treason denounced at the table which all share, and the ritual meal as one articulated whole. In this respect, the preparatory episode in 14:12–16 does not emphasize Jesus' omniscience for Mark. The important thing is that the preparations be made 'to eat the passover' and that this has to be done on the first day of azymes, alluding to the leaven of the Pharisees and that of Herod. Eating the Passover meal is in essence what Mark recounts in 14:17–25. But the negative moment throughout the narrative continues to invert the basically positive meaning of this gesture. To eat the Passover meal is an act with a wholly positive meaning, whether we emphasize the eschatological implication of the final banquet or the sacramental and ritual import of the instituting of the eucharistic meal. Yet the 'negative' constantly accompanies the 'positive' with its shadow. The pronouncement about treason is made right at the heart of the meal (14:18). Once again the sinister word 'betray' recurs: 'one of you will betray me, one who is eating with me'. Psalm 41 is made use of here, to tie together 'betray' and 'eating

with me'. At the same time, the connection between Judas and the twelve announce the secret bond between Judas's treason, Peter's denial and everyone's flight. The traitor is among the disciples at the meal. Treason is internal to the community. Perhaps we should even go further and, following structural analysis, emphasize the opposition between 'eating with' – that is, to nourish a body in a relationship of conviviality – and 'betray', that is, to hand over a body, by rupturing another space, that of community. In any case, Judas is not directly named: 'one who is eating with me'. In this way, the banquet of betrayal is the obligatory path to the eschatological banquet that breaks through the story as told. Absence is once again tied to being betrayed: 'the Son of Man goes as it is written of him' (14:21). (Matthew says the same thing, Luke has: 'the Son of Man goes', which attenuates the absence while increasing the manifestation of power.) As for the instituting of the eucharist, it too is as marked by absence as by presence. 'This is my body', 'this is my blood of the covenant' – indications of presence. 'Truly, I say to you, I shall not drink again of the fruit of the vine until that day when I drink it new in the kingdom of God' – absence. Final fulfillment is announced, but it is accompanied by a fearful warning: 'one of you will betray me . . . one who is dipping bread in the same dish with me'. One question marks his path: can one really be his disciple? Is this an impossible vocation, an impossible mission?

3. Next comes the narrative about Gethsemane (14:26–42). Is there no reason, I mean no narrative reason, why in 14:26 Mark has Jesus and the Twelve go out 'to the Mount of Olives', thereby making this indication a resting stone in view of the episode of Gethsemane, and before the announcing of Peter's denial, symmetrical in so many ways to Judas' treason? We most likely are meant to meditate on the pair Peter/Judas, where the helper Peter becomes an opponent on the figurative plane, while the opponent Judas secretly becomes the helper in the hero's qualifying test. Once again the individual figure of the one who denies Jesus is not left in isolation: 'You will all fall away' (14:27). It is this same 'you all' that is signified by the disciples falling asleep. What is more, they are successively designated as the 'disciples' in 14:32, then by the trio Peter, James and John in 14:33, which anticipates the more individualized narrative of Peter's denial, the epitome of all abandoning him. All, three, one.

As for Jesus at Gethsemane, I am struck by what so many commentators have said about it, when they oppose the stoic sovereignty of Jesus in Luke to his dereliction in Mark and even in Matthew: 'and he began to be greatly distressed and troubled' (14:33). We must not be afraid here to follow Frank Kermode's suggestion that the narrative deepens the mystery more than it clarifies the motivations. For here the theological line that ties the righteous one to death requires, on the narrative plane, an incomparable passage to the void. If it is true that the messianic mission passes through suffering and death, the anxiety and sense of horror that seize Jesus have to go so far as his plea that he be spared from such suffering; that is, that it be taken out of the messianic mission. Is this to say that for an instant Jesus wanted to avoid the cross? The text says instead that 'he fell on the ground and prayed that, if it were possible, the hour might pass [far] from him' (14:35). The very word 'hour' removes this agony from the chronological and narrative contingency. But it is, in fact, another hour, the one that designates the moment when the one who will betray Jesus 'is at hand'. For the Passion to 'come', the one who betrays Jesus must 'come': 'the hour has come' (14:41). Henceforth the eschatological hour and the chronological hour coincide. As for the flight of the disciples, readers will become less severe than they might have been when they read in 14:40 that 'they did not know how to answer him'. If Peter stands out from the chorus of misunderstanding, nevertheless he still belongs to it, too. At the last supper, everyone drinks the cup; at Gethsemane, 'they all forsook him, and fled' (14:50). What the disciples and Peter do not understand, refusing it in their hearts and through their flight, is Mark's christology of the Son of Man.

4. The arrest of Jesus is the pivotal event, the beginning of the short narrative, according to historical-critical exegesis. However the writer of the long narrative does not lose the guiding thread, the word 'betrayed': 'Now the betrayer . . .' (14:44). Structural analysis uncovers a still more subtle tie between the betraying kiss, which is a contact with the body, and the anointing touch, as though the first sign of the traitor stood in a relationship of parody to the anointing. The tie between the pericope of Gethsemane and that of the arrest is less subtle. It can be summed up in one word: abandonment. Those who were sleeping during the time of agony, flee at the time of arrest (14:51).[19]

All the pericopes that follow constitute so many illustrations of the notion of narrative as interpretation, that is, as contributing to a christological reading of the narratives relative to Jesus' Passion. Taken together, they assure a perfect narrative and theological coherence with what precedes, as well as with the passion narratives. If it is legitimate from a historical-critical point of view to inquire into the suture between the pericope about the agony at Gethsemane and that of the arrest, said to inaugurate the short narrative (arrest, trial, execution), the narrative and theological continuity between

Gethsemane and the arrest bear the mark of a clear literary art. This unity is assured by the theme of the 'betrayed' Son of Man. The conflict he gives rise to is merely raised to a higher level by the narrative of the events that carry through this betrayal in the narrative time. The slide in the meaning of the word 'hour' from the eschatological plane to the episodic plane had already prepared this tilting toward a more clearly event-based narrative, namely the events of the short narrative. But, if it is true that the disciples' rejection of the suffering Messiah is essential to the narrativization of the Markan narrative of the suffering Christ, then the episode at Gethsemane was necessary to his passion narrative.

5. Denial and trial. If this is what is kerygmatically at stake in the interpreting narrative, we can then give a more plausible explication of certain pure narrative features in the composition of the following episodes, in particular the fact that Mark interwove Peter's denial into the narrative of the double Jewish and Roman trial. (E.g. 14:54 sets the continuity of the theme into the account of the trial.)

The motif of denial leads quite far back in Mark's gospel, to the incident at Caesarea Philippi (7:27–30). From this moment on, it looks as though the confession about Christ was cut short and, in this sense, is misleading. What Peter had not accepted, beginning at this moment, was the necessity of the Cross. If it is true that at the end of the episode at Gethsemane everyone had fled, Peter is the only one to flee who, remembering what Jesus had said about his denying him, becomes aware of his own distress: 'And he broke down and wept' (14:73). (Matthew, followed by Luke, attenuates things: 'And he went out and wept bitterly.') Peter flees, just like at Gethsemane. This is the hyper-chronological and, if I may put it this way, the homological connection that, once again, ties the narrative to the kerygmatic by means of a kind of echo-phenomenon. The case of Judas has made us familiar with this kind of conjunction between two planes, that of inevitability and that of contingency. Inevitability: Jesus had told him what would happen and Peter remembers it. Contingency: the ancedotes about Peter warming himself, the servant recognizing him, and the cock who cries at just the right moment.

The embedding of the interrogation before the Sanhedrin within the narrative about Peter's denial and the cutting in two of this narrative has the striking effect of reinforcing the narrative pair questioning/denial (both episodes have the same introduction: 14:53–54).

However, the most intriguing pair is that of Peter and Judas. Peter is, of course, not the one who betrays (the body of Jesus, as Louis Marin emphasizes). He merely denies him in words. But speech is not innocent, as the incident at Caesarea Philippi just referred to made clear. His denial gets a special gravity, however, from its being interwoven with the interrogation before the High Priest. In a way, Peter too is a false witness. This underlines the peril of anti-testimony like a faultline in the disciple's service. It is this latter trait that makes the helper slip toward the side of the opponent. And what thereby becomes common to Judas and Peter is their comparable contribution to the righteous one's march toward death, in spite of the contingency proper to the pericope about each one of them. Inasmuch as his denial is that of the leader of the Apostles, Peter can be said to be an opponent more crushed by the narrative than Judas himself. In his denial culminates the scandal that brings the disciples' blindness to its highest point.

It is here that the narrative clouds over and leads to the unsayable. For if Peter is Satan, as we are told in the episode at Caesarea Philippi, is this not so because all the figures, when confronted by the enigma of Jesus, reply to the question 'Who do you say that I am?' with a comparable withdrawal. From Judas who betrays him, to the disciples who flee, to Peter who denies him, to the women who, they too, at the empty tomb are seized with horror and flee. It is against this shadowy background that Peter's denial takes on its full weight. Starting as a negative model of the condition of being a disciple, it becomes a source of uncertainty for the reader insofar as the reader is invited to proffer an affirmation of faith with such force that it will cut the ambiguity of everything that has gone before.

6. As for the crucifixion narrative (15:20b–41), its dramatic structure is not commanded by the polarity between the traitor and the helper, but rather by the dereliction that calls for the eclipsing of both of them. Suddenly, the dramatic effect is produced by another system of opposition that will henceforth play itself out on the level of the christological signification itself and that the narrative will interpret through recourse to the narrative resources belonging to it. If it is true that two theologies confront each other here, that of the divine man and that of the suffering Son of Man, it is by strictly narrative means that Mark separates these two theologies. The tour de force, it seems, is his having placed the theology of the divine man in the mouths of adversaries, who here are mockers: 'save yourself and come down from the cross'. 'He saved others; he cannot save himself.' The grotesque confusion of the cry 'Elo-i' as an appeal to Elijah, who was himself treated as a divine man, contributes to this repudiation of the theology of the divine man. Even more, the great cry, which for the latter theology should have been a cry of triumph, is transmuted into a cry of dereliction by borrowing from Psalm 22:1.

It is true that the centurion's confession, which uses the title Son of God (Mark 15:39), seems to attenuate this intra-theological conflict, but we may note that this title is emptied of its divine-man signification by the important addition that the centurion 'saw that he thus breathed his last'. It is because he saw how Jesus died that the centurion could give its correct theological signification to the episode of the crucifixion.

To the dereliction of Jesus left alone corresponds the displacement of the role of the opponent from the figure of the traitor to that of the mockers, a displacement that almost seems to indicate the extinction of this function. As for Jesus' cry, it brings to a peak his abandonment at Gethsemane. The disciples have fled, there remain the mockers – and the centurion.[20]

7. Just a few words, to conclude, about the narrative of the empty tomb.[21] I offer them from the perspective of this inquiry, namely how a narrative with an interpretative vocation functions. The formula for such a narrative will be the following. If Jesus lives and lives elsewhere, then here there has to be an empty tomb. It is in relation to this narrative structure with a kerygmatic function that we may attempt to interpret one unique feature of Mark's narrative, namely that the only ones present at the tomb are the women, no guards (as in Matthew), no disciples (as in Luke and John) and not even the figure of Jesus himself (as in Matthew and John). This 'parsimony of presence' is particularly appropriate to the general tone of the Markan passion narrative and accords quite easily with the hypothesis that the narrative of the empty tomb constituted the actual redactional conclusion of the gospel of Mark. What I have called narrative parsimony illustrates the following formula. The Lord resurrected, according to the kerygma, has as his narrative trace only the absence of the body of Jesus. If it is true that Mark here continues to oppose a christology that would immediately lead to a christology of glory, short-circuiting the Master's suffering and the difficulty of being a disciple, then the narrative that best interprets this theology of the suffering Son of man is one that does without an appearance of Jesus himself to Peter and the apostles. The only presence is the women – and a missing anointing. Even the vision of the 'young man' (*neaniskos*) does not contradict this parsimony of presence. He is a messenger who represents Jesus, but who is not Jesus (his position on the right is that of Christ next to the Father, his white robe is that of the elect in heaven). In the dimension of pure presence remains the voice, the voice that says, 'Do not be amazed; you seek Jesus of Nazareth, who was crucified. He has risen [from the dead], he is not here' (16:6). This negativity of presence belongs to

the guiding theme of the progressive disappearance of the body throughout the passion narrative. A decrease in the body, an increase in the word. A word that is not our own designates Jesus in the third person as 'risen absent' (note the anacoluthic form: 'he is risen, he is not here'). A message is contained in the command that follows ('go, tell his disciples and Peter'): 'that he is going before you to Galilee; there you will see him, as he told you' (16:7). Whatever may be said from a historical-critical point of view about the way that Galilee is a place indicated throughout the gospel of Mark, and whatever may be said about the allusions to the relationship between the community of Mark and that of Jerusalem, or about the question of the mission to the Jews and that to the gentiles, literary analysis will underscore the future tense of this announcement: there you will see him. This advance of Jesus over the disciples that the narrative presents allows it to stop at the threshold of the future as a narrative that cannot cross this threshold owing to its very narrative constraints. These constraints mean that the narrative finds its appropriate conclusion in the conjunction between the voice of an unidentified young man, even if he is a celestial character, and an awakening elsewhere, which the voice speaks of in the third person.

Is it not the case that we must say that the narrative not so much elucidates things as obscures them, in the sense that its manner of narratively interpreting the kerygma is to reinforce the enigmatic aspect of the events themselves? If not, why did Mark end this pericope, and quite probably his gospel, with the verse: 'And they went out and fled from the tomb; for trembling and astonishment had come upon them and they said nothing to anyone, for they were afraid' (16:8). Flight, fear, silence. We are not even told that the message conveyed by the young man was communicated. If we admit that the gospel narrative historicizes the kerygma of the risen Christ, must we not also say that the genius of Mark is to have placed all the resources of the narrative art for negativity and even obscurity at the service of his christology of a suffering and crucified Son of Man?

NOTES

1 Frank Kermode, *The Genesis of Secrecy: On the Interpretation of Narrative* (Harvard University Press, Cambridge, Mass., 1979).
2 Robert Alter, *The Art of Biblical Narrative* (Basic Books, New York, 1981).
3 Ibid., p. 24.
4 Eric Auerbach, *Mimesis: The Representation of Reality in Western Literature*, tr. Willard R. Trask (Princeton University Press, Princeton, 1953).

5 His most striking example is drawn from legendary narratives, such as the stories about Joseph, or from stories that come close to being chronicles, such as the story of the ascension of David to power or the well-known narratives about his succession.

6 Alter, *The Art of Biblical Narrative*, p. 33.

7 Ibid., p. 189.

8 Hans Frei, *The Identity of Jesus Christ: An Inquiry into the Hermeneutical Basis of Dogma Theology* (Fortress Press, Philadelphia, 1974).

9 Norman Perrin, *Rediscovering the Teaching of Jesus* (Harper & Row, New York, 1967).

10 Let me note in passing, without being able to give it the full development it deserves, the recourse to *testimonia*, to citations from the Old Testament. Contrary to what the modern reader may tend to think, the affirmation that a recounted event fulfills an earlier prophecy – itself quite arbitrarily taken out of context – does not make the narrative suspect but rather, augments its credibility, if we follow the criteria for reception of a text current among the first Christians. In this sense, it counts in the same way as does the anecdotal or material feature, which we may say reinforces what Frei has called the 'history-like' aspect of the narrative. We have here two converging procedures for conveying credibility.

11 Hans Frei, *The Eclipse of Biblical Narrative: A Study in Eighteenth and Nineteenth Century Hermeneutics* (Yale University Press, New Haven, 1974).

12 Louis Marin, *Semiotics of the Passion Narrative*, tr. Alfred M. Johnson, Jr, (Pickwick Press, Pittsburg, 1980).

13 Paul Ricoeur, *Time and Narrative*, tr. Katheleen McLaughlin and David Pellauer (University of Chicago Press, Chicago, 1984).

14 Erich Auerbach, 'Figura', in *Scenes from the Drama of European Literature* (Meridian Books, New York, 1959), pp. 11–76.

15 A.-J. Greimas, *Maupassant. La Semiotique du texte: Exercises practiques* (Seuil, Paris, 1976); Greimas, *Du Sens* (Seuil, Paris, 1983), vol. 2.

16 Gérard Genette, 'Frontiers of narrative', in *Figures of Literary Discourse*, tr. Alan Sheridan (Columbia University Press, New York, 1982), pp. 127–44; Genette, *Narrative Discourse: An Essay in Method*, tr. Jane E. Lewin (Cornell University Press, Ithaca, 1980); Dorrit Cohn, *Transparent Minds: Narrative Modes for Presenting Consciousness in Fiction* (Princeton University Press, Princeton, 1978).

17 Jurij Lotman, *The Structure of the Artistic Text*, tr. Ronald Vronn (University of Michigan Press, Ann Arbor, 1977); Mikhail Bakhtin, *Problems of Dostoevski's Poetics*, tr. R. W. Rotsel (Ardis Publications, Ann Arbor, 1973); Boris Uspensky, *A Poetics of Composition: The Structure of the Artistic Text and a Typology of Compositional Form*, tr. Valentina Zavanin and Susan Wittig (University of California Press, Berkeley, 1973).

18 I shall cite the Revised Standard Version text. Allow me also to acknowledge my dependence on the work of Xavier Léon-Dufour in his essays on 'Passion (Récits de la)', *Supplément Histoire/Bible*, cols

1419–92, and in *The Passion in Mark*, ed. Werner H. Kelber (Fortress Press, Philadelphia, 1976).

19 I must pass over the incident of the *Neaniskos*, clothed with a linen cloth, who runs away naked. Frank Kermode has given us a brilliant and troubling exegesis about him, from the point of view of a hermeneutic for which the narrative in obscuring more than clarifying things, engenders and preserves the secret.

20 Dan O. Via, in his *Kerygma and Comedy in the New Testament* (Fortress Press, Philadelphia, 1975), points to the theme of powerless death confronted by the struggle between power and not-power that takes place through the Passion narratives and in the whole Gospel. Power: the leaders of the Jews, soldiers, thieves, the centurion, Simon compelled to carry the cross. The narrative brings about a transvaluation of the images of coercion, by having the only bearer of power left on stage – the centurion – pronounce the confession of Christian faith. This dialectical reversal was anticipated in the figure of Simon of Cyrene, who, constrained to do something, is transformed into a model of service. Simon, literally, bears his cross. The reversal of the cry of triumph, if such is the case, into a cry of derelection belongs to the same reversal. What is more, the reversal brought about by the transvaluation of images of coercion, rejoins at an even deeper level the theme of the fulfilling of destiny – the Son of Man has to be betrayed – through the interplay of oppositions. It is through treason, denial, and, finally, the application of violence to the body of Jesus, that the destiny of the Son of Man is accomplished. The irony of the conclusion to the crucifixion narrative is to have the Son of Man proclaimed the Son of God by the one who has the mandate of power, who saw how Jesus died a death without power.

21 See John Dominic Crossan, 'Empty Tomb and Absent Lord', in Kebler (ed.), pp. 135–52.

11

The Gospel in Greco-Roman Culture

Mary Ann Tolbert

In a recent critique of the work of the 'new historicists' on
Renaissance drama, Edward Pechter argues that the essential
characteristic of this critical stance is 'its detachment from the text'.[1]
The detachment arises from an insistence on the integral relationship
of the text with its remote and alien cultural, political and social
milieu. The virtue of such a detached perspective is that 'by reducing
the power of the text, detachment increases the observer's power over
the text – the power to see through the surface, penetrate its
disguises.'[2] Although Pechter decides that such a stance may be
detrimental to a contemporary audience's involvement in Renaissance
literature and himself prefers a more benign view of the power of
texts and their contemporary appropriations, if it is the Bible rather
than Shakespeare or Jonson being considered, then the possibility of
detaching oneself from the coercive control of the text and its
generations of institutional interpreters becomes a political act of no
mean consequence.

For good or ill, and generally a considerable amount of both,
interpretations of biblical literature have molded the cultural, social
and political life of the Western world for many centuries to a degree
few other texts can boast. Moreover, new generations in quite
different cultural situations often read these works expecting some
direct relevance to their own particular experience, even when
maintaining such expectations required the development of elaborate
reading strategies like the four-fold allegorical method.[3] To historicize
the texts of the Bible by placing them within their own ancient and
alien era challenges the transcendent authority granted to them by
some ecclesial powers and potentially creates a space for liberation
from the oppressive uses to which these texts are sometimes put.
Thus, while gaining the power to penetrate the disguises of the text

may not make good theater,[4] acquiring a certain detachment from the dogmatic power of the Bible makes clear political sense.

The new-historicist agenda, however, in relation to biblical texts encounters a number of difficulties which are either lacking or much less severe in Renaissance drama. As an illustration of both the potential and problems of new-historicist analysis of biblical literature, I wish to explore the Gospel of Mark generally and in particular the Gethsemane episode in Mark 14:32–42 in light of its own literary-historical milieu. Modern biblical scholarship, beginning as it did in the positivistic historical currents of the Enlightenment period, employed the New Testament gospels as the primary sources for reconstructing the history of early Christianity or the historical Jesus, assuming all too often that the New Testament texts were fairly reliable windows onto that history rather than the ideological products of it. Only recently have biblical scholars begun studying the gospels in their own rights as narrative accounts of the life of Jesus written with very specific audiences and definite rhetorical goals in mind.[5] Moreover, the concomitant belief of positivistic historians in their own objective and value-neutral perspective in performing such reconstructions is only gradually fading from the scholarly scene under attack from feminists, Marxists and – yes – new historians.[6]

In attempting to situate the Gospel of Mark in its own history, I, as historian, am participating in the creation of that history not only by the selection and arrangement of data but also by the choice of hypotheses I find convincing for explaining that data.[7] In relation to ancient texts like Mark, where neither the author nor the place of origin nor the identity of the intended audience is known, the historian's role as imaginative creator is hard to overestimate or overlook. However visible Christianity would later become in Western culture, in the first century of the Common Era it was an obscure eastern Mediterranean sect essentially ignored by the artistic, intellectual and political authorities of the Greco-Roman world. Moreover, even the extant artifacts of the dominant elite culture of the period are the mere remnants of a lost civilization. And the dimensions of that loss are overwhelming. Whether out of ideological disagreement or simple unconcern or ignorance, most of the writings of the Greco-Roman world were destroyed during the long process of scribal copying and transmitting from ancient times through the Middle Ages. If our reconstructions of life among the most prolific aristocratic classes in the best documented cities of Rome and Alexandria can claim only partial and fragmentary adequacy, with how much less confidence can we reconstruct the social world of the urban masses out of whose ranks the early Christians came. Indeed, what little we do know about first-century Christians depends almost exclusively on their own scanty writings. Consequently, anyone who wants to historicize Mark seems to be placed in the frustratingly circular dilemma of having to use the gospel itself to reconstruct the history within which it is to be located historically.

For the literary historian, one possible path out of that circle might exist if one could study other texts of similar genre from the Greco-Roman world about which more information is available. By analyzing how certain generic expectations were used to mold the Christian proclamation concerning Jesus, one might be better able to delineate who the author and intended audience were, what social strata or roles they occupied in ancient society, and how they viewed themselves *vis-à-vis* the dominant Greco-Roman cultural milieu. But what is the gospel's genre? Suggestions range from a new genre, unique to Christianity – a suggestion obviously owing more to theological motives than literary sense – to types of ancient aretalogy (catalogues of the miraculous activities of divine men) or biography or history or memorabilia.[8] Each of these hypotheses has something to recommend it, but each also has objections lodged against it. For example, catalogues of the miracle-working activities of divine men in various literary forms may well have pre-existed the Gospel of Mark, but no such complete text is known nor does the label 'aretalogy' appear to be a recognizable or consistent designation for this multi-form group.[9] While biography (technically *bios*) is one of the earliest and most persistent scholarly hypotheses for the gospel genre, it generally charts the entire course of life from birth to death, which Mark, at any rate, does not, and its essential focus on the special character of the central figure seems to miss Mark's interest in the various responses to Jesus of the disciples, Jews and crowds. On the other hand, histories in the ancient world dealt mainly with the political and military struggles of city-states and nations rather than with the life and teachings of one individual and his followers.

The recent generic suggestion by Vernon Robbins of the memorabilia of a sage (technically *apomnemoneumata*) has the advantages of focusing mainly on adult life and death, emphasizing the relationship of the sage to disciples, existing as a recognized genre well before the first century CE, and being a term actually used of the gospels by some later patristic authors.[10] From a literary standpoint it also has the considerable advantage of being the first generic hypothesis to be argued on structural or rhetorical grounds rather than simply on generalized content. Robbins concentrates on the formal patterning of the teaching process between sage and disciples as the feature that links the Gospel of Mark to this ancient genre.

There are basic objections to all of these generic hypotheses. First, each of the main three – aretalogy, biography and memorabilia – by emphasizing so strongly one aspect of Mark's story, of necessity must omit or undervalue other parts of the story. In fact, if one could *combine* an aretalogy's focus on miracle-working, a biography's focus on the character of Jesus, and a memorabilia's focus on the teaching cycle between Jesus and the disciples, one would have almost created an adequate generic formulation for the Gospel of Mark. Second, the extant examples from the ancient world of all three of these genres exhibit far superior linguistic and technical skill and far more sophisticated literary and philosophical acumen than anything found in the Gospel of Mark. This second, overarching objection is especially damaging to Robbins' thesis, for, regardless of possible similarity in the patterns of teaching cycles, the rhetorical, philosophical and stylistic polish of Xenophon's *Memorabilia*, his generic exemplar, is as different from the Gospel of Mark as day is from night.

The simplicity of Greek style, the unpolished rhetorical development, the lack of philosophical or literary pretension, and the typological, conventional narration which characterize the Gospel of Mark – and, for that matter, the Gospels of Matthew, Luke and John – seem to place these texts on an entirely different plane from the majority of extant works from the Greco-Roman world. Attempting to account for that difference may provide a new starting-point in developing a plausible hypothesis concerning the genre of the gospels: perhaps they belong to the realm of popular culture and popular literature. If so, then Xenophon's *Memorabilia* stands in the same relationship to the Gospel of Mark that Dostoevski's *Crime and Punishment* stands to Agatha Christie's *The Murder of Roger Ackroyd*: one is written for the literate elite of culture, the other is accessible to middle- and lower-class masses; that is, one is purposely individualized, subtle, ambiguous and profound, according to reigning elite aesthetic values, while the other would be characterized as conventionalized, pellucid, stereotypical and repetitious; one is an example of self-conscious literate culture, the other of popular culture. The study of popular culture has been a major component of literary scholarship for many years, but only relatively recently have scholars begun to realize that popular cultures existed alongside 'elite' cultures well back in history, back behind the pulp novels of the nineteenth century, back behind the Middle English verse romances of the medieval period, back, in fact, at least to the Classical world.[11]

The Greco-Roman world was the first in Western history to develop numbers of sometimes quite large multi-national cities under a fairly uniform administrative system and employing similar educational, cultural, economic and legal structures. Furthermore, for the first time since the primordial Tower of Babel, people from different regions and tribes were able to speak the same language, *koine* Greek. Although the elite, cultivated tradition of arts and letters from which most of the extant works of the ancient world come never employ *koine*, for it was the Greek of the marketplace, of trade contracts and commerce, all of the texts of the New Testament are written in *koine* Greek. Understanding the New Testament as a product of popular culture, using the common language of the people, would account for its less polished character when compared to other 'classical' works and would also explain why no closely similar texts survived from the ancient world. Since the group controlling the processes of preservation and transmission of manuscripts, paintings and all the other artistic artifacts of an age are the privileged upper classes with the leisure and financial resources necessary for such activities, they naturally tended to preserve what they produced and liked. Popular literature then, as now, was generally disdained by the elite. Indeed, Augustine complained that he was initially poorly disposed towards Christianity because of the artlessness and crudeness of its writings.[12] However, it was not from the privileged, leisured, wealthy aristocracy that most of the earliest Christians came. They came instead from the growing middle stratum of society, the artisans, traders and freed slaves crowding into the large cities of the age,[13] whose language was *koine* Greek and whose cultural tradition was the result of popular experience. If the authors and original audiences of all the canonical gospels – indeed, of almost all early Christian writings of any type – belonged in the main to the middle and lower levels of society, it would be extremely odd not to find the evidence of popular literary techniques stamped on their works.

Providentially, examples of one other Greco-Roman popular prose literary genre endured the ravages of manuscript transmission: the ancient novel.[14] By describing and exploring the stylistic patterns, techniques and strategies of the Greek ancient novel, it may be possible to uncover connections between ancient popular literature and the Gospel of Mark. Five complete examples of the ancient novel exist along with numerous papyrus fragments of other novels. The five are Chariton's *Chaereas and Callirhoe*, Xenophon's *An Ephesian Tale*, Longus' *Daphnis and Chloe*, Achilles Tatius' *Leucippe and Clitophon* and Helidorus' *An Ethiopian Tale*. Of the five, only the first two display little 'Attic' influence from the Greek cultural revival of the first centuries CE, known as the Second Sophistic, and it is these earlier, non-Sophistic novels that show the clearest parallels to the gospels. Although dating is as difficult for these ancient novels as it is for Christian writings, papyrus fragments clearly date the genre to the first two centuries BCE. Chariton is usually dated between 100 BCE and 50 CE, while the dating of Xenophon varies from 50 CE to 263 CE, with the earlier rather than the later end of the spectrum being most probable.[15] About the authors themselves we know little. Chariton states in his opening line that he is Chariton of Aphrodisias (a city in Caria in southwest Asia Minor) and works as a clerk to the rhetor Athenagoras, and this information may well be true. Xenophon of Ephesus provides no personal reference, and the name Xenophon may be a pseudonym alluding to the famous Xenophon of Athens (author of the *Memorabilia*), who lived centuries earlier. The location of the authors and actions in all of the earliest ancient novels is the eastern Mediterranean world from Asia Minor to Egypt, the home also of early Christianity.

The five extant texts are all of the erotic variety of the ancient novel; that is, their basic plot details the familiar work of the god Eros: a young couple fall in love, are separated through evil or misadventure, endure great trials and testing, and are finally reunited. It would be a mistake, however, to think that the love theme is the primary focus of the story, for many ancient novelists, especially Xenophon, use the love–separation–reunion framework to concentrate on the exotic, painful, and thrilling adventures experienced by each of the lovers during their long separation. Travel, adventure, and violence are as much the point of these stories as love. Furthermore, a number of scholars argue that even this combination of themes is too restrictive in describing the ancient novel, for also included in this genre are the later writings *Apollonius of Tyre* and the pre-Christian revision of the Pseudo-Clementine *Recognitions* as well as the Christian apocryphal *Acts of the Apostles*, especially the *Acts of Paul and Thecla* and the *Acts of Thomas*.[16] Neither *Apollonius of Tyre* nor the *Recognitions* contain the conventional pair of lovers, although both have travel and adventure in large measure, and some of the earliest papyrus fragments seem to exhibit similar adventure plots without the love theme. On the other hand, perhaps the most rhetorically polished of the ancient novels, Longus' *Daphnis and Chloe*, lacks both adventure and travel, focusing solely on the pastoral, seasonal development of love between a shepherdess and a goatherd on Lesbos. The five extant erotic novels, then, might reasonably be described as one sub-type of the ancient novel that by the chance of history happened to escape the fate of most representatives of the broader genre.

What unites these works are a common myth, a common heritage, and a common conventionalized style, employed by the authors with varying degrees of technical skill. The myth is the Greco-Roman myth of the isolated individual in a dangerous world: 'Unaccommodated man, man alone and thus without security, seeks security, in God or his fellow man, or woman. Lacking a social identity, he seeks to create for himself a personal one by becoming the object of the affections of his own kind or of the providence of the Almighty. He identifies himself by loving God or man or both.'[17] The novels are full of religious concerns and themes. It is the gods who often step in to save or damn the hero and heroine. Indeed, one major thesis concerning the origin of the novel, not widely accepted at the present time, is that, with the exception of Chariton's, they are all *Mysterientexte*, cultic texts of Hellenistic mystery religions, fully understandable only to the initiated.[18] Whether one agrees with that hypothesis or not, the pattern of 'the separation, wanderings, trials, apparent deaths, and final reunion of the two lovers' is strikingly close to the myth of Isis and Osiris so important to the cult of Isis. Indeed, the gods or fate stand behind most of the action in these stories, and regardless of their clear relish for violence, exciting adventure, and entertainment, all of these ancient novels betray a very serious, very religious underlying concern: salvation from isolation, chaos and death.

The literary heritage of the Greek novel combines Greek drama and historiography. As prose writing, it takes its basic narrative structure from historiography but blends the manners, styles and concerns of drama and epic into its stories. The ancient novel is 'fundamentally drama in substance and historiography in its outward form'.[19] The major characters in the novels are often historical persons of earlier periods or the fictional sons and daughters of actual historical figures. The action takes place in real cities and involves practices and groups that truly existed (e.g. shipwrecks, pirates, slavery, crucifixion, etc.). This essential historiographic form gives verisimilitude to the conventionalized and formulaic plots themselves. The internal dynamics of the plots owe much to drama and epic: brief, dramatic scenes, dialogue with narrative summaries interspersed, episodic development, beginnings with minimal introductions or *in medias res*, central turning-points and final recognition scenes. The ancient novel, then, like the modern novel, was a remarkably synthesizing genre, pulling together a great variety of earlier forms and adapting them for a larger audience.

The Gospel of Mark is obviously not an ancient novel of the erotic type. However, its mixing together of historiographic form and dramatic force, its synthesizing of earlier genres like biography, memorabilia of a sage, aretalogy and apocalypse, its stylistic techniques of episodic plot, beginning with minimal introduction, central turning-point and final recognition scene, and most of all, its grammatically crude, repetitious and conventionalized narrative display striking *stylistic* similarities to the popular Greek ancient novel. There is, indeed, some fragmentary evidence for a more biographical, as opposed to erotic, type of the ancient novel, with Xenophon of Athens' *Cyropaedia* (rather than his *Memorabilia*) as its antecedent and the Alexander Romance and Philostratus' *Life of Apollonius of Tyana* as its heirs.[20] If such an historical/biographical type of ancient novel existed, it would clearly be the generic home of the gospels and would explain why Mark and John, if they were, indeed, completely independent of each other, should happen upon the same general format for the story of Jesus. Reference to ancient biographies of Pythagoras, a biography of Alexander (one of the possible sources of the later Alexander Romance), and perhaps the highly fragmentary *Ninus Romance*, dated to 100 BCE, would serve as possible candidates for this historical/biographical type of ancient novel. However, since none of these texts survived, or survived in sufficient quantity to be studied, the supposition of an historical/ biographical type of ancient novel must remain highly speculative; in fact, if the type existed, the only extant examples would be the gospels themselves, and of course, Christian monks made sure that they survived the medieval transcription process.

It is not necessary to posit the existence of an historical/biographical type in order to compare the Gospel of Mark usefully and appropriately to extant examples of the ancient novel. Because genre refers to shared expectations between author and audience, all I need argue is the plausibility of the authorial audience of Mark having some previous experience of the ancient novel in any of its types. Then, the kind of synthesizing style, rhetorical strategies, plot development and so on of the popular ancient novel could have been employed by the author of Mark and recognized by its readers or hearers. Manifestly, the historical data available on the ancient novel establishes the *possibility* of its membership in the generic repertoire of early Christians. Determining the *plausibility* of its presence might best be accomplished simply by indicating some of the literary, stylistic and rhetorical similarities between the Gospel of Mark and examples of the ancient novel.

Chariton and Xenophon of Ephesus, the authors of the non-Sophistic novels, provide the clearest comparisons in overall style, and while Chariton's work has strong similarities to Luke/Acts, it is

Xenophon of Ephesus, the least skillful of the ancient novelists, whose Greek style most resembles the Gospel of Mark. Besides the factors already mentioned – beginning with minimal introduction, journey motif, episodic plot, central turning-point (*peripeteia*) and final recognition scene, all of which find their ultimate ancestor in Homer – Xenophon, like Mark, supplies little descriptive detail to characters, places or events. Towns are only named; one stereotypical adjective, if that, is all most characters receive; and brief scenes of dialogue are surrounded by narrative summation.[21] There is a considerable amount of repetition, a characteristic of all the ancient novels, both in words and in similar episodes, whose major alterations are often simply that the actions take place in different towns. In Xenophon, as in Mark, these repetitions often take the form of doublets or pairs which help to structure the story. Such repetitions with variation in both the ancient novel and the Gospel of Mark are indications of their rhetorical heritage and their status as aural texts.

As with Mark, behind the human action in Xenophon stands divine decree and initiation which only occasionally enters the story concretely. This development of the action through both divine and human motivations simultaneously is another Homeric trait. Suspense is not an element in the ancient novel nor in Mark; early in the story, oracles or narrative reassurances of a successful conclusion are provided. The concern of the audience in both cases is not *what* is going to happen but *how* it will happen. In general, all the ancient novels, like Mark, use day and night sequences either to bind a series of actions together or to separate actions from each other. In Xenophon, the day and night sequences appear and disappear rather arbitrarily until the final action of the recognition scene which is, like Mark's passion narrative, organized strictly and carefully over a definite period of days.[22]

On the negative side, the plot of the *Ephesian Tale*, and those of the other erotic ancient novels, are considerably more complex than Mark's story line. The major reason for this greater complexity is the necessity of a *dual* plot in the erotic novels: one plot follows the heroine, the other the hero in their various separate adventures. Consequently, methods of alternation and transition play a larger part in the erotic novels than in the gospels. In Mark, only one plot line is followed, that of Jesus, and only rarely are transitions necessary (e.g. at Mark 6:14ff in the episode of the death of John the Baptist and at Mark 14:66ff for Peter's denial). While the novelists revel in shipwrecks (present in Luke/Acts but not in Mark), piracy, slavery and prostitution, all of which play little role in Mark, they also abound in apparent deaths, with awakenings in the tomb after burial, and unjust trials resulting in crucifixion, a form of death rarely present in the elite literature of the Greco-Roman period. These macabre devices and violent experiences serve the interests of entertainment to be sure, but they also provide occasions for serious moral instruction on the power of the divine to save or punish.

Finally, for anyone mostly familiar with the elite literature of the Greco-Roman world, one of the most striking similarities between Xenophon and the Gospel of Mark is the Greek they both use.[23] While Xenophon writes in Attic Greek rather than Mark's *koine*, the style of Attic employed by Xenophon is far from pure and shows much influence from *koine*. Indeed, although people trained only in New Testament Greek are rarely able to read most classical Greek texts, they could read Xenophon with ease. The vocabulary is simple and the language generally clear. In terms of language competency, Xenophon's audience and Mark's audience were on almost exactly the same level.

Whether these linguistic, stylistic and rhetorical similarities between the Gospel and extant examples of the ancient novel arise from actual familiarity with the erotic novel or from generic participation in another, now extinct historical/biographical sub-type of the ancient novel or from general mutual involvement in Greco-Roman popular literature with its synthesizing and formulaic stance toward elite culture, matters little. What does matter is the plausibility of locating the Gospel of Mark (and the other gospels as well) within the realm of popular literature, for that hypothesis provides concrete benefits for uncovering some of the conventional features of the narrative shared by these popular texts, for understanding more clearly the relationship of Mark to elite literary genres like memorabilia, biography, drama and apocalypse, and for opening up a whole new world of theoretical and textual analysis through the study of popular culture, which might allow a fuller picture of the social, cultural and political world of the early Christians to emerge.

If the Gospel of Mark is popular literature, composed in such a way as to be available to a wide spectrum of society, then its audience and that of the ancient erotic popular novel, also written so as to be available to a wide spectrum of readers, would share many of the same general characteristics. A number of studies of the ancient novel have attempted to evaluate its Greco-Roman audience.[24] 'Rootless, at a loss, restlessly searching, the people who needed and welcomed the novel are the same as those who are attracted by the mystery religions and Christianity: the people of Alexandria and other big cities round the Eastern Mediterranean.'[25]

The Greco-Roman period had seen an expanding level of literacy, especially in the fairly well-to-do sections of the working classes and among women. While their positions as artisans, traders, professional people and administrators were not always associated with high status, many from this expanding mainly urban class could amass sufficient income for the purchase of books and had developed a taste for episodic adventure stories through the use of Homer in the schools of grammar and rhetoric. Furthermore, since their fields of endeavor were primarily commercial, political or administrative rather than aesthetic and academic, they were not bound by the critical sensibilities of the cultivated aristic tradition nor were they likely to possess highly developed reading or writing skills. In addition to this newly literate group, the audience of the ancient novel probably also came from two other sections of Greco-Roman society: the traditional upper-class, educated aristocracy who could suspend their artistic judgment in the interest of an exciting story, and the illiterate.

The possibility of an illiterate component in the audience of the ancient novel has been proposed by Thomas Hägg in an interesting hypothesis about the use of the ancient novel as entertainment.[26] Hägg notes that the increased mobility of the Greco-Roman period forced an increasing dependence on written communication in letters, edicts, laws and other sorts of documents. Since the majority of people were illiterate, a class of scribes or secretaries developed who earned their living by reading or writing for others. Chariton, who described himself as a secretary to a lawyer, would be an example of such a group. Hägg, then, hypothesizes a reasonable consequence of this situation: 'The ability to read, and read easily and for pleasure, in a milieu where true literacy was not common, no doubt carried with it the obligation to read aloud to members of the household, to a circle of friends, perhaps even to a wider audience.'[27] As literacy grew, the opportunities for illiterate people to attend such recitations would also have grown. As Hägg points out, the many instances of repetition, regular plot summaries, and foreshadowings present in the ancient novels support the suggestion of their oral performance. Since the Gospel of Mark shares these stylistic features with the ancient novel, Hägg's hypothesis may describe Mark's audience as well. Indeed, the almost certain mixture of literate and illiterate people in the early Christian communities must have obliged the literate to read aloud for the benefit of all.[28]

The emerging consensus on the social description of early Christian communities seems to view them as a cross-section of Greco-Roman society with the very top level and very bottom level omitted.[29] The majority of first- and second-century Christians, moreover, came from the expanding urban class of artisans, traders and freed slaves, some of whom had considerable money and education. Speculations about the audience of the ancient novel point to precisely the same group. In addition, because of the general tendency of all the ancient erotic novels to portray the heroine as more admirable, more faithful and more chaste than the hero, some scholars have suggested that the rise of the popular novel should be linked to the increasing level of literacy among women and that women might have been the authors or formed a major part of the audience for the ancient novel.[30] Women, especially wealthy women, were clearly among the early leaders and patrons of the Christian movement as well and tended to be quite active in the propagation of Eastern cults like the cult of Isis.[31]

Besides its usefulness in providing this kind of additional data for social description, hypothesizing a popular origin for the Gospel of Mark can also inform its contemporary interpretation. As a concrete example of this latter benefit, I would like to look just at one passage, the Gethsemane episode in Mark 14:32–42. Gethsemane stands at the beginning of the final recognition scene of Mark. However, in the ancient erotic novels, speaking of a recognition scene is somewhat misleading, for the final events usually include a series of recognitions, culminating in the reunion of the lovers. In Xenophon's *Ephesian Tale*, for example, Habrocomes, the hero, is recognized for who he is after answering a series of questions by his old and faithful servants. The question and answer motif in recognition scenes probably derives from Homer's *Odyssey* and is a common feature.[32] Later the servants recognize a lock of hair placed as a votive offering in the temple to belong to the heroine, Anthia. Still later the servants observe a strange woman in the temple and recognize her as Anthia, although Anthia does not recognize them until they remind her who they are. Finally, through the servants, Habrocomes and Anthia are reunited and tell each other of their adventures. The whole sequence is carefully plotted over a three-day period and tied together by references to time: 'the following day', 'when night came', etc.

At the heart of a recognition scene is the question of identity, and the recognition sequence in the Gospel of Mark focuses on the issue of Jesus' true identity. During the question and answer scene with the high priest, Jesus openly confirms his identity (Mark 14:60–63): he is 'the Christ, the Son of the Blessed'. Later his rightful position as 'King of the Jews' is given backhanded recognition by Pilate in a question and answer exchange, and finally, after his death, the centurion recognizes him as 'Son of God' (Mark 15:39). In this light, it is interesting to note that Peter's denial (Mark 14:66–72), following immediately after the trial of Jesus, is almost an exact anti-type of the recognition scene. In a series of questions, a maid of the high priest recognizes Peter as one of Jesus' followers, but Peter three times denies this correct identification. To anyone familiar with the conventions of recognition scenes in the ancient world, such a denial of correct identification would rule out any final happy reunion. The recognition sequence in Mark, like those of the ancient novels, is carefully plotted over a series of days and uses time references to tie the events together.

Jesus' prayer in Gethsemane introduces these final events by showing his last actions and words as a free man. The *form* the words are given, a prayer spoken aloud to God when he was alone, would have alerted a Greco-Roman audience to the critical significance of the moment, for Jesus's prayer in Gethsemane, reported both in narrative summary ('he fell on the ground and prayed that, if it were possible the hour might pass from him', 14:35) and direct discourse ('Abba, father, all things are possible for you; take this cup from me; but not what I desire but what you desire', 14:36) is a superb example of what is technically called an 'interior monologue', a narrative soliloquy used at a critical moment to dramatize internal struggle.[33] Indeed, arguments for a factual basis for the prayer have always been difficult to mount for the simple reason that as Mark describes the scene, no one could have heard what Jesus said; thus, realizing that the episode is based on a literary convention shifts the discussion from its historical value to its narrative function.

Interior monologue and stream of consciousness are commonly found combined in extended format in modern narrative, and thus contemporary readers may not recognize the important but sparing use of interior monologue in ancient writings. Its earliest appearance can be found in Homer, but Apollonius Rhodius, Vergil, Ovid and Xenophon of Ephesus, the ancient novelist, also employed and developed the device. For illuminating Mark's use of the convention for Jesus in Gethsemane, Homer and Xenophon are especially helpful. Half of the interior monologues in the *Iliad* come at a crucial point when a character experiences fear on the verge of battle or some other risky venture and each of these repeats the same formulaic line: 'but why does my own heart dispute with me thus?' (Odysseus in XI, 402; Menelaus in XVII, 97; Agenor in XXI, 562; and Hector in XXII, 122).[34] For Homer, then, the interior monologue was particularly suited to those critical moments when 'a character seems to be giving way to the promptings of his *thymos* [heart or mind] but pulls himself together in the formulaic line . . . and proceeds to do the right thing'.[35]

While Homer's monologues are truly unspoken – that is, the character's internal dispute is not spoken aloud in the narrative – Xenophon of Ephesus and some other of the later writers tended to compose monologues in the form of prayers or laments spoken aloud, but in private, at a moment of crisis. For Xenophon the prayers were directed to Eros or Isis and were full of internal struggle; for example, at the beginning of the *Ephesian Tale* Habrocomes insults Eros with his arrogant good looks, and Eros decides to tempt him. After great inner conflict, Habrocomes yields in the following manner: 'And when he could withstand no longer he flung himself down upon the ground, and said, 'Thou hast conquered, Eros; great is thy trophy for victory over chaste Habrocomes. Thou seest him suppliant before thy feet. Preserve him who seeks asylum of thee, who art master of all creatures.'[36] Although the emotion dividing the will for Homer was mainly fear, and the resolution, after internal debate, was always for the right or courageous action, later writers like Xenophon applied the technique to a wider range of situations (e.g. love, honor, loyalty) but preserved the crisis nature of the scene. These ancient monologues, unlike their modern descendants, are not basically psychological but rather rhetorical. They are 'words artfully deployed so as to move the reader or audience',[37] and at the same time the form can be used to signal the start of crucial turns in the plot.

Jesus' prayer in Gethsemane clearly reflects the ancient convention. It comes at a moment of great crisis, for the hour is now upon him (Mark 14:41); the rhetorical play between the cup of testimony at the supper and the cup of suffering before him provides the audience with a profound sense of the sacrifice he is about to make 'for many' (Mark 14:24); and the agony inside him (14:34) is appropriately and heroically resolved in favor of God's will. Internal dispute is a typical feature of these monologues, and depicting Jesus as manifesting such ambivalence bonds him more firmly in the audience's sympathy, for he is human as they are and his correct resolution of the struggle can stand as an example to be imitated. Moreover, that his human anguish should be ignored and unsupported by his sleeping disciples serves to separate those disciples even more strongly from the audience's approval. Since convention dictated that such monologues occur at critical junctures, finding one here would alert the listening audience to the climactic nature of the events now beginning, just as hearing Jesus' prayer formulated in this familiar pattern would assure them not only of Jesus' full cognizance of what the future holds for him but also of his resolute willingness to face that future as

God wills. He is neither a joyful martyr bent on self-destruction nor an unwilling pawn forced into sacrifice; rather, like Odysseus, Menelaus or Hector, he is a courageous hero who knows what dangers lie ahead and resolves to do the will of God (see Mark 3:35). Historicizing Mark's Gethsemane story places Jesus' actions in the epic tradition of Greek literature that rises from Homer and flows through many centuries into the popular culture and literature of the Greco-Roman world. Nevertheless, the author of the Gospel of Mark did not choose to formulate the story of Jesus as an epic but rather as an ancient novel. While Jesus in Mark's eyes is indeed a conquering champion on the order of heroic figures from the past, the generic ideology evoked by the novelistic style of the narrative molds him also into a more familiar and imitable figure for the present. Jesus, for Mark, is not only hero but also example; his followers, drawn from the wide middle strata of Greco-Roman society, must not only be able to worship him but also able to live, act and die as he did. It is this image of Jesus that Mark intends to communicate to his audience. By failing to take seriously the ancient milieu of the Gospel, Mark's Jesus, an epic hero for the common people, is one that modern audiences rarely recognize.

NOTES

The material on the literary history of the Gospel of Mark in this article is adapted from my study of the entire gospel in *Sowing the Gospel: Mark's World in Literary-Historical Perspective* (Fortress Press, Minneapolis, 1989). For further discussion of all of the issues raised here, please consult that work.

1 Edward Pechter, 'The New Historicism and Its Discontents: Politicizing Renaissance Drama', *PMLA*, 102 (May 1987), p. 298.
2 Ibid., p. 299.
3 See, for example, the explanation of the fourfold method in Dante Alighieri, *Il Convivio*, or in *Letter to Can Grande Della Scala*. Dante is following the arguments of Thomas Aquinas, who elaborated the system of allegorical interpretation found in earlier Church Fathers like Augustine and Origen.
4 See Pechter, 'New historicism', pp. 299, 302.
5 See, for example, Werner H. Kelber, *The Oral and the Written Gospel* (Fortress Press, Philadelphia, 1983) and R. Alan Culpepper, *Anatomy of the Fourth Gospel: A Study in Literary Design* (Fortress Press, Philadelphia, 1983).
6 For New Testament studies, see the very important work of Elisabeth Schüssler-Fiorenza, *In Memory of Her: A Feminist Theological Reconstruction of Christian Origins* (Crossroad, New York, 1983).

 7 For a full discussion of this position, see Hayden White, *Metahistory: The Historical Imagination in Nineteenth-Century Europe* (Johns Hopkins University Press, Baltimore and London, 1973).

 8 For a discussion of most of these options, which ends by accepting biography as the most likely, see Charles Talbert, *What Is a Gospel? The Genre of the Canonical Gospels* (Fortress Press, Philadelphia, 1977).

 9 The most extensive criticisms of aretalogy as the designation of the gospel genre can be found in Howard Kee, 'Aretalogy and Gospel', *JBL*, 92 (1973), pp. 402–22.

10 Vernon Robbins, *Jesus the Teacher: A Socio-Rhetorical Interpretation of Mark* (Fortress Press, Philadelphia, 1984), pp. 60–7.

11 See the discussion in F. Schroeder, 'The Discovery of Popular Culture Before Printing', in *5000 Years of Popular Culture: Popular Culture Before Printing* (Bowling Green University Popular Press, Bowling Green, Ohio, 1980), pp. 4–15. See also, Norman F. Cantor and Michael S. Werthma (eds), *The History of Popular Culture to 1815* (Macmillan, New York, 1968); and particularly for Greek literature, see B. P. Reardon, 'Aspects of the Greek Novel', *Greece and Rome*, 23 (1976), p. 130. For the importance of the study of popular culture to the work of some new historicists, see Tony Bennett, Colin Mercer and Janet Woollacott (eds), *Popular Culture and Social Relations* (Open University Press, Philadelphia, 1986).

12 Augustine, *Confessions*, 5. 14; 6.4. His salvation from this problem came when he heard Ambrose preaching by allegorical interpretation. The 'rustic simplicity' of Scripture was but a veil over the riches of the spirit.

13 See, for example, Wayne Meeks, *The First Urban Christians: The Social World of the Apostle Paul* (Yale University Press, New Haven, 1983), pp. 51–73. The freed slaves of the ancient world came out of a culture-specific institution rather unlike the practice of racial slavery blighting recent North American history. Slavery in the ancient world was fed by economic and military goals. To pay debts or gain needed capital, ancient people sold themselves or their children into slavery; unwanted babies left exposed on village garbage heaps were sometimes rescued and raised as slaves by families with sufficient funds; and finally many slaves were claimed as captive booty through Roman military conquest, especially those with educational or craft skills. Besides domestic duties, slaves were used to perform jobs that were viewed as beneath contempt by their aristocratic owners: jobs like keeping accounts, negotiating trade deals, running businesses and all things related to commerce and the making of money. Needless to say, many of these slaves became quite accomplished at these 'morally degrading' occupations, and when they were freed (manumission was fairly common, although later curtailed somewhat by Roman law), they could accumulate considerable wealth for themselves, allowing them to become a ridiculed but powerful nouveau riche class quite disquieting to traditional Roman upper-class society.

14 This genre has also been called the romance. No designation was created for it in antiquity, although it was evidently a prolific class of literature;

however, as *popular* literature it was not deemed important enough for the cultivated theorists and critics of the ancient world to describe and name. The term 'romance' comes from the medieval world and was used initially to characterize writings done in vernacular languages ('Romance' languages) rather than Latin. Since the term 'romance' has come to have such narrow connotations in the present, several classicists have argued that the designation should be dropped in favor of the broader term 'ancient novel'. For this argument, see Tomas Hägg, *The Novel of Antiquity* (Basil Blackwell, Oxford, 1983), pp. 1–4.

15 Hägg, *The Novel*, pp. 3, 5–6, 20–1; G. L. Schmeling, *Xenophon of Ephesus* (Twayne Publishers, Boston, 1980), pp. 18–19; and Ben E. Perry, *The Ancient Romances: A Literary-Historical Account of Their Origins* (University of California Press, Berkeley, 1967), pp. 343–46. See also the review of various dating theories in R. Hock, 'The Greek Novel', in *Greco-Roman Literature and the New Testament*, ed. David Aune (SBLSBS 21, Scholars Press, Atlanta, 1988), pp. 127–9.

16 Perry, *The Ancient Romances*, pp. 27–36; Hägg, *The Novel*, pp. 147–65.

17 B. P. Reardon, 'The Greek Novel', *Phoenix*, 23 (1969), p. 294; see also Hägg, *The Novel*, pp. 89–90.

18 The position is most strongly argued by R. Merkelbach, *Roman und Mysterium in der Antike* (C. H. Beck, Munich, 1962).

19 Perry, *The Ancient Romances*, p. 140.

20 See Hägg, *The Novel*, pp. 115, 125–40.

21 For a discussion of some of these stylistic features in the ancient novels, see Tomas Hägg, *Narrative Technique in Ancient Greek Romances: Studies of Chariton, Xenophon Ephesius, and Achilles Tatius* (Acta Instituti Atheniensis Regni Sueciae, Stockholm, 1971).

22 Ibid., pp. 50–63.

23 For a careful comparison of Mark's Greek with that found in the ancient popular novels, see M. Reiser, *Syntax und Stil des Markusevangeliums im Licht der hellenistischen Volksliteratur* (Mohr-Siebeck, Tübingen, 1984).

24 See, for example, Hägg, *The Novel*, pp. 81–108; Schmeling, *Xenophon of Ephesus*, pp. 131–8.

25 Hägg, *The Novel*, p. 90.

26 *The Novel*, pp. 91–3.

27 Ibid., p. 93.

28 Several texts in the New Testament actually contain specific instructions that they be read aloud to the entire group; see, for example, Colossians 4:16, I Thessalonians 5:27, and Revelation 1:3. Indeed, the *anaginoskon* of Mark 13:14 may refer to the one reading the text aloud.

29 See, for example, Meeks, *The First Urban Christians*, pp. 72–3; A. Malherbe, *Social Aspects of Early Christianity* (Louisiana State University Press, Baton Rouge, 1977), pp. 29–59.

30 Hägg, *The Novel*, pp. 95–6.

31 See Meeks, *The First Urban Christians*, pp. 23–5, 58–63. For a thorough

attempt at reconstructing the role of women in early Christianity, see Schüssler-Fiorenza, *In Memory of Her.*

32 Schmeling, *Xenophon of Ephesus*, pp. 72–3. The recognition sequence in the *Ephesian Tale* begins at 5.11.2 and goes to 5.15.1.

33 For a general discussion of this device in ancient narrative, see Robert Scholes and Robert Kellogg, *The Nature of Narrative* (Oxford University Press, Oxford, 1966), pp. 177–94. For a discussion of the modern development of such monologues, which really begins with the work of Chaucer, see Adena Rosmarin, *The Power of Genre* (University of Minnesota Press, Minneapolis, 1985).

34 Scholes and Kellogg, *Nature of Narrative*, p. 179.

35 Ibid., p. 180.

36 *Ephesian Tale* 1.4.4. This translation comes from Moses Hadas, *Three Greek Romances: Longus, Xenophon, Dio Chrysostom* (Bobbs-Merrill, New York, 1953), p. 74. A partial translation of this same passage may be found in Scholes and Kellogg, *Nature of Narrative*, pp. 289–90.

37 Scholes and Kellogg, *Nature of Narrative*, p. 185.

12

'Buried with Christ': The Politics of Identity and the Poverty of Interpretation

Sheila Briggs

The hermeneutical shift from text to social practices

Marx wrote in the eleventh Feuerbach thesis, 'Philosophers have interpreted the world in various ways; the point, however, is to change it.' Does this statement imply that there is an incompatibility between the practice of interpretation and socially transformative praxis? Obviously, Marx's thesis has not operated as a ban on hermeneutics even within the Marxist tradition or within progressive movements of theology. The insistence on a 'hermeneutical privilege of the poor' (first advocated in Latin American Liberation Theology) as well as Elisabeth Schüssler-Fiorenza's proposal of a 'feminist critical hermeneutics' recognize the social position of the one who confronts the biblical text as crucial to how it is understood. The focus of liberation hermeneutics, however, is not on the text itself but on the community who produced the biblical text and the social practices they inscribed within it.

Is the liberative content of hermeneutics contained within this movement behind the text? Or put in a different way, is a socially transformative praxis based on a hermeneutics, not of the text itself, but of the social practices behind it? If one advances a hermeneutics of social practices, then one needs to define what 'interpreting' them means. One has to acount for why one privileges the hermeneutic over other epistemological categories in one's approach to the biblical texts. The claim to interpret social practices and the claim to interpret the biblical text are in themselves distinct, although they flow together in a liberation hermeneutics. What one has at stake in making the two claims simultaneously is twofold. First, one wishes to avoid with much other modern theology a biblical positivism and its concomitant authoritarian doctrine of revelation. One refutes the idea that scripture interprets itself, which objectifies the biblical text as revealed knowledge, universal, homogeneous and immutable. Second, one is arguing in distinction from other positions in modern theology that how one knows the biblical text is relative to one's consciousness of one's own and others' social position. Hence, 'interpreting' denotes the relativity of all knowledge, dependent on the social practices which construct gender, race and class in our own and in other societies. Further, one implies that there are criteria for adjudicating between the various and conflicting social positions and their knowledges/interpretative strategies, but that these are not knowledge-immanent. The liberation of oppressed groups and peoples is held to be the critical principle by which one judges between competing social positions and their knowledges/interpretive strategies. One has moved from the authority of the text to the authority of social practices, from orthodoxy to orthopraxis. This allows one to unmask the ideological character of the demand to engage in a *petitio principii*, a search for the grounding of the liberation of the oppressed in something external and supposedly more fundamental to it. Such a request itself can be seen as dependent on a particular social position and its form of knowledge and not as the appeal to a universal rule of rational argument. A transmutation and transvaluation of hermeneutical categories has taken place which places normative value in the kind of social practices which aim at liberation of the oppressed.

The politics of identity and the problem of cultural hegemony in interpretation

If one wants to cast the knowledge claims of liberation in the form of a hermeneutics of social practices, then one is confronted with two issues. There is the question of whether one can extend hermeneutics beyond texts to social practices. Furthermore, if one invests social practices with the authority with which one has traditionally endowed texts, especially religious texts, one has not by that move resolved the relationship of the normative to the hegemonic. The view that there are normative texts and its corollary that there are normative traditions, mediated through texts, is linked to the exercise of power. Hermeneutics seeks to be a normative discipline, although it shares the contemporary recognition of a plurality of traditions. Yet the acceptance of pluralism is not equivalent to the acknowledgement of difference, of the breaking of universal horizons, created by the totalizing discourses of an ontology of language or of history, or of both. The social reality constructed by the differences of gender, race and class is only reducible to the universally human through the various projects of cultural hegemony.

The definition of the universally human, stripped of all particularity, is an abstraction. It upholds the equality of all human beings on account of a shared human nature fundamental and prior to the differences of gender, race and class. The effect of equality, as it operates in society as access to equal treatment, has a very different impact on those who belong to the dominant gender, race and class than on those who do not. There is a commensurability between white, male, middle-class identity and equality. Those who do not share this identity have access to equal treatment when their identity is 'overlooked'. Hence, to be black or hispanic or female or on welfare would be detrimental to one's claim to equality without appeal to one's more fundamental human nature. It is unfair to treat such persons with regard to their sex, racial or social background because this would prejudice their rights. It is unfair to treat white, middle-class males with regard to their sex, racial and social background because this would grant them undue privilege. The liberal view of equality which accompanies the definition of the universally human, places a wedge between the culturally desirable and social equality. It sees the divergence in behaviors, attitudes and values, based on sex, race and class, as epiphenomenal to a basic core of humanity. To 'overlook' race, sex and class in order to see a basic and universal humanity is to take up a viewpoint which leaves out of account the cultural hegemony responsible for making some human identities more desirable than others.

Even when one argues that the cultural desirability of behaviors, attitudes and values, associated with some human identities and not with others, is based on unfounded prejudice, one is constrained in explaining how and why such prejudices arise. What is missing here is a recognition that the exercise of social control in a class-, sex- and race-divided society and the prevalence of cultural hegemony are coextensive. The actual society, in which all human beings are to be treated equally, is one controlled and developed in the interests and in the image of a white male middle class. To be, or at least to act and think like, a middle-class white male constitutes successful adaption to the dominant social structures. Since cultural preferences arise out of accommodation to a society, in which *de facto* hierarchies of race, sex and class exist, then their eradication requires the transformation of society as it currently exists. At this point, the definition of the universally human fails to offer us an anthropology upon which a society without inequality and cultural hegemony could be envisioned. A human being, devoid of all particularity, exists not in reality but only in abstraction. Why does human difference lead to inequality? If human beings in all times and in all places possess a common nature, then it becomes even more inexplicable why in any place and time human beings could deny this fundamental fact about other human beings. The question of the origins of human inequality, however, is not as interesting as that of the prospects for permanently eradicating it. Inequality may have arose as a result of historical accident or of a particular phase in the historical evolution of society. Overcoming inequality may be achieved when society develops cultural homogeneity, when that abstract being, possessing all the traits of universal humanity but no particularity other than the identity of a purely individual personality, takes on actual social flesh. I think that this view is implicitly and naïvely present in much liberal social theory and in Marxist theories which have a monocausal explanation of social oppression in terms of class. Ironically, it is when a universal humanity is explicitly denied that postmodern eclecticism celebrates the breakdown of cultural boundaries. If, on the other hand, one rejects cultural homogeneity as the form in which universal human nature would be realized in a society of genuine equality, then one is back to that troubling question as to how human differences are turned into social inequalities.

The attraction of a definition of the universally human lies in its strong warrants for a normative anthropology. One attempt to disconnect the normative from the hegemonic is to argue that discourses on universal humanity reflect particular human interests. Cultural hegemony is built into the definition of what is universally true of human beings. The abstract individual of liberal theories of equality and rights is unmasked as bourgeois, and also as white and male. One stands at the crossroads; one can give up all attempts to define what is universally and fundamentally human, or one can attempt to redefine the universally human in terms of an authentically universal human interest. Marxism criticizes preceding and competing universalistic anthropologies as being the ideological products of class interests. The particularity of class thus becomes the key to understanding what is universally human. Emancipatory consciousness becomes aware of human self-alienation in a class society as it engages in socially transformative praxis with and by the oppressed class. The ultimate goal of this praxis is not the social dominance and cultural hegemony of any one class – even in orthodox Marxist-Leninist theory the 'dictatorship of the proletariat' is only an intermediate stage in the revolutionary process and this doctrine has been rejected by Euro-communism. On the contrary, the ultimate development of history is the classless society. The particularity of class, therefore, yields a form of analysis which elucidates how human nature is universally formed within society. Yet the particularity of class itself will be finally transcended when human labor becomes a means of self-fulfillment, and solidarity replaces the social mode of self-alienation and social division. Marxism, even in its New Left varieties, has notoriously tended to subsume race and sex oppression within the overarching dynamics of class exploitation. The solution to racism and sexism has been seen as automatically given with the overthrow of class society. Although Antonio Gramsci in the earlier decades of this century proposed a Marxist theory of culture and cultural hegemony, orthodox Marxism and many socialist historians have been resistant to the notion of 'working-class culture'. The breach with orthodox Marxism has led to a widening of perspectives. One thinks of Eugene Genovese's work on Afro-Americans under slavery, of the London-based *History Workshop* group, where race and especially gender, as well as class, have been made central to socialist historical analysis.

The struggle in Marxist theory to recognize particularity as anything else but the product of social divisions, all ultimately reducible to the class base of society, should remind us that the identities of class, race and gender are inseparable from the hierarchical structuring of society. This does not mean that to be a member of an oppressed class, race or gender is to have one's existence solely determined by the nature of one's oppression. Yet, how one conceptualizes that 'surplus of identity' can lead not only to the problematic of a universalistic definition of the human but also to its opposite, and equally problematic: an essentialist view of particularity. An essentialist account of human differences rejects the concept of a universal human nature, of a common ontological ground between human beings in reason, language or history. This kind of theory has become prominent and highly controversial within feminist circles. Although it tends to eschew such terms as 'ontological' in describing human differences, it also deems social constructionist explanations of gender inadequate. Indeed, there is a widening gulf within feminist theory between those who see gender as socially constructed and who therefore privilege history and the other social sciences as tools for understanding women's reality, and those who see woman as the repressed reality of a psychic structure and who therefore work in the fields of psychoanalysis and the psychoanalytically informed literary and linguistic studies.

Social constructionists see gender polarization as shaping women's and men's social identities in the modern period. The separation of home and workplace during industrialization led to a stricter division of labor between the sexes and to segregation of women and men in separate spheres. The theoretical justification of separate spheres not only upheld the physical isolation of women's domesticity from men's work but also saw the separate spheres as predicated on distinct female and male natures. The notions of masculinity and femininity have prescribed social roles and opportunities on the basis of sex. Femininity is conceived not as the essential nature of women but as a social identity, which women have both internalized and resisted. Although I favor a social constructionist view, I recognize that there are two areas in which it remains unsatisfying. Some social constructionists seem to hold a weak version of a universalistic anthropology. One assumes that women want the same educational and work opportunities as men, if they are able to overcome their society's view that they are unfitted for such work. The culturally valued roles and activities of men provide the autonomy, choice and responsibility that any human being desires.[1] Yet this conception of the human being as autonomous and self-determining is itself socially constructed with its specific genesis in Enlightenment thought and the origins of modern society. As a social constructionist one sees both the construction of gender and the definition of the human as context-dependent. But what constraints or boundaries are there for the social construction of reality? One recognizes the continuity between cultural contexts, which is mediated by a major and long-lasting tradition, for example a religion such as Western Christianity.

Understandably, one recoils from giving a dominant tradition that has mediated certain forms of cultural hegemony, such as patriarchy, across centuries and epochs ontological status. One refrains from the type of argument, employed by Ernst Troeltsch in the *Absoluteness of Christianity* that, if not Christianity itself, then another religion, which in the essentials would be the same, would be required by human existence at a certain historical stage.[2] One stresses that behind such ideas as 'Western civilization' there are radical discontinuities in how one has conceived and experienced the social identity of gender or such institutions as the family or state. Still, one is confronted with the question what continuity is there to human experience outside of the social identities imposed by various projects of cultural hegemony? The best answer that one can give is that in any society where power and prestige is distributed unequally, those defined as less deserving or unworthy of power and prestige will always experience this cultural valuation of them as oppressive. They may internalize a sociocultural inferiority as their individual and collective identity, but behind such accommodation there is always the potential for resistance and subversion. There will be a desire to extend the social identity to include culturally desirable traits, which then can become the basis for expanded social demands. Some nineteenth-century feminists emphasized the moral superiority which had been allotted women in the domestic sphere by the modern construction of gender, in order to assert that the 'empire of the mother' contained distinctive values which were needed in the political community and could only find expression there through women's voice and vote.

Nonetheless, if women are able to resist the social identity which a patriarchal society seeks to impose upon them, then is the source for this resistance simply the reflexive reaction of the oppressed against their oppression, or is there some alternative identity upon which women can draw? Is there a continuity of women's identity which is not merely the other side of the coin to the enduring cultural traditions of patriarchy? Just as the universalist might object to a social constructionist view that there are no constraints placed upon the construction of social identity by human nature, so the essentialist might contend that women's identity goes deeper than social construction and is rooted in psychic structure. Luce Irigaray can analyze women's social identity in terms of the commodification of their sexuality, their reproductive capacities and their socially constructed femininity as objects of consumption for men. Yet behind this socially constructed woman there lurks another, repressed yet embedded in psychic structure. The power of patriarchal discourse prevails 'to such an extent that the existence of another sex, of an other, that would be woman, still seems, in its terms, unimaginable'.[3] The attraction of Irigaray's and similar statements, found in recent French feminist theory and elsewhere, is that it corresponds to how many women experience themselves. They cherish their particularity as women, they do not want to see their individual and collective identity as entirely socially determined, but they cannot articulate an alternative source of identity.

In the madhouse of identity

Universalist, essentialist and social constructionist accounts of women's identity are not merely debates of feminist theory; they are linked to distinct and competing political options. There is a rough correspondence between the universalist position and liberal feminism, between the essentialist and radical feminism and between the social constructionist and socialist feminism. Obviously there is much overlapping and more subtle distinctions. The issue of women's identity is a matter of practical politics. If women do not share in a significant common humanity, will not their struggle for liberation be placed on its customary back-burner in self-styled progressive political agendas to the detriment of all women? If women do not understand how they have been socialized into their behaviors, attitudes and values, how are they going to be able to change them? Within feminism there has been much discussion in recent years of the 'politics of identity', the need to claim one's own particular identity as an act of resistance to the cultural hegemony of white male middle-class society. Yet a woman's identity is not only female. She has also the particularities of race and class as well as those of sexual orientation, age, type of physical ability – the list could be lengthened not indefinitely and arbitrarily but to the extent to which actual women experience their lives in a multiplicity of identities. The anguished debate over racism and anti-semitism in the women's movement has shown that women of color and white women, Jewish women and Christian-born women, stand in terms of race and ethnicity in very different relations to the cultural hegemony.

The various forms of human particularity cannot be contained within a single concept or paradigm of human difference. The analyses of class, race and gender are not symmetrical. The identities of race, gender and class are not interchangeable in structure or in their historical development. Nor is the burden of difference equally distributed within the larger society. The convergence of women's studies and gender studies, and in some cases the replacement of the focus on women's lives by the analysis of gender relations, reinforces the role of woman as the signifier of otherness. Women's lives point to the reality of the gender from which we end up with men's studies and yet another vantage-point upon the lives of men. A similar phenomenon occurs when black people are expected to educate white people about race. Indeed, the phrases 'racial minority', 'ethnic minority' have no coordinates in the designation of a racial and ethnic majority. The problem of race is the problem of the black, the hispanic, the Native or Asian American. The problem is their very existence as the other, as the ones who introduce heterogeneity which taxes the cultural hegemony of the melting pot. Where differences cannot be ignored, one way of containing them is seeing in them an essential sameness. In the practical arena this is implemented in fostering the assumption that white women are competing for jobs and income with persons of color, that the senior citizens are competing with children for social welfare, while power and status remain in white male middle-class hands. This homogenization of particularity is internalized by oppressed groups not only in social but also in ideological competitiveness. Hence the futile debates over whether patriarchy or class society or racial oppression is the model of domination according to which all other forms of oppression are patterned in our society.

Although it is important to see the interrelationship between race, gender and class in contemporary systems of oppression, the term 'interrelationship' suggests a certain harmony in the identities which they configure. All individuals embody each of the particularities of gender, race and class, but without suggesting that human beings are inherently schizophrenic, these do not meld into a single, simply composite identity. A single individual's identities of class, race and gender, class, sexual orientation have their own histories, different ranges and textures of meaning. Thus individuals are faced with very and poor or black middle-class and male. The identities of race, gender class, sexual orientation have their own histories, different ranges and textures of meaning. Thus individual's are faced with very different identities to interpret. If one's existence adheres fully to the cultural norm, if one is white, middle-class, male, straight and in good health, neither too young or too old, then one does not experience a conflict in the lived experience of one's identities and the interpretations given to them in the way that a fully stigmatized person does, for instance, someone who is hispanic, female, poor and lesbian. Our different identities impose different loyalties upon us. Thus women of color experience ambivalence in the women's movement not, I would argue, because it is a white women's movement, since there is and there has long been autonomous feminisms of color. To be a black woman is to embody two identities which call for disparate analyses and political commitments. To live with differently stigmatized identities, with a combination of stigmatized and privileged identities makes it hard sometimes to find one's face in the mirror.

The past is one of the mirrors of our culture. The cultural hegemony of our society mediates the past to us as tradition. Within the tradition of Western civilization the white middle-class male can gaze and see his face reflected back as Plato. The Western white middle-class and male Plato is a distorting anachronism but a potent one, as Alan Bloom's latest diatribe against those who would take the mirror away from the likes of him has shown.[4] The identities of gender, race and class are not historically continuous; they have to be reinvented. Knowledge of the past is not a distant acquaintance with those who share our identities but a confrontation with alien identities, discontinuous with our own. It is here that we find the greatest divergence in the identities of race, gender and class. The construction of gender even within Western society has been so varied that the word 'woman' has denoted a very different existence in fifth-century Athens, in early Frankish society or contemporary suburban America. Women have not always been powerless; they have in some periods gained expanded social status and roles. Yet within Western society the word 'woman' has always designated persons of the same biological sex. This has given the construction of gender a peculiar stability and deceptive self-evidence which has cloaked the constructed character of gender relations with the aura of nature. Persons of female biological sex have had to contend with the historically accumulated meanings of inferiority, which the word 'woman' implies. Twentieth-century women are not the gender to which the New Testament household codes admonished obedience to their husbands. Yet by the sheer fact of her biological sex and its historically continuous identification with the sociocultural construct of 'woman' a present-day woman feels herself discussed and is, in fact, discussed by some of her contemporaries in the light of the first-century literature of a small and marginal religious sect.

Race is a very different cultural construct from that of gender. There is no biological group of persons to which a designation of race has been consistently applied over the same period of time as the gender of woman has been attributed to persons of biologically female sex. Race categories and racism are not, however, an invention of modern Western society. Yet the categories of race in other epochs of Western history were entirely different from their modern counterparts and stigmatized different groups of people. In the Greco-Roman world the word *ethnos* could function as a marker of ethnic difference and of ethnic inferiority. The *ethne* were, however, entirely different from contemporary racial designations. Persons of ancient African descent appear in the biblical texts, but black people are absent because black identity is historically situated in the victimization and survival of persons of African descent in modern Western society. To use race as a category of analysis for the biblical text is to use a category of race very different from that employed in the examination of contemporary society. Where one is not aware of this simple distinction, subtle distortions occur in the interpretation of biblical texts. Galatians 3:28 is conventionally described as the proclamation of the abolition or relativization of racial, class and sexual divisions in the Christian community. The statement that in Christ there is neither Jew nor Greek is taken to imply that Jewish claims to racial superiority were denied. Yet within the broader context of the Greco-Roman world the Jews were an *ethnos* whose rights were challenged in the Greek polis and whose very existence was threatened during the same period in which Paul wrote his letter to Galatian Christians.[5] Paul and other New Testament writers were, in fact, participants in an ancient discourse of anti-semitism which culminated in a series of genocides against the Jewish people in the second century. Ancient anti-semitism was, by the way, very different from its modern counterpart but equally deadly.

Race occupies an intermediate position on the spectrum of social construction between the naturalization of gender through biological sex and the category of class. The term 'class' itself achieved a denaturalized meaning of social status. In the modern period class displaced the older designation of 'estate' for a person's social status. With this change came a revolution in how social status was conceived. Previously, the hierarchical social order was seen as ontologically equivalent to a cosmic order, instituted by God. One was not only born into a social estate but was seen as innately possessing the social and moral traits that fitted one for it. Over against this older conception the rise of bourgeois democratic liberalism stressed the acquisition of social status through merit and evolved such concepts as the career open to talent and equal opportunities. Class is conceived neither as biologically based nor as an innate personal trait nor as a permanently fixed identity. One can change one's class in ways that one cannot change one's race or gender. Thus there is an in-built preference to some form of universalist anthropology in the category of class. Although a classless society is not present reality, one can have a reasonably coherent apprehension of what that society would be like. On the other hand, it is thoroughly unimaginable what it would be like to live without the particularities of gender and race, although the suspension of the social construction of gender and race is conceivable.

Despite the structural differences in the identities of class, gender and race, they do have in common that they are mediated by social practices. The politics of identity take place in a social world where to claim one's identity is to risk a conflict of identities, is to break the mirror with one's gaze. A hermeneutics of social practices cannot seek to piece together that broken mirror by a normative view of the human which is, in fact, to keep in place some form of cultural hegemony, the mirror of sameness.

Hermeneutics and the interpretation of social reality

Because my task here is to examine the viability of a hermeneutics of social practices, I am going to concentrate on those interpretive strategies that have as a major purpose the understanding of social reality. The hermeneutics of texts has always had a relationship to the social sciences, because historical texts have been its central concern. The historical discipline is poised between the social sciences and the humanities. On the one hand, it engages in the scientific investigation of the past. On the other hand, the reconstructed past is a cultural artifact of a special kind. The historian orders the 'facts' of the past into a context of meanings accessible to his or her contemporaries. It is out of the meaning given to the past by the historian that the concept and sense of a tradition emerges. The historian as a member of a culture is always in search of a 'usable past', although the uses of the past depend on the sociocultural identities of the historian and her or his audience. It is only within the past reconstructed as tradition, as 'Western Civilization' or 'the Rise of Christianity', that certain texts can take on significance. Therefore the hermeneutics of texts has never narrowly limited the *Geisteswissenschaften* or the *sciences humaines* to the narrow range of disciplinary approaches, implied by the English term 'humanities'.

In the nineteenth century, when the social sciences took on clear disciplinary contours distinct from those of philosophy, one was confronted with the problem of what was an appropriate methodology for them. The preceding emancipation of the natural sciences from the philosophy faculty provided one model. However, in the nineteenth century the natural sciences operated within a positivistic paradigm, and to assimilate the emergent social sciences to them one had to postulate laws of history and society, existing as an objective reality, which could be subjected to empirical tests of fact. Such a conceptualization of the social sciences ran counter to the distinction, familiar since Kant, between the objects of the external world and the human subject, endowed with a will. The causal determination of the external world of objects was the basic assumption of the methods in natural science, but to extend it to the social sciences, which investigated the behavior of human beings, was to deny the special status of human beings as subjects whose actions could be shaped by the exercise of their will rather than necessitated by natural forces. Johann Gustav Droysen and Wilhelm Dilthey attempted to place historical method on a different foundation from that of the natural sciences. In the nineteenth century the positivistic understanding of the natural sciences remained uncontested. Therefore Dilthey designated the method of the *Geisteswissenschaften* as 'understanding' (*verstehen*) and contrasted this with the method of 'explanation' (*erklären*) in the natural sciences. In the twentieth century, hermeneutics has largely abandoned this distinction as a result of the work of Hans-Georg

Gadamer and of the increasing acceptance within the philosophy of science of the idea that the paradigms and shifts of paradigm in the natural sciences are dependent more on human subjectivity than on the accumulation of empirical data.

Gadamer has insisted that hermeneutics is a universal dimension of all scientific enquiry. For Gadamer the social sciences have as their object social practices, and hermeneutics as the heir to an older Aristotelian practical philosophy can teach the social sciences the danger of the conflation of practical reason with technical skill, which he sees occurring in the modern concept of 'praxis'.[6] In the same essay Gadamer has repeated his criticism of Habermas' critical theory and has bewailed the lack of a common ground for political and social discourse, which he sees Habermas elevating as the normal context for sociocultural exchange. In contrast, Gadamer asserts, 'there can be no communication and no reflection without a prior basis of common agreement'.[7] Gadamer seems to have extended the hermeneutical principle of the 'Einverständnis mit dem Text', the operation through which the interpreter allows the text to correct his or her prior understanding of self and world, to the interpretation of social practices. In *Truth and Method* Gadamer praises Bultmann's hermeneutical approach to the New Testament because

it refers to the openness of the horizon of inquiry within which alone is understanding possible, but it does not mean that one's own fore-understanding should not be corrected by the encounter with the word of God (as, indeed, with any other word). On the contrary, the purpose of this concept is to make apparent the movement of understanding as precisely this process of correction.[8]

The process of correction which can eventuate in the agreement of a common ground between reader and text is, according to Gadamer, a universal hermeneutical structure. If one seeks an analogy to this agreement with the text in the social world, then I would contend that one comes up with a justification of cultural hegemony. Within the contemporary mainstream hermeneutics of Gadamer it does not seem possible to disconnect a universal hermeneutic dimension to all knowledge from the desire to create a universal political and social discourse, in which the disruptive effect of a 'politics of identities' will be bemoaned as the loss of a common ground and agreement.

Nonetheless, Gadamer's hermeneutics holds an attractiveness even for a progressive social theorist such as Anthony Giddens. Giddens' aim is to break away from a positivistic paradigm for the social sciences, and he is consequently impressed by Gadamer's overcoming of the dichotomy between explanation and understanding. Moreover,

Gadamer's insistence that knowledge is mediated through language and tradition is appropriated by Giddens in his call for a 'double hermeneutic'. Giddens offers a striking reformulation of Gadamer's universality of the hermeneutic dimension to knowledge. 'Hermeneutics, I wish to claim, does not find its central range of problems in the understanding of written texts as such, but in the mediation of frames of meaning in general.'[9] Giddens, indeed, assimilates Gadamerian tradition to paradigm, as understood in Thomas Kuhn's revision of the theory of scientific knowledge and its change, as well as to a more social-scientific concept of a 'frame of meaning'. What Giddens means by 'frame of meaning' is that human agents produce the social world from which both the professional sociologist and the ordinary social actor will draw in order to interpret social activity. Giddens accepts Gadamer's view that reason is tradition-immanent, and therefore rebuts the idea that the sociologist can through the possession of scientific rationality stand outside the frames of meaning of ordinary social actors and their language exchanges. The other side of the hermeneutic is that human beings 'are not merely inert objects of knowledge, but agents able to – and prone to – incorporate social theory and research within their own action'.[10] Especially fruitful in Giddens' opinion is Gadamer's concept of a dialogue between traditions which is equivalent to the mediation between different frames of meaning and therefore essentially the task of the social scientist. Again, the double hermeneutic implies that this task is not limited to the social scientist but is in fact part of the way in which ordinary members of society constitute their social world.[11] Giddens notes Gadamer's appeal to conformity with the tradition as a means of ruling out alternative readings, but still seems puzzled as to how readings from different traditions are to be compared, or for that matter different versions of the same tradition. Thus Giddens is able to appreciate Gadamer's view of a dialogue of traditions which seeks mutual knowledge in a common agreement, but fails to see that where a common agreement breaks down or is not achieved, Gadamer finds unmediated difference. Although Gadamer holds that one of the tasks of hermeneutics is to reveal such unmediated difference, this task is negatively valued in comparison to the discovery of agreement with tradition and between traditions.

Paul Ricoeur has offered a detailed analogy between the interpretation of texts and the interpretation of action.[12] Meaningful action is seen as being structurally similar to the speech-act and its fixation in writing. Ricoeur delineates three further characteristics of action. It can be detached from its agent whereby it takes on a social dimension and becomes the basis for institutions. Action, to be meaningful, must fulfill the dual criteria of relevance and importance. It must be relevant to its original context but it also 'transcends the social conditions of its production and may be re-enacted in new social contexts'. Third, human action is an 'open work', that is 'opened to anyone who *can read*' (original emphasis).[13] Ricoeur, like Gadamer, rejects the dichotomy between understanding and explanation and wishes to place them in a dialectical relationship to one another which culminates in act of personal commitment on the part of the inquirer. Social practices are obviously meaningful actions, which like texts in Ricoeur's opinion, interrogate not only a body of objective facts but also the existence of the reader-practitioner. Ricoeur's understanding of what it means to interpret texts or social practices is closely allied with how he views the function of history. Ricoeur does not propose a movement behind the text to the social practices which inform it, but a movement in front of the text to the *possible* world it discloses. History as the narrative of the past confronts us with realities of the past which make us aware of potentialities of the present, not revealed in its own realities. 'For to recognise the values of the past in their *differences* with respect to our values is already to open up the real towards the possible' (original emphasis).[14] Ricoeur's hermeneutics clearly allow for a positive articulation of human differences and locate a utopian and transformative element in the interpretation of social practices. Nonetheless, Ricoeur has not definitively removed hermeneutics from a project of cultural hegemony. One asks for whom does human difference exist and who is held to benefit from it. Part of the project of cultural hegemony is precisely to open up the expressions of the lived experience of those who are different for consumption by those who have the linguistic and social power to define them as different. The criterion of importance for meaningful action begs the questions *who* decides that it transcends its original context and what happens to the *integrity* of the action when it is re-enacted in new social contexts.

The Marxist literary hermeneutics of Fredric Jameson contain the same willingness to hypostatize history as Ricoeur. Both seem to hold that some form of totalizing concept of reality is unavoidable and that history is the best category in which to describe the totality of reality.[15] For Jameson a Marxist reading of literary texts is mandated because only the Marxist conception of history is a correct understanding of the totality of reality. Yet Jameson's Marxist view of history is not an optimistic one. History is 'nightmare' and the experience of necessity. The historical development of the means of production has led to the determinate failure of all revolutions, and the success of a socialist revolution presupposes the globalization of capitalism and its commodification of culture. Jameson seeks to detach his totalizing view of history from a version of cultural hegemony through his evaluation of the popular cultures of ethnic minorities and other marginalized people and his refusal to prioritize economic over sexual oppression. Nonetheless, the reconstruction of the past of oppressed groups finds its ultimate value in the recovery of their voices as subversive strategies 'in the dialogical system of the social class'.[16] Jameson's response to radical feminism's claim that the attack on patriarchy is the most radical political act is to recapitulate Engels' treatment of the emergence of patriarchy. Archaic modes of production and forms of alienation persist within capitalism in the form of patriarchy. To abrogate them is to dismantle the structure of capitalism itself.[17]

I have suggested that our identities, including our culturally stigmatized identities, embody in our individual and collective selves not only the potential richness of diversity and the breaking of cultural hegemony but also the pain of diversity and its fragmentation of selves. Interpretation of our socioculturally mediated identities will not heal the wound but can rather be the deceptive offer of a false comfort. In this light I approach Michael Walzer's attempt to give moral priority to interpretive strategies of social criticism. Walzer rejects the alternative modes of social criticism, discovery and invention as inadequate, or at best, interpretation in disguise. Discovery can take place in the religious form of a revelation of the divine law or in a secular version as the insight into the laws of nature. Invention is the attempt to design a moral world in which everyone would wish to live if he or she were removed from the social world and its prejudices in which that person actually lives. Walzer argues, in a similar vein to Gadamer, that criticism is tradition-immanent, that social criticism only makes sense where there is a basic agreement with the moral norms of one's social world:

The experience of moral argument is best understood in the interpretive mode. What we do when we argue is to give an account of the actually existing morality. That morality is authoritative for us because it is only by virtue of its existence that we exist as the moral beings we are. Our categories, relationships, commitments, and aspirations are all shaped by, expressed in terms of, the existing morality. Discovery and invention are efforts at escape, in the hope of finding some external and universal standard with which to judge moral existence. The effort may well be commendable, but it is, I think, unnecessary. The critique of existence begins, or can begin, from principles internal to existence itself.[18]

Walzer's criticism is aimed against the type of liberal theory of justice offered by John Rawls, which posits that a just society can be created when human particularities are ignored. What he gives us in exchange is just as, and perhaps, more disturbing than a Rawlsian claim to universal standards of justice. Walzer and other proponents of a narrative ethics of community assume the existence of a shared world of social and moral meanings. This world is, I believe, the process of cultural hegemony, and social criticism within it is a procedure of self-correction and therefore maintenance of the cultural hegemony. In reality the social world partakes of the same fragmentation as our identities despite the persistent exercise of the various forms of social control which seek to hide its fractures and contain oppositional voices and versions of reality within the boundaries of permitted criticism.

Early Christian baptism as a praxis interpreting identity

In reviewing some of the most important contributions to a hermeneutics of social reality, I have concluded that cultural hegemony is either tacitly implied or neglected as a problem. Before examining the ways in which cultural hegemony can be named within a hermeneutical project I want to explore what might be the source of theoretical inadequacies in *interpreting* social practices and therefore to what extent that they may be overcome. Obviously the lived experience of the intersection of language with social practices and their moral assessment constitutes the situation which can be hermeneutically grasped. One way to explore the viability of a hermeneutics of social practices is to see how certain practices and accompanying descriptions of them are adopted by groups of people as interpretations of their social existence. Baptism in early Christianity was such a practice which aimed at interpreting the social identities of its members both within the Christian community and outside it.

One of the most obvious texts to turn to in a discussion of the understanding of social identities among early Christians is Galatians 3:28. 'There is neither Greek nor Jew, there is neither slave nor free, there is neither male nor female; for you are all one in Christ Jesus' – what does this statement portend for the social identities of those Christians who defined themselves by this utterance? Paul is quoting here a baptismal formula and therefore referring to the act which was constitutive for Christian identity. One divested oneself of the identities of one's ethnic group, social status and sex on becoming a member of the Christian community. Wayne Meeks has borrowed the term 'performative utterance' from linguistic philosophy and social anthropology to describe how the declaration of the baptismal formula was experienced as actually ushering in a transformed reality for those initiated into the Christian community.[19] As he explains, the baptismal formula and its accompanying dramatic ritual action expressed the symbolic universe of the early Christians and demarcated it from that of the surrounding society. Baptism made claims that its representation of reality was at one and the same time symbolic and objective. Early Christians believed that it effectuated what it symbolized; it altered not only the cognitive state of the believer but made her or him an essentially new being. The language of baptism is radical for it does not simply displace or relativize existing social identities, but erases them. In the case of gender this erasure is especially marked through the use of the terms 'male' and 'female' instead of 'men' and 'women'. Hans-Dieter Betz has argued that this indicates that biological distinctions as well as social differences between men and women are obliterated in baptism.[20] The other identity categories of ethnicity and social status were also thought in the ancient world to carry inherent traits. This naturalization of ethnicity and social status, as well as gender, is in sharp contrast to modern anthropologies which separate person and social role. If baptism wrought change in an early Christian believer on an ontological level then *ipso facto* it also transformed social identity.

Obviously the early Christian understanding and practice of baptism had implications for the social roles connected to the social identities. The ways in which these were actually modified are the most difficult to ascertain. We have plenty of evidence both within the New Testament and in other early Christian literature that there were concerted attempts to refashion social roles in accordance with the new Christian identity. We are also informed of the tension between social roles in the Christian community and the larger society which led to conflict among Christians. Elizabeth Schüssler-Fiorenza has argued that the baptismal formula of Galatians 3:28 articulates the requirement of the early Christian community that one who wishes to enter it relinquish all forms of privilege, whether religious, social, cultural, national or gender-based. However, the 'egalitarian ethos of "oneness in Christ"' of pre-Pauline and Pauline missionary Christianity was lost in the later communities, represented in the New Testament by the deutero-Pauline writings.[21]

Conservative exegetes, on the other hand, simply assume that the patriarchalization and social hierarchalization of the Christian communities, typified by the household codes, upholds an authentic Pauline intention not to predicate the new life in Christ on any social arrangements. Christian identity does not necessitate social revolution, but accommodates itself to performing works of love within existing social structures.[22] The conservatives are undoubtedly wrong in their attempt to remove far-reaching social ramifications from early Christian belief and practice. Yet it is also reasonable to ask what were the concrete manifestations of baptismal identity in social reality. The notorious difficulties which confront one in the exegesis of such passages as I Corinthians 7:20–24 (on the Christian slave's attitude to his or her bondage) and I Corinthians 11:3–16 (on women's attire in public worship) leave one uncertain what the intended or actual change in social reality for early Christians was.[23] Indeed, what is unclear to present-day interpreters of the New Testament might also have been to early Christians. When Paul in his letter to Philemon urges him to receive back his escaped slave Onesimus 'no longer as a slave but more than a slave, as a beloved brother' (verse 16), what does he concretely intend their social relationship to be? The exegetical difficulties which we encounter in Paul's admonitions to slaves and women in I Corinthians may in fact be rooted in a confusion that Paul himself experienced in relating Christian baptismal identity to social roles.

I have spoken of confusion about social roles in Paul and among early Christians. It would, however, be wrong to suggest that the aporias encountered by later Christian moral traditions already exist *in nuce* in the very earliest period. Instead, the confusion as to appropriate social roles for Christians could in the early Church be integrated into a coherent account of the Christian's alienation from the world and the radical inauthenticity of the world's being. Whatever the actual social consequences of Galatians 3:28 were, its intention for the social identities of the present world order was their eschatological suspension. This eschatological suspension of social identity was only bearable because it was seen as temporary. Baptism was a form of 'realized eschatology', that is, it anticipated the conditions of the reign of God, the coming of which would bring about the destruction of the existing world. Such an anticipation was expected to be counterintuitive to ordinary experience of the social world. We should assume that early Christians expected conflict between their baptismal identity and their ordinary social identities, even though they might not have had the means to resolve it. The reign of God was imminent and hence the time of the conflict, when ordinary social identities were eschatologically suspended, was also limited.

Early Christian discourse was able to explain the conflict engendered by the eschatological suspension of social identities but could not resolve it. Early Christian literature testifies that the conflict intensified the longer the expected return of Christ and the abolition of the existing order were delayed. The theological language and the symbolism it employed in speaking of baptism became more urgent and more violent. The erasure of identity became total as it had to account for the persistence of social roles which prescribed human identities. This can be clearly seen in a closer examination of Paul's linking of baptism and death in Romans 6:3 and following, which was written against the background of Paul's instructions to Christian communities on the implications of baptism for social behavior. Paul's earlier use and interpretation of the baptismal formula in Galatians 3:26–28 was thus presupposed in Paul's further theological elaboration of the meaning of baptism in Romans 6.[24]

Paul stressed that a new identity is given in baptism, but, unlike the baptismal formula of Galatians 3:28, omitted any reference as to what this implied for existing social identities. The greater emphasis was placed on the deathlike destruction of the old identity implemented through baptism: 'Do you not know that all of us who have been baptized into Christ Jesus were baptized into his death? We were buried therefore with him by baptism into death, so that as Christ was raised from the dead by the glory of the Father, we too might walk in newness of life' (Romans 6:3–4). The violent imagery of death and being buried accentuates the difficulty as well as the completeness of erasing the former identity. The immediate context of this passage in Romans 6:1–2 was Paul's repetition and denial of a charge that his theology encouraged sin by its rejection of the Torah as the norm of Christian behavior. Paul was intent on showing that he took sin seriously but sin appeared to him as an existential human condition rather than as embedded in some forms of human behavior. New forms of Christian behavior arise out of the new Christian identity and not the other way round. In this point one already has a shift away from viewing the new Christian identity as the replacement of the former identity configured by one's social roles. Paul chose to explicate what he meant by 'walking in newness of life' not in reference to social roles and the identities they inscribed but through his doctrine of resurrection:

For if we have been united with him in a death like his, we shall certainly be united with him in a resurrection like his. We know that our old self was crucified with him so that the sinful body might be destroyed, and we might no longer be enslaved to sin. For he who has died is freed from sin. But if we have died with Christ we believe that we shall also live with him (Romans 6:5–8).

In this passage too one notes the violent imagery of death used to portray the present reality of the Christian (being crucified with

Christ, the destruction of the sinful body). The Christian has died to the old self and therefore is caught up in the acute process of the erasure of the old self. In contrast, the sharing of the Christian in the resurrection of Christ and the full assumption of the new self and the new identity will occur in the future. Paul uses the future tenses of the verb to describe in verse 5 the Christian participation in the resurrection (*esometha*) and in verse 8 the belief in a life with Christ (*syzēsomen*). The 'realized eschatology' of baptism has been modified to include a future dimension.[25] On the one hand, the eschatological suspension of social identities, expressed in Galatians 3:28 has been radicalized to a total cessation of identity. It seems to have been Paul's view that Christians living in the world were in a hiatus between death and resurrection. On the other hand, this interim condition, which is neither an affirmation of life within the existing order nor a full anticipation of existence in the coming reign of God, might allow former social identities to persist in a sort of limbo. This raises the question at what point does the 'walking in newness of life' (verse 4) begin. The verb here (*peripatēsōmen*) could refer to either the present or future reality of Christians.[26]

The inability of Christians to solve the tensions of the eschatological suspension of social identities seems to have led to a revision of how they conceived the transformation of reality through baptism. Baptism no longer brings an end to existing human identities and how they are inscribed in social roles, practices and institutions. Rather, it promises an end to them while at the same time initiating a process of eradicating the human self on what Paul seems to have believed was a deeper level than the surface reality of social identities. Ironically, when Paul sought metaphors for this process he drew from the oppressive social identities of the institutions of slavery and patriarchal marriage.[27] These two institutions provided Paul with the symbolism of the total absorption of one human being's identity within that of another. As such they were a social parallel to his theology of baptism, since the slave and the wife were dead to their social world, having no independent existence in it, but only continuing to exist subsumed in the lives of the master and husband.[28] In Romans 6:15–22 human beings are regarded as either 'slaves of sin' or 'slaves of righteousness'; to be free of one is to be enslaved to the other. Paul then proceeds to make a similar contrast between the Law and Christ in Romans 7:2–5 through the image of patriarchal marriage. A married woman is *hypandros*, that is under the power of her husband until her husband dies. At this point, Paul does not envisage the woman as becoming free from male authority but of being able to choose to place herself under the authority of another husband. In

Paul's view the human condition is total absorption of one's identity into the competing realities of sin or righteousness, the Law or Christ. Human beings cannot escape the erasure of their identity, but this occurs in two distinct and thoroughly opposed ways, either through the death of baptism or the death of sin. Slavery and patriarchal marriage provided a model of someone being dead and yet at the same time having another live through one's life. In his doctrine of baptism Paul reverses the parasitism of the social institutions by having the one who is dead live through the life of the other. This reversal is only partial since the identity of the Christian believer is totally subsumed in that of Christ.

Baptism was for early Christians a praxis through which they sought to reinterpret their identity. It sought to abolish the identities grounded in oppressive social roles and institutions, but was ambiguous in its conception of new identities and apparently lacked the means to create the new social roles and institutions to sustain these. Baptism as ritual action and declarative speech gave early Christians a language in which to construct new identities but not a material instrumentality through which to make these reconstructed identities effective in social relationships. The conflict around social roles in the early Christian community probably intensified the fragmentation of identity felt by its members. During this period the Christian communities gathered as house churches in the households of its wealthier members, many of whom were women. The Galatians baptismal formula asserted not only the equality of the *domina* but also that of her slave.[29] We do not have the details of the social adjustments made by servile and free women in the Christian communities. But we can see the analogy between their situation and that of women of different races and classes in contemporary society. The problem of a relative differential of social power between women, within a general disempowerment of all women, always pits solidarity on the basis of sex against that on the basis of social status. The fractured identity of the free and wealthier women in the early Christian communities as both oppressor and oppressed must have posed acute practical and ethical choices as some Christian communities in the late first and second century moved towards a general acceptance of both gender inequality and social hierarchy. The conflict of identities both within and between individuals led to the rapid division of the Christian communities. The battles over doctrine and church order between the socially conservative 'orthodox' and their often (though by no means invariably) socially radical opponents indicate the disintegration of the 'oneness in Christ' which Galatians 3:28 proclaimed as the result of baptism and its abolition of social distinctions.

Conclusion: interpretation and domination

A hermeneutics of social practices cannot accomplish through the theoretical activity of interpretation what the original praxis could not achieve. Admittedly, one could counter with Ricoeur that the values of the past, even if they were not realized in it, still hold possibilities for the present in which they might be realized. According to this argument a hermeneutics of social practices may be valuable not because of what it tells us about the past but on account of the commitment it demands from us in the present. I certainly agree that we should not conflate meaningful with successful action, but I also ask in what way understanding the past can redeem it. When Ricoeur renounces Hegel's total mediation of history through reason he must also abandon Hegel's view in the *Phenomenology of Spirit* that the Absolute Spirit takes back into itself the wounds inflicted by history, leaving no scar.[30] But it is precisely Hegel's insistence on an ultimate reconciliation which makes the concept of history as a totality bearable. Hegel affirms a radical openness of the past as the condition for reason to reconstruct history as a whole. In his view the past can be changed and its suffering abolished. What have the vanquished and the broken of the past to gain if the memory of their suffering and struggle *only* makes a succeeding generation, unknown and unknowable to them, aware of potentialities for this later world? They do not benefit from a hermeneutics of history which absorbs their past into the single history of a single humanity. If, additionally, subjectivity is attributed to this single humanity in its single history then one must ask, *whose* subjectivity? If it is not that of the Absolute Spirit then one can only assume that it is the interpreter's.

Ricoeur acknowledges 'the right to be different' as a counterbalance to the hegemony which a society or group of dominant societies might claim on the basis of the idea of a universal history.[31] John Brenkman has recently tried to construct a critical hermeneutics which would explicitly engage the problem of cultural hegemony in interpretation. He recognizes the plurality of social identities and that many individuals will have multiple identities, shaped by diverse cultural practices and traditions which may come into conflict with one another. Brenkman rightly sees the importance of cultural practices through which the oppressed and marginalized shape their identities over against those prescribed for them by the dominant culture. Cultural practices can be utilized by social movements of the oppressed as forms of resistance. Such cultural practices when they occurred in the past are or can be made part of the historical record. However, it is at this juncture that interpretation falls into the danger of becoming a hegemonic act. Brenkman gives us the following evaluation of the hermeneutic retrieval of the oppressed of the past: 'To preserve those heritages, indeed to recover them from beneath the rubble created by the victors, is to transmit an understanding of what Bloch called humanity's unfinished tasks.'[32]

Here, as with Ricoeur, one raises the question: *whose* humanity and *whose* unfinished tasks? Both Brenkman and Ricoeur perpetuate certain strands in the modern concept of history. This was the ideological product of an emergent bourgeois liberal society which sought to render the past transparent to the highest degree possible with the enhanced technical means at its disposal. Totalizations of history corresponded in their genesis to specific historiographical strategies. Nineteenth- and twentieth-century elites employed history to seek their genealogy in the hegemonic formations of the past. Contemporary historians would doubt that past subjective experiences are recoverable even in the abundant self-representations of earlier elites. The inability to recover past subjectivity is unlikely to deter those who wish to totalize history because it makes it all the more easy to make the interpreter's subjective position that from which the totality of history can be viewed. The hegemonic formations of the past are absorbed into the cultural hegemony of the present rather like the Hellenistic elites were integrated into and disempowered within the Roman Empire. One might perceive here a certain irony of retributive justice. Apply the same historical method to the traces of existence left behind by the oppressed of the past and the alienation suffered in their lived experience is transposed to the record of their past.

It is not my belief that interpretation must always result in a hegemonic act. Liberation theologies have portrayed how peoples of color, women, peasants and workers have appropriated the biblical tradition as a commitment to their own liberation. The interpretation or reinterpretation of religious texts by those stigmatized in their identities can be an act of resistance to cultural hegemony. Interpretation is inescapable. We can only 'know' the past within our own mental universe with its cultural assumptions, political commitments, and so on. A desire to avoid anachronism in our historical reconstructions can mask its own negative totalization of history. Claims that the past and the present are radically discontinuous with one another, and therefore the experiences and the identities of those who lived in the past must be fundamentally different from our own, seem to adopt the vantage-point of Absolute Spirit. However, this Spirit carries out a total mediation of history with irrationality.

It is obvious that I am using 'interpretation' in a much reduced sense to indicate the status of our knowledge of other cultural and historical contexts. Even the understanding of our own situation is restricted by the mistakes of our praxis and the limitations of our material and intellectual resources. Looking at the baptismal practice of early Christians we think we can see the past irrecoverable experience of fragmented, subjugated, yet resisting identities. The pain of the fracture and conflict of identities, we believe, was different but not unlike our own. The terms of this analogy we will never know with certainty. We think we can glimpse the possibilities they saw for the praxis of Christian baptism to reinterpret their social identities. These were potential existences for them, not possible worlds for us. They do not live through our interpretation, and our memory cannot heal their wounds. There is no totality of history in which we might finish their tasks. This fragile knowledge of the oppressed of the past calls us to reverence for the dead. It also summons us to commitment to the living, to those oppressed by race, class and gender. We, like the early Christians, wish to reinterpret our identities, but our reinterpretation too will falter unless it takes on the flesh of transformed social relationships. The elaborate programs of hermeneutics cannot themselves overcome the poverty of interpretation.

NOTES

This chapter is a revised version of a paper given at Princeton Theological Seminary in May 1988. It was part of the conference 'Gender, Race, Class: Implications for Interpreting Religious Texts', sponsored by Conversations: A Theological Project in Hermeneutics.

1 Since the publication of Carol Gilligan's *In a Different Voice: Psychological Theory and Women's Development* (Harvard University Press, Cambridge, Mass., 1982) there has been extensive debate on the respective merits of an 'ethics of care' and an 'ethics of justice'. The former is seen as stressing the connectedness of the moral self to others and the relativity of moral claims to contexts. The latter is held to stress the autonomy of the moral self and to demand that moral claims be universalizable. For further discussion of Gilligan's work, see especially Eva Feder Kittay and Diana T. Meyers (eds), *Women and Moral Theory* (Rowman & Littlefield, Totowa, NJ, 1987).

2 Ernst Troeltsch, *The Absoluteness of Christianity and the History of Religions*, tr. David Reid (John Knox Press, Richmond, 1971).

3 Luce Irigaray, *This Sex Which Is Not One*, tr. Catherine Porter (Cornell University Press, Ithaca, 1985), p. 85.

4 Allan Bloom, *The Closing of the American Mind* (Simon & Schuster, New York, 1987).

5 During the years 38–41 CE the Jews of Egypt were the victims of anti-semitic unrest in Alexandria, where the Greek and indigenous Egyptian population resented Jewish attempts to gain citizenship. These violent disturbances caused a significant loss of Jewish life and occurred shortly before Paul wrote his letter to the Galatian Christians. For an account of these events, see John Gager, *The Origins of Anti-Semitism: Attitudes toward Judaism in Pagan and Christian Antiquity* (Oxford University Press, New York, 1985), pp. 44–51.

6 Hans-Georg Gadamer, 'Hermeneutics and Social Science', *Cultural Hermeneutics*, 2 (1975), pp. 311ff.

7 Ibid., p. 315.

8 Hans-Georg Gadamer, *Truth and Method* (Sheed & Ward, London, 1975), p. 475.

9 Anthony Giddens, *New Rules of Sociological Method: A Positive Critique of Interpretative Sociologies* (Basic Books, New York, 1976), p. 64.

10 Anthony Giddens, *Profiles and Critiques in Social Theory* (University of California Press, Berkeley, 1982), p. 16.

11 Anthony Giddens, *Studies in Social and Political Theory* (Hutchinson, London, 1977), p. 172: 'Hermeneutics is not simply the privileged reserve of the professional social investigator, but is practised by everyone; mastery of such practice is the only avenue whereby professional social scientists, like lay actors themselves, are able to generate the descriptions of social life they use in their analyses.'

12 Paul Ricoeur, 'The Model of Text: Meaningful Action Considered as Text', in *Hermeneutics and the Human Sciences*, ed. and tr. John B. Thompson (Cambridge University Press, Cambridge, 1981), pp. 197–221.

13 Ibid., p. 205.

14 Ricoeur, 'Narrative Function', in *Hermeneutics and the Human Sciences*, p. 295. Notice the close correspondence in Ricoeur's language between the description of the function of historical narrative and that of the interpretation of text/action in the earlier essay, 'The Model of the Text': 'What has to be understood is not the initial situation of discourse, but what points toward a possible world' ('Narrative Function', p. 218).

15 Most recently Ricoeur has in the third volume of *Time and Narrative* (University of Chicago Press, Chicago, 1988) attempted to dissociate his own hermeneutics of history from the totalization found in the Hegelian tradition, which he admits has influenced him. A total mediation whereby reason in history and the reality of history would coincide seems no longer tenable. Ricoeur also rejects 'purely utopian expectations' in which 'the hopes of humanity lose their anchorage in acquired experience and are projected into an unprecedented future' (p. 215). Drawing on the work of Reinhart Koselleck, he develops a metahistorical analysis in which the categories 'space of experience' (corresponding to the temporalization of history in the present) and 'horizon of expectation' (corresponding to the temporalization of history in the future) are taken

to be transcendentals. These transcendentals lead to the postulating of a further one: a single humanity who is the 'subject as a collective singular' (ibid.) of a single history. On the basis of a single humanity with a single history, Ricoeur is then able to speak of 'effective-history'. The ability of human beings to inherit from the past provides a determination of the future which, in turn, permits one to conceive of the efficacy of history without postulating a ground for it in a total mediation, such as the Hegelian reason. Here once again the notion of the past as a possible world is crucial: 'the repercussion of our expectations relative to the future on the reinterpretation of the past may have as one of its major effects opening up forgotten possibilities, aborted potentialities, repressed endeavors in the supposedly closed past' (p. 227). The open past correlates with the determined future, requiring that 'the utopian imagination always be converted into specific expectations' (p. 258). Ricoeur characterizes this hermeneutics of history as a 'totalization through an imperfect mediation' (p. 256). I express my doubts on whether this limitation of the totalization of history frees it from the problematic of cultural hegemony on page 298.

16 Fredric Jameson, *The Political Unconscious: Narrative as a Socially Symbolic Act* (Cornell University Press, Ithaca, 1981), p. 86.

17 Ibid., p. 100.

18 Michael Walzer, *Interpretation and Social Criticism* (Harvard University Press, Cambridge, Mass., 1987), p. 21.

19 Wayne Meeks, 'The Image of the Androgyne: Some Uses of a Symbol in Earliest Christianity', *History of Religions*, 13 (1974), pp. 181f.

20 Hans-Dieter Betz, *Galatians: A Commentary on Paul's Letter to the Churches in Galatia* (Fortress, Philadelphia, 1979), p. 195.

21 Elizabeth Schüssler-Fiorenza, *In Memory of Her: A Feminist Theological Reconstruction of Christian Origins* (Crossroad, New York, 1983), pp. 205–18.

22 See, for example, James E. Crouch, *The Origin and Intention of the Colossian Haustafel* (Vandenhoeck & Ruprecht, Göttingen, 1972), p. 160: 'Genuine love may transcend the social order, but the forms through which it expresses itself do not.'

23 See S. Scott Bartchy, *First-Century Slavery and the Interpretation of I Corinthians 7:21*, SBL Dissertation Series 11 (rpt. edn: Scholars Press, Atlanta, 1985). The vast and ever-growing literature on I Corinthians 11 has not brought clarity to what Wayne Meeks has aptly called 'this confusing passage' ('The Image of the Androgyne', p. 201).

24 See Ulrich Wilckens, *Der Brief an die Römer*, Evangelische-Katholischer Kommentar zum Neuen Testament, vol. IV/2 (Benzinger/Neukirchener Verlag, Cologne and Neukirchen-Vluyn, 1980), p. 54.

25 Paul's use of the future tense is probably a revision of an already existing baptismal formula which saw the participation in both Christ's death and in his resurrection being given in baptism. Paul was, it seems, motivated to change the formula because of the consequences being drawn by the community in Corinth (which included the abandonment of conventional

social roles). See Gerhard Barth, *Die Taufe in frühchristlicher Zeit*, Biblisch-Theologische Studien, 4 (Neukirchener Verlag, Neukirchen-Vluyn, 1981), pp. 96–7.

26 The verb is subjunctive aorist in a final clause.

27 It is important to recognize that when, in Romans 6:12–20, Paul once more takes up the major theme of Romans, the righteousness brought by the Gospel of Christ, that he does so against the background of his doctrine of baptism. See Udo Schnelle, *Gerechtigkeit und Christusgegenwart. Vorpaulinische und paulinische Tauftheologie*, Göttinger Theologische Arbeiten, 17 (Vandenhoeck & Ruprecht, Göttingen, 1983), p. 87.

28 See my article 'Sexual Justice and the "Righteousness of God"', in *Sex and God: Some Varieties of Women's Religious Experience*, ed. Linda Hurcombe (Routledge & Kegan Paul, London, 1987), where I also comment on Romans 6 (pp. 258–9).

29 See Schüssler-Fiorenza, *In Memory of Her*, p. 250.

30 G. W. F. Hegel, *The Phenomenology of Spirit*, tr. A. V. Miller (Oxford University Press, Oxford, 1977), pp. 406f. See note 15, above, on Ricoeur's hermeneutics of history in *Time and Narrative*. For Ricoeur's treatment of Hegel, see *Time and Narrative*, pp. 193–206.

31 Ricoeur, *Time and Narrative*, p. 216.

32 John Brenkman, *Culture and Domination* (Cornell University Press, Ithaca, 1987), p. 230.

Index

Aaron 73, 184
Abaye 206
Abel 169, 172, 174, 179, 188
Abimelech, king of Gerar 84–5, 137, 138, 154–7, 180
Abimelech, son of Jerubaal 17, 35–6
Abraham: burial site 45–6, 55, 165, 173, 179; chronology 94, 95, 115, 116–17, 118; circumcision 167, 175; genealogy 119, 167, 168, 169, 171, 172, 173, 177, 181; in Gerar 149, 154–7, 160; Isaac's birth promised to 88, 94, 97, 105, 148–9, 151–2, 157, 160, 162, 166; Isaac's sacrifice 78, 166, 167, 181, 243; and Ishmael 125, 126–7, 162, 167; and Keturah 88–9, 92, 93, 119, 174; and Lot 179; and Sarah (marriage) 88, 94, 97, 157, 160, 162, 163, 164, 165, 166, 180, (pretends she is his sister) 149, 154, 155, 156, 160, 163, 164, 180; and Sodom 99, 150, 152, 153–4, 156, 160, 164
Abrams, M. H. 44
Absalom 97, 110
Achilles Tatius 262–5
Achish 103, 104
Achsah 20, 23
Acts of the Apostles 267
Acts of the Apostles, apocryphal 263

Acts of Paul and Thecla 263
Acts of Thomas 263
Adah 172
Adam 42, 115, 118, 169, 172; relationship to Eve 163, 164, 165–6, 173, 179
adoption 164, 169, 172, 177–8, 180–2, 185
Aggadah 5–6, 191
Aḥa, Rabbi 205
Ahab, king of Israel 93, 118–19
Akiba, Rabbi 202, 207, 208
Alexander Romance 265
Alexander the Great, biographies of 265
Alexandrian Fathers 4, 42; *see also* Origen
allegory 4–7, 11, 78, 206, 217, 223–6, 258
Alter, Robert 2, 20, 146–60, 237–9, 243, 247
Amalek 126
Ammonites 149, 152, 154, 163, 165
Amos 12, 62, 69, 78, 199
annunciation 62, 149, 157, 160, 166, 171, 178, 188
Antiochine Fathers 4, 42
Apel, Karl-Otto 189
Aphek 103
Apollonius Rhodius 270
Apollonius of Tyre 263
Aquiba, Rabbi 221–2, 225

Aristotle 81, 146, 242, 245, 288
Arpachshad 171
Assyria 97, 139–40
Auerbach, Erich 44, 238, 239, 245
Augustine of Hippo 60–1, 195,
    217, 247, 262
Austin, J. L. 233
Austruc, Jean 10

Ba'asha, king of Israel 118, 119
Babel 170, 173, 177
Bacon, Francis 8
Bakhtin, Mikhail M. 246, 247
Bal, Mieke 2–3, 12, 16–39
Balaam 94, 99, 105
Balak 105
baptism 292–7, 300
'Bath' *see* Jephthah, daughter of
Bathsheba 121–2, 183
Bauer, Ferdinand Christian 10
Baumgartner, Walter 26–7, 28
Becket, Samuel 65
Ben Azzai 191, 225
Benjamin 45, 51, 52, 131
Benjamin, Walter 53
Benjaminites 33, 86, 87, 158
Berechiah (Berekiah), Rabbi 196,
    203
Bereshit Rabbah 116
Berlin, Adele 13
Bernard of Clairvaux 5
'Beth' (raped concubine, Judges 19)
    17, 19, 20–1, 25–33, 36, 109,
    158
Bethany, anointing of Jesus at
    248–9
Bethel 187
Bethuel 180
Betz, Hans-Dieter 293
Bible: authority of 13–14; interpret-
    ation of *see* interpretation, bib-
    lical; narrative in 146–60 *passim*,
    161–88 *passim*, 237–57 *passim*,
    (gaps) 83, 93–6, 111, 113,
    129–31, 133–5, 140, 148, 218,
    (juxtaposition) 86, 87, 106–14,
    121, 130, 147, 154, 223, (repeti-

tion) 41, 51–5, 61, 73, 266, 269,
    (simultaneity) 85, 96–136, (suc-
    cessiveness) 123–36, (time)
    81–145 *passim*
Bilah 164, 187
Bloch, Ernst 299
Bloom, Alan 284
Bloom, Harold 77
Boaz 161
Boyarin, Daniel 3, 214–30
Brenkman, John 298–9
Briggs, Sheila 3, 276–303
Bruns, Gerald L. 3, 189–213,
    216–17, 219, 223
Bultmann, Rudolf Karl 288

Caesarea Philippi 252, 253
Cain, 51, 113, 163, 174, 188; city of
    177; genealogy 119, 120, 169,
    171, 172
Calvin, John 7
Canaanites 165
Cavell, Stanley 203
Cervantes, Miguel de 146
Chariton 262–5, 266, 268
Childs, Brevard S. 217
Christ 10, 34, 42–4, 173, 224,
    240–5, 247ff., 259–61, 270–2
Chronicles, Book I of 120
Chrysostom, John 4
class 277–80, 283–6, 297, 300
Clement, Pseudo-; *Recognitions* 263
Cohn, Dorrit 246, 248
concubine 17, 21, 22, 26, 29, 153,
    158, 186; raped (Judges 19) 17,
    19, 20–1, 25–33, 36, 109, 158
condensation 19–20, 23–5, 28, 37
Corinthians, Epistles to 4, 42,
    240–1, 294
covenant 148, 150, 157, 177

Danites 109
Dante Alighieri 64, 75
David, king of Israel 146, 238; and
    Absalom 97, 110; and Bathsheba
    121–2, 183; chronology 93,
    94–5, 97, 100, 102–5, 110, 126,

183; dual story of debut 134–6; and Saul 100, 102–5, 126, 134, 136; and sick baby 94–5
deconstruction 1, 46–55, 233–6
Deists 8
Delilah 18, 19, 36, 137, 138
Derchain, P. 34–5
Derrida, Jacques 14, 48, 247
Descartes, René 8, 198
Deuteronomy, Book of 54, 68, 91, 152, 167; chronology 82–3, 85, 137–8, 159; loss of text 46, 54; midrash and 199, 202
Dickens, Charles 147
Dilthey, Wilhelm 287
Dinah 102, 128–30, 137, 163, 164, 180–1
displacement 20, 36, 137
Dostoevsky, Fyodor 83, 261
Douglas, Mary 24
Droysen, Johann Gustav 9, 287

Eagleton, Terry 3, 231–6
Ecclesiastes, Book of 192–4, 196–7, 202, 205
Edom 120, 167, 174, 187
Eglon, king of Moab 84, 107, 108
Egypt: Abraham and Sarah in 154, 155, 156; nakedness of 50, 163; plagues 105, 156; *see also* Joseph
Ehud 84, 107, 108, 112, 113
Eleazar b. Azariah, Rabbi 193–4, 199, 201–2, 204, 207, 208
Eleazar Ḥisma, Rabbi 193
election 166–7, 173–8, 181, 238
Eliezar 179
Elkanah 166
Engels, Friedrich 291
Enoch 171; town of 169
Enosh 171, 172
Ephraim 54, 121, 122, 161, 162, 177; descendants of 166
Ephron the Hittite 45–6
Er 131, 132, 133
Eros 271
Esau: chronology 112, 113–14, 116, 118; and Edom 167, 174,

187; genealogy 120, 170, 171, 187; loss of birthright 125, 126–7, 162, 167, 174, 177, 182, 187; occupation 174
Ethiopian eunuch and Philip 41–2
Eucharist, institution of 249–50
Eve 84, 163, 164, 165–6, 173, 179
exegesis *see* interpretation
Exodus, Book of 187; chronology 82–3, 85, 110, 112, 138, 159; midrash on 218–23, 226; *see also* Moses
Ezekiel 55, 64, 67–8, 69, 76, 78–9
Ezra, Book of 140–1

feminism 1, 2, 14, 26, 259, 276, 280–3, 291
Fielding, Henry 83, 94, 147, 159
Flaubert, Gustave 146
Ford, Ford Madox 146
Formalists, Russian 81
Fowles, John 125, 126, 134
Frank, Joseph 81
Frei, Hans 11, 241, 242
Freud, Sigmund 20, 47–9, 67, 70, 71, 78, 235; on condensation 20; on displacement 20; on repression 46–9, 54–5; on stammering 70; on virginity 21, 24, 25
Frye, Northrop 43–5

Gabler, J. P. 9
Gadamer, Hans-Georg 189, 287–9, 290, 291
Galatians, Epistle to 286, 292, 293, 294, 295, 296, 297
Gamaliel II, Rabban 194, 205, 206–8
Gath 103
genealogy 162ff.
gender 17–18, 277–86, 297–300
Genesis 82–3, 98
Genesis, Book of; chronology 82–3, 85, 98, 115–18, 119–20, 123–5, 130–3, 138, 159; *see also* Abraham; Dinah; Jacob; Joseph; Judah

Genette, Gerard 246, 247
Genovese, Eugene 280
genre 147, 260 ff.; biography
    260–1, 265, 267; erotic novel
    262–7, 269–70; *fabula* 242, 246
Gerar 149, 154–7, 160; *see also*
    Abimelech
Gethsemane 245, 250–2, 254, 259,
    269–72
Gibbon, Edward 89
Gibeah, *see* concubine, raped
Gibeonites 177
Giddens, Anthony 288–9
Gilboa 102, 103
Gilgamesh Epic 84
Girard, René 32
Goldin, Judah 5
Goliath 134, 136
Gramsci, Antonio 280
Green, A. R. W. 32
Gregory of Nyssa 42
Greimas, A.-J. 243, 246

Habakkuk, Book of 62–3
Habermas, Jürgen 288
Hadad the Edomite 139, 141
Hagar 179, 181, 188
Hägg, Thomas 268–9
halakhah 5, 192, 194
Ham: genealogy 119, 169, 171,
    179; and Noah's drunkenness
    153, 163, 164, 165
Hamites 170, 172
Handmaid Tribes 163, 170, 171,
    172
Hanina, Rabbi 215
Hannah, mother of Samuel 166
Haran 168, 170, 171, 172, 173,
    179, 182, 185
Hazita *see* Song of Songs
Heber 170, 171
Hebrews 172
Hegel, Georg Wilhelm Friedrich
    298
hegemony 277–92, 298–300
Heinemann, Joseph 191
Helidorus 262–5

Herder, Johann Gottfried von 8
hermeneutics 1, 2, 14, 189–213
    passim, 238–9, 243, 276–7,
    286–92, 298–300; feminist 26,
    276
Hezekiah 97, 139–40, 141
Hillel, exegetic school of 5
Hirsch, Marianne 34
History Workshop 280
Hittites 45–6, 165, 179
Hivites 102, 128–30
Homer 81, 82, 83, 138, 151, 266,
    268, 269, 270, 271, 272
Horites 176
Humboldt, Wilhelm von 9

*Inanna's Descent to the Nether
    World* (Sumerian work) 84
incest 152–4, 163–5, 178, 187
interpretation 40–59 *passim*, 189–
    213 *passim*, 214–30 *passim*,
    276–304 *passim*; allegorical *see*
    allegory; biblical (early church) 4,
    41–3, 224–5, (eighteenth cen-
    tury) 7–9, (historical/critical)
    10–12, 49, 148, 237–8, 240–51,
    255, (history of) 14, (medieval)
    4–5, 153, (nineteenth century)
    9–10, (patristic) 4, 41–3, 224–5,
    (reformation), 6–7; rabbinic 5–6,
    83, 142, 189–213 *passim*,
    214–30 *passim*; *see also* mashal;
    midrash
Irad 171
Irenaeus 41
Irigaray, Luce 282
Isaac 126, 166, 174, 177, 187;
    chronology 116–17, 118, 119;
    genealogy 119, 120, 166, 167–8,
    170, 171; and Rebekah
    (betrothal) 29, 107, 182–6, (mar-
    riage) 88–9, 92, 93, 116, 161,
    162, 163, 164, 165, 167, 173,
    176–7, 179, 181, 186, (pretends
    she is his sister) 163, 164, 180; *see
    also under* Abraham
Isaiah 64, 65, 67, 68, 79; Book of

41–2, 74, 226–7, 241; Deutero-74
Iscah 179, 182
Ishmael 94, 118, 167, 174, 188; expulsion 125, 126–7, 162; genealogy 119, 120, 170, 178, 179; marriage 176, 181
Ishmael, Rabbi 218, 219
Ishmaelites 49, 172, 176
Isis, cult of 264, 269, 271

Jabal 169
Jacob: chronology 112, 113–14, 116, 117, 118; death 161; and Ephraim 162; and Esau 112, 113–14, 116, 125, 126–7, 167, 174, 177; funeral 45–6, 55; genealogy 120, 167, 168, 170, 171, 172, 176, 177; as Israel 174, 175, 187; and Joseph 45, 51, 101; marriages 29, 162, 163, 164, 175, 179; occupation 174; and rape of Dinah 128–30; shrewdness 186–7; wrestles with angel 175
James, apostle 83, 250
James, Henry 98, 100, 241
Jameson, Fredric 290–1
Janzen, Gerald 63
Japheth 119, 169, 171
Jared 171
Javanites 170, 172
Jay, Nancy 32
Jehoiachin, king of Judah 110
Jehoshaphat, king of Judah 118–19
Jephthah 20, 30, 97, 120–1, 122, 123; daughter of 17, 19, 20–5, 30, 31, 32, 33, 34, 36, 120–1, 122, 123
Jeremiah 64, 65, 68, 69, 73–4, 78; Book of 226–7; scroll of 46, 54
Jeremias, Joachim 241–2
Jerusalem, fall of 110
Jesus *see* Christ
Jezreel 103
Joḥanan b. Berok'a, Rabbi 193, 205, 207–8

John, Gospel of 62, 242, 248, 249, 250, 265
John the Baptist, death of 267
John of the Cross, St 64
Joktan 171
Jonah 71, 231–6
Jonson, Ben 147
Joseph 44–7, 49–55, 146, 162, 187–8; bones of 40, 55; and brothers 163, 167, 187; chronology 93, 94, 95, 97, 101–2, 104, 110, 123–4, 130–3; and dreams 40–1, 187
Joseph b. Dosethai, Abba 207–8
Joshua 41; Book of 82–3, 85, 91, 147, 159
Joshua, Rabbi 193, 198, 205, 206–8
Joyce, James 64, 84
Jubal 169
Judah, Rabbi 206, 216
Judah, son of Jacob 170; and Joseph 49, 52, 130–1; and Tamar 53, 101, 123–5, 130–3, 134, 135, 162, 163, 164, 178, 180–1, 187–8
Judas Iscariot 239, 242, 244, 249, 250, 252–3
Judges, Book of 16–39, 147; chronology 82–3, 85, 109, 114, 120–3, 159; *see also* concubine, raped; Ehud; Jephthah; Samson

Kahler, Martin 242
'Kallah' *see* Samson, bride of
Kant, Immanuel 61–2, 63, 64, 70, 73, 287
Karaites 6
Kaseman, Ernst 240
Kenan 171
Keret, Legend of King 84
Kermode, Frank 237
kerygma 237–57 *passim*
Keturah 88–9, 92, 93, 119, 174; descendants of 120, 170, 172, 174, 186
Kings, Books of 68, 147, 192;

Kings, Books of (*cont.*)
  chronology 82–3, 85, 110–11,
  118–19, 139–40, 159
  kinship 162–3, 166, 179–80; see
  also genealogy; marriage
Kish, asses of 86, 87, 137
Koehler, L. 26–7, 28
Kohelet *see* Solomon
Korah rebellion 138
Kuhn, Thomas 289

Laban: and daughters' marriage 29,
  162, 168, 175, 179, 182;
  genealogy 170, 180, 186; and
  Rebekah's marriage 184
Lacan, Jacques 14, 71
Lamech 169, 170, 171, 172, 188
Leach, Sir Edmund Ronald 148
Leah 162, 164, 170, 171, 175, 179,
  180, 187
Leitch, Vincent 189
Lesage, Alain René 146
Leviticus, Book of 82–3, 85, 159,
  205
literacy 268–9
Locke, John 8
Longus 262–5
loss 46, 49, 53
Lot 31, 54, 159–60, 179, 180; and
  destruction of Sodom 149–54,
  158, 164; incest with daughters
  152–4, 157, 158, 160, 162, 163,
  164–5; wife 149, 152, 165, 173
Lotman, Jurig 246
Luke, Gospel of 248, 249, 250, 267
Luther, Martin 6–7, 60, 192, 195,
  217

Machpelah, field of 45–6, 55, 165,
  173, 179
Mahalel 171
Maimonides, Moses 63, 206
Mallarmé, Stéphane 79
Man, Paul de 74–5, 233, 234, 235
Manassah 50, 54
Marin, Louis 244–5, 252
Mark, Gospel of: christology 240,

241, 243, 244, 245, 247–55;
  compared with Greco-Roman
  popular literature 259–60,
  264–72; interpretative narrative
  62, 237, 240, 247–55
Marks, Herbert 3, 60–80
marriage 23, 27–32, 161 ff.
Marx, Karl 235, 276
Marxism 2, 14, 259, 276, 279–80,
  290–1
Mary, mother of Jesus 42
mashal 215–23, 225–6
Masoretic Text 116
Matthew, Gospel of 242, 248, 249,
  250
Meeks, Wayne 292–3
Mehujael 171
Mekilta 218–23
Melchizedek 181
memory 24–5, 46–50, 53
Methuselah 171
Methushael 171
Micah 109
Micaiah ben Imla 68
Midian 49, 188
midrash, 189–213 *passim*, 214–30
  passim, 237; *see also* interpret-
  ation, rabbinic
Milcah 164, 179, 182, 185
Mill, John Stuart 196
Miller, J. Hillis 235
Milton, John 54, 55, 108, 165, 168
Miriam 42, 138
Moabites 149, 152, 154, 163, 165;
  see also Ehud
Morgenstern, Julian 27
Moriah, Mount 166, 181
Moses 55, 184, 188, 199–200; and
  bones of Joseph 40, 45; bride-
  groom of blood story 72–3, 148;
  call of 64, 66, 67, 68–9, 72–3;
  chronology 93, 95, 97; rabbis on
  202, 219–21; retrospect over
  leadership 137–8
Mowinckel, Sigmund 11

Nabokov, Vladimir 98

Nahor 168, 173; Abraham's alliance with descendants 167, 177, 181; genealogy 164, 168, 170, 171, 172, 180, 188; Milcah and 164, 179, 182
narrative 81–145 *passim*, 146–60 *passim*, 237–57 *passim*; semiotics of 243–7; *see also* Bible, narrative in
narratology 16, 18, 20, 21, 26–8, 36, 237
Nathan, Rabbi 194
Nehemiah, Book of 91, 140–1
new historicism 258–9
Niditch, Susan 31
Nietzsche, Friedrich 47, 54, 234
Nimrod 177
Nineveh 231–4
Ninus Romance 265
Noah 54, 174; drunkenness 153, 163, 164, 165; genealogy 119, 169, 170, 171, 172
Nohrnberg, James C. 3, 161–88
Numbers, Book of 66, 82–3, 85, 147, 159, 202

Oedipus 187, 216–17
Omri, king of Israel 118, 119
Onan 131, 132, 133
Onesimus 294
Origen 7, 224–5
Orpah 181
Othniel 20
Ouspensky, Gleb Ivanovich 246
Ovid 270

patriarchy 20, 37, 149, 281–2, 291
Paul 7, 45, 224, 285–6, 295; deutero-Paul 293; Philemon 294; *see also* Corinthians; Galatians; Romans
Pechter, Edward 258
Peleg 171
Peniel 175
Peraz 170
Perez 133, 161

performative 233–4, 292–3; *see also* speech-act
Perrin, Norman 241–2
Peter 244, 250, 252–3, 267, 270
Pharisees 201
Philemon, Epistle to 294
Philip, apostle 41–2
Philo 224, 225, 226
Philostratus 265
Pilate, Pontius 270
Plato 224–5, 284
politics 1, 188, 191, 197, 204–5, 258–9, 282–3; political action 234–6, 258, 289; *see also* praxis
popular culture 261 ff., 272
power 12, 32–4, 63, 192, 194, 202–5, 281
praxis 276–7, 279, 288, 300; *see also* politics
prophecy 60 ff., 233
Propp, Vladimir 243
Proverbs, Book of 215
Psalms 202, 220–1, 222, 241
psychoanalysis 1, 40–59 *passim*, 280
Pythagoras, biographies of 265

Quintilian 74

Raba 206
Rabbah, siege of 121, 122
race 163, 172–3, 187
Rachael 161, 166, 167, 170, 171, 180, 187; marriage 162, 164, 179, 187
Ranke, Leopold von 9
Rawls, John 291–2
Rebekah 29, 126, 177, 178, 180; *see also under* Isaac
Recognitions 263
Reimarus 8
Rembrandt van Rijn 34
remembering 25, 41, 46–51, 53–5
repetition 41, 51–5, 61, 73, 266, 269
resurrection 43, 45, 54, 55, 249, 254, 295–6

Reu 171
Reuben 49, 163, 164, 187
Reubenites 176
Revelation, Book of 69, 77
rhetoric 6, 62, 63–4, 74–5, 77, 91, 92, 120, 122, 136, 200, 221, 226, 233–4, 260, 261, 266, 268, 271
Ricoeur, Paul 3, 48, 237–57, 289–90, 298, 299
Robbins, Vernon 260, 261
Romans, Epistle to 295–6, 296–7
Romantic poetry 75 ff.
Roosevelt, Theodore 161
Ruth 82–3, 85, 114, 159, 161, 181, 182

Sa'adya, Pseudo- 214
Sa'dya Gaon, Rabbi 226
sacrifice 30, 32–3, 34, 72, 162, 166, 167, 243
Saducees 201
Said, Edward 53
Salmon 161
Samaritan Pentateuch 116
Samson 30, 33, 99, 105, 137, 138; bride of 17–18, 19, 30, 32, 34, 36
Samuel, call of 69
Samuel, Books of 159; chronology 82–3, 85, 130, 137, 159; *I Samuel* 86–8, 93, 97, 108, 110, 114–15, 125, 126, 134–6; *II Samuel* 95, 97, 120–3
Sandys, Edwin, Archbishop of York 42
Sarah: and Abimelech 84–5, 137, 138, 154–7, 180; barrenness 178, 179, 180–1; and Isaac's annunciation 88, 94, 97, 148–9, 151–2, 157, 160, 162, 166; and Ishmael 125, 181; *see also under* Abraham
Saul, king of Israel: chronology 86–8, 89, 93, 100, 102–5, 108, 126, 138; and David 100, 102–5, 126, 134, 136; rejection by God 125, 126–7
Schleiermacher, Friedrich Ernst Daniel 10

Schlüssler-Fiorenza, Elisabeth 276, 293
Schwartz, Regina M. 3, 40–59
Selah 171
semiotics 1, 243–7
Semites 170, 172
Semler, J. S. 9
Serug 171
Seth 112, 113, 115, 118, 119, 120, 164, 169, 171, 172, 180, 188
Sethites 164
Shakespeare, William 78
Shammai, exegetic school of 5
Shechemites 163, 176, 179
Shela, son of Judah 131, 132, 133
Shem 119, 164, 169, 170, 171, 180
Sheol 45
Shila, Rabbi 215
Shunem 103
Simeon, brother of Joseph 51
Simeon b. Ḥalafta, Rabbi 205
Sisera 17, 36
Smart, Christopher 60–1, 64
Sodom 149–54, 157–8, 158–60, 165–6; Abraham and 99, 156, 160, 164; *see also* Lot
Solomon, king of Israel 122, 139, 141, 161, 192; rabbis on 195, 202, 214–15
Song of Songs 195, 205, 214–30
Song of Songs Rabbah 214–18, 223
Sons of God episode 108, 114
Sophocles 147
Speiser, E. A. 49, 133
Spenser, Edmund 76
Spinoza, Benedictus de 8
stammering 60–80 *passim*, 159
Stein, Gertrude 66
Sternberg, Meir 2, 81–145
Sterne, Laurence 83, 107, 114
Story of Two Brothers (Egyptian) 84
Strauss, David 10
structuralism 1, 23, 246; *see also* structure
structuralists, Russian 242, 246
structure 18, 95, 146–58, 152, 159, 221, 239, 266

subject 18, 24, 32–3, 36, 61, 162, 192, 235
subjectivity 25, 34, 199, 235–6
sublime 61–3, 67, 70, 74, 79

Talmud 192; Babylonian 40
Tamar *see under* Judah, son of Jacob
Tanḥuma b. Abba, Rabbi 194
Tarshish 231, 232
Taylor, Charles 203
Terah: chronology 115, 118; genealogy 161, 168, 170, 171, 172, 176, 177, 178, 179; migration 173, 177, 180, 181
Terahites 161, 164, 179
theory *see* deconstruction; feminism; hermeneutics; interpretation; Marxism; narratology; new historicism; psychoanalysis; semiotics
Thucydides 94, 106, 113
Tiamat 168
Tindal, Matthew 8
Tiresias 216–17
Toland, John 8
Tolbert, Mary Ann 3, 258–75
Tolstoy, Leo 146
Torah: communal nature 192; midrash and 189–213; Moses receives 199–200; no earlier and later in 83, 86, 116; oral 5, 6, 201; Paul and 295; Solomon and 195, 214–15; Song of Songs as key to 214–30; survival of text 46, 54
Trible, Phyllis 26, 27
Troeltsch, Ernst 281
Tubal 169

Turner, Victor 23, 32
Twain, Mark 146–7
type-scene 20–1, 149, 157
typology 34, 41–5, 46, 54, 245, 261

Ur 170, 173, 177
Uriah the Hittite 84, 121–2

Vico, Gian Battista 64
Vincent of Lerins 4
violence 17–18, 32, 33, 264
Virgil 75, 270
virginity 20–1, 22, 24–5, 151, 180, 183

Walzer, Michael 44, 291–2
Weiskel, Thomas 61, 64, 67
Wellhausen, Julius 9–10
Wenham, G. J. 24–5
Wittgenstein, Ludwig 190, 203
Wordsworth, William 75–7

Xenophon (of Athens) 261, 265
Xenophon of Ephesus 262–5, 266–7, 269–70, 271

Yael 17, 36
Yahweh 20, 30, 62, 181
Yeats, W. B. 233
Yose, Rabbi 215

Zadok, Rabbi 207
Zephaniah, Book of 69–70
Zerah 170
Zillah 172
Zimmerli, Walter 65
Zimri, king of Israel 118, 119
Zipporah 72–3, 148
Zoar 152–3